Joseph Francis Thrupp

An Introduction to the Study and use of the Psalms

Vol. II.

Joseph Francis Thrupp

An Introduction to the Study and use of the Psalms
Vol. II.

ISBN/EAN: 9783744773171

Printed in Europe, USA, Canada, Australia, Japan

Cover: Foto ©Lupo / pixelio.de

More available books at **www.hansebooks.com**

INTRODUCTION TO THE PSALMS.

VOL. II.

AN INTRODUCTION

TO

THE STUDY AND USE

OF THE

PSALMS.

BY

JOSEPH FRANCIS THRUPP, M.A.

VICAR OF BARRINGTON,
AND LATE FELLOW OF TRINITY COLLEGE, CAMBRIDGE.

VOLUME II.

MACMILLAN AND CO.
Cambridge:
AND 23, HENRIETTA STREET, COVENT GARDEN,
London.
1860.

CONTENTS OF VOL. II.

BOOK III.

	PAGE
General account of this Book	3
Psalm LXXIII.	4
Psalm **LXXIV.**	7
Psalm **LXXV.**	12
Psalm **LXXVI.**	16
Psalm LXXVII. (The Church and the Ten Tribes)	19
Psalm LXXVIII.	23
Psalm LXXIX.	33
Psalm LXXX.	36
Psalm LXXXI.	46
Psalm LXXXII.	56
Psalm LXXXIII. (Typical characters of the enemies of Israel)	59
Psalm LXXXIV.	70
Psalm LXXXV.	76
Psalm LXXXVI. (Later psalms bearing David's name)	80
Psalm LXXXVII.	90
Psalm **LXXXVIII.**	96
Psalm LXXXIX.	103

BOOK IV.

General account of this Book	113
Psalm XC. (Prayer of Moses)	114
Psalm XCI.	120
Psalm XCII.	124

	PAGE
Psalm XCIII. (Advent Psalms)	126
Psalm XCIV.	131
Psalm XCV.	132
Psalm XCVI.	136
Psalm XCVII.	140
Psalm XCVIII.	143
Psalm XCIX.	144
Psalm C.	149
Psalm CI.	150
Psalm CII.	154
Psalm CIII.	170
Psalm CIV.	173
Psalms CV, CVI. (The Asaphic hymn in 1 Chron. xvi.)	179

BOOK V.

General account of this Book	187
Psalm CVII.	ib.
Psalm CVIII.	195
Psalm CIX.	198
Psalm CX.	203
Psalms CXI, CXII.	217
Psalm CXIII.	218
Psalms CXIV—CXVII. (The Hallel)	220
Psalm CXVIII.	231
Psalm CXIX.	244
Psalms CXX—CXXXIV. (Songs of Goings up)	256
Psalms CXXXV, CXXXVI.	280
Psalm CXXXVII.	284
Psalm CXXXVIII.	288
Psalm CXXXIX.	291
Psalm CXL.	300
Psalm CXLI.	304

CONTENTS.

	PAGE
Psalm CXLII.	306
Psalm CXLIII.	307
Psalm CXLIV.	309
Psalm CXLV.	313
Psalm CXLVI.	316
Psalm CXLVII.	318
Psalm CXLVIII.	321
Psalm CXLIX.	323
Psalm CL.	326

APPENDIX I.

On the Names of God in the Psalms   329

APPENDIX II.

On the Musical Instruments of the Jewish Psalmody   342

INDEX   351

BOOK III.

PSALMS LXXIII.—LXXXIX.

Therefore will I save my flock, and they shall no more be a prey; and I will judge between cattle and cattle. And I will set up **one** shepherd **over them, and he shall** feed them, even my servant David; he shall **feed them, and he shall be** their shepherd.

Ezek. xxxiv. 22, 23.

And other sheep I have, which are **not of this fold**: them also I must bring, and they shall hear my voice; and there shall be **one fold, and one shepherd.**

John x. 16.

BOOK III.

THE historical events which gave rise to the several psalms of the Third Book of the Psalter partly belong to the reign of **the good** king Hezekiah, partly group themselves naturally around it. Of the seventeen psalms comprised in the Book the first eleven bear the name **of Asaph**; and four, viz. Psalms lxxxiv, lxxxv, lxxxvii, **lxxxviii, that of the** Sons of Korah. The concluding psalm, **Psalm** lxxxix, bears the superscription "Maschil **of** Ethan the Ezrahite," in obvious analogy with the latter part of the superscription of the last psalm of the Sons of Korah, "Maschil of Heman **the** Ezrahite." All these psalms were composed by the various choirs **of** temple-singers, of whom a full account has been given in the Introduction to Book II. Psalm lxxxvi. is entitled "A Prayer of David;" and its authorship will be examined in its due place. These psalms were probably collected and arranged in the days of Josiah; and if so, then **by** a member of the choir of Asaph, the other **two** choirs having **at** that time already become **extinct**. The collector has accordingly in his arrangement made **the** Asaphic psalms stand **first**: in the Second Book, probably compiled by **a** Korhite, the psalms of the Sons of Korah **took** precedence. Of the psalms historically connected with the **reign** of Ahaz only those composed by the Korhites were included **in** the Second Book: that which proceeded from the Asaphic choir finds its place here. Of those psalms which belong to the reign of Hezekiah himself, there **is** apparently but one, the Korhite Psalm xlvi, which has its place elsewhere than in the Third Book; having been exceptionally permitted to appear in the Second Book, not long after the date at which it was composed, on account of its connexion in style and sentiment with Psalms xlvii, xlviii.

In the seventeen superscriptions of the **Third Book** the word *psalm* occurs twelve times, the word *song* five times, *maschil* four times, *prayer* once. It has been already observed, that from the Second Book onward these designations are occasionally used with great latitude of meaning, and are not available for a distinct classification of the psalms to which they are prefixed.

PSALM LXXIII.

In commencing the study of the **Third Book we can** scarcely fail to perceive **the contrast between** the deep **meditative thoughtfulness of the** psalms of the reign of **Hezekiah and the** mere strain of joyous exultation of **the days of** Jehoshaphat. **There** is a **more** truly Davidic feeling in the psalms on which **we are** now entering than in those which compose the earlier division of the Second Book. The heavy afflictions and the threatenings of yet worse misery by which in the days of Hezekiah Israel had **been** tried were gradually effecting for the nation at large what the tribulations and dangers of his early life had effected personally for Israel's greatest psalmist. **The** people were being educated into a sense of their own sin; and along with the **sense of sin came a** deeper **and more** earnest longing for deliverance.

It has been frequently maintained—by Theodoret among the ancients, and by several modern critics—that the psalm before us should be regarded as having a national reference to the circumstances of the Jewish people in the midst of their heathen oppressors. This view commends itself as correct. We have already remarked that the temple-singers were, unlike David, the mere spokesmen of the Church: they had no individuality of their own, nor ever ventured to put forth their mere private experiences. In case of by far the greater number of their psalms the national reference is at once apparent; and we are not justified in admitting, except upon clear evidence, any exception to so general a rule. But in the present psalm there is much that is confirmatory of its having been composed in reference to the trials of the Jewish people, more especially in the early part of Hezekiah's reign. The prototypes of the wicked whom the psalmist describes were the Assyrians, who were at that time in the full height of their power and the full tide of their success, having as yet met with no reverse. In the expressions of vv. 6, 7, we may trace a minuteness of allusion to their luxurious attire, their ornamental necklaces and bracelets, the artificial colouring of their eyelids[1]. Vv. 8, 9 are amply illustrated by the haughty and blasphemous speeches of Rab-shakeh at the siege of Jerusalem. And if indeed it were at that period that the psalm was written, we might compare with the words of v. 19 Hezekiah's resort, on two separate occasions, to the house of the Lord, once after tidings had been brought to him of the speech of Rabshakeh, and again on the receipt of the letter from Sennacherib. In the following verses of the psalm would be delineated in remarkably appropriate language (whether prophetically or not is uncertain) the awful discomfiture of the Assyrian host; to which event indeed it is difficult to suppose that the psalm was not intended to have some degree of reference. That the Greek translators took the same view may perhaps be inferred from a comparison of the addition which they

---

[1] See on all these Bonomi's *Nineveh and its Palaces*, pp. 319—324.

have made to the last verse, "in the gates of the daughter of Zion," with the opening words of the announcement of Isaiah respecting Sennacherib: "The virgin the daughter of Zion **hath** despised **thee** and laughed thee to scorn; the daughter of **Jerusalem** hath shaken her head at thee."

To the foregoing view it has been objected that the psalm makes mention of the wicked in general, not of the heathen. To this however it is easily replied that in the days when the Jews were receiving daily accounts of the cruelties that were being perpetrated by the Assyrian army, and of the language that was being held by Sennacherib and Rab-shakeh, the heathen **with** whom the Jews were brought **into contact** would be readily contemplated by them **as the living representatives** of wickedness. And **for the omission from the** psalm of **all** express mention of the heathen by name sufficient compensation is made by the use in v. 1 of the name "Israel." The struggle **between Israel** and Assyria in the days of Hezekiah **was a dramatic** exhibition, on a limited scale, of the universal struggle between faith and sin in the world at large.

But in maintaining the original national reference of the psalm, we have no need whatever **to** deny that it may be profitably used as a support to every individual believer, who is tempted by the seeming prosperity **of** the wicked with whom he has to deal to disbelieve in the moral government of the world, and to ask **whether** there be indeed knowledge in the Most High. (The words in **v. 11, it** may **be here** remarked, are not, as they are often understood, those of the wicked, but rather those **of** the faithful, uttered at the time when their steps **had** well nigh slipped, and when their faith was trembling **in** the balance.) As for the **rest,** the Christian, to whom is revealed the doctrine of a future judgment, will interpret the language of this psalm in the same extended sense with that of Psalms xxxvii. and xlix. He will, equally with the Old Testament believer, recognize the awfulness of God's retribution upon the wicked; but he will also know that as it is only in another world that that retribution will be complete, so the seeming prosperity of the wicked may endure in this world even to the day of his death; though he will find indeed that there are few cases wherein even the issues of this world will not in some degree bear witness to the certainty of a recompense to men according to their deeds.

PSALM LXXIV.

THE fundamental spirit of this psalm is embodied in the central verse (v. 12), by which the two strophes of eleven verses each (vv. 1—11, 13—23) are separated the one from the other: "For God is my King of old, working salvation in the midst of the earth." In this verse the "my King" accords remarkably with the similar expression in Psalm xliv, the general tone of which agrees also with that of the psalm before us. The latter part of the verse rests upon Exodus viii. 22, where God declares that he will send a plague of flies upon Pharaoh and the Egyptians, but will exempt the Israelites in the land of Goshen from its operation, "to the end thou mayest know that I am the LORD in the midst of the earth." The words point to the open manifestation of God's spiritual might, even in the midst of all the obstacles, whether apparent or real, which either the usual laws of physical operation, so far as they are understood by men, or the resistance of a proud and self-willed worldly tyranny, can threaten to oppose.

It is only by living critics that the true date of this psalm has been perceived. In general it either has been variously assigned to the period of the destruction of Jerusalem by the Chaldeans, or to that of **the persecution of Antiochus Epiphanes**; or else has been regarded as having a direct prophetical reference to the overthrow of Jerusalem by the Romans under Titus. This last view we may at once and without hesitation dismiss. The psalm was undoubtedly designed by the Holy Spirit for the use of the Church of God in all seasons of tribulation; but we should never be justified in seeking its only historical basis in definite events of the future, so long as there remained any possible origin for it in contemporaneous events to which, for aught that we know to the contrary, its language would exactly and literally apply. The hypothesis again of the Maccabean date, even setting aside for the moment the impossibility of reconciling it with the history of the completion of the Old Testament canon, labours under the disadvantage that its defenders have never explained how the Jews should lament that they had no more any prophet (v. 9) at an age when that order of men had ceased for more than two hundred years. And lastly, the hypothesis of the Chaldean date is also inadmissible, because the psalmist would not have bewailed the desecration (vv. 3, 4) and disfigurement (vv. 5, 6) of the temple at a time when it had been completely destroyed. To which it may be added that the words of v. 9, "neither is there among us any that knoweth how long," cannot well have been uttered at the Chaldean period, because a distinct intimation had then been given as to how long the captivity should last[1].

But when we carry back our thoughts to the period of the latter part of the reign of Ahaz, the same to

---

[1] Jer. xxv. 11; xxix. 10. Cf. 2 Chron. xxxvi. 21; Dan. ix. 2.

which we have already found Psalms xlii—xliv. to belong, we there find either a certain or probable correspondence of facts to all the indications of date which the psalm now before us presents[1]. We know that the solemn temple-worship was then suspended, the doors of the Lord's house closed, and the house itself treated with contempt by being made a receptacle for uncleanness[2]. The details of the desolation are not indeed fully recorded; but as it is stated that the ornaments of the temple-court were disfigured and plundered, we may without difficulty assume that the embellishments of the interior of the sanctuary fared no better. But the dwelling-place of God's name, although defiled, was not destroyed; and it is to be regretted that the **contrary** should be indirectly implied in so many versions **of** the psalm before us, in consequence of the failure of Hebrew scholars to perceive that the word rendered in v. 7, and in other passages of Scripture, *to the ground*, bears also the purely adverbial signification *thoroughly, utterly*[3]. But the persecution of the true worshippers of God which accompanied the desecration of the temple was undoubtedly severe; as **is** indeed shewn by the complaints of Psalm xliv. The threatened conflagration of all the synagogues of God in the land (v. 8) indicates (**whatever** be intended by the word *synagogue*) that the **persecution** was not confined to Jerusalem; and this agrees with the indications of Psalm xlii, where we find the ministers of the temple compelled to seek safety in temporary **exile across the Jordan.** The foolish people **were** reproaching God daily (vv. 10, 18, 22); and mean-

---

[1] The discovery of the true **date** of all these psalms is due to Mr Jebb; who has been followed, in part, by the author of the "Plain Commentary" recently published.

[2] 2 Chron. xxviii. 24; xxix. **16.** Also 2 Kings xvi.

[3] Cf. in proof of this, Psalm xii. 6 (*of earth*); lxxxix. 39; cxliii. 3; Isai. xxi. 9; Jer. xiv. 2.

while idolatry had been formally established in the place of the true religion: Ahaz had erected his altars in every corner of Jerusalem, and instead of the hallowed signs of the divine presence, the signs of an idolatrous worship had been set up in the temple-courts (v. 4).

In regard to the psalmist's complaint "There is no more any prophet, neither is there among us any that knoweth how long," it is not in the least necessary to suppose him to assert that no man then survived who had ever exercised the prophetical gift: the drift of the complaint is evidently that there was no more prophecy; that there was none to whom it was given to be a prophet to the people under their present distress, or to comfort them by a declaration of the counsels of God respecting the length of time through which that distress should last. And this was remarkably the case during the latter part of Ahaz' reign. The race of prophets was not utterly gone, for both Isaiah and Micah were living; but the very fact of their being alive made the absence of any prophetical announcement from them all the more bitter. When in the earlier days of Ahaz the kingdom of Judah was invaded by the confederate armies of Israel and Syria, God by his prophet Isaiah had given a sign to assure the people that within a definite time their enemies should disappear[1]; but now that the Assyrians under Tiglath-Pileser were masters of the country, the divine voice was silent, and none were commissioned to tell how long the desolation should continue.

Amid so much to tempt them to despondency, on what did God's true worshippers, as represented by the psalmist, rest for support? Whence did they draw their as yet unexhausted stores of comfort? First, from the thought (v. 2) that those who were now

---

[1] Isaiah vii. 14. seqq.

suffering from the blaze of persecution were still the people whom **God** had purchased, and that the now desolated Zion was still the Zion wherein God long had **dwelt**. The Church in her deepest abasement of suffering is **still God's** Church; and even when despoiled of her temples and deprived of her outward ministrations, still claims to belong to Him who changeth not. Secondly, they appeal (vv. 12—15) to the mighty deliverances which in the time of their forefathers God had wrought in their behalf. He who had erst broken the heads of the mighty leviathan of Egypt could equally overthrow the winged lion of Assyria[1]; he who had divided the Red **Sea** by his strength could equally **stem** the advancing flood of the overflowing **waters** of the Euphrates[2]; he who had cleft the fountain and the flood **and** dried up mighty rivers could equally make present streams of **grace** burst forth upon his people in the midst of their agony, and cause to evaporate those rivers of oppression **which** as yet seemed to be perpetually flowing. Thirdly, God's people behold even in the idolatrous worship of their oppressors a recognition of the mighty truth that the affairs of the world and of the universe are **ordered** by a more than human power. **And that God whom others** ignorantly acknowledge, *they* **are able to declare (vv. 16, 17).** "All the gods of **the nations** are idols: but the LORD made the heavens:" it is *their* God who ordered **the** day and the night, who prepared the light and **the** sun, who set all the **borders of** the earth, and made summer and winter. **And** having **thus no** need to put their trust in a lie, they **can look** forward with hope to the result. But fourthly and lastly, **they** rely on the stedfastness of God's promises: "Have respect unto the covenant (v. 20)." God had revealed himself to the Israelites by

---

[1] Daniel vii. 4. [2] Isaiah viii. 7, 8.

Moses as "the faithful God, which keepeth covenant and mercy with them that love him and keep his commandments to a thousand generations[1]." And although the earth might be full, as in the days of Noah, of the habitations of cruelty, yet even then there had been those who found grace in the eyes of the Lord; and with them on their coming forth from the ark he **had** established his covenant, setting the bow in the **cloud** for the token. How then should not his faithful servants in spite of the prevailing corruption still look for a renewal of his grace? How should they not plead that he would still remember that covenant which he had been pleased to make with Abraham? With confidence yet greater still may the **Church** of Christ rely on God's faithfulness to that covenant which has been ratified by the Redeemer's **blood; nor can** her members **find** much **difficulty in** discerning the bearing of the **several pleas in the** present psalm on their own earthly **struggles.**

PSALM LXXV.

THE following revised version will enable us to enter more conveniently into the meaning of this psalm.

1 We give thanks to thee O **God,** we give thanks;
And nigh is thy name:
They have recounted thy wondrous **deeds.**
2 "For I **will** seize an appointed time;
I will judge **uprightly:**
3 Dissolved **are the earth** and **all her inhabitants:**
I **poised** her **pillars."** Selah.
4 I **have** said to the foolish, **Deal** not foolishly,
And to the wicked, Lift **not up** the horn;
5 Lift not up your horn **on** high,
Nor utter bold words with erected neck.
6 For not from the east, nor **from** the west,

---
[1] Deut. vii. 9.

Nor yet from the mountain desert,—
7 No! **For God is** the judge:
He layeth low one, and setteth **up** another.
8 For a cup **there** is **in** the hand **of** the LORD, and the wine
 glows red,
It is full of mingled drink, and he poureth out **therefrom:**
The very **dregs** shall all the wicked of the earth
Suck out and swallow.
9 But I will declare forth for **ever,**
I will sing praises to the God **of Jacob;**
10 And all the horns of the wicked **shall I** cut off
That the horns of the righteous may be exalted.

The use of the first person plural **in** v. 1 shews that the speaker in this psalm is **the Church.** The date of composition must be sought in the early part **of the** reign **of Hezekiah: the** prototypes of the foolish boasters are as in Psalm lxxiii. the Assyrians, who had probably already **invaded** the Jewish land. Their overthrow is announced in **vv.** 2, 3, in words put into the mouth **of God himself: he** who poised the pillars of the earth at the creation will in his own **good** time, by a signal display of divine judgment, re-establish the tottering fabric of its political system. And accordingly the psalmist, in the person of the Church, basing his exhortation on this announcement, bids men calmly await **the** promised divine deliverance. They need not look anxiously for help to **the east or** to the west, for it is not **by** earthly means **that the** northern invader will be discomfited: they **need not** faithlessly sigh for the approach of the Egyptian **army** across the deserts **of** the south. God is the judge; and in his own due time **he will** execute vengeance both for himself and for his people. The latter then have only to place their entire confidence upon him: he has shewn himself nigh, and to him they may utter their thanks as well for those manifestations of **his** might which **are to** follow as for those which they have already experienced; nay, in his strength they may already view themselves as conquerors, and even as ministers of judgment, laying low the oppressors of the earth, that the righteous may be exalted. We assume that it is only in vv. 2, 3 that God can be regarded as speaking. Many recent interpreters would, and by no means without reason, put the concluding verse also into his mouth; but the transition from v. 9 to v. 10 becomes in this case so harsh that it is scarcely possible they can be right. The words of that verse may in fact be fairly treated as the words of the Church, if only it be understood, that they do not express her own determination of will, but merely indicate the career of judgment along which she will be divinely led. For one great lesson of the psalm is essentially this, that the Church must await God's time, and must not vainly seek to precipitate the hour of deliverance by a reliance on worldly succours or a resort to unlawful means. And this is implied in the motto *Al-taschith* with which the psalm is superscribed, and which indicates its agreement in spirit with those psalms of David to which the same motto is prefixed. The reader will refer to the remarks made upon the meaning of this motto in the Introd. to Psalm lvii.

One important feature in this psalm yet remains to be noticed: the extent to which its language is based on that of the song of Hannah in the First Book of Samuel. Compare v. 3 with the latter part of 1 Sam. ii. 8; v. 4 with 1 Sam. ii. 3; vv. 6, 7 with the latter part of 1 Sam. ii. 9, and the former part of 1 Sam. ii. 8; vv. 9, 10 with 1 Sam. ii. 1, 10. Now that that song—if acknowledged to be the song of Hannah—was essentially prophetical can scarcely be disputed. It spoke—openly spoke—of the Lord giving strength unto his king, and exalting the horn of his anointed, at a time when there was not yet an earthly king in Israel, and when therefore the only king of whom it was possible to conceive was the promised Messiah; of whose advent in due time the birth of every child in Israel was in some sort a pledge, and the assurance of whose coming could alone give meaning to the institutions of the Israelitish dispensation. And that a Jewish psalmist should so extensively have borrowed from the language of the song of Hannah without fully recognizing its prophetical character, or without consequently contemplating the same prophetical character as inherent in his own composition, is virtually impossible. The prophetical character of the one establishes the prophetical character of the other. The psalmist must have consciously looked forward to the days of the future Messiah as the days in which his own words should receive their highest fulfilment. The divine overthrow of the Assyrian host would necessarily, when it came, appear to him the earnest of a far mightier and more extended execution of judgment which was yet to follow upon the world. And though he could not fathom the full depths of that judgment; though he might not know how "nigh" God's "name" should be brought to men in the incarnation of Him in whom that name is; though he might not understand how He, without whom the foundations of the earth were not appointed, nor its pillars poised, nor any thing made that was made, should come, as man, for judgment into this world, that one might be laid low and another set up, that they which see not might see, and that they which see might be made blind; yet were his words, so far as they went, true, and holy, and wise; and as the same words, written under the Spirit's inspiration, are ever capable of bearing a deeper fulness of meaning according to the higher degree of instruction of those by whom they are employed, **so do** the words of faith of **the Jewish** psalmist still serve to express the faith of the Christian Church, that though by strength shall no man prevail, yet, through the strength imparted unto her King, shall all the horns of the righteous be in due time exalted.

PSALM LXXVI.

A TRIUMPHAL ode is before us; celebrating that manifestation of judgment which in the preceding psalm the Church had been led to expect upon her enemies. It was composed, as the Greek translators rightly judged, in immediate reference to the destruction of the Assyrian **host** of Sennacherib. **In proof** of this we have the evident completeness **of that** intervention of God which is here commemorated; the appropriate**ness** of **the** language of **vv. 5, 6** to the scene which **unfolded itself to** view in the Assyrian **camp** on the morning after the **deliverance; the** prominence given to the mention of Zion as God's dwelling-place, which renders it probable that the city of Jerusalem had been directly threatened by the enemy; the almost direct assertion in the opening word of v. 3, that it was at Jerusalem that the divine intervention took place; and lastly, the use that has been made of this psalm by the prophet Zechariah in delineating **the** overthrow of Jerusalem's enemies **in the final** prophetical struggle, for which overthrow he evidently found a type in the discomfiture of Sennacherib's army in the days of Hezekiah.

The psalm consists, in its formal arrangement, of a strophe (vv. 1—3), mesode (vv. 4—6; a verse of somewhat greater length enclosed by two verses of one line **each**), antistrophe (vv. 7—9), and epode (vv. 10—12).

The ends of the strophe and antistrophe are marked by the Selahs. The kernel of the descriptive portion of the psalm is contained in the mesode, and more especially in its central verse, v. 5: the epode supplies the moral.

The language of the earlier verses of this psalm is probably metaphorical. The God of Israel is represented under the image of a lion; having his 'leafy covert' in Salem (the poetical abbreviation for Jerusalem[1]) and his 'den' in Zion[2]; and 'from' his mountains of prey,—the mountains of Jerusalem, wherein he makes his lair,—bursting forth in the glory of resistless might to destroy the proud who in the insolence of their folly have made light of his majesty. With regard to v. 3, "There brake he the arrows of the bow (perhaps rather the 'flashings' of the bow; in other words, the flashings of the arrows from the bowstring), the shield, and the sword, and the battle," the meaning may simply be that by sending forth the angel of slaughter into the camp of the Assyrians, God rendered vain all those warlike preparations which they had made; for there is nothing in the scriptural narrative of what befell the Assyrians which would enable us to assign any more precise significance to these words. Still when we read Herodotus' account of the fate of Sennacherib's army at Pelusium, which is plainly nothing less than the discomfiture before Jerusalem in disguise; when we find him relating how the mice devoured the quivers, bows, and shield-straps of the invaders[3]; it is impossible to avoid the suspicion that the expressions of the verse before us may have been chosen with exact reference to what actually

---

[1] Bonar suggests that in the use of the name Salem there is a significant reminiscence of the reign of Melchizedek, and of the slaughter by Abraham of the former Asiatic kings by whom the realms of Canaan were invaded.

[2] See Stanley, *Sinai and Pal.* p. 170.

[3] Herodotus, II. 141.

occurred. And in this case a combination of the hints supplied respectively by the contemporary ode of the psalmist, by the subsequent allusions of Zechariah, and by the traditionary **record of** the Greek historian, would render it probable that **the destruction of the Assyrians themselves was, at least in part,** the result of a mutual **nocturnal** slaughter, consequent upon **the** hurried search in each other's tents for **weapons in lieu** of those **which had** been rendered useless[1]. **Nor is any** violence done by this supposition to the scriptural narrative; for the believer would as surely trace the hand of God in a destruction so effected as in the **mutual** slaughter **of the** Ammonites and Moabites in the days of Jehoshaphat[2]. It may be that mutual **violence completed the work which pestilence** had **begun.**

The main theme of the psalm may be deemed to consist in **the** threefold testimony to God's majesty, first, **in the** thankful worship of those that have been delivered, secondly in the overthrow **of** those that have perished, thirdly in the conversion of **the** once hostile remnant that were in the overthrow permitted to survive. It is better in v. 10, in preference to the reading of the Hebrew text presented by the Jewish editors, to adopt that sanctioned by the LXX, and remarkably confirmed by the parallel passage of Zechariah, xiv. 16[3]: the rendering will then be as follows:

> For the wrath **of** man shall praise thee:
> The remainder **of** wrath shall keep holyday to thee:

---

[1] Although the passive sense of the verb אשתוללו in v. 5, *are spoiled*, is not inadmissible, it would be in still more extensive accordance with Hebrew usage to assign it a reciprocal **sense,** *have spoiled each other*. Both senses are perhaps intended; their mutual spoiling of each **other** being the actual means by which **God's** spoiling of them was accomplished.

[2] 2 Chron. xx. 23.

[3] תחנך for תחגר: see Ewald, and **also** the *Journal of Class. and Sacred Philology*, Vol. IV. p. 260.

i. e. "Those of the wrathful who survive thy destroying judgment shall turn to thee, and shall come up to Jerusalem to the feast to adore thy name."

It is almost needless to point out that these words are a virtual prophecy of the general conversion of the heathen to the Church of Christ. For the Church Catholic is the Salem which God has now made his abode, the theatre of God's glory; and well may she, although the earthly struggle be not yet ended, give thanks for that enduring strength which has been vouchsafed her, and which the several attacks of the successive enemies of eighteen centuries have each in turn proved unable to impair.

PSALM LXXVII.

WE now enter upon a series of psalms, Psalms lxxvii, lxxviii, lxxx—lxxxv, lxxxvii, springing directly out of the relation of the Jewish Church to the ten tribes which had renounced the sovereignty of the house of David. This series has never yet been properly appreciated, owing to the fact that the historical reference of the psalms of which it is composed, although occasionally remarked in separate cases, has never been generally discerned. It is a series which should to the several branches of the Christian Church be of peculiar interest, as exhibiting the feelings which they should cherish towards the schismatic Christian bodies that have separated from their communion. It will on the one hand warn them how little reason they have to treat schism as a matter of indifference, to deny its guilt, or to think it can be healed by a compromise of principle. It will on the other hand teach them meanwhile not to refuse to those that are in schism the name of Christian, not to dare to deny that

God is truly among them, that he will defend them from the common enemies of all Christianity, or will bestow his blessing on those that seek to observe his statutes: it will teach them, while desiring and longing for the reunion of those that are separated, to regard them with the deepest love even in their state of separation, to manifest an earnest anxiety for their true spiritual welfare, and to bewail the calamities by which they are visited. There is not a word in Scripture to justify the ten tribes in the division which they introduced into Israel, or to shew that that division should be otherwise regarded than as a great national calamity. Yet we should also bear in mind that it was by that division that God punished the son and grandson of David for their transgressions; that he gave his sanction to the authority of the Israelitish kings, by ordering the unction of Jehu; that he did not withdraw from the ten tribes the gift of prophecy; and that he openly fought for them and saved them from their enemies in the days of Joash and Jeroboam II. And of all this the Church of Judah, much as she had suffered from Ephraimitish rivalry, was well aware.

The psalm before us is the lamentation of the Jewish Church for the carrying away of the ten tribes into captivity. It is therefore that the words of v. 2, "my soul refused to be comforted," recall the words of Jacob in Gen. xxxvii. 35, when tidings were brought to him of the fate of his son Joseph[1]. Jacob had now lost Joseph for the second time: the Israelitish nation had been bereft of all Joseph's descendants. It is for the same reason that the name Joseph is brought forward in v. 15. At a time when so heavy a blow had fallen upon the nation at large, all past rivalry and dissension would be forgotten. The faith, not the forbearance, of

[1] Hengstenberg.

the Church of Judah was now to be put to the proof: the extinction of the ten tribes seemed but the prelude for the extinction of Judah also: "Would the Lord cast off for ever? Had his promise failed for evermore?"

In this severity of affliction the psalmist's faith is upheld by the remembrances of the wonders by which God had effected the redemption of his people in the days when they yet were one; when among the sons of Jacob were numbered the sons also of Joseph; when the heathen wolves instead of succeeding in carrying off one half of God's flock into captivity, had, when they attempted to track God's footsteps through the bed of the Red Sea, suffered for their folly by perishing beneath the mass of returning waters. The lightnings which had then flashed from heaven upon the Egyptian shores, the thunders which had rolled around, however awful for even the Israelites to behold, had nevertheless conduced to their ultimate deliverance: it might be that the storm which had just burst upon Samaria would nevertheless prove the harbinger of a more prosperous period in Israel's history than had ever yet been known. Now as then, the earth trembled and shook; but who could tell what might result when once its sores were healed? For as the dark clouds had then 'been made to sweep the waters along¹ to cover again the marvellous pathway by which God's people had passed, thus rendering the footprints of their course undiscernible thenceforward by human eye; so did the darkness of the divine counsels shroud from mortal ken the path by which God was now conducting his people through seas of overwhelming tribulation to

---

¹ The verb זרם signifies, in Kal, to carry away as with a stream, Psalm xc. 5. The Piel might therefore, if used with a Hiphil sense, mean to make something carry or sweep something else away or along; and of this the Pual would be the passive.

ultimate safety and blessedness. But where discernment failed, there faith stepped in. God could not have forgotten his promise; and it was the remembrance of his past lovingkindness and of his wonders of old **which still** preserved **the** Church **from** the despair to which she was tempted by the awfulness of the surrounding **gloom**. The faith which believed God's way of old to have been in the sea, though that way was no more to be seen, acknowledged that **even now in his** holiness God was making a way for his people which no mortal eye could trace: "Thy way, O God, is in 'holiness': who is 'a great god like God'?"

Such is the general bearing on the theme of the psalm of the train of historical recollections in which the psalmist's sorrow finds vent. **But it is** left to be inferred: it is not expressed. The psalm, elegiac in its tone, as is shewn by **its** superscription[1], wears,—purposely wears,—an aspect of incompleteness. It is not irregular **in its** structure: vv. 1—3 **form the** prelude, vv. 4—9 the strophe, **vv. 10—15 the** antistrophe, vv. 16—20 the epode; the Selahs here indicating the divisions. And care has evidently been taken to mark, as regards the sense, the correspondence between the strophe and the antistrophe; the "I am so troubled" of v. 4 being repeated in the "my infirmity" of **v. 10**, the "days of old" of v. 5 in the "wonders of old" **of** v. 11, the calling to remembrance and the communing **of v. 6 in** the meditation and the talking of v. 12, while **vv. 7—9, 13—15 form the** two strains in which the psalmist actually unburdens his soul, **first** respecting his present distress, and secondly respecting his remembrance of God's former deeds. Yet when we come to the epode, (consisting, with the exception of the last verse, entirely of triplets,) we feel the termination is

---

[1] See above, Vol. I. p. 244.

abrupt[1]. The psalmist has reached the climax of his strain, he has found relief from his sorrow by forcing his thoughts into another channel, by dwelling on all God's mightiest wonders of **old**; but there he must end: **in** his present intensity of passion he cannot trust himself to draw forth in detail any mere *lessons* of comfort. There are seasons when even the holiest faith cannot bear to listen to words of reasoning; though it can still find a support whereon to rest, in the simple contemplation, in all their native grandeur, of the deeds that God hath wrought.

PSALM LXXVIII.

THE immediate purpose of this **long** homiletic psalm **was to** reconcile the Ephraimites, under which name are comprised the whole of the ten tribes, to the dominion of the house of David. But at what precise period the psalm was composed is more difficult to determine. Its date is certainly anterior to that of the destruction of the temple (cf. v. 69) and of the eclipse of the royalty of the Davidic house (cf. vv. 70—72) in the Babylonish captivity. Many critics have been induced by the prominence given to the events of the early Israelitish history, **and** to the record of the Israelitish idolatry in the days of the Judges, to assign the psalm to the period of **the** reign of David. But against this **we** observe that the exclusive mention of the Ephraimites as the leaders of the opposition to the Davidic sovereignty would in David's reign have been inappropriate: the resistance to David's rule came from the tribe of Benjamin rather than from that of Ephraim. The scions and kinsmen of the house of Saul, together with the rebel Sheba the son of Bichri, were all Ben-

---

[1] "Der Psalm erscheint **seinem** Ausgange nach als ein Torso," says Delitzsch.

jamites; and it was in the tribe of Benjamin, if anywhere, that Joab was afraid to carry out the census[1]. There is, moreover, in v. 69 of the psalm a clear allusion to the building of the temple; and the record of David's integrity, v. 72, would hardly have been penned while David was yet alive. Nor is it likely, considering how little the Israelites of the reign of David knew of the country of Egypt except from the annals of their past history, that a writer of that day would have spoken of the district of Egypt in which God's miracles were wrought as the field of Zoan (vv. 12, 43); of which name there is in the Pentateuch no trace to be found, except it be in one incidental notice of Zoan in the Book of Numbers[2].

From the times of the reign of Solomon to those of the captivity at Babylon we have still a wide period over which the date of the psalm may range. It has been confidently assigned to the reign of Solomon's grandson Abijah; but this theory rests on the most improbable hypothesis that v. 9 contains an allusion to Jeroboam's great defeat. We may therefore more reasonably suppose that the psalm was written in the reign of Hezekiah. In favour of this supposition are first, the place occupied by this psalm in the Psalter; secondly, the known effort which was made in the reign of Hezekiah to induce all Israel to come up to worship at Jerusalem. Which circumstances will, in the absence of demonstrative proof, have their due weight.

And in fact the resemblances between the tenor of this psalm and of Hezekiah's message of invitation to the Israelites[3] are by no means slight. In both the Israelites are bidden be not stiffnecked as were their fathers. In both they are expressly reminded of their fathers' trespasses. In both we have the occurrence of

[1] 1 Chron. xxi. 6. [2] Numb. xiii. 22. [3] 2 Chron. xxx. 6—9.

the expression "the fierceness of God's wrath." In both stress is laid on the perpetual sanctification of the sanctuary at Jerusalem. The main difference between the two lies in this, that whereas the latter concerns itself only with the question of religious worship, the former opens up the whole question of state government. And this is just the difference which we should expect. Hezekiah, full of zeal for the Lord, but hoping to heal the divisions of the nation by meekness and forbearance, invites the Israelites to worship at Jerusalem, but keeps in abeyance all claim to be their king. The psalmist, less hampered and no less zealous, boldly utters out the whole truth, and sets forth the divine claim of the house of David to the people's allegiance.

In the narrative portion of the psalm it is evidently the psalmist's main design to set forth, first, the early rebellions and punishments of the children of Israel in the wilderness (vv. 12—39); and secondly, their later disobedience and punishment in the land of Canaan (vv. 40—64). He descends no lower than the time of the Judges: their own experience would supply the rest. He has more delicacy than to reproach them with all the details of their present humiliation; there was no need to repeat them, for they knew them too well: he contents himself therefore with briefly and inferentially indicating the source of what had befallen them; the David from whose house they had withdrawn their allegiance was the king of God's appointment.

But although the psalmist carries the history of Israel's transgression no lower than the time of the Judges, it is certain that he takes especial pains to dwell on those features of their earlier history in the land of Canaan to which their later history furnished a resemblance. This will be made sufficiently clear if we but briefly peruse that portion of the psalm, beginning at v. 40, in which the disobedience of the people in the land of Canaan is narrated. The psalmist commences by lamenting that God's alternate wrath and mercy on the fathers who had rebelled in the wilderness should have produced so little impression upon the children who entered the promised land:

> Often as they had provoked him in the wilderness,
> And grieved him in the desert;
> Yet they tempted God anew,
> And crossed the Holy One of Israel[1].
> They remembered not, &c.

For although he had put an end to their oppression by the miraculous plagues which he had sent upon the Egyptians (vv. 43—51), and had safely guided the people into the land of their inheritance (vv. 52—55); yet notwithstanding, (v. 56 resumes or repeats v. 41,) they tempted and provoked the most high God, dealing unfaithfully like their fathers, provoking him to

---

[1] The true sense of התוו has been missed by critics. ות signifies a cross. The last letter of the alphabet, which bore this name, was in the old Hebrew of a cruciform shape; a shape which it retained in the Greek and Roman alphabets. Now a cross may be used as a mark: hence we have the word תוה used in the Hiphil of *setting a mark* upon any one, Ezek. ix. 4. It is also used in the Piel of *making marks or scrawls*, 1 Sam. xxi. 14. In a somewhat different form, the word is used of *marking out* boundaries, Numb. xxxiv. 7, 8. But furthermore, a cross is the symbol of thwarting; when we thwart a man, we cross his path or his purposes: hence the sense which the verb (in the Hiphil) bears in the present passage, which is exactly that of the English word *to cross*. The use of the English word *cross*, at least as a substantive, has doubtless been much influenced by Christian associations; and when we speak of the crosses which a man has to endure, it is perhaps doubtful whether we should explain the expression by a reference to the original symbolism of the cross, or by a reference to the instrument of our Saviour's sufferings. Yet we can hardly doubt that it was providentially designed that the instrument of our Saviour's death should be one which had already borne so appropriate a symbolical meaning. And it is difficult to resist the thought that in the verse before us the psalmist unconsciously gave vent to a symbolical prophecy of what afterwards befell, when the Jews filled up the measure of their guilt by "tempting" God manifest in the flesh amongst them, and by "crossing" the Holy One of Israel.

anger with their high places, and moving him to
jealousy with their graven images (vv. 56—58). And
for this those mighty calamities came upon them in the
days of the high-priest Eli (vv. 59—64). The bearing
of all that the psalmist thus recounted of the events of
olden time or the circumstances of the period at which
he wrote can scarcely be mistaken. The miracles by
which God had once delivered the Israelites from the
power of the Egyptians shewed that he could in like
manner now, if so he pleased, rescue them from the
grasp of the kings of Assyria, by whom, although
Samaria had not yet finally fallen, many of the Israelites had already been carried away captive[1]. The
victories by which he had put them in possession of
the land of Canaan, although far inferior in number to
the heathen whom they expelled, proclaimed to them,
that notwithstanding their present humiliation, their
God could still at his will re-establish for them the
rightful boundaries of their inheritance. The Philistine
subjection from which God had rescued them by the
hand of David was only an anticipation of what they
were suffering afresh from other foes, now that they
had separated themselves from David's rule; while yet
the single tribe of Judah, under the sway of a descendant of David, would, in a short time, without any
human assistance, prove able to resist the Assyrian ser-
vitude, and to reduce its ancient Philistine oppressors
to subjection[2]. But the present humiliation of the ten
tribes was the reward of the same sin for which they
had been smitten before the Philistines in the days of
Eli; the sin of which their high places and their graven
images were the standing monuments. And for this
sin, in a very few years, the whole people were to be
carried into captivity[3].

---

[1] 2 Chron. xxx. 9. [2] 2 Kings xviii. 7, 8. [3] 2 Kings xvii. 7 seqq.

But besides indirectly warning the Israelites to give over the imitation of their fathers' sins, it is also the psalmist's object to trace the history of the origin of those two institutions which they had contemned,—the sanctuary of Jerusalem, and the sovereignty of the house of David; to shew the chain of events through which Zion became the mountain, and David the king, of God's unalterable choice. As to the former, he observes (v. 54) that when the Israelites first entered God's 'holy territory' (not, as in E. V., *border of his sanctuary*) they were brought to "this mountain, which his right hand had purchased"; by which, as in Exod. xv. 17, we must evidently understand the whole mountain-range extending from the plain of Jezreel southward to the frontier of the Arabian desert[1]. Within the limits of this range stood those two sacred hills respecting which the direction had been given, "It shall come to pass, when the LORD thy God hath brought thee in unto the land whither thou goest to possess it, that thou shalt put the blessing upon Mount Gerizim, and the curse upon Mount Ebal[2]." These two hills were accordingly the first sacred resort of the Israelites on entering the land of Canaan; and on Mount Ebal, as we have already seen in the Introduction to Psalm lxviii, the first altar was built. In the partition of the land the greater part of the mountain-range was divided between the tribes of Ephraim and Judah, Mount Ebal falling within the limits of the inheritance of the former. As yet the entire range was all equally sacred. The special sanctity of Ebal was only temporary, and represented the sanctity of the whole; as was shewn by the circumstance that the tabernacle was set up not on Ebal, but at Shiloh, away

---

[1] See my *Ancient Jerusalem*, pp. 43 seqq.; where it is shewn that this was the extent of the mountain-district of Moriah. [2] Deut. xi. 29.

from Ebal, though still within the borders of the tribe of Ephraim. And for a while, **during the greater** part of the **period** of the Judges, Shiloh **remained the** religious **centre of** national unity; yet still not in such a way as **that any** permanent sanctity necessarily attached to it beyond what was accorded to the entire mountain-range; nor yet so **as that** Ephraim had in any way **permanently** become the leading tribe of Israel. There is in fact but little **mention made** of Shiloh in history; **nor are there indications of** any great preeminence on the part **of the tribe** of Ephraim. **Then** came the loss of the ark **in the days** of Eli; **when** God "forsook the tabernacle of **Shiloh, the** tent **which** he placed **among men; and delivered his** strength into captivity, **and** his **glory into the** enemy's hand." **And, from that day** forward, **to** Shiloh the ark never returned. God **now** made **a new** and **more** definite choice of the place where his sanctuary should be fixed. He did not leave **the** sacred mountain-range; but within the limits of the range, though not within the limits of that part **of** it which belonged to the tribe of Ephraim, he chose one **exclusive spot,** wherein to set his name,—even "the mount Zion, which he loved." In defending the site of **the sanctuary in Psalm lxviii.** against the reclamations **of the trans-jordanic tribes, David** appealed to the ancient sanctity of the western mountain-range of Moriah. In defending it in the psalm before us against the schismatic contumacy of all the **tribes** that were politically **associated** with Ephraim, the psalmist necessarily goes further, and appeals to the obligation arising from God's **deliberate choice.**

Next, **in regard to the** origin **of** the sovereignty of the house **of** David, the psalmist shews (v. 70) that it **was** from the distinct expression **of** God's will that this also took its rise. He does not enter fully into the circumstances; he omits all mention of the reign of Saul; he prefers connecting the establishment of the Davidic royalty with the deliverance of Israel from that Philistine oppression, which no doubt mainly awakened the people's desire for a king, and from which in fact they were never thoroughly rescued till David ascended the throne. Such then were the leading features in the history of the respective origins of that sanctuary on Mount Zion from which the ten tribes of Israel had separated, and of that sovereignty of David's house against which they had rebelled; and to both of which they were now, before the Assyrian had executed to the full the sentence of God's wrath upon them, solemnly invited to return.

The examination of the general scope of the psalm does not require that we should decide what particular interpretation should be given to v. 9, or how far the language of that verse is connected with the language of the latter part of v. 57. Both the meaning and the exact rendering of v. 9 have been much disputed. It is more probable that it is intended as a general delineation of the Ephraimitish character, than that it refers to any particular incident in the Ephraimitish history. We may perhaps understand its meaning to be this; that the Ephraimites, who had once taken the lead in war of all the tribes of Israel, had proved themselves unworthy of the honour they had then enjoyed by their defection from the commandments of God. Theirs had not been the courage to which Joshua had exhorted them, to keep and to do all that was written in the book of the law of Moses, and to turn not aside therefrom to the right hand or to the left[1]. This meaning of v. 9 is further developed in the two verses which follow; and if the verbs in these three verses be rendered in

---
[1] Josh. i. 7; xxiii. 6.

the perfect tense, we shall then **have in** them the argument or summary **of** the rest of **the psalm** (vv. 1—8 forming a mere prelude):

<blockquote>
The children of Ephraim, the bearers and drawers of the bow,
Have turned back in the day of battle.
They have not **kept** the covenant of God,
And in his law **they have** refused to walk,
And they have **forgotten** his works,
And **his** wonders **that he shewed them.**
</blockquote>

The narrative portion of the psalm, by which these **assertions** are made good, **then** commences.

In support **of the** above interpretation it may be observed, that **the bow was always** esteemed in olden times **an honourable weapon of warfare; and** indeed was **regarded** as the emblem of strength. **It had been a prominent** feature in Jacob's blessing **upon Joseph,** that **although the archers** had sorely grieved him **and** shot at him, **yet his bow** abode in strength[1]; and, viewed as **a prophecy, these** words had been fulfilled in the early prosperity **of the** Ephraimites. But, alas! that bow which had **for a** time abode in **strength** had also (as v. **57 of the psalm** assures us) proved deceitful; and the **Ephraimites had** forfeited their early prosperity and renown by **their** rebellious neglect of the commandments of God.

Respecting the Christian significance **of** the psalm **there can be little** room **for doubt. We know** the **dominion of David** and his **descendants to have** been a **direct type of the** dominion **of that Greatest of** David's **children, to whom in due** time **the throne of** his father **David** was **to be given,** who **was to reign over** the house **of** Jacob **for ever, and of whose kingdom there** should **be no end**[2]. The **last three verses of the psalm are** therefore a virtual warning to us, **that he who** was born

<hr>
[1] Gen. xlix. 23, 24.   [2] Luke i. 32, 33.

at Bethlehem has been exalted of God to be a Prince and a Saviour, and that by him alone is salvation. Again, as the ancient sanctuary of God on Mount Zion was a type of the New Testament Church, which God the Father, Son, and Holy Ghost hath chosen to cause his name to dwell there, the psalm is a standing testimony against the sin of religious separatism and schism, telling men that they shall not do that which is right in their own several eyes, but that to God's habitation they shall seek, and thither, to worship, they shall come[1]. The psalmist, speaking in the name of the Church, appeals to us, as he appealed to the Israelites his own contemporaries, by the examples of the events of former times, and by a recital of the evil results flowing from former rebellions. To use his own expression, he opens his mouth in a parable; his parable being taken from the occurrences in his own people's former national history, in the same manner as our Saviour's parables were drawn either from the ordinary occurrences of eastern domestic life, or from the well-known processes of nature[2]. There was however this difference between the parables of our Blessed Saviour and the parable of the psalmist; that whereas the former had to select from a boundless field such incidents or to construct for himself such tales as would serve his immediate purpose, the latter did little more than narrate the leading circumstances of the history which God had furnished ready to his hand. The whole Old Testament history was essentially a parable[3]. The parable had been acted long before it was uttered: the psalmist's office—

---

[1] Deut. xii.
[2] And therefore St Matthew traces in our Saviour's teaching the fulfilment of the psalmist's words; Matth. xiii. 35.
[3] For an instance of the general recognition of the parabolic character of the Old Testament history among the Jews, see John vi. 31; where they apparently quote from the present psalm.

an office which subsequently devolved on Stephen in the council-chamber at Jerusalem, and on Paul in the synagogue at Antioch—was to set it plainly forth.

PSALM LXXIX.

THE resemblance between the lamentations of this psalm and those of Psalm lxxiv. has been very generally remarked; but it would be rash on this account too hastily to conclude that they were composed at the same period; the more especially as, although both productions of the Asaphic choir, they are not placed together. Nor in fact does the state of misery described in Psalm lxxiv. come up to that depicted in the psalm now before us. It is probable that this psalm should be treated as the supplication of the faithful in the days of the impious Manasseh; and that that unworthy scion of a God-fearing parent, who being but a mere inexperienced boy at the time that he ascended the throne had most likely fallen into the hands of evil advisers, was himself the author of the terrible calamities which here meet our gaze. We remark in the first place that the opening words of the psalm, "O God, the heathen are come into thine inheritance" are even more applicable to the avowed adoption of heathen principles by the rulers of God's people than to the invasion of the holy land (for God's inheritance, if locally understood, must denote the whole land, not merely the site of the sanctuary) by a foreign heathen army. This latter calamity had become too familiar to the people in the evil days that were now gathering around them for them to speak of it as something new. The desecration of the temple by Manasseh—"thy holy temple have they defiled"—is fully recorded in history; and it may be that the words "they have laid Jerusalem on heaps," or "they have made Jerusalem into stone-heaps," should rather be understood as a figurative description of the desolate appearance that was coming over Jerusalem while idolatrous altars (many of them perhaps of a very rude character) were being everywhere erected in its streets, than of an actual overthrow of the city. Knowing what divine judgments Manasseh's idolatries were calling down, the faithful beheld in the changed appearance of Jerusalem the very beginning, as it were, of the fulfilment of the judgment denounced: "I will stretch over Jerusalem the line of Samaria, and the plummet of the house of Ahab: and I will wipe Jerusalem as a man wipeth a dish, wiping it, and turning it upside down[1]." The slaughter of the faithful servants of God, described in the second and third verses of the psalm, agrees with the historical record that "Manasseh shed innocent blood very much, till he had filled Jerusalem from one end to another[2]." Moreover the enquiry, "How long, LORD? wilt thou be angry for ever?" was one that even faith might well make, at a time when Manasseh's sins had provoked a sentence of national desolation which God would not recall[3]; and the form of expression in the ensuing words, "shall thy jealousy burn like fire?" would be remarkably appropriate in a season of general idolatry, seeing that the jealousy of God, in refusing to allow his own honour to be given to another, was just that divine attribute against which the sin of idolatry offended[4].

Arguments of a more critical kind may be also

---

[1] 2 Kings xxi. 13.
[2] Ibid. xxi. 16.
[3] Ibid. xxi. 12—15; cf. xxii. 19; Jer. xv. 4.
[4] It deserves consideration whether the singular number of the verb in the former clause of v. 7, אכל he hath devoured, may not be explained by a tacit reference to Manasseh as the author of all the misery. Some MSS. indeed, and all the ancient versions, as also our E. V., have the verb in the plural; but the *textus receptus* here merits respect from the very difficulty which it creates.

adduced in support of the assignment of this psalm to the period of the reign of Manasseh. We find that v. 4 is borrowed from Psalm xliv. 13. The two psalms can therefore not be of the same date; for a psalmist of the Asaphic choir would not have borrowed from a contemporary composition of the choir of the Korhites. But there would be on the other hand no reason why a Korhite psalm, composed during the reign of Ahaz, and arranged in its place in the Psalter during that of Hezekiah, should not influence the thoughts of an Asaphite writing in the days of Manasseh. Again, we cannot well assign to the psalm before us a much later date. For vv. 6, 7 are repeated, with slight variations, in Jer. x. 25; and from Jeremiah's habit of borrowing, as well as for other reasons (for which see Hengstenberg), it may be presumed that the passage in the psalm is the original. But that prophecy of Jeremiah was apparently uttered either in the reign of Josiah, or early in the reign of Jehoiakim,—more probably the former: the psalm therefore cannot well delineate the misery of the inhabitants of Jerusalem under any of her last three kings, and we are thus naturally led to date it as early as the reign of Manasseh. It will here be in place to remark that v. 2 is also cited, as a portion of canonical Scripture, by the author of the First Book of Maccabees, who traced a new fulfilment of the psalmist's words in the massacre perpetrated by Bacchides at Jerusalem[1].

In the structure of his composition the psalmist does not seem to have fettered himself by any rule save that of placing the short verse, v. 7, containing the kernel of the whole, in the centre.

The psalm is in its purport sufficiently simple. One point in it should not however be passed over without notice; the zeal, and one might almost say the entire

[1] 1 Macc. vii. 16, 17

singleness of desire, of the worshippers in it, notwithstanding their own abyss of misery, for the honour of their God. Even when they think of themselves, it is not in any feeling of selfishness, but rather through a just appreciation of their dignity as God's chosen people. "For the glory of his name" they beseech the God of their salvation to hear them; "for his name's sake" they pray him to purge away their sins; in order that his power may be known abroad they ask him to take vengeance on the heathen; because of the reproaches that have been poured upon him they appeal to him to reward their neighbours sevenfold; and the whole aim of their supplication for deliverance is that so they, "the people and sheep of his pasture," may render him thanks and praise for evermore. And from all this it will be evident in what spirit they utter the prayer at which many have stumbled, "Pour out thy wrath upon the heathen that have not known thee, and upon the kingdoms that have not called upon thy name." Not in malice; not even necessarily in indifference to the welfare of the whole mass of the heathen themselves; but to the end that God's Church may be kept alive upon earth; that he may still have on earth a people remaining to honour him, a people on whom his name shall rest, a people from whom as a centre, and through whose instrumentality, shall ultimately be diffused the richest of all blessings to the inhabitants of the world at large.

PSALM LXXX.

"To the Chief Musician, unto (or possibly, by a later and less correct usage of the preposition, *upon*¹) shoshannim (or lilies), a Testimony of Asaph, a Psalm."

---

¹ In the previous psalm, v. 6, "Pour out thy wrath *upon* the heathen," the preposition אל is used where we should have expected על.

For an explanation of this superscription the reader is referred to the Introduction to Psalm lx, to which this psalm bears a resemblance in its warlike tone, in the use of the phrase "thy right hand," and in its mention of some of the tribes of Israel by name. The full purport of the superscription is however obscure. In its structure this psalm resembles Psalm xlv, which is also "upon shoshannim:" it consists of three strophes, successively increasing in length, the concluding verses of which differ only in this, that for the word *God* in v. 3 we have the more solemn appellation *God of hosts* in v. 7, and the yet fuller name Lord **God** *of hosts* in v. 19.

With this psalm commences the second group of the series of psalms having their origin in the events which had befallen the kingdom of the ten tribes. Between the psalms on which we are now entering, and Psalms lxxvii, lxxviii, there is this difference; that whereas Psalm lxxviii. was the address of the Church of Judah to the Israelites, and Psalm lxxvii. the lamentation of the Church of Judah for their captivity, those from Psalm lxxx. onward seem to have been designed, at least in part, for the use of the Israelites themselves. As however their superscriptions shew them to have been composed by Levites from the choirs at Jerusalem, we may venture to suppose that they were the productions of persons who had gone among the Israelites in a missionary spirit, with a view of bringing before them the principles of godly obedience from which they had departed, and also of preparing the way for a reunion in due time of the two rival kingdoms. Knowing as we do from the evidence of Psalm xlii. how in the days of Ahaz during the "great persecution against the Church which was at Jerusalem" the Levites were "scattered abroad" through the neighbouring regions, we may well suppose that while some took refuge in exile in the districts across the Jordan, others made their way, like the early Christians in after times, to the city of Samaria, and there employed themselves in preaching the word. This however is a mere matter of conjecture; and the labours of the Levites in the kingdom of Israel must in fact have begun before the reign of Ahaz, if only it can be shewn that the psalms on which we are now entering are generally of earlier date.

Of the reference of the psalm now before us to the state of the kingdom of Israel there can be no doubt. It is sufficiently proved by the mention of Joseph in v. 1; as also by the title "Shepherd of Israel" by which God is addressed, a title derived from the language used by the patriarch Jacob both in his blessing upon Joseph's children, and also in his blessing upon Joseph himself[1]. In v. 2 we have mention by name of three of the most prominent of the ten schismatic tribes, Ephraim, Benjamin, and Manasseh[2]; specially of those

---

[1] Gen. xlviii. 15; xlix. 24.

[2] It would here have been necessary to refute the vulgar error that in the separation of the kingdoms the Benjamites adhered to the house of David, had not the task been already performed by Hengstenberg. At the time of the schism there were but eleven tribes; for the prophecy of Jacob upon Simeon and Levi had been fulfilled, and neither of those tribes could any longer claim to be reckoned in the enumeration. With the history of the Levites every one is acquainted: they never had an inheritance in the land. The Simeonites on the other hand, the weakest of all the tribes at the period of their entry into Canaan (see Numb. xxvi), had their inheritance within the inheritance of the children of Judah (Josh. xix), from whom therefore they could never have been politically separated, and among whom they become partially absorbed. We read indeed of their making invasions southward as late as the reign of Hezekiah, and of their expelling the Amalekites from Mount Seir (1 Chron. iv. 39 seqq.); but the very mention of the reign of Hezekiah as the date of their expedition shews that it was with the kingdom of Judah that they were connected. Of the eleven remaining tribes then, that had at the time of the schism a distinct political existence, ten rebelled (1 Kings xi. 31, 35) and but one adhered to Rehoboam (1 Kings xi. 13, 32, 36; xii. 20). A portion, however, of the Benjamites,— those, probably, who dwelt in the neighbourhood of Jerusalem,—appear to have been detached by Judah from the rest of the tribe; and it is of this portion that in treating of the affairs of the kingdom of Judah mention is fre-

three that had in old time in the journey through the wilderness marched immediately behind the tabernacle[1]; on which account God is here besought to stir up his strength before them, and is addressed in the words "**thou** that dwellest between the cherubim." Still further is the reference of the psalm to the state of the kingdom of Israel confirmed by the beautiful metaphor of the vine; which after it had been transplanted from Egypt into the land of Canaan, covered the hills with its shadow and the 'cedars of God' 'with' its 'branches,' and sent out its boughs to the sea and its 'suckers' to the river. In these words are marked out the limits of Israel's inheritance: the hills of **the** Arabian desert **on** the south, the cedar-nurturing heights of Lebanon **on** the north, the Mediterranean on the west, and the Euphrates on the east. These were the limits promised by Moses and Joshua, and actually reached in the days of Solomon[2]. And it may be observed by the way **how** accurately the psalmist marks the kind of tenure which the Israelites had of the territory eastward towards the Euphrates, a territory which although politically annexed could from its desert character not be occupied or inhabited: **he** represents the vine as putting forth thither not **its boughs or** its branches, but its suckers. Now granting that the vine was properly the emblem of the whole nation, we nevertheless observe

---

quently made under the name of Benjamin (1 Kings xii. 21, 23; seqq.). Of the Benjamite towns, Jericho (2 Kings ii.), Bethel (1 Kings xii. 29), and Ramah (1 Kings **xv.** 17; Jer. **xxxi. 15), were** included in the kingdoms **of** Israel; Geba (1 Kings xv 22), Mizpeh or Mizpah, if they be the same (ibid.), and probably Anathoth (Jer. i. 1), in that of Judah. Jerusalem itself, although locally situate within the original Ben- jamite inheritance, can hardly be reckoned a Benjamite city. It may be observed that the close alliance of some Benjamites with Judah, in opposition to the general leaning of the tribe, was of old standing; for even during the reign of the Benjamite Saul, several came to David at Ziklag (1 Chron. xii. 2, 16).

[1] Numb. ii. 17—24; x. 21—24.
[2] Deut. xi. 24; Josh i. 4; 1 Kings iv. 21—24.

that after the schism the kings of the ten tribes singly **still claimed** to reach, in three of the four quarters, the limits which marked the dominions of Solomon; nay, in the fourth quarter also, if the hills of the **south** may be understood as including not only those of **Edom**, the frontier of Judah, but also those of Moab, the frontier **of Reuben**. Respecting the kingdom of Judah it is obvious that **no such** assertion could be made. As applied therefore to Judah the image of the vine would be wholly out of place: as applied to the kingdom of **Israel** it possessed in a great measure the same force **and** beauty as if it had been applied to the undivided **realm** of Solomon. In **fact** the very name *kingdom of Israel* shews that although Judah more truly repre**sented the** Israelitish church as retaining possession **of** the sanctuary, and being governed by kings **of the house** from which the Messiah was to spring, it was the ten tribes that more truly represented the Israelitish nation, —the nation in all its rebelliousness and idolatry and apostasy from God.

Nor are we left without approximate indications of the period at which the psalm must have been composed. It was a period when the hedges round the vine had been broken down, when it was being plucked by all that passed by, when the **boar** out of the wood was wasting it and the wild beasts **devouring it**. This might be either **the period of the** reigns of **Jehu, Jehoahaz, and Jehoash,** when the Lord "began **to cut Israel short**[1]**,**" and when they were hard pressed by the **Syrians; or** else that later period, **more** immediately preceding the final overthrow of the kingdom, when the Israelites were being alternately plundered and carried captive by the **monarchs** of Assyria. The earlier period of the Syrian oppression seems the more probable. In

---

[1] 2 Kings x. 32.

favour of it is the circumstance that the earlier oppression would be the more acutely felt: the people had not then learnt to view humiliation **and misery as** their normal condition. The boar too may be preferably taken as an emblem of the Syrian rather than of the Assyrian king; inasmuch as the latter would be more consistently symbolized by the lion or the bull. **And** if the wild beasts[1] who are mentioned in connexion with the boar denote the subsidiary enemies of the Israelites, who took advantage of their humiliation to despoil them for themselves, it is worthy of note that we have a record of **a** Moabitish invasion of the kingdom of Israel during **the period of the** Syrian oppression[2], but none during the later period of the progress **of the** Assyrian **power.**

We find in the psalm one expression which will enable us to approximate even more nearly to the precise date at which it was composed. The use and even recurrence of the unusual phrase, "that thou madest strong for thyself" **(vv.** 15, 17), **can** scarcely be the result of accident. Assuming that there is in these words a general reference to the sovereignty of the house of David, it is not unnatural to suppose that they contain **also an** allusion to the name of the particular representative of that house,—AMAZIAH, "The LORD maketh strong,"—at the time that the psalm was written. Furthermore, as Amaziah had distinguished himself by his victory over the Edomites in the valley of salt, and by his capture of their strong city of Petra[3], **it is** at least possible that the author of this psalm may **have** been induced to imitate the superscription, and in some respects the tone and language of Psalm lx. by

---

[1] The word, although singular, seems to be used in a plural sense, as n Psalm l. 11.

[2] 2 Kings xiii. 20.
[3] Ibid. xiv. 7.

the circumstance that that psalm had celebrated the triumph of David over the same foes, and in the same valley.

Amaziah king of Judah was contemporary with Jehoash the son of Jehoahaz king of Israel. In the early years of their reigns the two monarchs were on friendly terms; and it may be that the alliance of Judah and Israel prompted the faithful to hope at that time more ardently than they would otherwise have done for the reunion of the two kingdoms under the sway of the house of David. If so, it was probably in the early part of Amaziah's reign that the psalm before us was composed. Nor is it any objection to this view that the alliance should have been so abruptly terminated, and the immediate hopes of the faithful disappointed. It was Amaziah's part to wait patiently and consistently for Israel's submission, not to anticipate the day by *hiring* the temporary obedience of the Israelitish army. Justly therefore in such a case did the prophet of God rebuke him for the compromise which through distrust of God he had made with schism: "O king, let not the army of Israel go with thee; for the LORD is not with Israel, to wit, with all the children of Ephraim[1]."

But it will be asked, by what process does the psalmist convert his lamentation for the calamities that had befallen the ten tribes of Israel into a prayer for blessings upon the king of the house of David? The answer to this will be found in the last six verses, the true interpretation of which, in consequence of their importance in reference to the general contents of the psalm, must not be here passed over. It will be observed that the psalmist prays in v. 15 for the branch (so E. V.) of the vine, in v. 17 for the son of man, that

---

[1] 2 Chron. xxv. 6, 7.

God has **made** strong for himself. The words rendered respectively *branch* and *son* are in Hebrew the same. Our **E. V.** has correctly noted the difference of usage of the **word in the** two verses; but has nevertheless **hardly** caught its exact meaning **in** the former verse in the choice of the English term *branch*. The "son of a vine" should be as strictly distinguished on the one hand from the boughs and branches of the tree (which would rather be, in Hebrew, the vine's *daughters*) as on the other hand from the mere suckers and offshoots. We should rather understand by it a young and healthy shoot, springing out **not** much above the ground from the parent stock, into which, when **all the** former growth of the vine has been cut down, the whole **strength** of the plant eventually passes, and from which **boughs** and branches thus spread forth anew[1]. In the **image** present to the psalmist's mind the vine was the whole nation of Israel; of whom the ten tribes formed **by** far the greater part. The shoot that God had made strong for himself was the house of David; from whom, according to the revelation made by Nathan, the Messiah was to spring, and to whom was given the promise of everlasting dominion. For a time the whole vine had appeared **to** flourish; and its various boughs—Ephraim **the** fruitful, and Benjamin the beloved, and **the** rest—had **shot forth** and blossomed in full life and beauty. But now the former beauty of the tree **had** passed away. It was "burned with fire," **it was** "cut down"; and though the whole tree was not **utterly** ruined, yet as each once gorgeous bough and **branch** was successively bruised, lopped off, or consumed, so did **it** become more and more difficult to

---

[1] The classical passage in which mention is made of the "son" **and** "daughters" of a tree is Gen. xlix. 22; where **our** English Version has employed the terms *bough* and *branches.*

hope for the restoration of the vine's former magnificence save by means of the shoot on which God had looked with peculiar favour, which had suffered no essential injury, and in which, as a new stem, the tree might yet fulfil the expectations that had been formed of it.

In v. 16 the simile of the vine is brought to a close. The latter half of that verse appears to be a prayer for the discomfiture of Israel's enemies: "'let them' perish, &c." However this may be, the following verse (v. 17) must unquestionably be regarded as an exposition of v. 15; the psalmist thus expressing in this verse in plain language what he had previously expressed in the language of allegory. The vine[1] which God's right hand had planted is here identified with "the man (or rather, the word being used collectively, the *men*) of his right hand"; i. e. the Israelites. Some interpreters have traced in this phrase an allusion to the name Benjamin, "son of the right hand." It seems difficult however to suppose that under the simile of the vine the psalmist intended to refer to one tribe more than another. On the other, the shoot of the vine which God had made strong for himself is identified with the "son of man" whom he has made strong for himself; in other words with the house of David, to whom the sovereignty of Israel had been for ever guaranteed, with Amaziah as the representative of the Davidic house at the time that the psalm was written, and with the Messiah as its future and greatest embodiment, in whom all the promises made both to the Davidic house and to Israel generally should receive

---

[1] The meaning of the word כנה (English Version *vineyard*), in v. 15, has been much disputed; some (with the LXX.) treating it as a verb; others (with the Targum and Jerome) as a substantive. It is probably a verbal substantive derived from the Infin. Piel of כנה *to surname, to regard as one's own, to look upon with peculiar affection;* and it will thus signify *property.*

their full accomplishment. The Targumist is therefore substantially right when he explains the "son of man" to denote the king Messiah. Still better Bossuet observes that the phrase refers to David who had been designated king and established on the throne by God, and also, under the figure of David, to Christ David's descendant.

How far in the days of Jehoash and Amaziah the hopes of any of the faithful among the schismatic Israelitish tribes had been once more fixed on the royal house of David it is impossible to determine. Those in whose hearts the spirit of the psalmist's prayer found an immediate response would undoubtedly be at best but few in number. It was a hard struggle which faith in God's promises to the nation of Israel and the family of David had to maintain against the general recklessness of everything sacred which must have been engendered by the career of wickedness through which the nation had passed, and which had in a measure been rendered chronic by the general gloom that had now set in. It is in like manner hard for the Christian Church in a season of general depression and apathy to realize the thought that Christ shall one day rule over all the earth. In such seasons this psalm will have its especial use. It will teach the faithful few not to "go back" from the Lord whom they have once acknowledged; but in the spirit of the psalmist continually to pray, "Turn us again, O LORD God of hosts, Father, Son, and Holy Spirit; cause thy face to shine upon the people upon whom thy holy name has been called; and so will salvation from on high be poured forth upon them."

PSALM LXXXI.

"Blow up the trumpet in the new moon, in the 'moon's change[1],' on our 'solemn' day" (v. 3). Among the Israelites the commencements of the several months, although generally speaking **not** strictly festivals, were marked **by the blowing** of silver trumpets, similar to those which **had** by divine direction been made in the wilderness. There was however one day in the year to **which the** blowing of trumpets imparted a special and distinctive character, and which was legitimately reckoned as a festival, and **was** ordered as such to be observed. This was the first **day** of the seventh month; on which we may venture to suppose that the blowing would be continued longer than usual, **and** the trumpets made to give forth a louder sound than on other days[2]. It was probably for this festival of trumpets that **the** psalm **before us** was written. To the interpretation of this **psalm it is** at all **events** quite **essential** that the **purport of the** blowing of trumpets should be well understood; **on** which account it will be **here** convenient

---

[1] The meaning of the word כסה (English Version *time appointed*), which recurs in the form כסא at Prov. vii. 20, has been the subject of much controversy. It probably denotes the commencement of any of the moon's quarters. It may therefore be applied either to **the** new moon, as in the present psalm; or **to** the first quarter; or to the full moon, **of** which the corresponding **Syriac** word **is used in the** Syriac **version of** 1 Kings xii. 32; **or** to the last quarter, of which the same **is** used in the Syriac version **of** 2 Chron. vii. 10. The word may be etymologically connected **with** the **Arabic** كسا (with last radical ي) *to put on (a garment)*; and would thus denote the season at which the moon *assumes* her new phase. The Jewish months were all lunar, and commenced with **the** new moon; the average length of the solar **year being preserved by the** intercalation **of a month at the** close of the year **as often as was necessary**; i.e. about every third year. And **the** observance **of the moon's changes is** shewn not only **by the celebration** of the Feast of Trumpets **on the** *first* day of **the** seventh month, but also by the commencement of **the** Feasts of Passover and Tabernacles on the *fifteenth* **days** of the first and seventh months respectively.

[2] See generally **Numb.** x. 1—10; xxix. 1; Lev. xxiii. 23—25.

to insert the following account of the subject from a work in which the typical significance of the various festivals and other religious institutions of the Israelites has been ably and lucidly treated[1].

"There can be no doubt," says the author of this work, "that the sacred use of the trumpet had its reason in the loud and stirring noise it emits. Hence it is described as a *cry* in Lev. xxv. 9 (the English word *sound* there is too feeble), which was to be heard throughout the whole land. The references to it in Scripture generally suggest the same idea (Zeph. i. 16; Isai. lviii. 1; Hos. viii. 1, &c.). On this account the sound of the trumpet is very commonly employed in Scripture as an image of the voice or word of God. The voice of God, and the voice of the trumpet on Mount Sinai, were heard together (Ex. xix. 5, 18, 19), first the trumpet-sound as the symbol, then the reality. So also St John heard the voice of the Lord as that of a trumpet (Rev. i. 10; iv. 1), and the sound of the trumpet is once and again spoken of as the harbinger of the Son of Man, when coming in power and great glory, to utter the almighty word which shall quicken the dead to life, and make all things new (Matth. xxiv. 31; 1 Cor. xv. 52; 1 Thess. iv. 16). The sound of the trumpet, then, was a symbol of the majestic, omnipotent voice or word of God; but of course only in those things in which it was employed in respect to what God had to say to men. It might be used also as from man to God, or by the people, as from one to another. In this case, it would be a call to a greater than the usual degree of alacrity and excitement in regard to the work and service of God. And such probably was the more peculiar design of the blowing of trumpets at the festivals generally, and especially at the festival of trumpets on the

---

[1] Fairbairn's *Typology*, II. pp. 413—415. ed. 2.

first day of the seventh month. That month was distinguished above all the other months of the year for the sacred services to be performed in it—it was emphatically the sacred month. Being the *seventh* month —bearing on its name the symbol of the covenant, and of covenant holiness—it was hallowed in its course by solemnities, which peculiarly displayed both God's goodness to his people and their delight in God. For, not only was its first day consecrated to sacred rest and spiritual employment, but the tenth was the great day of yearly atonement, when the high-priest was permitted to sprinkle the mercy-seat with the blood of sacrifice, and the liveliest exhibition was given which the materials of the earthly sanctuary could afford of the salvation of Christ. And then on the fifteenth of the same month commenced the Feast of Tabernacles, which was intended to present a striking image of the glory that should follow, as the former of the humiliation and sufferings by which the salvation was accomplished. In perfect accordance with all this, not only is the feast named the Feast of Trumpets, but "a memorial of blowing of trumpets," a bringing to remembrance, or putting God, as it were, in mind of the great things by which (symbolically) he was to distinguish the month that was thus introduced; precisely as when they went to war against an enemy that oppressed them, they were to blow the trumpet, and, it is added, "ye shall be remembered before the LORD your God, and ye shall be saved from your enemies" (Numb. x. 9).

In reference to these remarks it may be observed that the recognition of the trumpet-sound as the symbol of the voice of God may be carried somewhat further than they would seem to imply. For as it was by divine appointment that the blowings of the trumpets at the beginnings of the several months took place, so whatever other meaning they might have, they could not well but be in the first place regarded as a solemn summons from God to his people, not merely from the people one to another, to bestir themselves the more ardently in his worship and service; and at the same time, and as a legitimate consequence of this, as a warning to them to renew their obedience to whatever portions of his law had through negligence or through any other cause been suffered to lapse into temporary oblivion. And it is as the symbol of the voice of God thus calling to his people that the trumpet-blast furnishes the key to the whole train of thought in the psalm now before us. The leading truth which it seeks to set forth is this; that God is at this very time addressing his people even as he addressed them at the first. After therefore summoning the Israelites to the due observance of their customary solemnity (vv. 1—4), the psalmist proceeds to indicate the meaning of the solemnity (v. 5), and to shew by the lessons of past history the majesty of God's voice, and the obedience or disobedience with which it had been treated (vv. 6—12); and then affectionately warns the people to attend to the voice of God now addressing them, reminding them what mighty things that voice could in their behalf accomplish (vv. 13—16). And the voice of God being thus the psalmist's theme, the psalm itself is from v. 6 onward appropriately thrown into the form of an address from God, and is uttered in his person.

To this address from God v. 5 naturally leads. The true rendering of the verse is apparently as follows:

This he ordained in Joseph for a testimony,
(After he had gone forth against the land of Egypt,)

That I should listen to the utterance of him whom I might not know by sight[1]:—

In other words, this solemnity of trumpets did God, after he had gone forth to execute judgment upon the Egyptian oppressors, and had so by majestic displays of his power brought out his people from their bondage and conducted them to Sinai where his will was to be made known to them, ordain in Israel as a testimony that they should ever remember to listen to the voice of him who spake to them, and who by the voice which he uttered out of the midst of the fire and the darkness, and by the commandments and the statutes and the judgments which he delivered to them through Moses, revealed himself to them as the Lord their God, though they might not gaze on his face or behold his similitude. The name Joseph here stands for all Israel: the use of the name is justified by the circumstance that it was through Joseph, and as connected with him, that Israel had originally gone down to sojourn in Egypt: the reason for its employment is, as will presently appear, that it was to the tribes of whom Ephraim was the principal representative that the psalmist was addressing himself. With the use of the name Joseph here the introduction of the name into Psalm lxxvii. 15 may be compared. But it virtually includes all; and by the use of the first person in the last line of the verse the psalmist identifies himself with the people of whom he was one, and acknowledges that the obligation of listening to God's voice was as incumbent upon himself as upon the rest.

---

[1] The tense of the verb אשמע has, as in our English Version, been too generally disregarded; and the word עדות in the first line has in consequence been taken in the absolute sense, which it will hardly bear, of a mere religious rite; whereas it only denotes that rite as *witnessing* to something to be mentioned afterwards. With the second line cf. Exod. xi. 4. The infinitive after ב has here, as in other passages, the power of a preterite. Note, by the way, the general outward correspondence between this verse and v. 10.

And now therefore the voice of God is made to sound **forth**. The address of God **to** his people commences (**v. 6**) **with a** recital of what he had done in their **behalf: it is in** fact an expansion or exegesis of the psalmist's words in the previous verse respecting God's going forth against the land of Egypt:

"I removed his **shoulder** from the burden:
I caused that his **hands** should be delivered from the hod."

Of the language **of** this verse a remarkable illustration meets **us** in the circumstance mentioned by Tholuck and by other recent commentators **on** the Psalter, that among the remaining Egyptian sculptures **have** been found some representing, **as is supposed, the** Israelites with **the** vessels in which they carried the clay **and** the tiles. They had then groaned, almost in despair, **by reason of their** misery. But the voice of God had **spoken to Pharaoh** in the marvels of the ten **plagues:** it had achieved its divine purpose, and the Israelites had been set free. And yet again, when, commencing their **march,** they had been shut in by Pharaoh's army on the shore of the Red Sea, and had, **in** the language of the next verse, "called in trouble," **cried out in** their fear unto the Lord, he had delivered **them:** the voice of **the Lord,** speaking through the **uplifted** rod of Moses, had divided the sea for the people to pass through, and had then overwhelmed the Egyptians with the returning **waters.**

And all this he had done that he might then "answer them in the secret place of thunder," and might "prove them at the waters of Meribah." The former of **these** phrases refers to the impressive proof which the Israelites had had of the majesty of God's voice at the peaks **of** Sinai; when he had spoken to them "out **of** the **midst** of the fire, of the cloud, and of

4—2

the thick darkness, with a great voice;" and they had trembled to hear him, and had besought that he would rather speak unto them by Moses; promising that whatsoever he should say unto them, they would hear it and do it. And as regards the scene at Meribah, God had there vindicated the majesty of his voice by his sentence of punishment upon Moses and Aaron. He had bidden them *speak* to the rock before the eyes of the Israelites, that the water might flow forth: they by striking the rock instead of speaking to it had virtually dishonoured the majesty of the divine voice; and hence their exclusion from the promised land.

In vv. 8—12 the psalmist's strain reaches its highest pitch. God is represented as openly and expressly laying his bidding upon Israel, that they should hearken to his voice. Alas! as his mercy, so, almost, had been, through all history, their disobedience. They would not hearken to him. It was in his power to have satisfied their utmost desires: however wide they had opened their mouth, he, whose own voice was so majestic, could have filled it. But they had given themselves over to worship strange gods; and he had in return given them up unto their own hearts' lusts.

And yet God's mercy had not passed away. Notwithstanding the long catalogue of their transgressions, there still sounds forth the exhortation to renewed obedience (vv. 13—16). Our English Version, following in the wake of the ancient translations, has rendered this passage in the past tense; but it would be equally accordant to the Hebrew original, and more in conformity with the general tenor of the psalm, to render it in the present:

> Oh that my people would hearken unto me,
> And that Israel would walk in my ways!
> I should soon subdue, &c.

And it will be observed that this passage is based upon the words of God to Moses on the occasion to which the psalmist has already once referred, when the people, entreating that he would speak directly to them no more out of the secret place of thunder, had tendered their promise of obedience to all the commandments which by Moses he should lay upon them. God's words were these: "O that there were such a heart in them, that they would fear me, and keep all my commandments always, that it might be well with them, and with their children for ever[1]!" Rebellious as the people had been, all was not yet desperate; and even the very invitation to them to sing aloud unto God their strength, and to make a joyful noise unto the God of Jacob, was a virtual assurance of God's blessing upon them, if in true repentance they would only turn themselves to him.

Having thus developed the general purport of the psalm, it remains for us to investigate the historical circumstances out of which it probably arose. And when we note the apparent comprisal of the whole Israelitish people among Joseph's descendants (v. 5); the continued use of the name Israel (vv. 4, 8, 13), and of the title "God of Jacob" (vv. 1, 4); and the absence of even the slightest allusion to the tribe of Judah, the royal family of David, or the sanctuary at Jerusalem; there can be little doubt that the psalm was, like that which precedes it, composed for the more immediate use of the people of the ten tribes.

And to them, even in their separation from Judah, a psalm which should help them to enter aright into the spirit of the Feast of Trumpets would not be out of place. The other feasts were solemnized only within the limits of the holy city of Jerusalem, whither all

[1] Deut. v. 29.

were for that purpose commanded to repair: the celebration of this extended, we may well believe, throughout the whole land. We have, it is true, no record whatever of either the manner or the place in which the blowing of trumpets was observed. In the days of the institution of the festival, when the Israelites, still in the wilderness, were gathered together within the limits of a single encampment, there had been but two trumpets in use, and therefore of necessity but one place within the encampment where the trumpets were blown. But that after the Israelites were settled in the land of their inheritance trumpets were blown at the appointed seasons in every city of importance may be gathered from the following circumstances. First, the blowing of trumpets had a meaning for the whole nation; yet the people were not commanded to assemble at God's sanctuary either on the new moons generally or at the Feast of Trumpets in particular. In the second place, the Feast of Trumpets at the beginning of the seventh month was evidently intended to serve as a warning to the people to observe duly the ensuing holy solemnities which in the course of that month were to be celebrated; but such a warning would be but to little purpose, unless it were uttered throughout the length and breadth of the land so that all might hear it.

It is thus easily conceivable that the Feast of Trumpets may have been one of the few religious institutions of the law of Moses that survived in the kingdom of Israel. There could be small political motive on the part of the rulers of Israel for abolishing it; whatever religious significance it had would by them be overlooked; nor did it of necessity require the assemblage of all the people to the sanctuary at Jerusalem. And thus at a time when the Passover, and the Feast of Pentecost, and the Feast of Tabernacles had long since been superseded by the feast in the eighth month of Jeroboam's devising, and when the Great Day of Atonement had been utterly forgotten, the blowing of trumpets on the first day of every month, and even the more solemn Feast of Trumpets on the first day of the seventh month, may have perpetuated itself from sheer force of custom, though its origin and its religious significance were alike unheeded[1].

And if so, let us endeavour to realize the feelings with which the spectacle of this ancient solemnity would be regarded by a Levite of Jerusalem, travelling in an earnest missionary spirit, in the days of the division of the kingdoms, into the realm of Israel. It would be his endeavour to remind the people of the real meaning of the custom which they had not abandoned; and thus to awaken these schismatic churchmen to a sense of the divine teaching conveyed by the one church ordinance, which, however ill appreciated, still held its ground amongst them. He would tell them that the blowing of trumpets which they still kept up was "a statute for Israel, and a law of the God of Jacob (v. 4)." He would shew them that it was a symbol of the voice of God continually proclaiming aloud, "I am the LORD your God (v. 10)[2]," and calling on his people for obedience; and he would seize the opportunity to exhort them to give heed to that divine voice which they had so long and so bitterly neglected.

Pondering at the same time on the depressed political condition of those whom he was addressing, and receiving from time to time tidings of the ground they were losing before their Syrian enemies,—for in all probability this psalm is of the same general period with the preceding,—he would call to mind the words

[1] Cf. Hos. ii. 11, "her new moons."   [2] Numb. x. 10.

of the olden promise, "If ye go to war in your land against the enemy that oppresseth you, then ye shall blow an alarm with the trumpets; and ye shall be remembered before the LORD your God, and ye shall be saved from your enemies[1]." And in reliance on this promise he would aver how soon, if the people would only heed the divine call, God would subdue their enemies and turn his hand against their adversaries, and force all that opposed them to crouch before them. It was perhaps not many years after the date of the composition of this psalm, that God, looking with the deepest tenderness on the bitter affliction of Israel, gave one more earnest of what he was still willing to do for his people, in the victories which he granted to the younger Jeroboam[2]. But alas, notwithstanding his promises and pledges of mercy, the people would not hearken; and were after a temporary respite overtaken by the ruin by which they had been already threatened.

Have we, the members of Christ's Church, no need to be reminded of the voice of God which is continually addressing us? And is it not well that we should be advised how many of the institutions connected with our Christian worship,—for example, the Church-season of Advent, the commencement of the ecclesiastical year,—bear witness of the continual call which is sounding forth from God to our hearts?

PSALM LXXXII.

A PSALM reproving the iniquitous perversion of justice by those who, as judges in Israel, were the human representatives of God the Great Judge of all; and who ought therefore in their judicial proceedings to have set

---

[1] Numb. x. 9. [2] 2 Kings xiv. 26, 27.

forth that equitable and impartial righteousness, from the very necessity of which, as the foundation of all order in earthly affairs, their own authority sprang. In **v. 1**, the psalmist gives utterance to the important truth that God himself is invisibly present in every judicial assembly; conveying authority to those who judge, sanctioning the justice which they administer, receiving appeals from their wrongful decisions, and reserving to himself the right to call the judges to account for their shortcomings in integrity or wisdom. **In vv.** 2—7 God is accordingly **introduced,** reproving **and** warning those who have forgotten his presence **among** them. In v. 8 (which recalls before us the concluding verse of Psalm lviii.) the psalmist, **weary of the** injustice which **he had beheld** perpetrated, and recognizing the eternal sovereignty **of him from** whom all judgment ultimately proceeds, **calls on God to** arise and assume back into his own hands the administration of justice throughout the earth.

In regard of the strophical arrangement, v. 5, consisting of three lines, is the emphatic verse round which the rest are grouped. Vv. 1—4 hang together, so also vv. 6, 7: v. 8 forms the conclusion of the whole.

It has been rather strangely supposed by many students of this psalm, that it was composed at the time that Jehoshaphat set judges throughout the kingdom of **Judah**[1]. They have overlooked the fact that the psalm is obviously not an exhortation to officers newly **appointed, but** a stern reproof **to** those **who** had **long abused** and perverted their office. The vice against **which it** testifies **is** that oppression of the poor which prevailed so largely **in** the kingdom of Judah in the days of the prophet Isaiah[2], but which was denounced even more severely at a somewhat earlier period in the

---

[1] 2 Chron. xix. 5, seqq.   [2] Isaiah iii. 13—15.

kingdom of Israel by the prophet Amos[1]. It is probably to the state of affairs in the kingdom of the ten tribes that the psalm mainly refers; and it is in connexion with the prophecy of Amos that it should be read. The words of the last verse, "Arise, O God, judge the earth," strikingly coincide with the denunciations of judgment in the opening of the Book of Amos upon eight several countries; and the remaining words, "Thou shalt inherit all nations," may be compared with the train of thought in the nine verses with which the prophecy of Amos concludes. The exact date of the psalm cannot be precisely determined. Amos prophesied in the days of Jeroboam II.; but the eleven years' anarchy which followed on the decease of Jeroboam and the subsequent violent deaths of Zachariah, Shallum, and Pekahiah so strikingly illustrate the force of the words of v. 7, "ye shall fall like one of the princes," that we might almost venture to assume that the psalm was not written till after those scenes of anarchy and murder had commenced.

Remarkable, both on their own account, and also on account of the manner in which they are cited by our Saviour in the New Testament[2], are the words put into God's mouth in v. 6, "I have said, Ye are gods;" of which the words of the following clause, "and all of you are children of the most High," may be taken as a sort of exegetical paraphrase. They rest on the fact that in several passages of the Book of Exodus the Hebrew term *elohim* (*gods* or *powers*) is applied to those who exercised the office of judge[3]. They are so called, as our Saviour explains, because to them "the word of God came"; that word by which chosen men

---

[1] Amos ii. 6, 7; v. 6—15; &c.
[2] John x. 34.
[3] Ex. xxi. 6; xxii. 8, 9, 28; in which last passage our English Version has retained the rendering *gods*. On other uses of the term *elohim*, see above, Vol. I. p. 85, note 2.

were variously qualified for the discharge of their judicial or prophetical functions; in the one case the word of prophetical wisdom; in the other the word of prophecy. It is well known how frequently the announcements of the prophets of the Old Testament are prefaced by the phrase "Then came the word of the LORD unto, &c." The very existence of both judges and prophets, both of them in their respective modes God's earthly representatives, was a token that God had in old time not left himself without witness even in the persons of men. And if they might be called gods, whom God had appointed or accepted from among men to be his ministers, sending his word unto them to fit them for their ministerial office; how much more might the term be applied to him who exhibited in his own person the works of his Father; who had not been chosen out of the world to be God's minister, but had been expressly sent into it for that purpose, having been consecrated to his high office before he was conceived in the womb; and who, we may add, was himself the Revealing Word through whose agency the divine will had in every age been made known to the inferior judges and prophets!

PSALM LXXXIII.

THE psalmist calls upon God to discomfit the extensive hostile confederacy that had been formed against the people of Israel; and in order to add force to his prayer, puts God in mind of the former victories which he had granted for his people's deliverance. The instances of these deliverances are taken exclusively from the history of the period of the Judges; they are those of Deborah and of Gideon; in the which, or in the one of them, shared the tribes of Ephraim, Manasseh,

Benjamin, Issachar, Zebulun, Naphtali, and Asher, but not the tribe of Judah. Of the subsequent successes of David no mention is made. From all which it appears that the psalm was composed in reference to a danger which especially threatened the kingdom of the ten tribes.

Of the hostile confederacy which had been formed we have no direct historical record; but one or two scattered notices will enable us to ascertain its approximate date. The psalmist enumerates ten nations as concerned in it; possibly with reference to the ten tribes of Israel against whom they were confederate. These are the Edomites; the Ishmaelites; the Moabites; the Hagarenes, who had probably become the neighbours of the Moabites after their expulsion by the Reubenites and Gadites from the land of Gilead[1]; the Giblites, supposed by some to be the citizens of the Phœnician city Gebal, mentioned by Ezekiel, but more probably, from the connexion in which they here stand, the inhabitants of the mountain-district to the southeast of the Dead Sea still bearing the name Jebâl, the Gebalene of the Romans, the Gobolitis of Josephus; the Ammonites (the leading people of the triad in which they are enumerated); the Amalekites; the Philistines; the Tyrians; and the Assyrians. Now of these the Amalekites were extirpated by the Simeonites in the days of Hezekiah[2], and thenceforth disappeared from history: the confederacy therefore of which the psalm speaks must have been prior to the date of that occurrence. Again, as the list includes the Assyrians, but yet only as the auxiliary allies of the Moabites and Ammonites, who seem to have formed the mainstay of the league, we must assume a date sufficiently late for the Assyrians to be already rising into importance, but

---

[1] 1 Chron. v. 10, 20—22.   [2] 1 Chron. iv. 39—43.

yet not so late as the time when they approached the zenith of their power under Pul and Tiglath-pileser. This would lead us to the period of the reigns of Jehoash and of his son Jeroboam II. Now in the opening of the Book of Amos (who prophesied at some time during the last twenty-six years of the reign of Jeroboam) we have judgments denounced on eight several nations, and among them on the Philistines, Tyrians, Edomites, Ammonites, and Moabites. That on the Philistines of Gaza is denounced, "because they carried away captive the whole captivity, to deliver them up to Edom:" that on the Tyrians, "because they delivered up the whole captivity to Edom, and remembered not the brotherly covenant." Here are evidently the traces of that extensive confederacy of Israel's north-western, south-western, and south-eastern enemies, which the psalmist more fully lays open. Judgment is denounced upon Edom, "because he did pursue his brother with the sword, and did cast off all pity, and his anger did tear perpetually, and he kept his wrath for ever:" upon the children of Ammon, "because they have ripped up the women with child of Gilead, that they might enlarge their border." And there is a resemblance well worthy of note between the words of the prophet's judgment, and those of the psalmist's prayer. The former run thus: "I will kindle a fire in the wall of Rabbah, and it shall devour the palaces thereof, with shouting in the day of battle, with a tempest in the day of the whirlwind." They were probably suggested by the following (vv. 14, 15):

> As the fire burneth a wood,
> And as the flame setteth the mountains on fire,
> So persecute them with thy tempest,
> And make them afraid with thy 'whirlwind'.

¹ The Hebrew word here, although rendered in our English Version *storm*, is the same as that translated *whirlwind* in Amos i. 14.

It is only at this one period that we have any indication of the Phœnicians of Tyre being in league with the eastern enemies of the Israelites. Their object in entering into the league, as also that of the Philistines, seems to have been to carry on a traffic in Israelitish slaves; as appears from the writings of Joel, who prophesied but shortly before Amos, and who, being a prophet of the kingdom of Judah, condemns the Phœnicians and Philistines for having sold into slavery the children of Judah and the children of Jerusalem[1]. The nations of whom the hostile confederacy was formed were indeed at this time the common enemies of both Judah and Israel; and it is thus that we have another trace of the confederacy in the historical notice of the successes of king Uzziah, the contemporary of Jeroboam, "against the Philistines, and against the Arabians that dwelt in Gur-baal, and the Mehunims"; the Ammonites at the same time bringing him gifts[2]. It was probably by the contemporaneous victories of Uzziah and Jeroboam that the confederacy against which the psalmist prayed was finally broken up.

In respect of its structure the psalm consists of four strophes, vv. 1—4, 5—8, 9—12, 13—18. Of these the second and third, divided from each other by the Selah, form together the central portion of the psalm: the one enumerates the enemies by whom Israel was now assailed, the other the triumphs which in the strength of God she had won over her former foes; the one details the danger, the other the pledges of victory. As regards the other two strophes it is worthy of note that while the one records the desire of the surrounding heathen to consign the *name* of Israel to oblivion, the other sets forth the universal sovereignty of him whose *name* is Jehovah.

[1] Joel iii. 6.   [2] 2 Chron. xxvi. 7, 8.

In its Christian use, this psalm is admirably adapted both to express the supplications and to sustain the hopes of God's "hidden ones," when they behold, as is too frequently the case, the multifarious enemies of God's truth and Church all combining together against them. Different as were the designs with which the Edomites and Moabites and other enemies of God's Israel in ancient times entered into the ungodly confederacy, so different are the motives and principles which now influence those who are actively or passively combining to uproot the Church of Christ. And in the case of a psalm which enumerates in so distinct a catalogue the ancient enemies of the literal Israel, the question naturally arises, whether that tendency ought to be altogether checked, which would seek to trace out in each of the nations enumerated the type of a separate and recognizable class of the enemies, or of some separate feature in the general character of the enemies, by whom the Christian Church is assailed.

No hesitation was felt in this matter by Augustine and the interpreters of his school. They took, as was their wont, the *names* of the several enemies enumerated by the psalmist; they asked what those names signified in the Hebrew language; they found, rightly or wrongly,—and certainly the scraps of Hebrew lore which they contrived to pick up were none of the most accurate,—that the name Edomite denoted *earthy*, or *bloody*; Ishmaelite, *one who obeys himself*; and so for the rest. And these renderings of Hebrew names they proceeded to apply after a spiritual sort to the various characters of men in the world. They believed that in each separate Hebrew name there lurked some mystery which it was their business to search out; they urged that in doing this they were not unravelling some mere passage of rhetoric, but were endeavouring to interpret that which had been written by the Holy Spirit; and they asked the not altogether unreasonable question, If we do not thus interpret, what can it profit the Churches of Christ to read about the tabernacles of the Edomites, and the Ishmaelites, and the like? But estimable as may have been their intention in thus endeavouring to draw instruction out of every single Scriptural word, such a scheme of interpretation is evidently unsatisfactory, because it leaves so much to be accomplished by the mere arbitrary exercise of the fancy. In how few cases could those who interpreted the Old Testament in this manner venture to assert with any degree of confidence that the lessons which they had thus drawn out of a passage were those which the passage was intended to convey! The defect of their system was this: they forgot that on mere names we can reason only so far as they represent or embody facts. A name can only be invested with a typical importance if it have reference to some typical feature or peculiarity in the history or character of the person, nation, or place originally designated. The name Balaam, or a Greek rendering of it, is used in the New Testament with manifest reference to its assumed etymological meaning, "destroyer of the people," to denote a class of early heretics in the Christian Church; but it would not have been so employed had it not happily delineated the character of the original Balaam, who destroyed the people of Israel by consenting to entice them to sins of idolatry and uncleanness. That so many of the personal Old Testament names should be full of etymological interest, arises from the fact that they were so frequently appropriate to the persons to whom they were originally given.

Passing then from the mere names of the enemies of the Israelites, we ask whether there be aught in the origins, histories, or characters of the several nations or of the progenitors from whom they sprang, which may fairly mark them as the types of particular classes of those against whom the Church of Christ has to contend. The mention of the different nations whom the psalmist enumerates would undoubtedly call up very various associations to the minds of the Israelites for whose use the psalm was originally written, exciting in them corresponding modifications of devotional feeling. Must it not be that each of these associations will find something akin to itself among the differing aspects in which to the view of the faithful of the Church of Christ is continually displayed the manifold hostility of the world against the Lord whose sacred name they bear? The enemies of Israel, as enumerated by the psalmist, fall into four main divisions: 1st, those most nearly connected with the Israelites themselves by the ties of blood-relationship, the descendants of Esau and Ishmael; 2ndly, the two branches of the descendants of Lot along with their respective Arabian auxiliaries, viz. the Moabites, who had engaged the assistance of the Hagarenes, and the Ammonites, who had gathered round their standard the Giblites and Amalekites; 3rdly, the inhabitants of the coast, the Philistines and Tyrians; 4thly, the more distant Assyrians.

Of all these the bitterest in their hostility to Israel were those who were the most nearly allied to them in blood,—the Edomites. Their hostility was founded upon hatred. From their conduct to the Israelites through a long course of ages it would seem as though in them were lastingly perpetuated that olden hatred wherewith their forefather Esau had hated Jacob because of Isaac's blessing. And though they had once and again succeeded, according to the prophecy, in breaking Israel's yoke from off their neck, yet they never could wrest away from Israel the possession of the birthright, and with it of the promises, which their ancestor had profanely despised: from Israel, not from Edom, was the Redeemer of the world to spring, and in Israel were all the families of the earth to be blessed. The Edomites may accordingly be appropriately viewed as the types of those whom the Church of Christ has ever found her bitterest foes, the sceptics who have refused to acknowledge that redemption through a personal Redeemer, on which, as on a basis, the Church is founded; whose intellectual pride is offended by the humbling doctrines of Christianity, and who hate those that hold them for their possession of blessings which *they* have wilfully rejected; whose human learning has nevertheless all along been rendered subservient on the whole to the edification of the Church, in spite of the violence with which they have striven, and for a while, as it would sometimes appear, successfully, to gain the mastery over her by opposing her, and to exercise a temporary dominion. Dwelling themselves in tabernacles, they cannot bear that others, more blessed than they, should have the houses of God in possession: "owning themselves to be astray, and unable to find the way to the truth, they are yet most importunate and imperious that others should come away from the ancient paths, and try to join them, or at least, wander as they are wandering[1]." In conjunction with the Edomites the psalmist makes mention of the Ishmaelites. And these, as the descendants of the bondwoman, may fitly represent those Jewish opponents of Christianity, still, perhaps, locally, if not generally, formidable, who in their rejection of Christian doctrine have been swayed by the same feelings of intellectual

---

[1] From *Strength in Trouble*, a Sermon by the Master of Trinity College, p. 12.

pride as the sceptics of Christian descent; who professing to hold fast to **that** covenant of Mount Sinai which gendereth to bondage, persecuted, **so** long as they **were able,** those born after the Spirit, and having been finally cast out from the spiritual family of Abraham, have ended by their hand being against every man, and every man's hand against them, even at the very time that in spite of their wildness they everywhere dwell, throughout the civilized world, in the presence of their more fortunate brethren.

In the descendants of Lot and their Arabian auxiliaries we have the types of a different class of **foes.** The historical origin of the former marks them **as** the appropriate representatives of the slaves of sinful lusts; who hate the Church not for the humbling tone of **her** doctrines, **but for** the standard of holiness which she exacts **and for** which she is continually witnessing. And experience shews how such persons are wont, in their attacks **upon the** Church, to enlist into their service those who **are** more wildly, **but at** the same time more ignorantly, unholy than themselves; how in order, if possible, **to** uproot those fences and safeguards of the law of holiness on which, having transgressed them, they hate to look, they appeal to the unbridled passions of the lawless multitude by whom the very existence of the fences had been utterly disregarded.

From the enemies of the Church who are animated by feelings of positive hatred, **we** pass to those who act from calculation rather than passion, and whose proceedings are all directed with a view to their own earthly aggrandisement. The Philistines and Tyrians had engaged in the hostile confederacy with the hope of obtaining Israelitish captives, from whom they might reap a profit by selling them abroad as slaves. It does not appear that they regarded the Israelites in themselves with other feelings than those of mere selfish indifference. Both nations had tendered their services to Israel in the days of Israel's prosperity; for the Philistines had probably furnished the Cherethites and Pelethites of David's body-guard, and the Tyrians had furnished Solomon with materials and workmen for the building of the temple: both nations were now seeking to enrich themselves at Israel's expense in the days of Israel's adversity. And these then are the fitting types of all who in their varying professions of friendliness or hostility to the Church of God are actuated by the mere mercenary desire of lucre; favouring, and even zealously favouring her interests, when they can procure a good recompense for their services; unhesitatingly combining with her bitterest enemies to vilify and despoil her, whenever the opportunity offer of increasing their worldly substance thereby.

The last class of enemies are those of whom Assyria is the type; the worldly potentates, whether ecclesiastical or temporal, papal or imperial, who are unscrupulously ready to employ all means for the ultimate accomplishment of their one object, that of extending and consolidating their dominion. Gradual in their growth, but with the single aim of their ambition continually before them; with well-organized forces ever ready at their command; able from their distance either to take an active part in the conflict whensoever it may befurther their views, or else to maintain an attitude of haughty and apparently dignified reserve; with sufficient self-control to watch their opportunities, and to bide their time; with sufficient shrewdness to side with either party in the conflicts in which they interfere, according as it may best advance their ultimate design of rivetting their fetters equally upon all; gladly welcoming such schisms and divisions in church and in state as may induce either party to claim their patronage and protection; gladly accepting, like Tiglath-pileser from Ahaz, an invitation from the rulers of God's Church to aid them to quell the unhappy attacks of those who have seceded from their communion; eagerly carrying all before them, yet affecting a moderation in their success; impeded **by no** religious or moral restraint, and yet able to **make** a display of forbearance; such potentates seem to represent **most** truly that determined and resolute selfishness, which, to eyes that are not dazzled by the grandeur **of** its proportions or the gorgeousness in which it is arrayed, must ever appear as one of the most terrible embodiments of the **enmity** of the world to God.

Pride of intellect **and** unbelief,—unholiness and lawlessness of life,—covetousness,—worldly ambition,— such are the characteristics of four important classes of those by whom God's Church is threatened. And meanwhile the danger **is** aggravated by the circumstance that God's "hidden ones" are sundered into different communions; Israel does not all come up to worship at the temple in Jerusalem where God has set his name; and bitter jealousies are raging between those who tread the courts of the Christian Zion, and **those** who sullenly refuse or are morally unable thither **to** repair. We have already observed that although both the kingdom of the ten tribes and the kingdom of Judah were threatened by the confederacy against which the psalmist prays, it was yet for the especial **use of** the worshippers of the former that the psalm **itself was** composed. Christian experience seems to have shewn that when God's worshippers are assailed by their foes, it is on those that are in secession from the unity of the Church that the storm will generally fall the heaviest; and however much we may both bewail and condemn the schisms in the Church which wilfulness has created, we cannot in charity or consistency do otherwise than bid God speed to all, be they who they may, who against the combined hostile efforts are defending God's cause.

PSALM LXXXIV.

With the death of Jeroboam II. the temporary sunshine which had gleamed on the political fortunes of the Israelites departed. The horizon was again overcast; and with clouds of more lowering hue and more impenetrable gloom. From the north-east steadily onward the Assyrian desolator was advancing, and cutting short the limits of the sacred inheritance. In the midst of this political darkness, when the crisis was almost at hand, it pleased God to vouchsafe to the Israelites a season of spiritual refreshment. Hezekiah, king of Judah, having on his accession to the throne reopened and purified the temple which the impiety of his father had plundered and defiled, had determined "to make proclamation throughout all Israel, from Beersheba even to Dan," inviting the people of both kingdoms to repair to Jerusalem in the following month to celebrate the passover; at which the Israelites of the ten tribes had not been present for a period of two hundred and fifty years. The result shewed that the past missionary efforts of the Levites in the kingdom of Israel had not been wholly ineffectual. That Hezekiah's messengers should be publicly laughed to scorn and insulted was no more than might be reasonably anticipated; but the invitation which was rejected by the many was not lost upon the religious few; and "divers," we read, "of Asher and Manasseh and of Zebulun humbled themselves, and came to Jerusalem."

It was apparently in order to give utterance to the awakened devotional feelings of these Israelitish pilgrims that the Korhites composed the present psalm. Like all the psalms "upon Gittith," it is of a joyful character; though, as we might expect, its joy is tinged with melancholy. It expresses the feelings of those who were too *deeply* thankful to be jubilant; who moreover, although they saw before them the accomplishment of their warmest aspirations, could not forget the manifold sorrows by which they were surrounded. They were, in more than one sense, pilgrims.

There are two passages in the psalm in which they are virtually made to depict their own condition. The first is the often misunderstood v. 3: "Yea, the sparrow hath found, &c." The true meaning of this verse is well given by Bossuet: "Such a home as the sparrow hath found for herself in the retreat of her nest, hath my soul discovered in thy altars, O Lord: here therefore will it repose after all its previous wanderings and disquietude[1]." The other passage is vv. 5—7; in which the pilgrimage of the Israelite to Jerusalem becomes an image of the pilgrimage of the soul to full communion with God. The passage is difficult to translate, because there are in v. 6 no fewer than three words admitting a double sense, a play on the two meanings of the word being in each case evidently intended. The word Baca may either signify *weeping*, or else denote a certain tree resembling the balsam-tree, whence distilled white drops of a cold and pungent taste, and the name of which was probably derived from its weeping property. Again, the word rendered in our E. V. *rain* may signify either *the early rain*, or *a teacher:* doctrine, be it observed, is compared to rain

---

[1] In the language of the psalms worshippers frequently compare themselves to birds: Psalm xi. 1; lv. 6; lvi. superscription; lxxiv. 19; cii. 6, 7.

in other passages of Scripture[1]. Lastly, the same **Hebrew word may be** rendered either *pools* or *blessings*. And thus adopting in this passage one set of meanings of the ambiguous words, we have a sort of parable or allegory of which the other set of meanings supply the interpretation. As the diligent pilgrim, travelling through some **dry** valley where nought but the weeping balsam **is to be seen, is** glad to find even in the droppings of this tree the means of slaking his **thirst, so** the true **pilgrim** of Zion will find even in affliction itself a source of religious comfort and improvement; and furthermore as God, who never leaves nor fails to protect them that seek him, can cheer the visible path **of** the traveller in that thirsty vale by making the early rain descend **from heaven,** and unexpectedly cover the surface of the ground with pools of water, **so will he** oftentimes of his goodness visit the believer in his affliction, by seizing the opportunity to instruct him in divine truth, and thus to cover him **with** the truest blessings. **We should also remark that** the word in v. 5 rendered *ways* denotes the public highways leading to the sanctuary; and that the word in v. 7 rendered *strength* denotes a force or company of people; the sense being that as the pilgrim-companies become more numerous to view the nearer that **they approach to** Jerusalem, so does the spiritual **pilgrim** receive continual accessions of inward **strength** the nearer that he **draws to** his God. The following is an attempt to exhibit the import of the passage:

> Blessed is the man **whose strength is in thee;**
> (They in whose heart **are the** pilgrim-roads:
> Passing through the valley of the weeping-tree, they render it a spring;
> Yea, and the heavenly **shower** covereth it with pools of blessing:
> They go forward, **ever** stronger and stronger;)
> He appeareth unto God **in Zion.**

[1] Deut. xxxii. 2; Isaiah lv. 10.

Herein we find described, **first,** the pilgrim's source of strength; secondly, the holiness of his aspirations; then **the use** which he prudently makes of the most seemingly unpromising circumstances; next, the unexpected further outpouring of divine blessing upon him; after this, his continual increase of strength as he goes on advancing; and lastly, the full accomplishment of all his hopes.

And this may **be** the best opportunity for observing that it was when the schism had been healed, by the coming up of the Israelites to worship at Jerusalem, that the psalms which had been previously composed by the Levites for their use became, happily, songs of Zion. They would hardly have found an appropriate place in the Psalter of the Jewish Church so long **as** those for whose especial use they were designed failed to worship in the Jewish sanctuary. This may be partly the reason why Psalms lxxx—lxxxiii, although anterior in date to the reign of Hezekiah, do not appear in the Second Book of the Psalter: it was the religious reconciliation in Hezekiah's reign which first gave them a full claim to be included in the Psalter at all.

On resuming the consideration of the psalm now strictly before us, it is time that we observe its structural arrangement. **It consists of** three strophes, of three, four, and five verses respectively; vv. 1—3, 4—7, 8—12. The opening and close of the first and last strophes are solemnized by the occurrence **of** the sacred name LORD of hosts (once, more fully, LORD God of **hosts**) in the **first** and last verses of each: in the middle strophe that name **is not** employed. Furthermore, in all three strophes, **by a** somewhat unusual device, the first verse is made to **serve as a** motto to what follows; on which account, in the latter two strophes, a special and distinctive emphasis is imparted **to** it **by** the introduction of the Selah. And thus the theme of the first strophe is the loveliness of God's courts (v. 1): that of the second, the blessedness of those that abide in them (v. 4), the natural expansion of this thought being that picture of the Zionward pilgrimage which has already engaged our attention. We pass to the third strophe. It is, as its opening verse (v. 8) implies, a prayer; but in whose behalf is the prayer offered?

Gladdened by the prospect of worshipping once more, after a lapse of from two to three centuries, in the courts of Zion, the pilgrims could not in gratitude forget the human king by whose instrumentality this privilege had been vouchsafed them. They had long been taught by their Israelitish sovereigns to look on the tents of wickedness as their home; and had been encouraged to content themselves with assembling before the calves of Bethel and of Dan instead of pressing on to the sanctuary of Jerusalem where God had set his name. They now hoped to stand once more— even though it were but as visitors[1]—on the threshold of the house of their God; and for this they were indebted to the piety of the royal descendant of David, the sovereignty of whose family had long since by their tribes been cast off and forgotten. Hezekiah, himself in this a true type of Christ, had sought to awaken new feelings of repentance and devotion in those who had so long been perpetuating the sins of their fathers in transgressing the statutes of their God. He had striven to gather together in one the children of God that were virtually scattered abroad. Because they had hitherto

---

[1] Our English Version has *I had rather be a doorkeeper;* and Bossuet and Bonar remark that this sentiment would come appropriately from the lips of the Korhites, some of whom were employed to keep the gates of the sanctuary, 1 Chron. ix. 19. But the Korhite psalmists spoke in the name of the Israelite pilgrims; and the *visiting* in God's house contrasts better with the *dwelling* in the tents of wickedness.

in habitual disobedience kept aloof from the place of God's name, therefore he had affectionately sent forth to them the message of invitation to attend; hoping thus solemnly to reconcile the whole nation once more to God. And the pilgrims, reflecting on all this, and discerning in the piety and prosperity of the house of David the only hope of the future habitual appearance of all Israel before God's presence, might well intercede for him to whom they owed so much, "Behold, O God our shield, and look upon the face of thine anointed." And there is no reason to doubt that in uttering these words, the psalmist thought not only of Hezekiah, but also of that greater scion, yet to come, of Hezekiah's race, to whom all the promises made to David, to Israel, and to the patriarchs, should be fulfilled, and in whom all families of the earth should be blessed.

To the Christian worshipper the "anointed" of this psalm is Christ Jesus of Nazareth. Through him have those who were before estranged from God through disobedience and ignorance been made not merely visitors on God's threshold, but fellow-citizens with the saints, and members of God's household. And from those who have thus been made through Christ partakers of God's grace the prayer of gratitude may well be asked in return. They are of course not bidden intercede for their Anointed King in his own now glorified Person; but they may well pray that his glory may be more fully manifested upon earth, and that his earthly kingdom may be prosperous; they may intercede for him in the person of the Church, his great representative upon earth, and also in the persons of his inferior and more individual representatives, the earthly rulers and ministers by whom his Church is governed and served. A prayer for Christ, "Look upon the face of thine anointed," is virtually a prayer for the Church; for the Church is the great witness for the sovereignty of Christ, even as Christ is the **witness** for the sovereignty of God. It should also be remembered that the pilgrims are not the only intercessors. Perhaps at one of the times when the pilgrims of the ten tribes of Israel were pouring forth the strains of this psalm, Hezekiah, mindful of their unsanctified state, was interceding for *them*, "The good LORD pardon every one, that prepareth his heart to seek God, the LORD God of his fathers, though he be not cleansed according to the purification of the sanctuary." For in fact, in consequence of their unsanctified state, it had been necessary that the passover should be slain and its blood sprinkled not *by them*, but *for them*, "for every one that was not clean to sanctify them unto the LORD[1]." In like manner for us, *for* whom Christ our passover has been sacrificed, our Anointed King is, while we are interceding for him on earth, himself interceding in heaven; for "if any man sin," we read, "we have an advocate with the Father, Jesus Christ the righteous: and he is the propitiation for our sins."

PSALM LXXXV.

THE internal indications **of the date of** this psalm are **but** slight; but when we **read** it in connexion with **the preceding, it** becomes **probable** that it was composed **at the same** period, on **the** occasion of Hezekiah's first **passover. It** would be equally appropriate in the mouths **of the worshippers of** both kingdoms who were present at that **feast.** The Jews had but lately beheld the restoration **of their** national religion, and the reinauguration of their temple-worship, and had now the

---

[1] 2 Chron. xxx. 15—20.

additional satisfaction of welcoming their Israelitish brethren back to Jerusalem: the Israelites on the other hand might well regard their own presence at the feast **as** an earnest of the return of all the inhabitants of the **land to** obedience to the laws of Moses: and under such circumstances both might well feel that God had indeed been favourable unto his land, and had given a proof of his willingness **to** pardon his people's sins. The mingling together through all the earlier portion of the psalm of thanks and entreaties, of declarations that God had already laid aside his wrath, and of supplications that he would not be angry for ever, shews that it was written at a time when days of new blessing and prosperity were only just dawning; which indeed **was** remarkably **the** case at the commencement of Hezekiah's reign. It is only through a misunderstanding of the phrase in v. 1 "thou hast brought back the captivity," (for the true interpretation of which see the Introd. to **Psalm xiv,**) that many persons have supposed the psalm to date from the return of the captives from Babylon. The general tone of the psalm does not carry the impression **that** the whole political existence **of the Israelitish nation was** commencing anew: **it implies a past** season of national humiliation, and more **especially** of the hiding of **God's face** and of spiritual **wretchedness,** but not one of utter political ruin.

The kernel of the psalm, **on** which both the thanks and prayers **of** vv. 1—7 and the glorious anticipations of vv. 9—13 depend, is to be found in **the** record of **God's** announcement **of** mercy in v. 8. **This,** from its length, **is** evidently the emphatic verse of the whole; and it will stand in the very centre of the main portion of the psalm, if, as is probable, **vv.** 1, 2, terminated by the **Selah,** should (after the manner of **vv.** 1, 4, 8 in **the** preceding psalm) be regarded in the light of a mere motto or preface to the rest[1]. In interpreting the language of this central verse we are not to assume that the psalmist had been personally honoured by any special revelation from above. The substance of the divine message which he puts forth was to be found in various passages of the prophet Hosea: ii. 19—23; iii. 5; vi. 1—3; xiv. 4; and the appearance of the Israelitish pilgrims at the passover at Jerusalem seemed already to the psalmist an earnest of the time when the children of Israel should "return, and seek the LORD their God, and David their king," and should "fear the LORD and his goodness in the latter days."

Enkindled into rapture by the remembrance of that divine word which could not fail, the psalmist breaks out, in the latter verses of the psalm, into a glowing and imaginative delineation of the blessings in store for God's people. "Mercy and truth," he exclaims, "are met together." The same future dealings of God with his people which would testify to his *merciful* forgiveness of their long transgressions, would exhibit also his *faithful* fulfilment of the promises which he had made to the patriarchs and to David. "Righteousness and peace have kissed each other." The psalmist recognizes that the restoration of Israel to a *righteousness* which of themselves they had never realized must be an act of divine grace: God himself must heal their backslidings: the righteousness, from lack of which all their wretchedness had proceeded, must descend upon them from on high (v. 11), must publicly go forth at God's command (v. 13, former clause), and must make her own footsteps a pathway in which they might tread and

---

[1] V. 1 contains the summary of vv. 9—13, v 2 of vv. 3—7; the order of the topics of the two verses, salvation in its positive and negative aspects, being inverted when they are expanded. So, nearly, Jebb, II. p. 40, to whom I am indebted for the remark: whatever imperfection his analysis exhibits is probably due to a misunderstanding of the phrase "to bring back the captivity."

follow (v. 13, latter clause)[1]. And then, when righteousness thus remained "in the fruitful field,"—for simultaneously with the descent of righteousness the land was to yield forth her increase (v. 12) and all God's varied blessings were thus to be poured upon his justified people,—then should "the work of righteousness be *peace*, and the effect of righteousness quietness and assurance for ever[2]."

That the prosperous commencement of Hezekiah's reign should have served as an earnest to the psalmist of the ultimate fulfilment of all God's promises, shews how the longings of God's people for a full redemption were continually kept alive by the alternations of mercy which amid their various calamities they experienced. It was probably the same bright period in the history of the Jewish kingdom which gave occasion to the evangelical prophecy in the thirty-second chapter of Isaiah. To the Christian Church has been vouchsafed a far more important and effectual pledge of the redemption of all mankind, in the coming upon earth of the Incarnate Son of God; and the psalm before us has accordingly formed a portion of the regular praises of Christmas-day. Mercy and Truth met together indeed in the birth at Bethlehem of Him in whose person the grace and truth of God were fully revealed to men. And as in his birth of a mortal womb Truth sprang out of the earth, so in the free justification of man by God's grace through the redemption by his blood, Righteousness looked down from heaven[3]. And then the kiss was interchanged

---

[1] Render v. 13 thus:
Righteousness shall go before him (God)
And shall render her footsteps a pathway.
In Hebrew, Righteousness, although personified, remains of the masculine gender.

[2] Isaiah xxxii. 16, 17.

[3] See Augustine's interpretation of this verse.

between Righteousness and Peace; and through the Lord Jesus Christ those who were justified by faith had peace with God. It is not however necessary to restrict the righteousness of the psalm to the righteousness of justification; it may include that of sanctification also; and peace is confessedly one of the fruits of the Spirit. The point of real importance is that both the justifying and sanctifying of men should be acknowledged to be God's work; and that it should thus be confessed that only through the lovingkindness of God can that normal order of things be restored which man's transgression has disturbed.

PSALM LXXXVI.

"A Prayer of David." Very little examination of this psalm is needed in order to establish the propriety of its being styled a *prayer*. In respect of its authorship a longer investigation will be necessary. If it be David's, as is commonly supposed by those who acknowledge the authority of the superscriptions, how came it to its present place in the Psalter? Of the psalms over which we have already travelled those ascribed, either expressly or by implication, to David have formed two large groups, viz. Psalms i.—xli, and Psalms li.—lxxi. (see the respective Introductions to Books I. and II.) The present psalm, as a Davidic psalm, stands alone: it is the only psalm in the Third Book which bears David's name; and from any other psalm bearing his name, whether previous or subsequent, it is in the Psalter separated by no fewer than fourteen places.

And when we peruse it, fresh grounds present themselves for demurring to the view that it proceeded directly from David[1]. Holy as are the sentiments that breathe through it, **it** nevertheless in the general tone of its language lacks that freshness which characterizes even the most plaintive and the most supplicative of David's **psalms**. The verses have often no direct connexion one with another, a feature which we elsewhere find only in the case of the alphabetical psalms. And this again is explained by the fact that many of the verses are extracted, with but slight variations, from the earlier psalms of David: cf. v. 1 with Psalm xl. 17; **v.** 4 with xxv. 1; v. 9 with xxii. **27**; v. 10 with lxxii. 18; v. 11 with xxv. 4, 5, xxvii. **11**; v. 13 with lvi. 13; v. 14 with liv. 3 (the words *proud* and *strangers* differ in Hebrew but by a single letter); **v. 16** with xxv. **16**. Such **a** drawing together of passages from many previous **psalms** is unparalleled in all the earlier portion of the Psalter. In addition to this the train of thought (see especially vv. 2, **13**, 16) is decidedly influenced by **the** latter part of Psalm xvi; the suppliant expressing **a** confidence that as **he** is *holy*, God will not give him over to the grave. **V. 15** is extracted from God's announcement of **himself** to Moses on Mount Sinai, Exod. xxxiv. **6**: **v. 8** from Exod. xv. 11 and Deut. iii. 24.

We have hitherto spoken **of** this psalm alone. None **of the** psalms bearing David's **name** shew upon their surface so plainly as this the marks of not having proceeded **from** David's hand. **But in fact** with regard **to** those psalms of the Fourth **and** Fifth Books which **bear** the name of David, there exist in many cases, even when we contemplate them severally and singly, strong difficulties in the way of our allowing their Davidic

---

[1] That it is not directly **David's** is, I find, acknowledged by Delitzsch; who explains the superscription by a reference to the Davidic materials from which the psalm is constructed. This is partially also the view of Hengstenberg.

authorship. The following is a list of them: Psalms ci, ciii; cviii.—cx; cxxii, cxxiv, cxxxi, cxxxiii. (these four are all included in the series of "Songs of Degrees"); cxxxviii.—cxlv. Of these, one, Psalm cxliv, is, like the psalm before us, made up in great measure of passages from previous Davidic psalms; another, Psalm cviii, is entirely constructed from portions of Psalms lvii. and lx, and in a way to which David's own use of portions of previous psalms by way of preface to Psalm lxxi. can hardly be deemed parallel. There are some again, e. g. Psalm ci, the language of which can ill be reconciled with the historical circumstances of any period of David's life. Above all, the Hebrew text of many is marked by grammatical Chaldaisms, the sure proof of their comparatively recent date.

And again when we contemplate these psalms as a whole, the fact of their being scattered through the later books of the Psalter hardly admits of any satisfactory explanation on the hypothesis of their Davidic authorship. For when we observe that the First Book of the Psalter contains only psalms of David, and does not include his latest compositions, that the Second Book contains no psalms of a later date than the reign of Hezekiah, and the Third none (apparently) of later date than the reign of Manasseh; and when we further take these circumstances in connexion with the known characters of David, Hezekiah, and Josiah, and the attention which was paid by them to the orderly arrangement of the temple-service; we have before us a presumptive proof that the three several Books were respectively compiled in the reign of these three monarchs. We have seen that for certain reasons David excluded from the First Book a large number of his own psalms, as inappropriate at that time to the temple-service; and that of these and of his later compositions no fewer than twenty-one were included in the collection formed in the reign of Hezekiah. It is obviously to be presumed that these were all the psalms of David which remained; for on what ground should any have been then excluded? What is there in any one of the eighteen psalms which, bearing the name of David, are scattered through the last three Books of the Psalter, to have disentitled it to a place in the earlier collections, were it truly the composition of David? But we are not left here to mere presumptive inference. A note at the end of Psalm lxxii, appended to the doxology which there marks the close of the Second Book, explicitly states that "the prayers of David the son of Jesse are ended." Critical ingenuity has in vain endeavoured to evade the force of this distinct announcement. "Because," it is urged, "in the Book of Job, Job appears speaking in Chaps. xl, xlii, notwithstanding the announcement at the end of Chap. xxxi. that the words of Job are ended, therefore notwithstanding the notice at the end of Psalm lxxii, there may yet be other psalms of David the son of Jesse to follow." But a very slight examination will shew that the assumed analogy between the announcement in the Book of Job and the notice in the Psalter altogether fails. With Chap. xxxi. of the Book of Job terminates, finally and unreservedly, the discussion of Job with his three friends; and the announcement "The words of Job are ended" is probably intended to come from Job's own lips. Elihu then appears, and afterwards God himself speaks to Job out of the whirlwind; and then certainly Job again opens his mouth; not however to argue with his friends, but to confess his presumption before God. The discussion with his friends was a thing of the past: he now only speaks to acknowledge to God the error of which he had been convicted. Where is there any such fundamental distinction, or even any approach to it, between the earlier and the later psalms of the Psalter?

And yet the authority of the superscriptions of the later psalms should not be needlessly rejected. Their *apparent* inconsistency with the notice at the end of Psalm lxxii. must have been as discernible by the sacred editor of the Psalter as by ourselves; and is therefore evidence rather of their genuineness than of the contrary. There is yet one way in which their truth may be reconciled with that of the notice. The latter informs us that the prayers of *David the son of Jesse* are ended; not all the prayers or psalms which might in any sense be called Davidic, but those which were composed by the individual David, Jesse's son. But we find that in Scripture the name David is used, long after the original David's death, to denote the representative for the time being of the Davidic family, and more especially, in prophecy, the great future Messiah, of the seed of David, who was to sit on David's throne. When the Israelites were rebelling against Rehoboam their language was, "What portion have we in David? neither have we inheritance in the son of Jesse: to your tents, O Israel: now see to thine own house, David[1]." Hosea predicted a time when the children of Israel should "return, and seek the LORD their God, and David their king[2]." Isaiah, speaking in God's name, says, "Hear,.... and I will make an everlasting covenant with you, even the sure mercies of David. Behold, I have given him for a witness to the people, a leader and commander to the people[3]." In this latter verse the original David is obviously not the person intended. Similar is the prophecy in Jeremiah, "They shall serve the LORD their

---

[1] 1 Kings xii. 16.   [2] Hosea iii. 5.   [3] Isaiah lv. 3, 4.

God, and David their king, whom I will raise up unto them[1];" as also that in Ezekiel, "I will set up one shepherd over them, and he shall feed them, even my servant **David**; he shall feed them, and he shall be their shepherd. And I the LORD will be their God, and my servant David a prince among them; I the LORD have spoken it[2]." Under these circumstances, why may not the superscription "Psalm of David" in the later portions of the Psalter designate those psalms which were composed by the subsequent representatives of the house of the original psalmist?

That more than one descendant of David should have been among the number of the psalmists cannot be deemed improbable. In the case of a sovereign like Hezekiah, his personal character, combined with his royal dignity, rendered him, as his ancestor David had been in former time, the foremost man in the realm. His zeal in the restoration of the temple-service is matter of recorded history; and we can thus easily suppose that as in other things he did "according to all that David his father had done," so also he would be prompted to essay an imitation of the lyrics in which David had poured forth, both for himself and his people, the devotion of his heart to God. Since the days of Asa and Jehoshaphat, the voice of Israel had repeatedly sounded forth to God in the strains of the Asaphite and Korhite choirs: the voice of Israel's king needed yet again to be heard. Hezekiah, as the anointed of the Lord, and as the inheritor of the promise which had been made to David respecting the everlasting establishment of the kingdom of his seed, could do that which was never permitted to any mere temple-singer: he could speak not merely in the person of the Church, but also in that of the future Messiah.

---

[1] Jerem. xxx. 9. [2] Ezek. xxxiv. 23, 24.

And in so doing, he would obviously superscribe his psalm not with his own personal name, but with the name of him, from whom his title to speak in the person of Israel's future King was by inheritance derived. If in the times posterior to those of David the Levite choirs prefixed the names of their ancestors Asaph, Heman, and Ethan to the psalms which they composed, out of a mere feeling of veneration for their ancestors' memories; how well might the name of David be prefixed to the utterances of those who were not merely his descendants, but also the representatives for the time being, and so in some sort the pledges, of the perpetual royalty of his lineage! For that as such the kings of Judah were regarded is evident from the contents of Psalm lxxxix.

We conclude then that while the "Psalms of David" in the first two Books of the Psalter are the compositions of "David the son of Jesse," those in the last three Books are the productions of some from among his posterity. And this being established, there can be little room for doubt that the first of these latter psalms, the psalm now before us, Psalm lxxxvi, must be assigned to Hezekiah. This is, indeed, sufficiently proved by the place which it occupies among the other psalms of Hezekiah's reign. Not remarkable, perhaps, among its fellows in a purely poetical point of view, which indeed it could not well be, in consequence of its large dependence on the earlier psalms of David, it has nevertheless its own special claims to distinction. It is the first extant lyrical composition of any monarch of Israel after Solomon. It is the first sure evidence of an Israelitish heart after the death of David thoroughly imbued with David's piety and David's spirit. We have already observed that it was only the spirit of Solomon that was revived in the days of Jehoshaphat.

Hezekiah was the first to rekindle the deeper devotion of David. "He trusted in the LORD God of Israel," says the history, "so that after him was none like him among all the kings of Judah, nor any that were before him." Thus it was that while Jehoshaphat left the high places standing, Hezekiah destroyed them. The relative characters of the two men may to some extent be gathered from a comparison of the present psalm with the prayer of Jehoshaphat in 2 Chron. xx. 6—12. That prayer is mainly based on the dedication-prayer of Solomon: the psalm of Hezekiah rests on the earlier supplications of David. Jehoshaphat addresses God as the Sovereign Protector of his people. Hezekiah addresses him as also the Merciful Redeemer both of the people at large and of every individual amongst them. And there is in Hezekiah's prayer a deeper feeling of the necessity of holiness on the worshipper's part in order to render his prayer effectual. We may here observe how well the words of the psalm "Preserve my soul, for I am holy (v. 2)," correspond with Hezekiah's prayer on the receipt of the message of death in his sickness, "Remember now, O LORD, I beseech thee, how I have walked before thee in truth and with a perfect heart, and have done that which is good in thy sight[1]." With deeper convictions of sin, Hezekiah shewed also a more just appreciation than Jehoshaphat of the true dignity and position of the Church over which he ruled. The one entered into alliance, on equal terms, with the Baal-worshipping king of the schismatic tribes; the other invited all the Israelites to assemble themselves once more to the sanctuary where God had set his name. And in spite of the gilded protestations of friendship with which the courtesies of Jehoshaphat were answered, and the scorn

---

[1] Isaiah xxxviii. 3.

and mockery with which the **posts of** Hezekiah were **generally received**, it can scarcely be doubted that **of the two** Hezekiah **rendered** God the better service. Again in respect of the heathen, although Jehoshaphat as well as Hezekiah acknowledged God to be **the ruler of all the kingdoms** of the earth[1], yet it was only the **latter who**, in supplicating for deliverance for Israel, **openly prayed** that the salvation which God should bestow upon them might be **the means of** bringing the heathen to the knowledge of the Lord[2], or **who looked forward to** the time when all nations should come and worship before him, and should glorify his name[3]. It is thus that, through uncompromising faith, the **Church**, even in her most humiliated condition, (and Hezekiah succeeded to the throne under far **less** prosperous **circumstances** than Jehoshaphat,) realizes the true dignity of her calling, and looks forward to a bright future of growth, triumph, and glory.

This anticipation of the time when all nations should come to worship before the Lord proves on closer examination to be the **central thought of the psalm**. Although the structure of the psalm is not very strongly marked, there are sufficient indications of its being designedly arranged backwards and forwards from **the** centre. The close of v. 1 rhymes in the Hebrew **to the close** of v. 17; and that of **v. 2** to that of **v. 16**. Again, v. 1 and v. 17 both contain the **sacred name** Jehovah (LORD); v. 2 and v. 16 the expression "**thy** servant"; v. 4 and v. 14, "**my** soul"; v. 3 and v. 15, v. 5 and v. 13 all speak of God's mercy; v. 8 and v. 10 of God's **greatness**; and these last **two** enclose the central verse, v. 9. And when once we have discerned the hope of the future assemblage of the heathen to God's sanc-

---

[1] 2 Chron. xx. 6; Isaiah xxxvii. 16.   [2] Isaiah xxxvii. 20.
[3] Psalm lxxxvi. 9.

tuary to be the central feature of the psalm, we are enabled to explain the reason why this "Prayer of David" should have its place in the Psalter in the midst of the psalms of the Korhites. It is obviously connected in subject with the psalm which succeeds it. In Psalm lxxxv,—or rather in Psalms lxxx.—lxxxv,— we behold the Church of God bringing back those that had seceded from her communion to worship with her in the courts of Zion. In Psalms lxxxvi, lxxxvii. we behold the same Church looking forward to a far wider diffusion of God's glory, and anticipating the time when those courts should be trodden by worshippers from all nations of the world. That time is now in a measure arrived; and from every quarter of the globe Gentile believers are come unto Mount Zion, and unto the city of the living God, the heavenly Jerusalem; though much still remains to be accomplished before the earthly work of the Church shall be complete.

At what period of Hezekiah's reign this and the following psalm were written can perhaps not be exactly or certainly determined. It was however not improbably after the overthrow of Sennacherib, when "many brought gifts unto the LORD to Jerusalem, and presents to Hezekiah king of Judah, so that he was magnified in the sight of all nations from thenceforth[1]." And if Psalm lxxxvi. be subsequent in date to Hezekiah's recovery from his sickness, we might trace in the words of v. 13 a reference to that event.

As uttered in the person of the Messiah, the "holy" one whose "soul was preserved" and was "delivered from the hell 'beneath,'" the psalm seems typically to set forth how he, the "son of God's handmaid" of the house of David at a time when the glories of that house had apparently passed away, and thus from his very

[1] 2 Chron. xxxii. 23.

birth brought up in poverty and need, should be strengthened on his father David's throne, and should behold the fulfilment of his desires in the glorification of God's name through all the nations of the earth. There is however nought in the psalm which should prevent its being appropriated by every holy Christian worshipper; and the remarks which were made in reference to the Christian use of the earlier Davidic psalms may be also generally applied in the present case.

PSALM LXXXVII.

"A Psalm and Song of the Sons of Korah." The appropriate position of this psalm after the Davidic psalm immediately preceding has been already remarked. It was doubtless composed in the reign of Hezekiah. Its theme is "Jerusalem, the mother of us all." The following is a translation, or rather a paraphrase; for the terseness of the original can scarcely be transferred into any other tongue:

1 'Tis His foundation!
  Upon the holy mountains!
2 The LORD hath loved the gates of Zion
  More than all the dwellings of Jacob:
3 With glorious promises he claimeth thee for his bride[1],
  O city of God! (Selah)

---

[1] The word דבר in Piel, followed by ב, signifies in 1 Sam. xxv. 39 *to ask a woman in marriage*. In Pual it is used impersonally in a corresponding passive sense, followed, as before, by ב of the *woman:* see Cant. viii. 8, the only passage, besides the present psalm, in which the Pual occurs. The use of the word is here exactly the same as in the Canticles; and נכבדות is the accusative after the Piel verb implied in the impersonal Pual: it expresses the *words* in which the demand is made. The ordinary rendering of this verse is in itself not free from objection: the preposition ב after a word of speaking signifies by general usage (though in 1 Sam. xix. 3 there is an instance to the contrary) not merely *concerning*, but *against*. Accordingly Jerome conscientiously wrote not *de te*, but *in te;* but what meaning he attached to his own rendering is not clear.

"I will record Rahab and Babylon as of the number of them that
   know me:
"Behold Philistia and Tyre with Ethiopia!
"This one was born there."
5 And of Zion it shall be said, "Each several man was born
   in her;"
   And the Most High himself shall establish her;
6 The LORD shall reckon, when he writeth up the nations,
   "This one was born there;" (Selah)
7 And they, singing as well as playing, shall say,
   "All my springs are in thee."

Notwithstanding its brevity, the psalm is regular in its structure. Of the seven verses of which it consists, the two extreme verses are the shortest, the central verse the longest. In the first three verses the relation of the Lord to Zion is set forth. He founded her, he has loved her, he claims her. She is the "city of God"; not merely as the holy city, but as God's chosen bride. Similar representations are found in the prophecies of Isaiah, liv. 5; lxii. 5. The central verse of the psalm contains the words of God himself: they are the glorious promises to which reference had been made in v. 3. They are to the effect that all the people of the various Gentile realms (this one, viz. every one) should be reckoned among the worshippers of the Lord, and so among Zion's children. The glory which God promises to Zion is thus the glory of motherhood. In the last three verses we have the testimony, first of general report, secondly of God's book, thirdly of Zion's children themselves, to Zion's glory and richness. The singing and playing of these last are the symptoms of their joy; (we may remark, by the way, what love the Korhite author of this psalm evidently felt for his own art;) and the spring of their joy is that they have been made children of Zion; with joy they draw water from Zion's wells of salvation; and in Zion's glory they find a fitting theme for their praises.

In the enumeration (v. 4) of the nations that shall be brought to know the Lord, Assyria, as the principal enemy of Israel in Hezekiah's reign, and therefore the most appropriate representative at that time of the continued opposition of worldly power to the kingdom of God, is omitted. It is different in the prophecy of Isaiah, Chap. xix, where even Assyria is mentioned as one of those that shall be joined in covenant with Israel. The list of the psalmist comprises four nations who had either like Israel been engaged, or else were about to be engaged, in hostility with Assyria; viz. Egypt (named here, as in other passages, Rahab[1]), Ethiopia[2], Philistia, and Tyre: it comprises also the Babylonians, who were at this time disconnected from the Assyrians, and who sent a friendly embassy to Hezekiah after his recovery from sickness.

The true purport of this psalm is amply illustrated in the writings of the New Testament. We at once recognize in the ancient Zion, the former abode of God's presence, the type and the Jewish anticipation of the Christian Church. The imperfect knowledge and consequently imperfect conceptions of the prophets and psalmists forced them to clothe in local associations those spiritual truths respecting the Church of God's redeemed to which they gave utterance: it remained for the apostles to shew that the Jerusalem respecting which they had prophesied was not the Jerusalem "which now is, and is in bondage with her children," (St Paul wrote before the earthly Jerusalem's great overthrow), but the free Jerusalem "which is above," and "is the mother of us all[3]." It was that city respecting which the Christian believers were reminded

---

[1] Psalm lxxxix. 10; Isaiah xxx. 7, where see the rendering of Bp Lowth; li. 9. The origin of the name is unknown; but it is used by Isaiah with allusion to its etymological meaning in Hebrew, *insolence*, *pride*.

[2] Cf. Isaiah xxxvii. 9.

[3] Gal. iv. 25, 26.

that they were come unto Mount Zion, "and unto the city of the living God, the heavenly Jerusalem[1]." The psalmist speaks of it as God's foundation; and in like manner we are told in the New Testament of even Abraham, that "he looked for a city which hath foundations whose builder and maker is God[2]." The holy mountains on which the ancient Zion stood betokened in respect of their height both the near communion of the Church with God, and her shining as a beacon-light to the world. Their one symbolical import is illustrated by the almost universal choice in patriarchal times of mountain-tops as the places of religious worship: their other by the prophecies of Isaiah and Micah, "It shall come to pass in the last days, that the mountain of the LORD's house shall be established in the top of the mountains, and shall be exalted above the hills; and all nations shall flow unto it[3];" as also by our Saviour's words, "A city that is set on an hill cannot be hid[4]." In v. 2 the question arises why special mention should be made of the *gates* of Zion as the objects of God's love. Theodoret understands by them the churches upon earth as forming the approaches to the heavenly Jerusalem: "it is in these," he says, "that men are disciplined and exercised beforehand, in order to learn how to live as citizens of that city." But this explanation is inadmissible. Holy Scripture draws no such distinction between the Church triumphant in heaven and the Church militant on earth; it speaks of but one body and one family, including alike the sanctified below and the glorified above; it tells Christians that to the heavenly Jerusalem they are already come; and although it allows the accomplishment of Christ's redeeming work to be as yet imperfect, it recognizes no

---

[1] Heb. xii. 22.   [2] Heb. xi. 10.   [3] Isaiah ii. 2; Micah iv. 1.
[4] Matth. v. 14.

separate ideal of the Church in her present and the Church in her future condition. And the prophets, even when foretelling the actual events that shall befall the Church during the period of her militancy upon earth, never view her in any other than an ideal light. We may therefore more appropriately discern in the *gates* of Zion the symbol of the universal admission, of all who will enter, into the Church of Christ. In the city of the vision of Ezekiel there are twelve gates, named after the twelve tribes of Israel: this betokened that all God's people should be admitted into his presence. The same feature occurs in the vision of St John; but there, in order that it may more clearly appear that the catholic Israel is intended, the twelve foundations of the city-wall are marked with the names of the twelve apostles, Christ's chosen ambassadors to all nations. The meaning therefore of v. 2 of the psalm may be taken as follows: "God hath loved the city of Zion with her open gates more than all the land of Jacob with its private abodes: his love is fixed not so much on any single nation in its exclusive nationality as on that Church into which the redeemed of all nations shall enter: hitherto God's preservation of the descendants of Jacob in the land assigned them has been more or less identified with his care of the Church; a time shall ere long come, when the latter shall be seen not to depend upon the former, and when it shall be made manifest that though he love nations much, he loves the Church still more." That time was indeed already dawning at the date of the composition of this psalm; for Hezekiah's reign witnessed a large accession to the number of worshippers in the courts of Zion, though it also witnessed the carrying away into captivity of ten of the tribes of Israel. To pass to v. 3, which speaks of God claiming Zion for his bride: we at once call to mind, amongst other passages, that in which St John describes the new Jerusalem, "coming down from God out of heaven, prepared as a bride adorned for her **husband**." And here again it must be borne in mind that the bridal of the Church ideally dates from the day that her Lord gave himself for her through the shedding of his blood upon the **cross**. She is already his bride in so **far** as she realizes that spotlessness to which she has been redeemed, and in which she will at **the** last shine forth, all-glorious.

The later verses of the psalm unfold the dignity of the espousals by declaring how many and how various **the** children whom **the** Church **thus** wedded to her **Lord** shall divinely number. Literally rendered indeed, **the words** of the psalm speak only of being "born *in* her;" nevertheless it is evidently as the *mother* of those that **shall be** born that the Church is here contemplated. **Their** spiritual birth of their mother, the Church, **stands** in contrast to their first birth of the various nations whence they originally sprang. The different appearance which the doctrine of the second birth presents in this psalm and in the New Testament respectively is mainly owing to the circumstance that in the one it is contemplated in its human, in the other in its **divine aspect**. The object of the psalmist is simply **to set forth** the **glorious** motherhood of the Church; **that** of Christ and his apostles is to trace the primary source of man's new spiritual life, his being born of the Spirit, his being begotten of the will of the **Father** with the **word** of truth, and, **so** born not of corruptible seed, but **of** incorruptible. The motherhood of Mary was the subsequent type of the one; the overshadowing power of the Holy Ghost by which she conceived was the divine pledge of the other.

PSALM LXXXVIII.

The alternating fortunes of Israelitish history have entered a new phase: the bright hopes which had been raised by Hezekiah's reign have passed away, and are followed by calamities apparently more dark than any which the nation, or at least the kingdom of Judah, has yet experienced. Manasseh the son of Hezekiah has by his career of apostasy brought down an irrevocable doom of destruction upon Jerusalem, to be executed in due season; and at the period at which this and the following psalm were written he was probably already undergoing the more immediate and personal punishment of his transgression in the endurance of captivity in a foreign land. The place of these psalms in the Psalter exactly harmonizes with the above view of their date: they can hardly be brought down to any later period, if the Book of which they form the conclusion was arranged in the reign of Josiah.

The authorship of Psalm lxxxviii. is ascribed in the superscription to the Sons of Korah; but it is also entitled "Maschil of Heman the Ezrahite;" manifestly because the Korhites thus wished, in imitation of the previous practice of their Asaphite brethren, to assign the imaginary authorship of their psalm to the founder of their choir. To Psalm lxxxix, the companion-psalm of Psalm lxxxviii, the similar title "Maschil of Ethan the Ezrahite" is in like manner prefixed. Maschils, i. e. homilies, or psalms of instruction, might well be made to proceed from the lips of Heman and Ethan, who were proverbially known for their wisdom; and Hengstenberg very properly remarks that the Sons of Korah were desirous of honouring their own poem and of strengthening its impression by prefixing to it the name of Heman next after their own. The question however still remains, Why should they have introduced the name of Heman into the superscriptions of their psalms only in this single instance? Was it that the present crisis, when for the first time in history the representative of the royal house of David had been carried into captivity, might well move them to imagine the lamentation which they had composed for the Israelitish people as coming from the pen of the contemporary of the original David? Or was it that the Korhite choir were at this time themselves in captivity along with Manasseh, and that, anticipating their own extinction, they wished to provide for the perpetuation of their founder's memory before they themselves had ceased to exist? These are but conjectures. The latter of the two however derives support from the circumstance that the Korhite choir did probably not survive Manasseh's reign; as also from the deep melancholy of the psalm, which, though uttered in the name of the Israelitish people, might derive somewhat of the impress of its tone from the more private feelings of the Levitical choir from some member of which it proceeded.

This seems the appropriate place for offering an explanation of the term *Ezrahite*, applied to Heman and Ethan in the superscriptions of this and the following psalm, and to Ethan (and perhaps even there also, by implication, to Heman) in 1 Kings iv. 31. It cannot, as many have supposed, and as the Hebrew form of the word might at first lead us to conclude, be a patronymic; for as Heman was a Kohathite and Ethan a Merarite, they had no common ancestor below Levi. Again the rendering *native*, adopted by the Targumist, is not satisfactory either in respect of etymology or meaning: the rendering *laureate*, put forth by Dr Mason Good, is in respect of etymology utterly inadmissible. The Hebrew scholar will find in the note below the reasons for interpreting the word to mean a *chantsman* or *chanter*[1]. And this meaning is especially appropriate, not only because of the sacred office which Heman and **Ethan** filled, but also because thus in 1 Kings iv. 31 **we have Ethan** the "chanter"—the

---

[1] The Targumist derives אֶזְרָחִי from the root זרח; but the word for *native*, the rendering which he adopts, is not אֶזְרָחִי, but אֶזְרָח; cf. Lev. xvi. 29, &c. Dr Mason Good, in deriving the word from the root אזר takes no account of the ח. There seems no reason why it may not come rather from the root רזח (akin to צרח), to be traced in the word which appears in Jer. xvi. 5 as מַרְזֵחַ and in Amos vi. 7, in the construct state, as מִרְזַח; and which, being applied in the former passage to a funeral feast, in the latter to a convivial banquet, seems strictly to denote *a chant*, which according to its character might be used on occasions of either mourning or rejoicing. From the root רזח would be derived, with א prosthetic, אֶזְרָח, or by transposition for the sake of euphony אֶזְרָח, *a chant*: analogous formations are אֶזְרָע from זרע, אֶקְדָּח, אֶשְׁפָּר. And from אֶזְרָח, *a chant*, would naturally come אֶזְרָחִי, *one of the chant, a chanter*.

No reference has been made in the text to the occurrence of the names of Ethan and Heman along with those of Calcol and Dara (doubtless a mere variation for Darda) in 1 Chron. ii. 6. In reference to the genealogy there given it may be observed, 1st, that men who lived in the reign of David could certainly not have been grandsons or even near descendants of one of the twelve patriarchs; 2ndly, that Heman and Ethan, being Levites, could not have been the children of a son of Judah. (Hengstenberg's explanation, that they were the adopted sons, is unsatisfactory; and the passages which he cites specify only the tribes in which the Levites lived and to which they were attached: they would never be enumerated in genealogies of those tribes.) But on further examination, the present text of that genealogy bears marks of corruption. It omits to give the pedigree of Carmi, mentioned in v. 7; though that pedigree was certainly known, being preserved in Joshua vii. 1, where we find that Carmi was the son of Zabdi the son of Zerah. It is therefore probable that the latter part of v. 6 originally contained a record of the parentage of Carmi: the Zimri mentioned in the beginning of the verse may either be an error for Zabdi, or Zabdi may have been the brother of Zimri. The copyist, however, seeing the name Ethan (which is undoubtedly genuine, cf. v. 8), and possibly also the name Heman (which may or may not be genuine), rashly concluded, as others have done since, that this Ethan the son of Zerah was Ethan the Ezrahite; and assuming also that the Heman, Chalcol, and Darda of 1 Kings iv. 31 were Ethan's brothers, determined to insert their names in the genealogy; to effect which he erased the latter part of the verse containing the pedigree of Carmi. That Ethan the son of Zerah was not the same with Ethan the Ezrahite may be further shewn by the circumstance that to the former the Book of Chronicles assigns only one son, Azariah; whereas it enumerates five sons of the latter (1 Chron. xxv. 3; six with Shimei, v. 17), but no Azariah amongst them.

"son of the chant," the "child of song," as we may style him, in order to bring out the force of the patronymic form—mentioned in connexion with Chalcol and Darda, the "children of the dance"; there being no occasion to follow our English Version in taking the word *mahol* for a proper name.

Besides designating the authors, both real and imaginary, the superscription of this psalm further contains the words "upon Mahalath, to afflict" (for such is the meaning of *leannoth*—the same word is used, in a different inflexion, in v. 7, "Thou hast afflicted me, &c."). The words *upon Mahalath* may here merely imply that the psalm is composed in the same style, or was intended to be sung in the same manner, as David's Mahalath-psalm, Psalm liii; which, like this, is very desolate in its tone. This part of the superscription will thus be nearly analogous to the "on Jeduthun" in the superscriptions of Psalms lxii, lxxvii. The words "to afflict," i. e. "to afflict the soul," mark the character of the psalm: we may compare the words "to bring to remembrance," prefixed to Psalms xxxviii, lxx, and "to thank," in 1 Chron. xvi. 7. The psalm before us should be regarded as a solemn exercise of humiliation: it is more deeply melancholy than any other in the Psalter[1].

That this psalm was uttered in the name of the people of Israel when in captivity was the general view of the ancient interpreters; as also of the Rabbinic commentators among the Jews. But even setting aside all considerations of the place of the psalm in the Psalter, it is preferable to suppose that it was written

---

[1] In the misery which it depicts it has its points of contact with the Book of Job; and outward correspondences between the two have been also noticed by Köster and Delitzsch; correspondences on which the latter seems disposed to lay considerable stress.

in the days of Manasseh; that it represented the feelings of the Church of Israel at a time of very bitter distress, though not of universal captivity; but at the same time that the imagery in which the distress of Israel is described was suggested by the captivity which Israel's anointed sovereign was known to be enduring. We can hardly allow that during the period of the Babylonish captivity psalms were composed at all: the nation was then in a state of comparative abeyance, and the harps hung upon the willow-trees, unused, and unexercised. The psalm is no doubt one of the nearest approaches in the Old Testament to a genuine utterance of the dead; still it is only an approach: the suppliant is indeed *counted* with them that go down into the pit; yet the actual fact is only that his life is *drawing nigh* to the grave. We need not be surprised at the continual afflictions under which the Church of Israel groaned: as Christ's members in these last days, so the Church of Israel in those days of old always bore about in her body the dying of the Lord Jesus, that the life also of Jesus might be made manifest in her body. Dying, yet preserved unto life, chastened, yet not killed, her continual deliverances unto death were all so many foreshadowings of the death of Him by whose death she was to be redeemed from all her iniquities.

We have already learnt from other psalms, such as Psalm xxv, to view in the nation of Israel a type of Christ, in Christ the consummation of the nation of Israel. In Psalm xxv. the suppliant bewailed his youthful sins. In the psalm now before us he complains that from his youth up he has been on the verge of death. To a contemplative Israelite the calamities which had befallen the nation in the captivity of its king would easily call up the remembrance of all the early struggles through which the nation had had to pass. Not to speak of the oppressions in the days of the judges, and of the journey through the wilderness, the psalmist might well also bethink him how when the nation was yet but in its earliest infancy, the patriarch Jacob and his family had been only kept alive through the providential adventures of Joseph and the subsequent sojourn in Egypt. In due time, when that land had become rather a prison-house of bondage than a refuge of safety, God had brought forth his people: "When Israel was a child, then I loved him, and called my son out of Egypt[1]." And in after times, in order that the human life of Christ might be visibly marked as the fulfilment and concentration of all the past history of Israel, it was ordered that he should be carried in infancy to the same land in which the forefathers of the Israelites had sojourned. He too had been ready to die from his youth up; no sooner was he born in Bethlehem, than Herod had sought the young child to destroy him; and Egypt had been the place of his refuge. That the Christian Church may well make the same confession with respect to herself, "I am afflicted and ready to die from my youth up," must be obvious to every one acquainted with her early perils and struggles. And in her present seasons of distress, it is well that she should summon to her recollection the long-continued scenes of persecution and suffering in the midst of which she grew up.

The deep gloom of this psalm forms, as we have already observed, the nearest approach in the Psalter to an actual utterance of the dead. The language is apparently that of utter despair: from first to last it contains hardly one expression of hope. And yet we feel that the very fact of the suppliant lifting up his voice

---

[1] Hosea xi. 1.

to God is a proof that hope still animates him. The theme of the psalm is the apparent inability of even divine succour to reach him: "Wilt thou shew wonders to the dead?" And yet the very circumstance that he enlarges on the difficulty tells of his expectation that in some as yet unrevealed way it will be surmounted. "In the measure as the night of melancholy is gloomy" (writes Tholuck) "and enwraps all around in her sable fold, must our admiration rise for the faith of him who withal continues in prayer. The faith of the tempted may appear like an extremely slender thread,—for such is the effect of melancholy,—but the thread, which under such serious circumstances does not break, cannot be altogether powerless; it is stronger than the most courageous confidence of sunny days. The psalmist, as he states in v. 8, sees no outlet; but he *believes* in one, else why should he pray?"

The feelings to which this psalm gives utterance would be those of the faithful apostles, in sympathy with their Master, during the interval between his death and resurrection. They are however those which will always animate faithful men when still relying on the love of God in the face of obstacles from which they can discern no prospect of deliverance. In reference to the living sense of death, and of separation from God, which the psalm exhibits, the reader may refer back to the Introd. to Psalm vi. The word rendered *free* in the opening of v. 5 (etymologically connected with that rendered *several* in 2 Kings xv. 5; 2 Chron. xxvi. 21) admirably expresses this feeling of perdition. It denotes one who is separated or cast aside; cast out from other men, and above all from the presence of God; one who is freed from the organic bonds which constituted his life, and who is thus in utter misery; one who is *loosed*, and who therefore is *lost*.

PSALM LXXXIX.

"Maschil of Ethan the Ezrahite." The psalm was obviously not composed by a contemporary of King David (see vv. 38, seqq.); and the foregoing superscription would in subsequent times hardly have been prefixed to it by any but a member of the choir of which Ethan was the patriarch and founder. We may therefore assume that the present psalm was composed by some member of the Ethanite or Merarite choir. It is their only production; and was doubtless written at the same time as the preceding Korhite psalm, to which it forms the companion, and with the superscription of which its own superscription is connected.

The suggestion has been occasionally thrown out that the author of this noble strain was none other than the prophet Isaiah. The evidence in favour of this hypothesis is not, it must be confessed, overwhelmingly strong: the fact that other pieces of a partially lyrical character are found interspersed among the prophecies of Isaiah, Chaps. xiv, xxv, xxvi, the general sublimity of style, and lastly the parallelisms between vv. 10, 49, and Isaiah li. 9; lv. 3, are all perhaps that can be fairly urged in its behalf. An external probability however that the prophet Isaiah belonged to the Merarite branch of the tribe of Levi arises from the fact that the name Isaiah (or Jeshaiah) occurs among those of the sons of Ethan (Jeduthun), 1 Chron. xxv. 3, and that the names Amaziah and Amzi, both cognate to Amoz, the name of Isaiah's father, occur in the genealogy of Ethan's ancestors, 1 Chron. vi. 45, 46. It is known that it was the practice of Jewish families to make repeated use either of the names which had occurred in the family before, or of names etymologically derived from the same root; these latter being to a certain extent regarded as interchangeable[1]. Of the recurrence of names we have in fact one other instance in the Merarite family in the case of the name Hashabiah, 1 Chron. vi. 45; xxv. 3. It may here be not amiss to make mention of a Rabbinic tradition that Amoz the father of Isaiah was brother of Amaziah[2]. If the king of the last name be the person intended, the dates barely suit; nor indeed could Isaiah, if a Levite, have belonged to the royal family. But however worthless in itself, the tradition is at least a testimony to the habitual connexion among the Jews of cognate family names. It needs only to be further observed in respect of the authorship of this psalm that even should it be assigned to the prophet Isaiah, he must have composed it not in his prophetical but in his choral capacity; and it should therefore be subjected to the same canons of criticism as the other psalms of the temple-singers.

The psalm was manifestly written at a season when the kingdom of David was in a state of extreme humiliation. The place which it occupies in the Psalter naturally conducts us, as in the case of Psalm lxxxviii, to the period of the captivity of King Manasseh; and even internal evidence is on the whole in favour rather of this date than of that to which many critics assign it, viz. the period immediately preceding the Babylonish captivity. It is, for example, more probable that the psalmist had respect in vv. 44, 45 to the captivity of Manasseh than to that of Jeconiah. For he is evidently bewailing the calamities not of any mere individual person, but of the representative for the time being of the Davidic sovereignty: now Manasseh was the only example of a sovereign of Judah in captivity; in the case of Jeconiah, the sovereignty passed from

---

[1] See Lord A. Hervey's work on the Genealogies of our Lord.

[2] Gem. Megilla, 10, 2: Winer, Realwörterbuch, s. v. Jesaias.

him, at the time of his being carried captive, to his uncle Zedekiah, who continued to rule in Jerusalem. Again, **we** have in this psalm the designation of Egypt by the **name** Rahab, which only occurs elsewhere in a psalm of the reign of Hezekiah, and in the prophecies of Isaiah, nowhere in the writings of the Babylonish period; and which indeed, considering its Hebrew significance, "pride," "insolence," would hardly have been applicable to Egypt after the power of that kingdom had been broken by Nebuchadnezzar at the battle of Carchemish.

The psalm is uttered in the name of the people of Israel: see especially vv. 17, 18, 50. It consists of two parts; vv. 1—37, **38—51**. In the former the psalmist celebrates God's promises respecting the **house of** David; in the latter **he** bewails the apparent contradiction **which is** presented to those promises by the calamities which now surround him.

The substance of the former part of the psalm is comprised in its central and longest verse, v. 19: "Then thou spakest in vision to thy 'holy ones' (the chosen people)[1], and saidst, I have laid help upon one that is mighty; I have exalted one chosen out of the people." What God had uttered in vision to his prophets he had virtually uttered **through** them to the whole nation. For the sake therefore of **his** holy ones, the Israelites whom he had taken to himself **for** an inheritance, he had **spoken** in turn with **Samuel** and with Nathan. He had bidden Samuel anoint David **to** be king, and forthwith David, thus chosen out of the people, had **been** exalted to be the deliverer of the Israelites from their foreign oppressors. By Nathan God had revealed that the throne of the kingdom of David's seed should be established for ever; and that his mercy

---

[1] There can be no reasonable **doubt** of the correctness of the plural reading; which **is** sanctioned by about half the MSS. and by all the ancient versions.

should not depart away from him as it had already departed from Saul. The substance of Nathan's message is recounted by the psalmist in full; it was his object to exhibit in all their expressness the richness and perpetuity of these promises. But it should be observed that although relating to the Davidic house, the psalmist views them as having been made for the sake of all God's holy ones, the people at large. It is not merely the sovereign of Israel, but the people, who in this psalm appeal to God for the continuance of his lovingkindness; in the preservation of their Davidic sovereign they behold the pledge of their own salvation; and hence in v. 18 they celebrate God's mercy as displayed towards them in the exaltation of the house of David, "'From the LORD is our shield, and from the Holy One of Israel is our king[1].'"

If we proceed to analyse still further this earlier portion of the psalm, we find that the first eighteen verses, vv. 1—18, are made to run inversely parallel to the last eighteen, vv. 20—37; the central verse, v. 19, forming the culminating point of the whole. Thus vv. 36, 37, which insist on the perpetuity of God's faithfulness, correspond to vv. 1, 2; vv. 34, 35, which speak of God's sworn covenant with David, correspond to vv. 3, 4; and so in other cases: compare, for instance, v. 13 with v. 25. Again there is a minor inverted correspondence (already noticed in the Preliminary Essay, Vol. I. p. 19) between the verses of the portion vv. 28—37 taken by itself: compare vv. 28, 37, vv. 29, 36, and also vv. 31, 34 ("if they *break*"—"will I not *break*"). But to return to the earlier portion of the

---

[1] See the English marginal reading. And note by the way, that a reminiscence of the language of this psalm, v. 20, meets us in St Paul's speech in the synagogue at Antioch, Acts xiii. 22; the "I have found" of the words which he there puts into God's mouth occurring only here, not in the history.

psalm in its entirety. The more especial theme of the first eighteen verses culminates in the two central verses, vv. 9, 10, which celebrate the *completeness* of God's earlier deliverances of his people. In like manner the theme of the last eighteen verses culminates in vv. 28, 29, which allege in the most explicit terms the promised perpetuity of the Davidic sovereignty. But that God's faithfulness to his oath to David is the grand theme of the whole thirty-seven verses, is evident from the mention of this oath as early as v. 3. The contents therefore of this portion of the psalm may be thus briefly summed up: "For our sakes God exalted his servant David to be our deliverer, and promised that his throne should continue for ever. Knowing therefore from experience the proofs of God's power and love in his deliverances of his people in olden time, and knowing also the explicit promise of perpetuity which he has since made to the chosen house of David, we may rest confident of the certainty of our ultimate salvation, may in gratitude sing of God's mercies, and in faith proclaim God's faithfulness."

From the recital of God's promises the psalmist passes to rehearse the present calamities of the people and their king. The latter portion of the psalm subdivides itself into two parts. First, we have the description of the effects of God's present displeasure, vv. 38—45; and of these verses again it may be observed that they are in a measure complete in themselves, the last four running inversely parallel to the first four[1], and the whole being terminated by the Selah. As regards their contents they remind us of the complaints of Psalm xliv, which they resemble. Then lastly we have the efforts of faith to pierce through

---

[1] The correspondences, somewhat faint, are traced by Forbes, *Symm. Struct. of Scripture*, p. 41.

the gloom, and the appeal to God to attest by visible tokens his faithfulness to the promises he has sworn, vv. 46—51. These verses are divided by the Selah into a strophe and an antistrophe of three each: compare the interrogations in vv. 46, 49, and the calls for remembrance in vv. 47, 50. They give utterance to terrible cries, which hardly yield in depth of melancholy and apparent despondency to the cries of Psalm lxxxviii. They lift not the veil of the future; they disclose not the secret outlet of mercy; yet they are evidently the utterances of faith; of a faith which, while complaining of the deep darkness of the night, and of the absence of any glimmer to guide the footsteps onward, still leans on the past experiences of God's love, and clings to the sure promises of his word.

And for a long time the problem how God's promise respecting the house of David should be fulfilled remained unsolved. The sovereignty of that family, which had continued almost without interruption for three centuries and a half from the days of David to those of the captivity of Manasseh, lingered on for near another century after Manasseh's return till the Chaldean destruction of Jerusalem, and left behind its vestige in the subsequent princedom of Zerubbabel: it then for five centuries disappeared; nor after the time of Zechariah did any fresh prophet arise to confirm anew the expectation of the fulfilment of that promise which, so far as human ken could discern, had already failed. At length the mystery was cleared up. The throne of David was established for ever; more spiritually, and therefore in real truth more gloriously, than the most sanguine of the "holy ones" of old had ever ventured to anticipate. The promised Christ, of the seed of David, was born in David's city Bethlehem; and the Lord God gave unto him the throne of his father David, with the assurance that he should reign over the house of Jacob for ever, and that of his kingdom there should be no end.

The general prospective bearing of the psalm, and the realization in the kingdom of Christ of all for which the psalmist sought, are thus clear; nor will it on these points be necessary to enlarge. It may be well however to point out two special instances in which the phraseology of this psalm has either anticipated or influenced that of the New Testament. First, it will be observed that the key-note, as it were, of this psalm lies in the words "Mercy and Faithfulness:" see particularly vv. 1, 2, 5, 8, 14, 24, 28, 33, 49. These are in substance the same as that "Grace and Truth" of which St John tells us that "the law was given by Moses, but grace and truth came by Jesus Christ:" "the Word was made flesh and dwelt among us,..... full of grace and truth[1]." God's mercy and faithfulness were not merely exemplified in the sending of his Son into the world: the Incarnate Word was himself the living human impersonation of those attributes. Secondly, the earlier portion of the psalm concludes (in the E. V.) with these words: "His (David's) seed shall endure for ever, and his throne as the sun before me. It shall be established for ever as the moon, and as a faithful witness in heaven, (or, 'and faithful is the witness in heaven')." What is meant by the faithful witness in heaven? Various answers are given: the moon—the sun and moon—the rainbow—some or any faithful heavenly witness—God himself. None of these explanations are altogether satisfactory. It seems preferable to understand the eternal wisdom of which Solomon had spoken in the Proverbs: "The LORD possessed me in the beginning of his way, before his works of old. I was set up from everlasting, from the beginning, or ever the

[1] John i. 14, 17.

earth was.........I was by him, as one brought up with him[1], &c." We shall then have Jesus Christ in the Revelation identifying himself with the witness in heaven of whom, in his imperfect knowledge, the psalmist had conceived: "Jesus Christ who is the faithful witness;" "These things saith the Amen, the faithful and true witness, the beginning of the creation of God[2]." There is no passage in Scripture, except that in the psalm before us, from which the expression "faithful witness" can well have been derived. Jesus Christ is the witness to men both of the fulfilment of the divine oath to David, and of all God's truth; even the witness of God himself.

Although in these Christian times there will be scarcely room for doubt, as in the days of the psalmist, of the fulfilment of the promise made to David, yet there will undoubtedly be seasons at which and aspects under which the analogous question will present itself to the Christian Church, Is Jesus Christ to be Lord over all? When wickedness abounds; when those who have been called by Christ's name own not his supremacy in their hearts and lives; when his truth seems to be making no progress; when the Christian Church or any portion of it seems to be outwardly contracting rather than expanding; when the people that know the joyful sound and that walk in the light of God's countenance are but a scattered few, and bear in their bosom the reproach of all the numerous enemies of the Lord's Anointed; then will Christian faith be tried as was the faith of the psalmist; then will his utterances find an echo in the hearts of those likeminded with himself, and his words will help others still to confide with unabated trust in God's mercy and faithfulness.

The doxology, v. 52, marks the end of the Third Book of the Psalter.

---

[1] Prov. viii. 22 seqq. [2] Rev. i. 5; iii. 14.

BOOK IV.

PSALMS XC.—CVI.

O LORD, I have heard thy speech, **and** was afraid: O LORD, **revive thy work** in the midst of the years, in the midst of the years make **known**; **in wrath remember mercy.**
Habakkuk iii. 2.

And they cried with **a** loud voice, saying, **How long, O Lord, holy and true,** dost thou not judge and avenge our blood on **them that dwell on the earth?**
Rev. vi. 10.

BOOK IV.

THE Fourth Book of the Psalter numbers, like the Third Book, seventeen psalms. It comprises, along with the psalm of Moses, those of the last hundred years of the Jewish monarchy, up to the date of the Babylonish captivity. At what time they were collected and arranged in their present order there is no certain evidence to shew: perhaps not till the days of Nehemiah, when the Fifth Book of the Psalter was also arranged, and the canon of Old Testament Scripture closed. Of the psalms composing the Fourth Book Psalm xc. is entitled "A Prayer of Moses the man of God;" Psalms ci, ciii. bear the name of David; Psalm cii. is "A Prayer of the afflicted, &c." In the superscriptions of the rest there is no indication of the authorship: they are probably the productions of the Sons of Asaph, who formed during this period the only surviving temple-choir.

These psalms do not reflect, to the same extent as those of Book III, the political events and vicissitudes of their period. They were all written (excepting, of course, the Prayer of Moses) after the irrevocable doom of destruction upon Jerusalem for the wickedness of Manasseh had been solemnly pronounced. In consequence of that doom, the expected full redemption of Israel and the glorification of the sovereignty of the house of David in the person of the promised Messiah were in the eyes of the people indefinitely deferred; and the continuity of progress to the future of glory being thus destroyed, the immediate political events of the times lost in great measure their prospective interest.

Whatever impatient hopes the events of the reign of Hezekiah had served to nurture of a speedy fulfilment of God's promises to Israel must have yielded with many to the recklessness of despair and indifference; but meanwhile the faith of the true servants of God was being disciplined, and their expectations spiritualized. Deeply prophetical as are many of the psalms on which we now enter, the result of the dissociation of the anticipations of the future from the contemplations of the present is that they depict the events of the future rather in their divine than in their human aspect; they speak not so much of the truth which should spring out of the earth as of the righteousness which should look down from heaven. These psalms have a freshness of their own; not the freshness of national youth, nor that of national rejuvenescence; but rather the freshness which will ever spring from solid depth of faith. They are the utterance of the traveller who, finding but little of interest in the long weary plain that extends around him, rejoices nevertheless in gazing on the glories of the distant hills; and in the assurance that he will not fail to reach them in the end, contentedly plods on along his level road, aware that the journey, however dull, is necessary, and trusting that in the Lord even his present labours will not have been in vain.

PSALM XC.

There is no valid reason to doubt that this psalm was really, as its superscription would imply, a prayer of Moses. Saadia, the Jewish translator of the Pentateuch into Arabic, who lived in the tenth century A.D., threw out the suggestion that by "Moses" might here be meant the children of Moses, i. e. the Levites; and the way in which we have found that the names of David, Asaph, Heman, and Ethan were prefixed by their several descendants to the psalms of their own composition, **might** possibly dispose us to look with favour on **this** view. But the individuality of the ancient lawgiver seems to be marked by the words "the man of God" affixed to his name, just as the individuality of the original David, as distinguished from his descendants, is marked by the adjunct "the son of Jesse[1]." And all objections to the Mosaic authorship of this psalm arising from the fact that in respect of its antiquity it stands alone in the Psalter are more than counterbalanced by the unlikelihood that any merely **imitative** writer would have succeeded, **in** a psalm the sublimity and grandeur of which do not depend on passionate excitement, in realizing so completely the impress of the Mosaic age, of the history of the wanderings, and of the scenery of the desert. The history of this psalm, and of its place in the Psalter, is unknown to us: we can only speculate upon it. It may be either that, after having been long lost, it was newly discovered in the reign of Josiah along with the book of the law; or else that, having been previously known, it received in the reign of Josiah increased attention in consequence of the increased respect with which the book of the law of the Lord, given by Moses, was after its rediscovery regarded. Again, it is possible that it had been excluded from the earlier portions of the Psalter on account of the reverence due to its antiquity, and that **it** was now first embodied in the Psalter by the collector of the Fourth Book because he wished to render the collection of the Songs of Israel complete. And lastly, there is also room for the surmise that its

---

[1] Psalm lxxii. 20.

place in the Psalter, at the head of the psalms of the last years of the monarchy, may be in some way due to that special harmony of its sentiments, which we shall presently observe, with those of the faithful in Josiah's reign.

Viewed then with reference to its author, this psalm is the utterance of the feelings of the great prophet and lawgiver of Israel during his pilgrimage through the wilderness. It was probably written towards the end of the forty years' wanderings (see v. 15); but its solemnity makes it more likely that it was the result of the long and habitual contemplations of Moses during those wanderings, than that it was occasioned by any single incident. The leading thought of the psalm is that to which vent is given in the first verse; that God is the eternal abiding-place of his people. This thought is first expanded in v. 2. "There is indeed,"—so runs the current of the prophet's meditation,—"an earth, which some might deem their home, and which, with all its ancient hills, might verily be called permanent as compared with the shortlived beings that inhabit it; for across its fields have flitted the living bodies and beneath its soil have rested the bones of successive generations of men, who from the swiftness with which they passed away knew nothing of each other, though the earth meanwhile remained the same and experienced no sensible change. Yet even this earth is itself but the thing of a day in comparison of Him whose infinity of existence no language can express, and who from everlasting to everlasting is God: it is therefore in the Creator, rather than in the creature, that we recognize our true abiding-place." In order further to illustrate the everlastingness and power of God, they are contrasted in vv. 3—6 with the transitoriness of man; as also, in vv. 7—11, with his misery, the result **of the divine wrath** upon his sin. V. 12, which stands in connexion with the preceding, contains a short **petition that by the** contemplation of his own impotence **man may** acquire a heart of wisdom, **so** as to learn **that God is his** abiding-place indeed.

The truth **of this** being now assumed, the last five verses, vv. 13—17, contain the prophet's main prayer. God is implored to extend his grace and blessing to those whose abiding-place he is. One and all, prophet and people, were weary of the sins and miseries of their long dreary pilgrimage: they asked that mercy and gladness might at length take the place of wrath and calamity. They asked in patient faith. They had little expectation that they themselves should during their lifetime behold that season of prosperity in which the memories of their past sufferings should be wiped out. They knew—Moses among the number—that for themselves, they must perish in the wilderness. Still, though the sentence of death was upon them, and though after a few more years of labour and sorrow they must turn to destruction, and must rest beneath the wastes of the desert, they felt that those barren rocks, those burning sands, were not their true home; the God of Abraham, of Isaac, and of Jacob would yet prove himself their abiding-place by granting to them, in the persons of their children, the promised blessings which had been denied to themselves. **Hence** their prayer: "Let thy *work* appear unto *thy servants,* **and** thy *glory* unto *their children.*" They were content to live and to die as pilgrims, provided **only** they could feel that in his sterner dealings with them God was, however slowly, preparing the way for that display of glorious blessedness which should be the lot of their descendants. In a similar spirit they ask God to establish the work of their hands, though they reckoned not that they should behold its results. Their comfort in sowing was the belief that their children would reap.

It is easy to perceive how similar to the historical position of the generation of the exodus, after they had been condemned to die in the wilderness, was that of the Jews of the century preceding the Babylonish captivity, after the sentence of destruction had for the sins of Manasseh been formally pronounced upon Jerusalem. In each case the promise remained; the promise on which the thoughts of the older generation were centred being that of the inheritance of Canaan, while the attention of the later Jews was more distinctly directed to that of the advent of the Messiah. But in each case there was also a moral certainty that no approach to the fulfilment of the promise would be witnessed by the suppliants themselves. The aged Moses when he reproclaimed the law in the plains of Moab, and the young Josiah, when he publicly read in the temple the words of the book of the covenant which he had so providentially discovered, were alike labouring less for themselves than for posterity. The task of Josiah was indeed, of the two, that which apparently required the greater faith. The work of Moses might be uninterruptedly carried on by his successor and thus continuously progress to maturity; but of whatever Josiah could immediately achieve, the greater part must unavoidably perish in the evil which was to ensue so soon as he was gathered into his grave[1].

How universally the zealous members of the Christian Church have been obliged to employ themselves in labours of which they could not reasonably hope to behold the fruits, and how applicable under such circumstances the prayer of this psalm must at all times be, will be easily discerned by every one; nor need we

---

[1] 2 Kings xxii. 20.

here enlarge upon it. But there is another application of the psalm which demands a few words of explanation. It has been shewn in the Introd. to Psalm xxxvii. that in the desire so ardently cherished by the Old Testament saints of being perpetuated in their posterity we may trace the germ of our belief in the resurrection of the dead. No religious man could, even in olden times, be content to think that he had no interest in what should occur after his death. And as, in his degree of knowledge, the phrase "his children's days" expressed his whole conception of the future, we too must, in order not unduly to narrow its significance, regard it as including all that is yet to come, whether in this world or in another. In asking that his children might behold God's glory, the Old Testament saint virtually prayed that he himself might behold it in that way (the only way known to him) in which it was possible for him to behold it after his own death. We know of another way; and part of the Christian sense of the last two verses of the psalm may therefore be legitimately developed as follows: "Let thy work appear unto thy servants in this world, and thy glory to them in the world to come; .... and so establish thou the work of our hands upon us, that what we have here sown, we may reap in life eternal."

And thus each time that we the survivors repeat the words of this psalm at the burial of our departed friends, they should warn us that neither God's present dealings with us nor our own present deeds cease to operate at our deaths. The extent of their consequences cannot be measured. Whether for good or for evil, they follow our children in their future careers in this world: they follow us to the judgment. In respect of the influence which they exert upon our own future lots, they seem indeed for a time to be lost.

Their results are in abeyance. While sleeps the man in death, pending the resurrection unto judgment, they, it may be, sleep also. And thus each living man's faith and energy are tried, to a greater extent than is commonly supposed, by the discouraging conviction that the ultimate consequences of his deeds to himself will, like the ultimate consequences of the work of Josiah to his posterity, not immediately appear. But over such discouragement the faith of true obedience triumphs; the Christian believes that in every way his work will be established, even though he behold it not; and so having served God in his generation, he lies down to die, and to await in the Lord the resurrection-day, knowing that though meanwhile he rest from his labours, yet his works do follow him.

PSALM XCI.

A RABBINIC canon, referred to by Hilary and Jerome[1],—probably a mere hasty generalization from what is really the case in the first three Books of the Psalter,—enacts that all anonymous psalms shall be deemed the compositions of the authors named in the superscriptions last preceding. In virtue of this canon the Jewish critics from the time of Jerome downwards have assigned the ninety-first and nine following psalms to Moses. It is fatal to the authority of the canon that the prophet Samuel is mentioned by name in Psalm xcix; but in addition to this we may observe that the canon was either unknown to or repudiated by the Targumist, who, if he did not regard David and Solomon as the actual authors of the psalm before us, at least supposed them to be introduced as the imaginary speakers in it.

---

[1] Hilar. *Prolog. in Psalmos.* Sect. 3; Hieron. *Epist. ad Cyprianum*, Opp. Tom. i. p. 1050, ed Vallarsi.

To the existence of this assumed canon it was however necessary to allude, because many modern critics, who have allowed themselves to argue from internal evidence for the Mosaic authorship of this single psalm, Psalm xci, have supported their argument by the authority of the canon which they nevertheless fairly admit to be generally untenable. There are undoubtedly points of contact between Psalms xc. and xci; thus with xc. 1 cf. xci. 1, 9; with xc. 3, 7, xci. 6; with xc. 14, xci. 16; but yet the solemnity and archaism of tone of the former are wholly wanting in the latter. Like the psalm which follows it, Psalm xci. bears the marks of having been written in what we may call the Byzantine period of Jewish history, when national life was on the wane, and when the true servants of God, finding comparatively little opportunity for employing themselves in the duties of active patriotism, and weary of the political confusion and of the general apostasy and wickedness which they could do but little to alleviate, were glad to seek in the peace of the sanctuary that repose which the world denied them. The psalm was probably composed for a directly liturgical purpose. The blessedness of dwelling in the secret place of the Most High would be a natural thought with those who valued the privilege of regularly worshipping within the precincts of the temple. And could we be but certain that the psalm was, as many have supposed, intended to be sung by alternating choruses, its original liturgical character would be placed beyond a doubt[1].

All resemblances between this and the preceding

---

[1] If this theory be correct, we may suppose that vv. 1, 2, 9, 10, were severally divided in lines between the two choruses; and that the other parts of the psalm, vv. 3—8, 11—16, were sung by the choruses combined. The whole psalm will thus be divided into two equal corresponding portions, vv. 1—8, 9—16, each commenced by the alternating choruses. A different scheme is given by J. D. Michaelis, in note 3 to Lowth's *Prælectio* xxvi.

psalm may be easily explained by assuming that the author of Psalm xci. had Psalm xc. before him. And in fact, as he wrote without any special reference to the events of his own time, he seems to have drawn his imagery rather from the circumstances attendant on the historical march through the wilderness than from those with which he was himself familiar; just as a preacher or sacred poet of our own day would, in depicting the life of the individual Christian, generally prefer the imagery furnished by the scriptural records of the Israelites to that suggested by the events passing immediately around him. Hence the mention of the desert-beasts, "the lion and adder, the young lion and the dragon," to represent the believer's foes, whether open or secret. Hence the mention also of the ordinary desert-dangers, "the terror by night" and "the arrow that flieth by day," "the pestilence that walketh in darkness" and "the destruction that wasteth at noonday;" the latter words, at least, referring to plagues such as those by which, for their rebellions in the wilderness, the Israelites had more than once been visited; and the whole of the dangers enumerated being "the types of all the moral evil and spiritual pestilence which either secretly or openly have afflicted mankind since sin entered into the world[1]." Hence, lastly, the expression in v. 11, "to keep thee in all thy ways," apparently suggested by a remembrance of those divinely-appointed journeyings of the Israelites through the wilderness, in which they had been so remarkably kept

---

[1] Jebb, II. p. 205; who regards the expressions in v. 5 as allusions to those threatened plagues, by night and by day, which are viewed in v. 6 as in actual operation. Theodoret, with the majority of modern critics, refers the expressions in v. 5 to the stratagems and attacks of enemies: καὶ διαφεύξῃ καὶ τὰς νύκτωρ ἐπιούσας ἐπιβουλάς, καὶ τὰς μεθ' ἡμέραν γενομένας παρὰ τῶν ἐχθρῶν προσβολάς. But even such dangers would be especially experienced by those surrounded by the wild tribes of the desert.

by the ever-present power of God[1]. It was probably from those journeyings that the phrase "to walk in God's ways," which first occurs in the book of Deuteronomy, originally arose[2].

And as the imagery and phraseology of the psalm are thus derived from the circumstances of former times, so also the blessings which in the end of the psalm God is represented as promising, more especially that of length of days, are the same which the psalmist found promised in the older scriptures; cf. especially Prov. iii. 2. They have no particular reference to the circumstances of the psalmist's own time: on the contrary, the defeat and early death of Josiah must, so soon as they occurred, have stood out in strong apparent contrast to them. And though long life had in many cases, as in those of Abraham, David, and Job, been a visible token of the blessing of God; yet the universal truth of such promises to the righteous as those which the psalmist brings forward must have become more and more difficult to reconcile with the general experience of mankind, until life and immortality were brought to light through the gospel, and until it thus became known that length of days and fruition of God's salvation did not finally terminate with man's death.

In reference to the devil's quotation of the text "He shall give his angels charge over thee, to keep thee, &c.," it should be remarked that he omitted the important words "in all thy ways," by which, as we have already indicated, are virtually intended those ways of duty directly or indirectly marked out for us by God[3]. And

---

[1] Cf. Deut. ii. 7; viii. 2—4.

[2] Deut. viii. 6 (following close upon viii. 2—4). Cf. also Exod. xviii. 20, Deut. v. 33; but in both these passages the word is, in the Hebrew, in the singular.

[3] Matth. iv. 6; Luke iv. 10, 11. In both evangelists the quotation is, so far as it goes, taken correctly from the LXX. It is curious that our English version of the passage, both as it stands in the Old Testament, and as it is quoted

such was not that way along which Satan would have led our Saviour when he bade him attempt an exploit of selfish vanity and presumption. "Had the Lord Jesus," remarks Stier, "wished to make a special exegesis of the passage in the psalm, he might have replied, That is not the *way* for me to follow!" This was indeed indirectly the force of the answer which he actually gave: "It is written again, Thou shalt not tempt the Lord thy God."

PSALM XCII.

"A PSALM and Song for the Sabbath-day." We have before us a psalm of much beauty both of language and sentiment, and which will on that account ever remain one of the most pleasing hymns in the Psalter; but which in the artificial evenness of its melodious flow carries proof of having been composed not with immediate reference to the circumstances of the psalmist's own time, but rather as a pious reiteration of the truths embodied in older psalms. Original in its details, it bears nevertheless the general impress of the influence of the strains both of David and of the Asaphite author of Psalm lxxiii; but is at the same time hardly

---

in the New Testament, contains an erroneous rendering which neither the Hebrew nor the Greek will bear. For "*in* their hands," we should read "*on* their hands." The false rendering, although here happily of no great importance, is thus precisely parallel to that at Psalm xvi. 10 (*in* for *to:* see the Introd. to that Psalm), which is in like manner warranted neither by the Hebrew original nor by the Greek of the LXX, as quoted in the New Testament. Thus unaccountably do indefensible errors of translation creep in and become perpetuated in the best known passages, in spite of the check imposed by the existence of a double original. The difference between "in their hands" and "on their hands," is nearly the same with that difference between "under his wings," and "on her wings," which Mr Jebb, and after him the author of the *Plain Commentary*, have neglected, when they assert Psalm xci. 4 to be parallel to Deut. xxxii. 11, 12. The images in the two passages are by no means the same: the one illustrates the love with which God protects, the other that with which he schooled his people.

less different in tone from David's own strains than is the preceding psalm from the hymns of Moses. It is symmetrical in its formal arrangement. The central verse is **v. 8, comprised** in a single line, and standing between two verses of three lines each: all the other verses of the psalm consist of two lines. In respect of their mutual coherence the verses may be thus distributed: vv. 1—4; 5, 6; 7—9; 10, 11; 12—15; the first four and the **last** four **verses** forming the most joyous portions of the psalm.

From the generality of its character it is sufficiently evident that the psalm **is** uttered in the name of the whole church; and that v. 10 has **no** reference **to** any individual preeminence. **It** was also certainly composed for a directly liturgical purpose. Hence the mention **by** name of some of the musical instruments that were used in the temple-worship, v. 3. Hence also the comparison of the righteous in the last four verses to the palm and the cedar-tree; cedars furnishing the material out of which the sanctuary was in great measure constructed, and palm-trees being the objects with which its walls were sculptured. From the superscription we learn that the psalm was more especially designed for use **on** the sabbath-day; and Hengstenberg throws out **the suggestion that** from the mention of the morning **and night in v. 2,** it may have been intended to be sung at the bringing forward of the morning and evening sacrifice. As a sabbath-song, and as the only psalm in the Psalter so designated, it has its appropriate theme. It is a meditation **on** the works of God, **v.** 5. As on the sabbath-day God rested from all his works which **he** had created and made, so on that day might men most fittingly contemplate the wonders of his work **by** which they had been gladdened. The opening **verses** shew that the sabbath was designed not merely for a day of rest, but also for a day of worship; the object for which men on that day ceased from **their** own works being that they might celebrate the works **of** God. But furthermore, the older sabbath was a type of our rest in Christ from **sin**; and therefore the final extirpation **of sin** forms **one of** the leading subjects of the psalm; **it being** declared that though the wicked prosper for a season, it is only that they may at the last be destroyed for ever, while the righteous **shall** still flourish **in** never-fading beauty. The doctrine thus delivered by the psalmist is that which he found in older psalms, e. g. Psalms xxxvii, xlix; and which in faith he received, though its universal truth could (like that of the promise of long life in Psalm xci.) be **only** thoroughly understood when **the** doctrines of a future resurrection and of **a** future judgment were also revealed. To us the resurrection of Christ has marked out **another** and a more appropriate day for special holy meditation on the general greatness of the divine works; the day of the week on which God rested from **the work of** creation has given way to that on which the most stupendous of his deeds was achieved; and the ancient holy day which typified our rest in Christ from sin, has since the fulfilment of the type been replaced by one that symbolizes **our** uprising to new holiness of life. But the **psalm before us is as a hymn of praise** hardly less adapted **to** the Christian Lord's **day** than to the Jewish sabbath; and thus in the Church **of the new covenant** is the worship of the Church of **the old** perpetuated.

PSALM XCIII.

WE here enter upon a series of **eight** psalms, evidently composed **at the** same time and by the same hand, and designed **by** their author to form together one lyric poem[1]. They bear evidence of having, like the two preceding psalms, been expressly intended for the temple-worship[2]; but they are more spirited in their tone, and of a far more extended significance. Though there be in them no trace of any allusion to the political events, they yet carry a certain reference to the political prospects, of the period at which they were written; but their main and distinguishing feature is the prophetical clearness with which they herald from afar the approach of the divine kingdom; that kingdom which had formed the theme of a large part of the predictions of Isaiah. They are hymns of thanksgiving for the future blessings which Isaiah had foretold; and from the evangelical prophecies of Isaiah their substance is in great measure derived.

The opening words of the first psalm of the series strike the key-note to the theme of the whole: "The LORD reigneth"; or as our older version more expressively translates, "The Lord is king." Such is the grand announcement: it is repeated in the openings of Psalms xcvii, xcix, and substantially also in Psalms xcv. 3, xcviii. 6; and in Psalm xcvi. 10 the worshippers are bidden proclaim it to all the world. There is in the words themselves, as Hengstenberg justly remarks, an allusion to the form used at the proclamation of the commencement of the reign of an earthly sovereign[3];

---

[1] Hengstenberg would make the series commence earlier; and would treat Psalm xciii. as a pair to Psalm xcii. But putting aside his questionable argument from the symbolical arithmetic, the utmost to be gathered from the slight resemblance between xcii. 8, xciii. 4, and from the occurrence in both psalms of the same form of anadiplosis, xcii. 9, xciii. 3, is that they may have been composed by the same author. Who can fail to perceive the difference in character between the melodious flow of the one psalm, and the proclamatory triumph of the other? Bp. Horsley makes the series commence at Psalm xcv; but is properly corrected by Jebb, II. p. 258.

[2] Cf. Psalm xciii. 5; xcv. 2; xcvi. 8, 9; c. 2, 4.

[3] Cf. 2 Sam. xv. 10; 1 Kings i. 11, 13; 2 Kings ix. 13.

and hence it follows that the language does not apply to the constant government of God, but to a new glorious manifestation of his dominion. The same thing is also evident from the call, in Psalms xcvi, xcviii, to sing unto the Lord a *new* song: that which demanded the new song being not God's rightful sovereignty of old, but the new assertion of that sovereignty in the work which he was accomplishing for his own glory and for the salvation of his people.

And in the celebration of this advent of the manifestation of God's kingdom, each psalm in the series has its own particular branch of the general theme of which it treats. The outline of their respective contents is as follows. Psalm xciii. sets forth God's claim to be king by right of eternal dominion. Psalm xciv. shews how the claim is resisted: the throne of iniquity has set itself up against the throne of God, and the wicked are in apparent triumph. Hence the necessity of some means by which the sovereignty of God shall be made good. The succeeding psalms exhibit the process of God's work. Psalm xcv. shews how he has called and is educating unto himself a peculiar people who shall shew forth his praise. Psalm xcvii. tells of the deliverance of that holy people out of the hands of the wicked, and of the latter's confusion and destruction. Psalm xcix. has for its theme the future worship of God in perfect holiness after the judgment shall be complete. And of these three psalms the alternate three are the respective companions; Psalm xcvi. being a thanksgiving for the establishment of the sanctuary as a witness for God in the world; Psalm xcviii. a thanksgiving for the divine victory in the ensuing struggle; Psalm c. an invitation to the universal redeemed to adore the Eternal Creator of all, whose sovereignty has now been confirmed beyond dispute.

It remains for us to investigate the date at which this series of psalms was written. The principal indications are to be found in Psalms xciii, xciv. In the former we read of the floods lifting up their voice and their waves; by which we must understand that some mighty hostile power was exalting itself against God. In the latter we read of "the throne of iniquity," "which frameth mischief by a law;" or rather, which 'fashioneth misery after the pattern of an appointed task'; viz. by substituting the burden of sheer misery for the burden of compulsory labour which others had laid upon their subjects, and by meting out misery to every one with as much regularity as that with which Pharaoh's taskmasters meted out to the Israelites their daily tasks[1]. And in other parts of the psalm the enormities which this throne of iniquity was perpetrating are more fully described. Thus from both psalms alike we may gather that God's people were at this time either actually sustaining or gloomily expecting a conflict with either the Assyrian or Chaldean power. It is probable that of the two the Chaldeans were the enemies contemplated, inasmuch as psalms of the Assyrian period would have found their place in the Third Book. Now the invasion of the Chaldeans, "that bitter and hasty nation," was foretold, probably in the days of Josiah, by the prophet Habakkuk[2]; and as the signs of their advance became from that time discernible, it will not be unreasonable to suppose that the psalms of which we are speaking were written shortly afterwards in the middle or latter part of Josiah's reign. The psalmist's account of the cruelties of God's enemies may

---

[1] Psalm xciv. 20. The word חק denotes anything *appointed*; hence a *prescribed task*, cf. Exod. v. 14. The preposition על signifies *after the manner of*, cf. Psalm cx. 4.

[2] The arguments of Delitzsch for assigning the prophecy of Habakkuk to the 12th or 13th year of the reign of Josiah are epitomised in Smith's *Dictionary of the Bible*, Art. Habakkuk.

well be compared with the account of those of the Chaldeans in Habakkuk; to whose prophecy indeed Theodoret repeatedly refers in illustrating the language of the first two of the psalms in the present series[1].

To these two psalms the LXX. have prefixed superscriptions, which, besides assigning the authorship of them to David, appropriate them respectively "to the day before the sabbath, after the earth has been peopled," and "to the fourth day of the week"; superscriptions obviously suggested by that of Psalm xcii. Psalm xxiv. had in like manner been specially connected by the LXX. with the first day of the week. It is possible that these superscriptions may simply embody the private view which the Greek translators took of the contents of those psalms: more probably they represent the liturgical use which was made of them at Alexandria at the time when the translation was executed. The Jewish liturgical arrangement of the psalms would probably not be everywhere the same.

And thus much then respecting the general purport of the eight psalms now before us. The opening words of Psalm xciii. must be regarded, as we have already shewn, as the theme of the entire series, inasmuch as they virtually announce not the existence of God's dominion of old but its new approaching manifestation. But the main design of that psalm is to set forth God's *title* to dominion: he has been king from the beginning. And this is most emphatically announced in v. 2, which, as the kernel of the psalm, is distinguished by its brevity, consisting of only two lines, whereas all the other verses contain three. Vv. 3, 4 briefly declare that God the Creator shall prove superior to all the assaults of his rebellious creatures; and v. 5 contains the immediate

---

[1] Cf. Psalm xciii. 3, 4 with Hab. 2 with Hab. ii. 5—8; xciv. 21 with iii. 8; xciii. 5 with Hab. ii. 20; xciv. Hab. i. 13; &c.

moral; viz. that as God never faileth, so neither will he ever suffer either his testimonies or his Church to fail. His word shall be ever fulfilled; and he will ever preserve unto himself a holy house upon earth. Let his people therefore not dread the violence or might of their foes.

PSALM XCIV.

The purport of this psalm in its relation to the entire series of which it forms a part has been already explained. Delineating in vv. 3—11, and again, incidentally, in vv. 20, 21, the wickedness in consequence of which the sovereignty of God remained as it were for a time in abeyance, it shews how in order to re-establish his dominion the Lord must first appear as a God of vengeance; and it accordingly opens by announcing with prophetical anticipation the approaching manifestation of God in that character. Our E. V. renders the verb of v. 1 in the imperative; but that rendering is not borne out by the Hebrew[1], and the indicative, besides being supported by the parallel passage Psalm l. 2, agrees better with the openings of Psalms xciii, xcvii, xcix:

> The God of vengeance, even the Lord,
> The God of vengeance shineth forth.

The latter portion of the psalm, vv. 12 seqq., is designed to administer comfort in the meanwhile to God's afflicted people; until the days of adversity be ended, the expected vengeance be accomplished, and judgment be again exercised in conformity with the eternal principles of righteousness (v. 15) instead of being perverted by the usurping thrones of iniquity.

[1] And therefore Maurer, who advocates the imperative rendering, candidly alters the Hebrew text. The LXX and Vulgate render in the indicative.

That it is the heathen who in this psalm are contemplated as the types of ungodliness, seems probable from the **opposition in** which the wicked are represented as standing to God's *heritage* (vv. 5, 14), and also from the **use of the** phrase "the throne of iniquity," with apparent allusion to the might of the Chaldean monarchy. Yet much of the language would also apply to the **heathen-minded** in Israel, to the world within the Church as well as to the world without; and it should be remembered that the prophet Habakkuk, whose writings furnish the best illustrations of this psalm, complained of the iniquity of his own land before he complained of that of its heathen invaders[1]. And how little right we have to limit the fair import of the psalmist's words is shewn by the example of St Paul, who in quoting v. 11 substitutes "the thoughts of the wise" for "the thoughts of man[2]"; not as though it were the worldly-wise of whom the psalmist had been intentionally speaking, **but because such were** virtually guilty of the follies against which the psalmist had testified.

PSALM XCV.

THE psalm is an invitation to the **chosen** people, the flock of God's pasture, **to worship their** divine Shepherd and **to** serve him with sincerity and willingness. The calling and training of a peculiar people were the means by which from an early period God had unfolded his design of bringing all mankind to a recognition of his sovereignty. Israel was thus the light that was to give light to the whole world; and in the dealings of God with Israel and of Israel with God were to be practically exemplified the mutual relation of the sheep and their Creator-shepherd. Hence the solemn summons

---

[1] Hab. i. 2—4.   [2] 1 Cor. iii. 20.

to Israel to worship and bow down, and kneel before the Lord their maker, who was their God, they being **the people** of his pasture and the sheep of his hand. **But what if** the light should itself become darkness? What if those who were to be the special witnesses for God's sovereignty should themselves become like the world who despised it? What if those whose history was designed specially to illustrate the blessings of obedience to God's shepherd-rule should themselves tempt **and** provoke the God who had called them? Alas! the fathers of the Israelites had already thus transgressed, and God had been forced to punish them by not suffering them to enter into his rest. And hence the solemn warning, in the latter part of the psalm, to succeeding generations of the chosen flock not to harden their hearts in like manner.

The particular appropriateness of such a warning in the days of Josiah's reign, when this psalm was probably written, was long ago noticed by Theodoret. The discovery of the lost book of the law had then shewn how fearfully the Israelites of that and the preceding generations had departed from the precepts that had been given for their observance. And the spirit of God's sentence **upon** the rebellious generation of the wilderness, that they should not enter into his rest, had been then again displayed **in** the doom uttered by the prophetess Huldah: "Thus saith the LORD, Behold, I will bring evil upon this place, and upon the inhabitants thereof, even all the words of the book which the king of Judah **hath** read: because they have forsaken me, and **have burned** incense unto other gods, that they might provoke me to anger with all the works of their hands; therefore my wrath shall be kindled against this place, and shall not **be** quenched¹." The indirect evi-

---
¹ 2 Kings xxii. 16, 17.

dence thus afforded of the date at which the psalm was written is corroborated by the protests which are introduced into the earlier portion of the psalm against the follies of idolatry, vv. 3, 4, 5; idolatry being the special sin for which the doom of God was in Josiah's reign hanging over the city of Jerusalem.

It would however have been mere mockery, after the doom of destruction on Jerusalem was pronounced, to bid the people be not hard-hearted like their fathers, had nothing more remained to which they might still look forward. But there were blessings in store. The series of psalms of which this forms a part, Psalms xciii—c, is, as we have already explained, essentially prophetical. Behind the darkness of the approaching Chaldean catastrophe the prophets had already hailed the advancing light of the future manifestation of God's kingdom; and it was to this that the people's expectations were now being directed by the psalmist. In closing his psalm with an allusion to God's promised rest he implied that for the people of God a rest still remained. His own generation might at least welcome from afar that promised glory of God which their children should behold; and in that prospect might, with Moses towards the close of the wanderings in the wilderness, seek to be taught to apply their hearts to wisdom.

With the above view of the import of this psalm agrees the practical exposition of its latter verses given in the Epistle to the Hebrews[1]; if at least we allow for

---

[1] Heb. iii, iv. The quotation in iii. 7—11 accords with the LXX. except at the commencement of v. 10; where the words τεσσαράκοντα ἔτη are thrown into the preceding verse, and the word διό inserted before προσώχθισα. The former objectionable arrangement may be due to the copy of the LXX. which the writer used. But in inserting the word διό he has given a more correct rendering of the Hebrew original than most other translators, ancient and modern, who have overlooked the tense of the verb אמרתי. The historical

the fact that the New Testament writer, living under the Christian dispensation, necessarily looked forward not to the first but to the second advent. For it has been the property of each divine dispensation under which **men have** lived to shew the incompleteness of past events with reference to the promises which God has made. The Israelites after entering Canaan found that God's rest would not be theirs till God's Messiah should appear: hence the "To-day if ye will hear his voice" of the psalmist. And in like manner after the coming of the Messiah and the proclamation of the divine kingdom, Christian believers still found that God's rest could not be fully theirs till all earthly toil and sin should be ended by the second appearance of their King in glory: hence the "To-day if ye will hear his voice" of the apostle. The name David, Heb. iv. 7, is, it need scarcely be remarked, a general designation of the Psalter, and does not indicate the authorship of the particular psalm quoted: we in like manner still apply the name Samuel to two historical books narrating events long posterior to that prophet's death.

fact narrated is not **that God's** displeasure lasted forty years: **this** would require the preterite, and moreover **the** subsequent insertion in the same verse **of** words uttered on the day of provocation would be manifestly illogical. What the psalmist asserts is that the people's disobedience *led to* that displeasure of God, whereby, as they learnt and eventually found, they *would be* precluded **for** forty years from entering into the land of promise. The reference **is** to what occurred on the day of the return of the spies to Kadesh, Num. xiv.

1—35. Our English translators, following the Targum, LXX, and Jerome, and wiser than Luther, who has been followed by many moderns, saw that the words *meribah* (contention, provocation) and *massah* (temptation) in **v.** 8 were not to be taken as proper names. It is true that Kadesh was one of the two places to which the name Meribah was given; but the occasion on which it was so given **was long** subsequent to that provocation of **which** the psalmist speaks.

PSALM XCVI.

The Alexandrine translation, which does not suffer any psalm of the present series to pass without a superscription, has here the following: "A Psalm of David, when the house was being built after the captivity;" a superscription in which two views of the origin of the psalm, scarcely consistent with each other, have been amalgamated together. In ascribing the psalm, along with those among which it stands, to David, the translators or annotators may have been influenced by the insertion of it, almost entire, in 1 Chron. xvi, in the middle of the account of David's establishment of the ark on Mount Zion. The real reason of this insertion we shall examine in the Introduction to Psalms cv, cvi. The other part of the superscription, though equally incorrect, may have sprung from the allusion to the sanctuary and its ritual in vv. 6—9, which are in fact an expansion, though with a new force, of Psalm xxix. 1, 2; and the opening words, "O sing unto the Lord a *new* song," would readily suggest the imaginary connexion of the psalm with the building of the second rather than of the older temple.

We shall only arrive at a true appreciation of the contents of the psalm before us, when we perceive that it is the companion-psalm to Psalm xcv. It is in some sort the jubilant outpouring of praise to which Psalm xcv. had invited. Being too purely lyrical, too much a mere utterance of the joyousness of thanksgiving, to stand alone, it attaches itself to the preceding psalm, which was in part of a hortatory character. The subject which lies at the basis of each psalm is substantially the same; viz. Israel a witness to the world for the sovereignty of God. But this witness was twofold. There was the witness of the people, and the witness of the sanctuary.

Psalm xcv. dwells upon the former: **Psalm xcvi.** upon **the latter.** The Israelitish people witnessed for the sovereignty of God, or so should have witnessed, by a holy and dutiful obedience to his commandments. The Israelitish sanctuary witnessed for the sovereignty of God by being the symbol of his divine presence in the midst of his people on earth, by the consequent reverence with which it was regarded, and by the purity and solemnity of its ritual. The "honour and majesty," the "strength and beauty" of the Lord God of Israel, **the King** of the whole earth, were symbolized in various ways within the wall of the sanctuary of Zion; e. g. in the figures of the cherubim overshadowing the mercy-seat. The reverence which was paid to the sanctuary by the Israelites, **and which** they claimed for it from all the **world,** was shewn by the offerings which they brought into the temple-courts. The ritual of the sanctuary was pure; it repudiated the use of idols and likenesses, and bade the people bow down and worship the very LORD: it was also solemn; it ordered the use of holy apparel (E. V. *beauty of holiness*) and forbade such personal disfigurements as the heathen practised[1].

Such being the witness borne to the sovereignty of God by his dwelling-place, the Israelitish sanctuary, the people are in this psalm invited to sing a *new* song, in anticipation of that future manifestation of God's sovereignty for which the establishment of his sanctuary in Israel was helping to prepare the way. They are bidden shew forth day by day that salvation which they had been taught that he was working out. They are bidden proclaim in prophetical anticipation among the heathen that "the LORD reigneth"; in other words, that he has publicly assumed and displayed abroad his sovereignty. And at the tidings of his approaching

[1] Lev. xxi. 5; 1 Kings xviii. 28.

advent to judge the world in righteousness all creation also is summoned to rejoice; which, had it but the needful consciousness, it well might do, seeing that the Lord's coming would be the signal for the removal of that curse which had been inflicted even on the ground for man's sake.

In illustration of the close alliance between the contents of this psalm and those of the latter part of the prophecy of Isaiah, Hengstenberg notes the literal agreement in particular expressions between vv. 1, 11, and Isaiah xlii. 10. "The verbal reference to Isaiah in v. 1," he justly remarks, "is designedly placed at the beginning, for the purpose of pointing out the prophetical fountain from which the lyric stream has flowed." It may deserve notice that the same chapter of Isaiah furnishes towards the close,—more especially in v. 19,—the best illustration of the subject treated in the preceding psalm, viz. the shortcomings of that Israel who had been expressly designed to be the messenger and witness for God in the world; but who would only fully realize that high calling in the person of the Servant-Son, in whom the Father should be well pleased. The true Israel was Christ.

In reference to the present use by the Christian Church of Psalm xcvi. it is sufficiently obvious that we, whose lot is cast upon these latter days, intervening between the two advents of Christ, occupy a place in the midst of the fulfilment of the events to which the worshippers of the days of the psalmist looked forward. Now already, we are told, is the day of salvation; yet still we expect a salvation to come, and rejoice that it should be nearer than when we first believed. Long ago did the herald proclaim the time fulfilled, and the kingdom of heaven at hand; yet "Thy kingdom come" is still our prayer. We have known of one who for judgment came into this world; yet to the great day of judgment we still look forward. And the result is that while we have already a new song to sing for what has been achieved, and find the psalms of Israel practically insufficient to express the manifold mercies of redemption which we have received of God through Christ, there must still be another new song for blessings yet to come; and thus the whole creation, which was to rejoice for the advent of the Lord to judgment, still groaneth and **travaileth** in pain together, even until now. Under these circumstances **the** Church of Christ, both in the several members of whom she consists, and also in her collective capacity, **must** like the Israelitish people and sanctuary of olden times, still witness for God's sovereignty to the world. "Say among the heathen that the LORD reigneth" must be the Christian's as it was the Israelite's motto. The earliest preaching of our Saviour and his disciples was the preaching of **the** gospel of the *kingdom*[1]. It was because *all power was given unto him in heaven and in earth*, that, after his resurrection **from the** dead, Jesus sent forth his apostles to go and teach all nations[2]. The substance of the apostles' subsequent preaching was, confessedly, the *kingdom* of God[3]. The Jewish sanctuary was, in its testimony to God's sovereignty, a type of the Church of Christ. That divine honour and majesty and strength and beauty which the one testified by its symbols the other testifies by its doctrines. The temple of Solomon did **not** contrast so favourably in solidity and magnificence with other material buildings as the Church of Christ contrasts with all other human societies in catholicity and permanence. And there can be no doubt that in the mysterious bond of union by which it has

---

[1] Matth. ix. 35.
[2] Matth. xxviii. 18, 19.
[3] **Acts** viii. 12; xix. 8; xx. 25; xxviii. 23, 31.

been so long held together, although composed of people of every earthly realm and clime, as also in the solemnity and truthful majesty of its worship, it has, in spite of the shortcomings and wickednesses of its individual members, proved a mighty witness for the claim of God to the allegiance of all mankind. We may therefore in using this psalm fitly appropriate to the Christian Church the language which was originally suggested by the structure and ritual of the Jewish temple[1].

PSALM XCVII.

THE two preceding psalms shewed how God had called and educated a peculiar people, and in the midst of that people had established a ritual of pure worship

---

[1] An early Christian reading of this psalm added after "the Lord reigneth," in v. 10, the words "from the tree;" and Justin Martyr brings against the Jews the charge of having cancelled these words from the Greek text of the translation of the LXX, as being too clear a prophecy of the crucifixion of the Messiah. (*Dialog. Tryph.* 73; where see Otto's note. It is worthy of notice that Justin here quotes the psalm without the disputed words; though he inserts them when he again quotes the psalm in *Apolog.* I. 41; his editor, Otto, on his own authority, supplies them also in the former passage.) In the Latin these words are found in the passage as quoted by Lactantius, Tertullian, Arnobius, Augustine, Cassiodorus; and they form the basis of one of the stanzas in the well-known Latin Passion-hymn "Vexilla Regis prodeunt." The Roman Psalter contains them: from the Gallican they were excluded, and they consequently do not appear in the modern Vulgate. In Greek Justin alone openly brings them forward; and if they are also apparently embodied in a passage of Barnabas and in one of Celsus, those authors' knowledge of them may nevertheless have been derived from the Latin. From the Latin also they were probably translated by some unscholarlike transcriber of the Greek Psalter, in whose copy they appear in the form ἀπὸ τῷ ξύλῳ (sic); for no vestige of them has been discovered in any other manuscript of the version of the LXX, with which in other respects, barring one or two slight discrepancies, Justin's version coincides. It is almost needless to say that no trace of them occurs in the Hebrew, or in any other version directly derived from the Hebrew original. Yet they probably sprang, through the carelessness of some sciolist, from the misreading of a Hebrew word; for אף *also* was substituted עץ, the Chaldee for עץ *wood;* and having been once broached they were afterwards ignorantly cherished by those who prized them for the prophecy that they seemed to contain.

to witness for him in the earth. But these were only the beginnings of his dealings with mankind in order to enforce among them a general recognition of his sovereignty. The righteous people must be delivered out of the hands of the wicked who surrounded them; and purity of worship must obtain a universal prevalence through the extermination of idolatry. In due time therefore God would appear in all his majesty, to judge those that should resist him, and to overthrow all idol-worship. **The** accomplishment of these objects is prophetically celebrated in the psalm before us. **The** psalm divides itself into three portions. Vv. 1—5 describe the majesty of the Lord's coming. Vv. 6—9 tell the result: God's glory is publicly revealed, **idolatry is overthrown, and** all true worshippers rejoice. This forms **the most** important portion of the psalm, and is perhaps marked as such by its structure: it consists of two verses of three lines each enclosed by two more each containing two lines. Vv. 10—12 form **the** moral: let the righteous remain faithful in their obedience, and expect with certainty **the** deliverance that awaits them.

Here as elsewhere we have compressed into a single scene what would prove to **be** a work of gradual accomplishment. The first great earnest of the fulfilment of the psalm was the deliverance of Israel from captivity by the overthrow of Babylon; an event which had already been clearly foretold by Isaiah, and in language borrowed from which much of that prophet's evangelical predictions had been clothed[1]. The coming of Christ upon earth prepared the way for a more extended fulfilment of the psalmist's language; it has since been partially verified in **each** successive triumph of the Christian Church over surrounding heathenism; and

[1] Isaiah xliii—xlviii.

the fulfilment will be consummated in the second coming of Christ to final judgment. We, living between the two advents, may justly use the psalm as a thanksgiving both for what has been already achieved, and also, by anticipation, for the certainty of those events which still remain to be accomplished.

It has been frequently assumed that the words quoted in Heb. i. 6, "And let all the angels of God worship him," are taken from the Greek version of v. 7 of the psalm before us; and hence some difficulty has arisen; for while the "gods" of the psalmist are here (as the context shews) evidently the false gods of the heathen, "poetically viewed as gifted for the moment with life and feeling," the argument of the New Testament writer, who is shewing the inferiority of the angels to Christ, would oblige us to suppose, along with the Greek translators of the psalm, that these "gods" were here, as elsewhere, the angels. It will therefore be proper to observe that the quotation in the Epistle to the Hebrews is really taken from an addition which the Greek translators here made to Deut. xxxii. 43. With that, and with that alone, it verbally agrees[1]; and the mention of "sons of God" in the Greek version of that passage will account for the designation of Christ in Heb. i. 6 as "the first-begotten." We may add that the points of resemblance between the present psalm and Deut. xxxii. seem to have led the Greek translators to suppose the psalm to be a thanksgiving for that mercy of God to his land of which Moses had spoken; and hence they have somewhat strangely entitled it a psalm "of David, when his land is settled, or established"; whatever that may mean.

---

[1] In Deuteronomy and in the Epistle to the Hebrews the words run thus: καὶ προσκυνησάτωσαν αὐτῷ πάντες ἄγγελοι θεοῦ. But the psalm has προσκυνήσατε αὐτῷ πάντες οἱ ἄγγελοι αὐτοῦ without καὶ at the beginning.

PSALM XCVIII.

This psalm, observes Theodoret, treats of the same subject as the preceding: it foreannounces both the advents of our Saviour. It is the only piece in the Psalter which, without any author's name attached, bears in the Hebrew the simple title *Mizmor*—"A Psalm." This marks it as emphatically a psalm among psalms, a genuine lyrical effusion: it forms in fact the lyrical complement to the more decidedly prophetical psalm by which it is preceded; standing to it in nearly the same relation as Psalm xcvi. to Psalm xcv, or as Psalm xxxiii. to Psalm xxxii. It is the "new song" of praise for the victory which the previous psalm represented the Lord as gaining, in behalf of his true worshippers, and for his own glory's sake, over the wicked and over all that boasted themselves of idols. It contains however one new feature: the victory for which in Psalm xcvii. only Zion and the daughters of Judah were pictured as rejoicing is in Psalm xcviii. treated as a source of gladness to all the earth. Thus almost instinctively, as it were, did the Jewish psalmists, especially at seasons when their hearts were most expanded in praise, recognize the world-wide importance of God's dealings with their own little nation, and virtually anticipate the day of the catholicity of Zion, when there should be neither Greek nor Jew, circumcision nor uncircumcision, Barbarian, Scythian, bond nor free; but Christ should be all, and in all. That this levelling of all distinction between Jew and Gentile was never clearly present to their minds we may reasonably admit; but yet it was the legitimate development of their invitation to all the world to rejoice. In its formal structure the psalm falls into three parts. Announcing in the opening verses the victory that has been gained, and implying in the concluding words of v. 6 "before the LORD, the King," that by that victory God has publicly vindicated his sovereignty abroad, the psalmist calls first on Israel (vv. 1—3), then on all mankind (vv. 4—6), lastly on all creation (vv. 7—9), to testify their joy. With regard to the use of this psalm by the Christian Church the remarks already made on Psalm xcvii. will suffice.

PSALM XCIX.

THE struggle is over; the victory has been gained; God has vindicated his sovereignty beyond further dispute; and now the psalmist prophetically celebrates the holy worship of the redeemed Church. The psalm consists, after the manner of Psalms xlv, lxxx, of three strophes ending with nearly the same words; the second strophe being here the shortest of the three. Certain difficulties which the psalm presents may render the following version acceptable.

1 The LORD is king,—let the nations tremble,—
   Seated on the cherubim,—let the earth be moved!
2 The LORD is great in Zion;
   And high is he over all the nations.
3 They shall praise thy name, great and dread:
   Holy is he!

4 And they shall praise the strength of the king who hath loved judgment:
   Thou hast established equity;
   Thou hast executed judgment and righteousness in Jacob.
5 Exalt ye the LORD our God, and worship at his footstool:
   Holy is he!

6 Moses and Aaron among his priests and Samuel among them that call upon his name
   Call upon the LORD, and he answereth them.

7   In the pillar of cloud he speaketh unto them:
    They have kept his testimonies and the ordinances that
    he gave them.
8   Thou, O LORD our God, hast answered them;
    Thou hast been a God that forgivest them,
    Though taking vengeance of their inventions.
9   Exalt ye the LORD our God, and worship at his holy hill;
    For holy is the LORD our God!

In interpreting this psalm, it will be well by a few preliminary remarks to endeavour to obviate some erroneous conceptions which might otherwise be formed either respecting the general contents of the psalm or respecting the meaning of particular expressions in it. First, in v. 1 we read of the nations trembling and the earth being moved: are we to behold in this a description of the advent of the Lord to judgment? The general tenor of the psalm forbids it: we have to look yet further onward, to a time when the judgment shall be already complete. The meaning therefore is that God will then reveal himself in the fulness of that majesty at which even now all things, both animate and inanimate, may well be confounded. The psalmist portrays the dreadness of God's future reign in imagery borrowed from scenes with which he is himself familiar. Secondly, as no mention is made in this psalm of any adoration of God by the heathen, are we therefore to assert, with Calvin, that, "unlike the psalms which precede, it does not extend the divine kingdom and the ensuing blessedness beyond the limits of Judea; but rather separates off the children of Abraham, in virtue of the privilege of their adoption, from the surrounding nations, and confines more peculiarly to them its invitation to praise God"? Or are we, with Bishop Horsley and the modern Judaizers, to go even yet further, and suppose the psalm to allude to a literal "reign of Jehovah in Zion subsequent to the restoration of the Jewish nation, when Moses, Aaron, and Samuel are to bear a part in the general worship,"—conducted, apparently, after the old Jewish model? Our Saviour's own words expressly forbid it: the hour, he told us, was coming, when no longer at Jerusalem should men worship the Father, but when the true worshippers should worship him in spirit and in truth. And clearly we need not so interpret any psalm as to make it directly contradict the tenor of Christ's teaching. The theme of the psalm is the future holy worship of the company of the universal redeemed; the citizens of that true Zion of which the New Testament speaks[1], the *general* assembly and Church of the firstborn. In delineating this under its positive aspect, the psalmist was almost necessarily constrained, on account of the position which he occupied, to represent it under an Old Testament *form*. Nor was this a disadvantage. For it was no part of his immediate purpose to contrast the spiritual worship of the future with the typical worship of the Jewish sanctuary and ritual,—a task for which indeed he may not have been prepared; nor yet to assert the catholicity of the future Church, which he himself may have but imperfectly understood. His aim was to set forth the adoration of the future as the *holy* worship of a *redeemed* people; and as such it was shadowed forth in that divinely appointed ritual, which, although not the very image of good things to come, was nevertheless a faithful shadow of those things.

It is therefore of great importance in our own interpretation and employment of this and other psalms to distinguish between the substance of the doctrine which they contain and the mere Old Testament form in which that doctrine is clothed. For it is but trifling with the

[1] Heb. xii. 22.

sacred word of God and with the devotions which for eighteen centuries the Church Catholic has claimed for her own, **to restrict the** signification of the name Jacob **to** persons of one particular natural descent, when **we** know that **others** also, who were not **a** people at the time that the psalm was written, have now become the people of God[1]. **It** is trifling with God's word and with the Christian faith to think that God can now be more acceptably worshipped at the old typical holy hill than at any other place, when the Church Catholic has been manifestly revealed as that "mountain of the LORD" unto which, according to prophecy, all nations were **to** flow. Nor can we reasonably believe that **either Jew** or Gentile will hereafter be summoned to worship before God's material footstool,—that ark of the covenant, the receptacle of the tables of the law, which was covered by the mercy-seat, the emblem of God's atoning love, and which God, the ancient throne of whose divine presence was the cherubim overshadowing the mercy-seat, was consequently represented as touching with his feet. But that the whole redeemed family of mankind will hereafter render adoration to their Almighty and All-gracious Sovereign, who shall **dwell in** the midst of them in the new Jerusalem in mingled majesty and love, and that they will then ascribe to him the praise of their salvation and of their elevation to the highest region of life and blessedness and glory,—this is what the daylight of the sacred writings of **the New** Testament, as well as the twilight **of those** of the Old, leads us with sure confidence to await.

Each strophe of the psalm has its own especial theme. The first sets forth the future manifestation of the greatness and majesty of God; the second, the

---

[1] 1 Pet. ii. 10.

manifestation of his eternal righteousness. In order that the two may not be too widely separated, the theme of the first is carried on into the first line of the second: "And they shall praise the *strength* of the king, &c." The sense is apparently as follows: "This same king, whom they have praised for his strength, they shall also praise for the judgment that he has loved, &c."

But it is in the third strophe that the fullest details are to be found. This has been often understood, especially by those who treat the distinction of the tenses of Hebrew verbs as a matter of no importance, as a record of the former supplications of Moses, Aaron, and Samuel, by way of incitement to God's people to follow their example. It is in reality a prophetical picture of the future holy worship of God, in which Moses, Aaron, and Samuel appear as the living representatives of the redeemed Church, like the four and twenty elders in the more fully developed Apocalyptic scene of St John[1]. The image of the pillar of cloud (expressive of the close communion of the worshippers with God) is, like the personages of the worshippers themselves, borrowed from past history; but it is nevertheless of the future that the psalmist is speaking. For like Moses and Aaron, who had formerly been God's priests on earth, (Moses himself had actually exercised the priestly office at the period of Aaron's consecration, Lev. viii.) and like Samuel, who had been one of the most eminent patterns of a true and faithful worshipper, so would all the redeemed hereafter appear as priests before God, and worship him in his presence. They would then be for evermore with that God who had in time past from the cloudy pillar spoken unto Moses "face to face as a man speaketh unto his friend[2]," nay, who had honoured even Aaron and Miriam by speaking to them to rebuke

[1] Rev. v.   [2] Exod xxxiii. 9—11.

them for their folly[1]; and they would own that though in wisdom God had chastised even his servants' faults, and though in righteousness he had taken eternal vengeance of the inventions of those that obstinately resisted his will, yet had all his dealings with mankind, viewed as a whole, **been** those of mercy and forgiveness. And thus as the **earlier** portions of the psalm had shewn how God should be adored for his greatness and his righteousness, so the last tells how he shall be praised for his redeeming love.

PSALM C.

"A Psalm, for thanksgiving." **Such is the** title. The **psalm is** the lyrical companion to Psalm xcix, as Psalm xcviii **to** Psalm xcvii. It is, in substance, the strain of holy praise and thanksgiving which the universal redeemed of **the** Church triumphant shall pour forth, and which for **the** present it is the privilege of the Church militant by faith to anticipate. And most appropriately is it used **in** the English morning service after the second lesson, as being the strain which the gospel of Christ, the power of God unto salvation **to every one that believeth,** will have prepared every **one to sing.**

The grand announcement **in this** thanksgiving strain is that the **Lord** hath made us, and we are his[2]. Contemplating the relations of God to us in their logical **order, we** should speak of him as our Creator, King, and Redeemer; but when with the psalmist we trace

---

[1] Numb. xii.

[2] The received text of v. 3, **as rendered** in our E. V., "It is he **that** hath made **us** and not (לֹא) we ourselves," is decidedly inferior to the לוֹ, "It is he that hath made us and his (לוֹ) we are;" and the authority of the Targum and Jerome, supported by that of a few MSS., places the correctness of the latter almost beyond doubt.

the sequence of those dealings by which God is bringing mankind to recognize the relations in which he stands to them, the order is necessarily reversed: God is then our Redeemer, King, Creator. Thus to know God for our Creator implies that we have previously known him for our Redeemer and our King, and in the acknowledgment of him as Creator the entire fulness of his praise is summed up. The devotional praises of the psalmist are brought back to the point from which they started; Psalm c. bears in its language more resemblance to Psalm xcv. than to any of the psalms which intervene: to know that "the Lord he is God" was the beginning of all religion; it is also the highest pinnacle which knowledge can ever reach. The same image of the pasture-sheep which the psalmist had applied to the Church in its infancy he now applies also to the Church in its final triumph. The most glowing terms which the New Testament seer could find to express the future relations of God and men are in like manner almost the same with those that had been used by the prophets of old: "Behold, the tabernacle of God is with men, and he will dwell with them, and they shall be his people, and God himself shall dwell with them, and be their God[1]."

PSALM CI.

"A Psalm of David." The psalm is obviously of a personal character; and has been generally supposed, even by neologian critics, to proceed from David himself. But the Davidic authorship is rendered improbable by the late place occupied by the psalm in the Psalter; which, considering that we have before us the outpouring of the pious heart of a young monarch, on

---

[1] Rev. xxi. 3.

first assuming the reins of government, leads at once to the assumption that it was written by Josiah, of whose early fear of God it would be the natural embodiment. **Most suitable in his** mouth would be the aspirations of the opening verse:

> Of piety and truth **let me** sing: unto thee, O LORD, let me make melody[1];

(for the substantives in the first line seem rather, as the whole of the subsequent verses shew, to refer to the gracious dispositions of the heart of the worshipper, than, as our English Translators have supposed, to the mercy and judgment of God). The meaning of the superscription "Psalm of David," when prefixed **to** psalms not proceeding **from** David himself, has **been** already explained in the Introduction to Psalm lxxxvi. And in the present psalm every indication directs us to Josiah **rather** than to David as the author. Thus, in regard of the historical facts embodied in it, it could not have been uttered at the beginning of David's reign; for Jerusalem, to which, as the city of the Lord, reference is evidently made in v. 8, was still in possession of the Jebusites not **only** when David became ruler of Judah in Hebron, but also even when all the tribes of Israel **first acknowledged his** sway. Besides which, the **expression** "within my house," **or** literally, "in the midst of my house," which occurs in **v. 2** and again in v. 7, receives its explanation in the promise respecting David's house made by God through Nathan, and could **not** well have been penned till after the date of that

---

[1] The two Hebrew verbs employed in this verse are the respective **correlatives** of the nouns *song* and *psalm;* and should have been distinguished from each other in our E. V, **as the** corresponding **Greek** words in Eph. **v.** 19. *To sing* (שיר, ᾄδω) is a term having respect to the *subject* of the song: *to make melody* (זמר, ψάλλω) to the *manner* in which it was sung, with instrumental accompaniment. See above, Vol. 1. pp. 245, **246**.

promise; of which, be it remembered, the successive kings of Judah, including Josiah, were the subsequent heirs. Then again when we recognize the reference to that promise in v. 2, we must needs acknowledge that the ensuing question in that verse, "When wilt thou come unto me?" is altogether unsuited to David, who was rather overwhelmed by the exceeding graciousness with which God had visited him[1]; while on the other hand it is perfectly natural in the mouth of Josiah, who lived at a period when, for the wickedness of his grandfather, God seemed almost to have forgotten his promise, and to have forsaken the house of David for ever[2]. Moreover in regard of its general tone, the psalm seems to flow more naturally from the lips of one who was attempting to restore than of one who was seeking to inaugurate a kingdom of righteousness. In harmony also with the supposition that Josiah was the author of this psalm are the resemblances which have been noticed between it and the Book of Proverbs. The fruits of familiarity with that book might well display themselves in his writings if they also displayed themselves in the whole tenor of his subsequent life. It may be further remarked that the connexion of this psalm with the opening of Josiah's reign was distinctly brought out by Theodoret.

The psalm, which consists entirely of long lines, generally pentatonic, occasionally, perhaps, hexatonic, falls into two portions, vv. 1—3, 4—8, each of which commences with a one-line verse, the remaining verses all containing two lines. In the first portion the king sets forth the principles by which his own private demeanour, in the second those by which his public government will be guided.

Like most of his forefather David's psalms, those of

---

[1] 2 Sam. vii. 18, 19.   [2] Psalm lxxxix. 38 seqq.

Josiah, who holds his own place in the gospel genealogy of Jesus Christ the son of David, must be viewed as uttered in the person of his Great Descendant. But even **when so viewed** they still have, in consequence of the **historical** circumstances under which they were written, their own distinctive character. They do not, like David's, carry our thoughts exultingly forward to scenes of boundless triumph; but rather, while acknowledging the longsuffering of God, who would not that **any** should perish but that all should come to repentance, they lead us with chastened hope to seek humbly **for** acceptance in the day of inevitable doom. The sentence that had already in the days **of** Josiah gone forth upon Jerusalem was the earnest **of the sentence of final** destruction **upon** a guilty world. In gathering around him a righteous generation, and in cutting off all wicked doers **from** the city of the Lord, Josiah felt that the judgment was meanwhile hanging in suspense overhead. And so too, although there be times when we may think of Christ as the Captain of his people's salvation, going forth like David at their head, conquering and to conquer, there are also times when we should contemplate him as the antitype of Josiah, teaching and training men to flee from **the** wrath to come, sparing not some **to the** end that others **may** be saved, and bidding his disciples watch and pray **always** that they may be accounted worthy to escape all **the** things that shall come **to** pass, and to stand before the Son of man. The manifold relations of Christ to his people could not **be** fully foreshadowed **in** the case of a single typical person; and Josiah fills up **a** space in typical history which David had left **void**.

In repeating this **psalm with our** own lips, we can only truly utter it in virtue of our mysterious oneness with Christ. To Christians severally **and** individually has not been committed the authority to cut off all wicked doers from the city of the Lord. But through that sympathy with their Redeeming Lord which is nourished by a purified heart, they may spiritually view themselves as effecting even this; and while diligently reforming their own ways, and extirpating from those bosoms which the Spirit of grace hath made his own every sin that defileth, may look forward in true faith to the time when all public enemies of God shall be consumed with the spirit of the Lord's mouth, and destroyed with the brightness of his coming.

PSALM CII.

This psalm, taken apart from the unique superscription by which it is surmounted, falls into three portions. The first two are strophes of eleven verses each. The one (vv. 1—11) contains the complaint: the worshipper is in misery and loneliness, and his days are, to all appearance, numbered. The other (vv. 12—22) embodies the prophetical anticipation of deliverance: the Lord, whose days none can number, shall in his appointed time regard the prayer of the destitute and put an end to their groaning; and in that Zion which God in his indignation now permits all the enemies to reproach, the heathen shall hereafter assemble to praise his holy name. The leading thought of the psalm is that the eternity of God is the guarantee of his people's continuance. He is, as Psalm xc. had taught, the dwelling-place of his people in all generations; and therefore even when they are seemingly on the verge of a premature death, they yet possess a sure ground of hope in the contemplation of an eternity and immutability beyond their own. This is in the concluding portion of the psalm (vv. 23—28) brought out in a very remarkable manner; but before we can fully enter into the import of those verses, **we** must direct our attention to the **historical** circumstances and prospects out of which **the psalm** sprang, and with which its language **is connected.**

There can be no doubt that it is uttered in the name of the Church, as represented **by** the Israelitish people. It will **be** sufficient **to** refer in proof of this, to the language of verses 14, 17, 20, 28. But at what date was it composed? Some have brought it down to near the close of the Babylonish captivity, laying especial stress on the words of v. 13: "Thou shalt arise, and have mercy upon Zion: for the time to favour her, **yea,** the set time, is **come." In** this view, however, it **is, on a** more attentive examination of the whole, impossible to concur. Notwithstanding the abyss of misery in the midst of which the psalmist appears to be already set, there is enough **to** indicate that the extremity of his distress was approaching rather than already arrived. Whether **we** look **to** v. 11, "My days are like a shadow that declineth," i. e. like a shadow which becomes longer as the evening draws on, and the outline of which will soon, after the sun has set, be no more visible; or whether we look to v. 23, which in our English Bibles **runs thus,** "He weakened my strength in the way; he shortened my days"; it is evident that **the** suppliant beholds **in** the calamities which he delineates the termination of **a** once hopeful career. **He** contrasts his present abandonment with the progress to which he had **been** looking forward. Now such contrast would **be** natural, by anticipation, so soon as ruin had begun to stare him vividly in the face; but it would scarcely be natural after many **years** of his captivity were past, because then, although his previous hopes might not be altogether forgotten, the keen sense of **the** arrest of his former career would nevertheless be lost. Internal evidence will thus justify us in assigning this psalm to the reign of Josiah, when the evil which God was about to bring upon Jerusalem was already unmistakeably announced; and this date is fully confirmed by the place occupied by the psalm in the Psalter. As to v. 13, the language there employed is the language of anticipation. The author of this psalm is, as is well known, not the only sacred writer who foretold the future deliverance from calamity before the calamity itself had reached its height. The psalmist takes his stand on the certainty of the fate which is impending over Jerusalem; but he evidently relies on a divine promise that Zion shall be restored. Many passages of the prophecies of Jeremiah distinctly unfold that promise. In general they seem to belong to a later period than that of the reign of Josiah: there is however one passage in that prophet's writings (iii. 14—18), relating to the future glory of Jerusalem, which, coupled with the prophecies of Isaiah (especially Isaiah lx.), may have formed the basis of the prophetical portion of the psalm before us, and which probably dates from the 13th year of Josiah's reign, five years before the great reformation. It is not unlikely that that was the very date of the composition of the psalm.

Connected with the question of the historical period to which the psalm belongs, is the question of its authorship. Although the psalm, as we possess it, can hardly be called other than anonymous, still the remarkable superscription which stands at its head seems to warrant the belief that it may be distinguished from those which proceeded from the ordinary temple-singers. If this be so, and if we may lawfully surmise to whom the psalm should be attributed, to none so readily as to the prophet Jeremiah himself would our thoughts naturally turn. It would be in full harmony with his subsequent **Lamentations,** written after that Jerusalem had actually **fallen; and he who spoke** forty years after in the name **of the** desolate nation as "the man that had seen affliction by the rod of God's wrath[1]," might **well also** in his earlier days utter **forth** his prayer in the person "of the afflicted, when he is overwhelmed, and poureth out his complaint before the LORD." And his prophetical office, which imparted a permanently sacred character to his subsequent wailings, would equally warrant the reception into the Psalter of the lyrical supplication now before us.

The prophet knew that **his** supplication would **be** heard. However long the time that might elapse ere its fulfilment, he knew that the Lord would "regard the prayer of the destitute, and not despise their prayer (v. 17)." He avowedly wrote for future generations **(v.** 18); and vv. 19—22 contain the song of praise **which,** in anticipation of the eventual deliverance, he already puts into their lips:

> This shall be written for a generation to come,
> The Hallelujah of **a** people new-created,
> That from the height of his sanctuary he hath looked down,
> **That** the LORD hath **from** heaven beheld unto the earth,
> **To hear** the groaning of the **prisoner,**
> To **loose** the children of death,
> That **the** name of the LORD **may be declared in** Zion,
> And **his praise in** Jerusalem,
> When the nations are gathered together,
> And **the** kingdoms, to serve the LORD.

Those interpreters **who** still look for a literal restoration **of the** Jews to **their** own land, and for a future rebuilding of the material temple,—contingencies of which, as some of them confess, no mention is made in

---

[1] Lam. iii. 1.

the New Testament,—lay much stress upon the language in which these anticipations are clothed, as favouring their views. Those on the other hand who unreservedly hold that in Christ Jesus there is "neither Jew nor Greek," but that the Songs of Israel are the common heritage of believers of every natural descent, will not lose sight of the substance of the psalmist's anticipations in the contemplation of the mere drapery in which they were almost necessarily invested. Recognizing the Apostles as adequate expositors of the Prophets, they will interpret the whole of the prophetical scriptures by the analogy of the construction which the New Testament writers have put upon those passages of them which they quote. They will see no adequate reason for dissevering, on no authority but their own, that hearing of the groaning of the prisoner of which the psalmist speaks from the predicted proclamation of liberty to the captives and of the acceptable year of the Lord which our Saviour himself, in the synagogue at Nazareth, declared to be that day fulfilled in the ears of those whom he addressed[1]. Fully admitting then, along with the literal interpreters, that the psalmist's hymn was "written for a generation to come," and that his anticipations were not finally accomplished in the restoration of the Jews by Cyrus, they will nevertheless maintain that now, once, in the person of the Incarnate Saviour, the Lord hath appeared in his glory; and that the Church Catholic which he founded is, in the truest sense, the Zion of which the psalmist spoke; the very image of that purified fellowship of which the old material sanctuary was but the shadow: "Ye are come unto mount Sion, and unto the city of the living God, the heavenly Jerusalem,......and to Jesus the mediator of the new covenant[2]." This is indeed the only Zion in

---

[1] Isai. lxi. 1, 2; Luke iv. 21.   [2] Heb. xii. 22—24.

which the nations and kingdoms could be "gathered together" to serve the Lord: the fulfilment of the psalmist's words in any but the spiritual Zion, the antitype of the old, is, on the face of it, plainly impossible; and it is only by sacrificing, openly or implicitly, one part of the description, that the literalists can contend for a future literal accomplishment of the other. In the true Zion, the Catholic Church of Christ, the nations and kingdoms already have to a certain extent been assembled: **she** is God's instrument for the world's conversion; and the more that she be inwardly "built up" or "edified" (v. 16), the more will she be outwardly **increased or** "multiplied[1]"; **every** fresh conquest that **she make** being in very truth a fresh display of the glory **of the** Lord, till **the** day when the Incarnate Redeemer shall appear **the** second time to perfect for ever his earthly work.

To this blessedness then of the latter days the Church **of** Israel looked forward, in pious hope, though with imperfect knowledge. Her own career was, in God's good providence, preparing the way for that which was to follow. Meanwhile **a** melancholy **and** bitter interruption awaited her in her progress to the desired goal. **At** the time that the psalmist wrote, the sentence of doom had gone forth upon Jerusalem; and the Church of Israel complained that God had shortened **her** days. "He 'hath **afflicted**' 'his' strength in the way," **is** her cry[2]. And then, because of the

---

[1] Cf. Acts ix. 31; the true text of which runs thus: Ἡ μὲν οὖν ἐκκλησία... εἶχεν εἰρήνην οἰκοδομουμένη **καὶ πορευο**μένη τῷ φόβῳ τοῦ κυρίου καὶ τῇ **παρα**κλήσει τοῦ ἁγίου πνεύματος ἐπληθύνετο.

[2] Our E. V. gives *my strength*, following the קֹרִי, which is supported **by** nearly one-third **of** the MSS., by **the** Syriac, the **Targum**, Symmachus, **and** Jerome. But the כְּתִיב is upheld by the preponderance of MS. authority, and by the LXX; and, being the more apparently difficult, is probably the original reading. Any moulder may have altered *his strength* into *my strength*, on account of the *my days* in the same verse: the opposite change would not be likely to **suggest** itself.

threatened shortening of her days, follows her account of the petition which her state of affliction suggests to her: "I 'say'," or "I 'will say'"—the tense is the present or future—"O my God (El, not Elohim)"—so it begins; but the syntax of the clauses will more clearly appear if vv. 23, 24 be exhibited according to their poetical structure:

> He hath afflicted his strength in the way,
>   Hath shortened my days:
> I say, O my God, Take me not away
>   When but a half are my days,
>   When from generation to generation are thy years[1].

The question now arises, To whom, and in what character, is this petition, along with the verses which follow it, directed?

There can be no doubt that, according to the view now generally taken, the petition is, in common with the supplications in the earlier portion of the psalm, regarded as addressed, simply and directly, to Almighty God; to the God who had made known his perfections and his ways to Israel, and on whom it was the privilege of every Israelite psalmist and of every Israelite worshipper to call. No distinction is thus, in fact, made between this prayer and any other in the Psalter. Yet such could hardly have been the way in which among the Jews themselves this passage was treated. In the Epistle to the Hebrews vv. 25—27 of the psalm are quoted in proof of the dignity of the Son; they are coupled with the address to the Messiah from Psalm

---

[1] The repetition of the ימי and of the ב (בדור, בחצי) can hardly be accidental; and a similar inverted arrangement of the lines is found in vv. 25—28, where the last two lines of v. 26 form the centre, v. 27 corresponds to the early part of v. 26, v. 28 to v. 25. This attention to the poetical structure helps to separate off vv. 23—28 from the rest of the psalm. The meaning of אל־תעלני is somewhat doubtful: our E. V. gives the sense usually adopted.

xlv, "Thy throne, O God, is for ever and ever, &c."; and as no explanation of them is there offered, nor any vindication of the propriety of the purpose with which they are cited, it must be inferred that the general interpretation put upon these words among those to whom the epistle was written would be that they were addressed to the Mediator. And to us that interpretation is now sanctioned by the authority of the inspired writer himself.

With this remarkable quotation Christian students of the Bible, whatever view they might be disposed to take of the purport of the psalm, could hardly fail to be struck. Some of them have indeed contented themselves with observing upon it that whatever is addressed generally to God may be applied to Christ; and that in the Epistle to the Hebrews such application was fully justified by the circumstance that Christ's divinity had been already shewn. And it is doubtless true that whatever is addressed to God the Christian will deem to be addressed to all the Three several Persons of the Ever-blessed Trinity[1]. But this consideration, although it would sufficiently establish the doctrinal propriety of the application, cannot establish the appropriateness of the quotation as illustrative of the apostolic argument.

Again, the view ordinarily taken of the latter portion of the psalm is hardly reconciled with the use made of it in the Epistle to the Hebrews by the assertion that the Jews would recognize the object of the psalmist's longings to be the divine kingdom of Christ. True it is that it was in the person of the Son, the brightness of his glory and the express image of his own person, that the Lord appeared "in his glory," as

---

[1] Theodoret: Ταῦτα μέντοι ὁ θεῖος ἀπόστολος τῇ τοῦ υἱοῦ περιέθεικεν ἰδιότητι, ἐν τῇ πρὸς Ἑβραίους ἐπιστολῇ. ἀλλ' ὅμως ἐν τῷ υἱῷ θεωροῦμεν τὸν πατέρα, ᾧ γὰρ ἂν ἐκεῖνος ποιεῖ, ταῦτα καὶ ὁ υἱὸς ὡσαύτως ποιεῖ· καὶ τὸ ταύτην τῆς φύσεως ἐν ἑκατέρῳ γνωρίζεται· μίαν γὰρ ἴσμεν τὴν τῆς τριάδος ἐνέργειαν.

he had promised: true it is that he commenced building up Zion "by his word," in accordance with the interpretation given by the Targumist of the earlier portion of v. 16, by coming unto his own in the person of the Incarnate Word, and so giving power to become the sons of God to as many as believed on his name: true it is that by the Word he had in the beginning made the worlds. Still if the words quoted be merely applied to Christ in virtue of his being the promised manifestation of the Father, what do they add to the proof of the superiority of his dignity to that of the angels? The force of the quotation from Psalm xlv. evidently lies in this, that an address directed expressly and exclusively to the Messiah designates him by the title God: unless it can be made to appear that the cited words of Psalm cii. were similarly addressed, expressly and exclusively, to the Messiah, or to the Word or Son of God as contradistinguished from the Father, they do, as it would seem, but illustrate a truth which hardly an infidel would dispute, that the dignity of the angels is excelled by that of God himself.

Hence it is that at various times some students of the psalm, among whom Stier and Bonar may be mentioned as the most recent[1], have been induced to interpret it according to a different plan. They conceive that up to the middle of v. 24, Israel, or Christ as typified by Israel, speaks in his humiliation; but that from that point the psalm enters a new phase; and that the silence above being broken, God, in the words "Thy years are throughout all generations," and in what follows, replies to the invocations of the suppliant.

---

[1] Stier makes mention of A. H. Francke as one who had previously taken the view which he adopts; and Michaelis, in his notes on Lowth, says generally, "fuerunt, quibus prior pars Psalmi cii. usque ad illa verba: *ne tolle me in dimidio dierum*, oratio Christi viderentur, reliqua inde a verbis ejusdem versus, *in seculum seculorum sunt anni tui*, Dei patris responsio."

According to this view the latter verses of the psalm will, prophetically, be the address of the Father to the Son. In support of it Stier refers to the Greek rendering of v. 23 and the beginning of v. 24, "He answered him in the way of his strength: tell me the shortness of my days[1]": which, he argues, either correctly expresses the genuine reading, in which case the apparently unsuitable return to complaint will disappear, and the quotation in the Epistle to the Hebrews will be completely justified; or else, although erroneous, bears witness to an authentic and correct tradition that the closing portion of the psalm contained an answer from God; a tradition which the LXX. accordingly embodied in their rendering, although they made the answer commence too soon. Of this view it may best be said that it is almost impossible to persuade oneself that it can be correct. The sudden change of persons cannot but appear unnatural in the extreme: even Bishop Horsley, so fond of disturbing the currents of supplication in the psalms by the introduction of oracular responses, here holds aloof his hand, and lets the petition flow on. Moreover it is no light objection to this view that such an address as it contemplates from God the Father to the Son, setting forth, not his glorification in his mediatorial kingdom, but his divine majesty which he had from all eternity, is unparalleled in any part of Holy Scripture.

The words of the latter portion of the psalm are still then the words of the suppliant, the expression of his worship and of his trust. But are they therefore necessarily addressed to the same Divine Person to whom his previous supplications had been poured? Not

---

[1] ἀπεκρίθη αὐτῷ ἐν ὁδῷ ἰσχύος αὐτοῦ· τὴν ὀλιγότητα τῶν ἡμερῶν μου ἀνάγγειλόν μοι. The Greek translators read the Hebrew as follows: עִנָּה בְדֶרֶךְ כֹּחוֹ קֹצֶר יָמַי אֱמֹר אֵלָי:

necessarily. Even the structure of the psalm would rather lead to the opposite conclusion. For after the prophetical anticipations which terminate with v. 22, the renewed complaint of the shortness of the suppliant's days in v. 23, to be again followed by a contemplation of the glories of the divine majesty, can scarcely be explained except on the supposition that those concluding verses are to contain either a richer or a more special consolation than that which had been afforded by what went before. Yet if vv. 24 seqq. be addressed to the same Divine Person, and in the same character, as vv. 12 seqq., the transition from v. 23 to v. 24 hardly forms any sensible advance on the transition from v. 11 to v. 12. Does v. 24 speak of the divine years extending throughout all generations? V. 12 had previously declared that the Lord should endure for ever, and his remembrance unto all generations; and although the thought of v. 24 is in the succeeding verses enlarged upon and expanded, it does not appear that it is materially altered or heightened. The inference is that the real advance of vv. 24 seqq. on v. 12 consists in their being more special in their reference.

Now as regards the address "O my God" in v. 24, it is to be observed that the term *El*, which we are constrained to render *God*, but which we are thus unable to discriminate in English from the higher *Elohim*, and which, although generally applied to Him who is Very Strength, is occasionally,—at least once[1],—used to designate a purely human potentate, is in two prophecies of Isaiah employed of the promised Messiah. The first is Isaiah vii. 14: "Behold, a virgin shall conceive, and bear a son, and shall call his name Immanu-el, With us God." The second is that contained

[1] Ezek. xxxi. 11.

in Isaiah ix, x. In ix. 6 we read: "For unto us a child is born, unto us a son is given ...... and his name shall be called ...... The mighty God (*El gibbor*)." And in a later passage of the same prophecy, x. 21, we have the announcement that "the remnant shall return, even the remnant of Jacob, unto the mighty God (*El gibbor*)," where the same title manifestly designates the same wondrous personage; though it is there ordinarily, but incorrectly, interpreted simply of God. And to the Messiah the term *El* was particularly appropriate, as indicating that it was through him that the *strength* of God was to be manifested forth in the world: he was to be the very strength of God in the hearts of his people[1].

But again, he who was in due time to appear as the Messiah had existed from the first; and even before his incarnation as man the same office had been his, of unfolding upon earth the hidden strength of God. The records of the Exodus told the Israelites explicitly of that not only superhuman but also super-angelic guide who had conducted them up out of the land of Egypt. God had said of him, "Behold, I send an Angel before thee, to keep thee in the way, and to bring thee into the place which I have prepared. Beware of him, and obey his voice, provoke him not; for he will not pardon your transgressions: for my name is in him[2]." His office had more recently been recognized by the prophet Isaiah, who had styled him the "angel of the LORD's presence," that "saved them[3]." It was of his

---

[1] Worthy of notice is the circumstance that while the name אלהים may be construed with any suffix (*my God, thy God, his God*), the name אל admits, in the Bible, the suffix of the first person only. As the object of our worship, we speak of God indifferently in his relation to ourselves or to others: as the source of inward strength, we more readily contemplate him from our own experience alone.

[2] Exod. xxiii. 20, 21.

[3] Isaiah lxiii. 9.

guiding presence that the portentous pillar of fire and cloud had been the visible display.

If the believing Israelites, foreseeing for themselves a state of desolation and captivity impending immediately over their heads, looked forward also through the present gloom to a second mighty deliverance from bondage, and to a salvation which as yet they had never fully realized, would they not also naturally and legitimately anticipate its accomplishment through the agency of the same heavenly guide? Or if, to put the matter in a truer light, their whole history, past and present, was but the history of a journey conducting them, as they hoped, to future glory, even as their journey through the wilderness had conducted them to their inheritance in Canaan, must not their career be one along which they had been led, wittingly or unwittingly to themselves, by the same Angel of the Lord's presence who had led them forth from Egypt? And if that career seemed to be violently interrupted, or if, as the psalmist describes it, God was afflicting his strength in the journey, what was it but that, as he had once threatened to do in the wilderness[1], he was withdrawing the Angel of his presence from them? To that very Angel then, as it would appear, the psalmist appeals, not so to deal with them as to bring their days to an untimely end.

And if this be so, it seems in every way probable, from a comparison of the address "O my God" with the prophecies of Isaiah already cited, that in the Guiding Angel of Israel the psalmist recognized him who was eventually to appear as Israel's promised Messiah. It has been stated indeed by Hengstenberg in his Christology, that "it was only at a late period, in Malachi iii. 1, that the doctrine of the Angel of the

[1] Exod. xxxiii.

Lord was expressly brought into connexion with that of Christ." But the same author truly observes that "a knowledge of the divine nature of the Messiah is found at a much earlier period; and we can certainly not suppose that the doctrine of the Angel of the Lord, and that of a truly divine Saviour, should have existed by the side of each other, and yet that manifold forebodings regarding the close connexion of things which lay so very near should not have been awakened in the mind." There is no more difficulty in supposing that the Angel of the Lord and the future Messiah were expressly identified in the days of Jeremiah than in the days of Malachi. The declaration of the eternal existence of him to whom the psalmist addresses himself will then moreover find a clear support in the previous prophecy of Micah, in which he speaks of the future Bethlehemite ruler of Israel as him "whose goings forth have been from of old, from everlasting[1]."

Interpreted as above, the latter portion of the psalm before us is admirably adapted to the purpose for which in the Epistle to the Hebrews it is quoted. The object is to shew the superiority of the dignity of the Son of God to that of the angels. A passage from the Old Testament Scriptures is accordingly adduced in which he who had in those Scriptures been frequently designated as an angel, the Angel of the Lord, and whom through a misunderstanding of that title many might view as a mere angelic being, has nevertheless an eternity ascribed to him, and a participation in the work of creation, which are not ascribed to the angels generally. In the Greek translation of the LXX, from which the quotation is made, the word "Lord" is introduced into the beginning of v. 25, without authority

[1] Micah v. 2.

from the Hebrew; but whether that word be there viewed as representing the Hebrew Adonai or the sacred name Jehovah, the introduction of it does not substantially alter the sense which may be legitimately drawn from the psalmist's own words[1].

It only remains to produce some corroborative evidence, if any can be found, in proof that the above interpretation of the psalm was among the Jews actually received. Such evidence the following passage of Philo may perhaps be deemed to supply. Anticipating the future blessings which his nation should live to enjoy, he declares that those who were scattered abroad in the world shall, "rising up with one impulse, and coming from all the different quarters imaginable, all hasten to one place pointed out to them, under the guidance of a form (ὄψεως) more divine than that of man, unseen by all beside, and visible only to those who are being saved...; and when they come cities will be rebuilt which but a short time ago were in complete ruins, and the desert will be filled with inhabitants, and the barren land will change and become fertile...; and they will revert to the ancient prosperity of their ancestors, completing their course back to the point from which they started, those alone excepted who make shipwreck altogether[2]." The mention of the rebuilding of cities, and the stress laid upon the journey of return, make it probable that Philo had the psalm before us in his mind; the guiding form or vision is manifestly that Presence of the Lord which led the Israelites through the wilderness; and if Philo found any mention of that guiding Presence in this psalm,

---

[1] The Vatican copy of the LXX. begins v. 25 thus: κατ' ἀρχὰς τὴν γῆν σὺ Κύριε ἐθεμελίωσας. The Alexandrine reads thus: κατ' ἀρχὰς σὺ Κύριε τὴν γῆν ἐθεμελίωσας. In the New Testament quotation, the words are yet differently arranged: σὺ κατ' ἀρχὰς Κύριε τὴν γῆν ἐθεμελίωσας.

[2] Philo *De Execrationibus*, 8, 9.

where did he find it but in the divine person who is addressed in the last five verses?

And in connexion with this we have lastly to refer to a remarkable passage in the New Testament, in which St Paul speaks of our "looking for that blessed hope and the glorious appearing of the great God and our Saviour Jesus Christ[1]." Why the *great* God? Neither those who refer the expression to God the Father nor those who, more correctly, interpret it of Jesus Christ, have, so far as I can find, given any explanation of the epithet. But let the expression be viewed as a Pauline translation of *El gibbor*, "the mighty God;" let it be remembered that it was as "the mighty God" of whom Isaiah had prophesied, and to whom the psalmist had prayed, that the Lord Jesus Christ was to appear; let it be further borne in mind that though the anticipations of both the prophet and the psalmist had in the Incarnation and in the founding of the Christian Church been already fulfilled, there nevertheless remained a second and more glorious divine appearing to follow; and then the whole purport of the apostle's language is apparent. Between the two advents of the Son of God the Christian Church has still the days of her pilgrimage, corresponding to those of the Church of Israel while yet anticipating the first appearance of her promised Messiah. And there are seasons in which the Christian Church, like the Church of Israel, may well feel herself desolate, and may mourn as though God's strength had departed from her. But her Saviour, the Brightness of the glory of the Father, hath promised to be with her alway, even unto the end of the world; and to Him, in her faintness, she may ever pour forth her prayers, in the full confidence that she shall be heard,

---

[1] Titus ii. 13.

and that his unchangeableness remains the sure pledge of her own continuance.

PSALM CIII.

"OF David;" that is, (as we have already explained in the Introductions to Psalms lxxxvi, ci,) composed by the representative for the time being of David's royal house. There can be little room for doubt that the present psalm was written by Josiah, in or subsequently to his 18th year, the year of the great reformation in Judah. It would thus naturally occupy a place after Psalm ci, which was written by him on assuming the reins of government, and Psalm cii, which probably also dates in the earlier portion of his reign. The abruptness with which at v. 9 reference is made to God's revelation of his ways unto Moses may be explained by the circumstance that the newly discovered book of the law and its contents must have been the theme on which in the reformation-year every one was dwelling. The sentiment of vv. 17, 18 would come with especial force at that time from the lips of Josiah, who, solemnly vowing "to walk after the LORD, and to keep his commandments, and his testimonies, and his statutes, with all his heart, and with all his soul, to perform the words of the covenant which were written in the book[1]," was seeking, by walking "in the ways of David his father," a continuance of that divine mercy which had been poured forth upon David. An unsuspecting testimony to the propriety of the language of this psalm in the lips of a royal descendant of David has been borne by Hengstenberg, who "finds in vv. 1—5 an individual person speaking, *the seed of David;*" although his assumption that David was the author of the psalm obliges

---

[1] 2 Chron. xxxiv. 31.

him somewhat awkwardly to conclude that "*from the soul of that seed* David himself gives thanks." It is evident that he was fettered by an incorrect view of the meaning of the superscription, in consequence of which he felt himself constrained, in spite of all evidence to the contrary, to admit the Davidic authorship. Those who are acquainted with the Commentary of Theodoret are aware how continually he was in like manner fettered by the arbitrary belief, prevalent in his day, that David was the author of the whole of the Psalter; in consequence of which he was compelled, whenever he recognized the reference of a psalm to particular events in the subsequent Jewish history, to maintain that David was himself made acquainted beforehand with those events, and composed his psalm in reference to them in the spirit of prophecy. That prophets and psalmists were indeed continually enabled to take their stand in the future, and thus to throw forward not only their gaze, but their very point of view, is certain; but we are not on this account, in the absence of sufficient and reasonable proof, to refer back writings to an earlier date than that to which they may be deemed more naturally to belong.

It is probable that in giving vent to vv. 14—16 Josiah had before him the language of that Mosaic psalm (Psalm xc.) which now stands at the head of the Fourth Book of the Psalter. We may also observe that already, at the date of the composition of this psalm, Chaldean influences were beginning to make themselves felt in Judea. In the Hebrew text of vv. 3, 4 we discern what are perhaps the earliest instances of the effects of a Chaldean influence upon the grammatical inflexions of the Hebrew language; while the unusual details into which the royal psalmist enters in vv. 20, 21 with reference to God's angelic ministers seem to shew that special attention had been excited in such subjects through acquaintance with the Chaldean philosophy[1], and that in opposition to the errors of that philosophy God was now seasonably providing that true views of the office of the heavenly host should be set forth by those who wrote under his inspiration and guidance.

The number of verses in this psalm is that of the letters of the Hebrew alphabet; and the completeness of the whole is further testified by its return at the close to the words with which it started, "Bless the LORD, O my soul." In the middle of the psalm indeed the individual devotions are gradually merged in those of the community, as is clear from the use of the first person plural in vv. 10 seqq. Otherwise its general spirit is akin to that of Psalm ci. It is replete throughout with the acknowledgment of that richness of divine mercy and fatherly tenderness which God pours forth upon those that humbly seek him, even at the time that his judgments are all prepared, ready to fall upon a guilty world. And so the two verses in which the doctrine of the fulness of God's forgiveness is most loudly proclaimed (vv. 11, 12) are purposely rendered as prominent as possible by being placed in the very centre of the psalm. For indeed the graciousness of God has often most strongly revealed itself in the breathing-time that has preceded the lightning-flash of his displeasure. The promises by which his chosen nation of old had been cheered for more than a thousand years were fulfilled to the devout few who waited for the consolation of Israel just as the great bulk of the nation was filling up the measure of its guilt; and when the Jews in their obduracy put a crown to all their previous iniquities, and drew down upon themselves the sentence of final

---

[1] In reference to which see the article so headed in Kitto's *Cyclopædia*.

doom, the very death of him whom they crucified proclaimed to the faithful and penitent how God had indeed removed their transgressions from them.

PSALM CIV.

A NOBLE hymn of praise, breathing throughout of the peacefulness of the sanctuary, and illustrating the spirit in which the wonders of the natural creation will be contemplated by one who has been educated as a member of the Church of God. Its uniform evenness of flow marks it indeed, like Psalm xcii, to which it is somewhat akin, as a composition of late date; but perhaps its very smoothness impresses it the more strongly on the memory, and commends it the more effectually to many who but imperfectly appreciate the impassioned outbursts, the stirring depths, and the rapid transitions of the older psalms of David.

This psalm has been not unfrequently characterized as a pure hymn of praise to God from the book of nature. A hymn of praise from the book of nature it certainly is, and as such may be most appropriately and legitimately used: the assertion of Augustine, that some passages in it could not be literally understood, rested on a mere error of translation, and will probably now be universally repudiated. But at the same time an attentive examination of the psalm renders it almost impossible to doubt that to set forth the wonders of the natural creation was not the only object that the psalmist had in view; that in those wonders he beheld the types of the yet greater marvels of the spiritual world; that in God's watchfulness over the welfare of his material creatures he recognized a pledge of his watchfulness over the interests of his Church; that in some particular details of the phenomena of the material world he discerned special tokens of encouragement to the Church in the trials she must needs encounter; and that in particular his more immediate aim was to stir up himself and the Church in whose name he spoke to continued reliance upon God amid the present declining prospects and approaching dissolution of the Jewish monarchy. The psalm was doubtless written during the reign either of Josiah or of one of his successors. We may perhaps allow that Augustine carried the under-meaning of the psalm too far when he sought to give a spiritual interpretation to each several verse[1]. But the broad lessons which the psalmist intended to inculcate can hardly be mistaken; and it was certainly with reference to those lessons that some of the details of his description were selected.

Thus, firstly, he renders prominent the principle of order and harmony which reigns throughout the material creation. All is so contrived that the several creatures shall minister to each other's needs. The streams supply moisture to the trees; these serve in turn as dwelling-places for the birds; while the hills amid which the streams run form a refuge for the wild goats and conies. Could it be doubted then that a similar order and interchange of beneficial ministering was intended to obtain among God's reasonable creatures in regard of their mutual moral relationships? At present men too often met, as Israel well knew, only to injure, kill, and destroy; but this could not last for ever; and the believer would in faith look forward to the day when a divine harmony should be re-established, when the enemies of order should be removed,

---

[1] "Psalmus qui lectus est, prope totus figuris rerum mysteriisque contexitur, ... quanquam etiam cuncta quæ dicta sunt, possint ad literam religiose accipi," (which afterwards, in discoursing on v. 17, he disallows.)..."Tamen in omnibus quæ dicta sunt, quærendus est etiam intellectus spiritualis, &c."

when the sinners should "be consumed out of the earth," and the wicked "be no more" (v. 35).

But again the psalmist noticed how providentially God had ordered the various times and seasons. It was not always daylight; the sun knew his going down; darkness came on, and the beasts of the forest crept forth, and the young lions were permitted to seize the prey after which they roared. Yet this too was only for a season; for "the sun ariseth, they gather themselves together, and lay them down in their dens;" and then man goeth forth to resume in cheerfulness his work and his labour until the evening. In all this there was a mysterious lesson for the Church. For at the time that this was written a night-season in the life of the Jewish nation was at hand. The sunshine of God's visible favour was about to be withdrawn from his people; and the heathen beasts of Chaldea were about to make good their opportunity, to issue forth in all the lust of ravening, and to pounce upon the heir of David's line and the city of David's rule as their appointed prey. But the night would have its limits; the beams of God's mercy would again dawn upon his people; their heathen foes would slink back into their hiding-places, and the Church would once more manifestly and energetically enter on her divine work. The history of the Christian Church has supplied many similar illustrations of the alternation of night and day, and will doubtless continue so to do till that last great evening when all earthly work shall be ended, and its eternal fruits alone shall remain. There will here be but space for noticing what befell when the Incarnate Sun of Righteousness knew his going down, he the Prince of Life submitting to the temporary grasp of death. That was the hour of his enemies; and the power of darkness was by the determinate counsel and foreknowledge of God permitted to exercise its sway. But the Sun once more "arose;" the enemies were confounded; and, in the light of the Sun, man,—redeemed and Christian man,—went forth to his new and holy labour.

Another type of the enemies of the Church the psalmist beheld in those waters which had once extended over the whole face of the earth, but which at God's rebuke had fled and wasted away, leaving clear both the elevations of the mountains and the depressions of the valleys. The psalmist intended perhaps mainly to speak of that separation of land and sea which is recorded in the first chapter of Genesis; but his words may also be applied to what took place after the deluge. From that time forward God set a bound to the deeps that they should not pass over; and as the earth had her charter, that the waters should cover her no more, so the Church had also her charter, that the gates of hell should not prevail against her.

In connexion with this attention should be directed to that continual renewal of the earth of which the psalmist speaks. "Thou hidest thy face, they are troubled: thou takest away their breath, they die, and return to their dust. Thou sendest forth thy spirit, they are created: and thou renewest the face of the earth." "The period after the flood," remarks Hengstenberg, "furnishes us with the most visible picture of such a renewal as it exists after every ruinous catastrophe; and in a certain measure each spring. These renewals of the earth furnish a type and a pledge of the renewal of the condition of the Church, until the final perfect regeneration (Matth. xix. 28)." The most striking natural illustration however of the psalmist's words, and therefore the most striking pledge of the successive divine renewals of the Church, may be now legitimately traced in the discoveries of modern science with regard to the successive breakings up and renewals of the surface of the globe in the early geological **periods**.

But the **great lesson of** the psalm still remains. It will be observed that throughout the earlier portion it is on the details connected with the *waters* of the earth that the psalmist mainly dwells. By water the earth is fertilized. Without due supply **of** moisture there could **be neither grass** for the cattle (v. 14), nor corn, nor oil, nor wine **for** the service of man (v. 15), nor trees, the earth's chief natural ornament (v. 16). But this needful moisture is derived **from** above **(v.** 13), from the watery chambers which **God** has constructed above the firmament (v. 3; cf. Gen. i. 6, 7); and these heavenly water-chambers (for as such the Hebrews regarded them[1]) are the material types of those inexhaustible treasures of spiritual grace which God is continually pouring down for the sustenance and renewal **of** his Church. Without such supplies of grace the Church would necessarily perish. By heavenly grace alone is continual life and vigour ministered to the Lord's noblest trees, the spiritual cedars of Lebanon, the "trees of righteousness" of his planting[2]. And **it is** because the **psalm** thus **bears** so strongly upon the life-giving operation **of** the grace **of** God's Spirit, that it has been appropriated **by** the Church as one of her Whitsuntide hymns.

---

[1] A different view of these chambers is taken by Bp. Lowth, *Prælectio* VIII. He supposes all the imagery of **the** early part of the psalm to be borrowed from the earthly sanctuary, and more particularly from the structure of the tabernacle. To this view it is almost fatal, that the psalm was written long after the tabernacle had disappeared. Could it have been **shewn** that the details of the psalmist's imagery accorded with those of the fabric **of** the temple (the chambers, for instance, corresponding to those over the Holy Place and the Holy of Holies, 2 Chron. iii. 9), there would have been some degree of probability in the hypothesis that the sanctuary supplied the basis of the imagery of this psalm equally with that of Psalm xcii.

[2] Isaiah lxi. 3.

Nor is it perhaps without a determinate undersense that the psalmist speaks of the springs of waters giving drink "to every beast of the field" (v. 11). He seems to have intended to imply that all spiritual life, whether within the visible Church or without it, whether recognized or unrecognized, whether in a David and a Josiah or in a Naaman and a Cyrus, proceeded from the same divine source. The time would come when the Israelites would acknowledge the true dignity of those whom they now regarded as "beasts of the field"; when God would bear public witness of his having cleansed those who now were treated as unclean, and when the visible Church would become the true antitype of the patriarchal ark, into which there entered male and female of all flesh wherein was the breath of life. The same watchfulness of God over the people of every nation, the same ultimate extension of the Church, seems to be indicated in a different manner at v. 25, where the psalmist, having recorded how full of divine riches was the earth, turns to speak of the wonders of the sea and of God's bounty to the creatures that moved therein. If the earth—and the psalmist's description of its appearance is entirely drawn from the natural features of the land of Canaan[1]—if the earth might be treated more especially as the emblem of the Jewish Church, then by contrast the sea would well represent the vast, restless, heaving world. Yet the creatures of the deep were not forgotten of God; from the smallest to the greatest, from the 'nautilus[2]' to the leviathan, all were the objects

---

[1] "Feeble as its brooks might be,—though, doubtless, they were then more frequently filled than now—yet still Palestine was the only country where an Eastern could have been familiar with the image of Ps. civ. 10." Stanley, *Sinai and Palestine*, p. 123.

[2] So the word in v. 26 usually translated *ships* is, with much apparent probability, but I know not on what authority, rendered by French and Skinner.

of his care; the types in this of those living souls of the heathen world who were now unconsciously waiting on God, **but who** would surely receive of him their meat in due season.

V. 7 of the psalm before us is quoted in the Epistle to Hebrews, **i.** 7, **in** illustration of the angelic office and character. It has not however been yet decided whether the LXX. translation, from which the quotation is made, here correctly represents the meaning of the Hebrew text; or whether the latter should not rather be rendered, "Who maketh winds his messengers, flames of fire his ministers." This latter rendering is more agreeable to the context of the psalm, and is supported by such parallel passages **as Ps.** cxlviii. 8, Job xxxviii. 35; while the meaning thus elicited would not be inappropriate in the Epistle to the Hebrews, as illustrating the important truth that the office of the angels, God's personal messengers, is **as** purely ministerial **as** that of his impersonal messen**gers,** the wind and the lightning.

PSALMS CV, CVI.

These two psalms, which are closely connected together, were apparently composed in the immediate prospect of the Babylonish captivity; as we gather more especially from the concluding verses of Psalm cvi. They have been sometimes assigned to **the** period of the captivity itself. But their language seems equally capable of explanation **on** the supposition that the psalmist, writing before **the** captivity, regarded that event as already certain; and the bond which exists between them and Psalm civ, which last can hardly have been written after the removal from Canaan, and the general connexion between the psalms and the sanctuary-worship at Jerusalem, renders this the preferable view.

The two psalms before us are outwardly united to Psalm civ. by the Hallelujah (Praise ye the LORD) which is found, for the first time in the Psalter, at the end of Psalm civ, and which occurs also at the end of Psalm cv, and at the beginning and end of Psalm cvi. The immediate object of all three psalms seems to have been to help to sustain the faith of the Jewish church through the long period of trial which was about to be her lot. But in Psalm civ. the psalmist drew his parable from the wonders of God's work in the natural world; in Psalms cv, cvi. from the wonders of his dealings with his people as displayed in past history.

The difference in character between the two psalms with which we are now more immediately concerned is itself very strongly marked. Psalm cv. recounts the history of God's faithfulness; Psalm cvi. the history of the people's transgressions, to which in Psalm cv. not even the most indirect allusion had been made. The theme of Psalm cv. is the bestowal on the Israelites of the promised land of their inheritance; the theme of Psalm cvi. their temporary forfeiture of that inheritance in consequence of the sins of which they had been guilty. The lands of the heathen had been given them that they might observe God's statutes and keep his laws (cv. 44, 45). This they had not done; yet their prayer was that in remembrance of his covenant, God would still gather them from among the heathen, to shew forth his praise (cvi. 47).

In each psalm it will be found that the details dwelt on are selected with reference to the main end in view; which is in both cases entirely different to that which formed the end in view of the author of the historical Psalm lxxviii. But in each psalm also the details on which the psalmist dwells must have been of special interest to the people under the trial which they were about to encounter. They would naturally compare their migration from Judea to Babylon with the journeys "from one nation to another" of the patriarchs of old, and their sojourn in the land of Babylon with the sojourning of their forefathers in Egypt (cv. 13, 23); and it would comfort them to think both how wondrously God had protected their forefathers wherever they went, and how he had made their very wanderings the means of his ultimate fulfilment of his covenant with Abraham. Again they would learn that in delivering them into their captors' hands God was only fully executing upon them that judgment with which for their sins he had once threatened their forefathers (cvi. 27), and which more than once in past time he had brought partially to pass (cvi. 41); while yet they would see how in every case he had in judgment remembered mercy, and had healed his people's affliction for his own covenant's sake.

The appropriateness of these psalms to us in our seasons of affliction will at once be understood from the circumstance that the nation of Israel was but a type of the Church of Christ, to whom richer promises have been made than those relating to the mere possession of the land of Canaan.

With these psalms the Fourth Book of the Psalter concludes. V. 48 of Psalm cvi. is the doxology to the whole Book; and in that verse the words "and let all the people say" seem to be a mere rubrical direction: as indeed we may gather from the circumstance that when we turn to the verse as inserted in the historical narrative of 1 Chron. xvi. we find there substituted the corresponding words "and all the people said."

On that historical narrative a few remarks will now be necessary. The chapter 1 Chron. xvi. contains a hymn of considerable length, which proves on examination to be constructed, with a few unimportant variations, of the first fifteen verses of Psalm cv, of Psalm xcvi almost entire, of the first and last verses of Psalm cvi, and of the doxology by which that psalm is followed. As this hymn is inserted in the middle of the account of the arrangements made by David for the tabernacle-service, it has been frequently assumed that we have the authority of the Books of Chronicles for assigning to David's pen the psalms out of which it is constructed. This assumption is, unfortunately, strongly countenanced by the rendering which our English Version gives of 1 Chron. xvi. 7: "Then on that day David delivered first this psalm to thank the LORD into the hand of Asaph and his brethren." The words "this psalm" have however no existence in the Hebrew; and the verse may be more correctly rendered as follows: "Then on that day did David first appoint"—or still better, "Then on that day did David lay a charge upon—the chief (i. e. the head of all the choirs, cf. v. 5) to thank the LORD by Asaph and his brethren." It would thus seem that the author of the Book of Chronicles was recording the source whence the temple-choirs drew their authority to officiate in the temple-service, and indirectly also their authority to introduce into that service psalms of their own composition; and it may further be that he was speaking with more especial reference to the choir of the Sons of Asaph, which alone of the three choirs returned from the captivity, and with which he himself was not improbably connected. Having thus recorded the original charge laid upon Asaph, he interrupts his narrative to take the opportunity of shewing how Asaph's descendants had fulfilled the trust thus committed to their ancestor; for which purpose he introduces a sort of compendium of those Asaphic psalms which would be likely at the period **of** the **return from** the captivity to possess the greatest national interest. Hence the hymn, if such we may **call it,** which has proved the occasion of so much misapprehension. We have already observed that the descendants of Asaph must be deemed the authors **of** most of the anonymous psalms in the Fourth Book of the Psalter; and it is among these that we find the three psalms from which the extracts in the First Book **of** Chronicles are made.

BOOK V.

PSALMS CVII.—CL.

And the ransomed of the Lord shall return, and come to Zion with songs and everlasting joy upon their heads: they shall obtain joy and gladness, and sorrow and sighing shall flee away.

Isaiah xxxv. 10.

And they shall come from the east, and from the west, and from the north, and from the south, and shall sit down in the kingdom of God.

Luke xiii. 29.

BOOK V.

THE psalms of the Fifth Book of the Psalter belong to the period of the return from the Babylonish captivity, and extend in date from the days of Zerubbabel to those of Nehemiah, during whose administration they were probably collected and arranged in their present order. Fifteen of them bear the name of David in the superscription, as having been composed by the representatives of David's house. The authorship of Psalm cxxvii, "A Song of degrees 'of' Solomon," may best be ascribed to one of the same persons: the reason of the superscription will come before us in its due place. The remaining twenty-eight psalms are anonymous; and may, with the exception of Psalm cxix, be deemed the productions of the Sons of Asaph.

PSALM CVII.

THE opening psalm of the Fifth Book of the Psalter at once awakens visions of the dawn of the new life of the Jewish nation after the return from Babylon. It is emphatically a strain of redemption; the first public thanksgiving of the Jewish people for restoration to their land. It was probably sung at the celebration of the Feast of Tabernacles in the first year of the return (Ezra iii. 1 seqq.), when the whole of the people "gathered themselves together as one man to Jerusalem," and when the national worship was resumed by the offering of sacrifice upon the newly-erected altar. Two passages in the psalm may incidentally serve to corroborate the supposition that it was composed at that season of the year; vv. 25—27, and v. 37. The description in the former passage of the dangers of the sea would be especially natural during the season of the equinoctial storms, which was popularly reckoned to commence at the fast, five days before the Feast of Tabernacles[1]; and the allusion in the latter passage to the fruits of increase would be particularly suitable at the feast which was purposely designed to mark the season of ingathering. No reference is made in this psalm to the temple: the building of the new temple was not commenced till afterwards.

The plan of the psalm is remarkably regular. In order, seventy years before, to express the completeness of the judgments by which the Jews were to be visited, the prophet Jeremiah had represented them as delivered over to four different kinds of punishment; death, the sword, famine, and captivity,—or again, the sword, the dogs, the fowls, and the beasts: he had moreover declared that they should be removed into all kingdoms of the earth[2]. In the present psalm, sung at the return from the captivity, the restoration of Israel is celebrated in a corresponding manner. The redeemed of the Lord are represented (vv. 1—3) as gathered out of the lands, from the east, and from the west, from the north, and from the sea; or in other words from as many places as the heaven has quarters. Without exactly naming each several quarter of the heavens, (for the sea would according to Hebrew usage denote the west rather than the south,) the psalmist nevertheless, after the example of Isaiah (xlix. 12), preserves the *number* of the quarters; the number four, the symbol of universal space, indicating here the completeness of the redemption, as it had in the prophecy of Jeremiah

---

[1] Acts xxvii. 9.   [2] Jerem. xv. 2—4.

indicated the completeness of the judgment. Each of the four places named, the east, the west, the north, the sea, suggests the picture of some particular form of misery from which in the ensuing portions of the psalm Israel is represented as rescued; though it must be borne in mind that each picture is to be taken not as a literal delineation of the afflictions of any portion of Israel, but as a figurative representation of the wretchedness of the whole. Some of the pictures, e. g. the second, may have been partly suggested by what particular Israelites had experienced; but there is no reason to suppose that any considerable number of the people had been in more peril at sea during the captivity than at any other time. It is characteristic of this psalm that the variety of pictures presented to the imagination and the generality of the expressions employed render it an easy and appropriate hymn of praise for the rescued of every age and clime. The four portions of the psalm in which the four pictures are respectively contained are purposely made to correspond: in each we have the people's cry unto the Lord in their trouble (vv. 6, 13, 19, 28), in each the call to praise the Lord for his goodness (vv. 8, 15, 21, 31). The Hebrew phrase for "in their trouble" has a peculiarity which disappears in translation: it is borrowed from Psalm cvi. 44, and thus forms a connecting link between the two psalms.

The first picture (vv. 4—9) is suggested by the mention of the east, the quarter in which lay the wilderness. A traveller in the wilderness, ignorant of the road he should follow, is fainting for hunger and thirst: the Lord in answer to his cry leads him forth by the right way, that he may come to a city of habitation. In this phrase, "city of habitation," which occurs thrice in the psalm (vv. 4, 7, 36), there is manifestly a covert allusion to Jerusalem, whither the Israelites had returned.

Again, the mention of the west leads the psalmist's thoughts to Egypt; and the remembrance of the bondage and labours of the ancestors of the Israelites in Egypt, coupled with the description in a previous psalm (cv. 17) of the imprisonment of Joseph, and possibly with the recollection of the fate of Jehoahaz the son of Josiah, who had perished a captive in that country[1], suggest the picture of a bondman (vv. 10—16), ground down with heavy toil, and pining in almost hopeless captivity; unable to devise, or even to conjecture any possible means by which the bars that fasten the doors of his prison-house may be undrawn. But he cries unto the Lord; and as he cries, there bursts upon him an unexpected light: the bars are cleft in twain, the doors themselves are broken in, his fetters are loosed, and his liberty is restored.

The third picture (vv. 17—22) is connected with the mention of the north, the land into which the Israelites had been actually led captive. The gross idolatry for which that captivity was the punishment; the distaste for the worship of the true God which their long sojourn in the land of their captivity and their consequent deprival of the more solemn means of grace would create; the danger in which they lay of being permanently cut off from being God's people; their sudden restoration by the edict of Cyrus, whose spirit the Lord had stirred up to rebuild the temple at Jerusalem, are all represented under the image of a man who by his brutishness has brought upon himself a dangerous and well-merited sickness, who now loathes his food and is in imminent peril of death, but who is healed as in an instant by the power of the word of the Lord.

[1] 2 Kings xxiii. 33, 34.

The last picture (vv. 23—32) springs naturally from the mention in v. 3 of the sea; and here the psalmist may have directed his imagination not only to the usual tempestuousness of the season at which the psalm was sung (see above), but also to the description of the storm in the Book of Jonah. Israel appears under the image of a ship's crew, beset by a fearful tempest, but rescued by the rapid subsiding of the wind, and brought safe to shore. They have thus beheld "the works of the Lord, and his wonders in the deep;" in other words, the marvellous power with which he stills the raging of the waves.

In each of the four pictures stress is laid not merely on the fulness but also on the suddenness of the deliverance. The restoration of Israel to their own land might well be deemed sudden, considering how little, a few years or perhaps even a few months before, it could, humanly speaking, have been anticipated.

The New Testament furnishes some striking exemplifications of the pictures here presented to us; in the deliverance of Peter from prison, in the healing of the centurion's servant by Jesus' word, and in the subduing, on more than one occasion, of the storm on the lake of Gennesaret. All these however were only fresh types of that great deliverance which was foreshadowed by the restoration of Israel, and which is therefore the true subject of each separate portion of the psalm: our redemption from sin and from spiritual death in Christ Jesus.

But we must pursue the course of the psalmist's strain. In the pictures as yet presented to us, the pleasantness of the land of liberty and safety, if it can only be reached, the permanent continuance of the city of habitation, if it can only be found, are tacitly assumed. It is equally assumed that the wilderness must ever remain barren, and the sea dangerous. Certain limitations to God's power had been thus virtually implied. These limitations the psalmist now removes (vv. 33 seqq.) God can not only conduct his people from the wilderness into the fertile country: he can also transform the very face of the earth itself; can make the wilderness fruitful and the fertile land barren. A wondrously prophetical acknowledgment of *His* almighty power, who has visited all the once heathen lands of Europe with the rain of his grace, and has made them yield forth the fruits of righteousness, even the fruits of Christian faith; and has on the other hand rendered barren the land in which he had once fixed his dwelling-place, by delivering it over to the blighting influences of a corrupt Christianity and of Muhammedan misbelief! Full moreover of important instruction to us in our anticipations of the future; that so from it, instead of mistakenly looking for any future literal restoration of the Jews to their former country, we may learn that *wheresoever* men shall hunger and thirst after righteousness, even *there* God can satisfy them, can turn the wilderness for them into a standing water and dry ground into watersprings, and *there*, even *there*, make the hungry to dwell, that they may prepare a city for habitation!

But the latter portion of the psalm is no mere general assertion of God's power, no mere indefinite anticipation of the wonders which that power should achieve. It will be found, when closely analysed, to contain, in common with the writings of Daniel and Zechariah, a minutely-detailed prophecy of the events which were to befall the Jews and neighbouring nations during the centuries following the restoration of the former to their land. And although the immediate interest of these events in themselves be now in a considerable degree passed away, yet it is not unfitting that they should still furnish the language in which the Christian worshipper may express his confidence in the continuance of God's protection, inasmuch as they **had a** typical character, and, along with the Old Testament prophecies relating to them, supplied much of the groundwork of the Apocalyptic representation given by the apostle St John of the perils, struggles, deliverances, and triumphs of the Church of the New Covenant.

The psalmist's thoughts turn first to Babylon, whence the Israelites had returned, and to whose desolation, as may be shewn by the parallel passages in the prophecies, the expressions in vv. 33, **34, "He turneth** rivers into a wilderness, &c." immediately refer[1]. And here we must remember that the capture and destruction of Babylon, although they had (in accordance with the prophetic style[2]) been foretold as consecutive or connected events, were actually separated by a period of several centuries. The former had been already achieved by Cyrus: the latter still remained to be accomplished. At the very outset therefore of this portion of the psalm we enter on the region of prophecy: the great historical fact which lies at the basis of the language employed **by the** psalmist was to him still future. He knew however **that** the time must come when the predictions of **Isaiah** and Jeremiah respecting Babylon should be fulfilled; and in v. 34 he, after the example of the prophet Isaiah[3], sets forth the desolation of her land in language suggested by the ancient fate of Sodom and Gomorrha[4].

In contrast to the destruction in store for Babylon

---

[1] Cf. Isaiah xxi. 1; l. 2; Jer. l. 38; li. 36. (Hengstenberg.)

[2] See Fairbairn *On Prophecy,* Cap. v. sec. 5; or Lee *On Inspiration of Scripture,* p. 185.

[3] Isaiah xiii. 19.

[4] As was justly perceived by the Targumist.

stand the blessings (vv. 35—38) of which the Israelites at the date of the composition of the psalm were anticipating for themselves the long enjoyment. The language of blessing (v. 35) is purposely made to correspond to that of the curse upon the oppressor (v. 33); but the pools and springs thus mentioned may be appropriately taken in a figurative sense as pools of spiritual refreshment and springs of grace. For although the Israelites undoubtedly set great store on the blessings of temporal prosperity, yet the great change to which they were now looking forward was not a physical change in the features of their land, but the revival of their public worship of God and of their religious national life.

But prosperity could not be unchequered. The following verse (v. 39) carries us on to anticipations of new trials in store for God's people; for no one who has not been prejudiced by exegetical difficulties can well read that verse in connexion with the preceding, without feeling that it refers to events following on those last described. It is indeed easy to recognize in it the prophetical allusion to the time when the Jews were subsequently "minished and brought low" through the corruption of their rulers in the days of Antiochus Epiphanes. But with oppression came also renewed deliverance. The words of v. 40, "He poureth contempt upon princes," (themselves borrowed from the Book of Job,) received ample fulfilment in the ultimate discomfiture of the armies of the Greek monarch; while those of v. 41, "Yet setteth he the poor on high from affliction," were notably verified in the elevation of the Maccabean family; an elevation which not merely delivered them from affliction, but also had its very source in the persecution to which they had been previously exposed. Intimations of what should come to pass had already been given by the prophet Daniel (xi. 30 seqq.). Subsequently the Maccabean deliverance was more distinctly foretold by Zechariah (ix. 12—17); and it would seem that from v. 41 of the present psalm, "and maketh ...families like a flock," was derived Zech. ix. 16, "And the LORD their God shall save them in that day, 'his people as a flock'." The peaceful happiness enjoyed by the people under Simon Maccabeus became in after times proverbial; so that to no other period of Jewish history could the psalmist's words more properly apply.

It is for the Church of Christ's redeemed wisely to observe (v. 43) these events in the history of the Church of the elder dispensation. She must herself in like manner look for many alternations of prosperity and adversity; and may in the trials of the more ancient Church read the prognostications of her own. She must expect to be both assailed by the fury of persecutors from without, and also betrayed and brought down by the unfaithfulness of unworthy rulers and false brethren within; yet will she have learnt from observation of the past to "understand the lovingkindness of the LORD," and will amid all difficulties look for His protection, who hath promised that the gates of hell shall not prevail against her.

PSALM CVIII.

FROM the superscriptions of this and the two following psalms it may be gathered, according to the explanation already given in the Introduction to Psalm lxxxvi, that they were composed by the representative of David's house. There can certainly be no improbability in attributing them to Zerubbabel, whose name occurs in both the gospel genealogies of our Saviour, and who was the foremost man in the Jewish state during the early years of the return from Babylon. His dignity is attested by the office which he held (at least during the reign of Darius Hystaspis) of Persian governor or captain of Judah[1]; and along with the high-priest Jeshua he took from the first the leading part in the re-establishment of the appointed worship and in the rebuilding of the temple. The prophets Haggai and Zechariah were both entrusted with special divine messages to him; and in the writings of both those prophets he appears as bearing a typical or representative character[2].

Nor can there in the case of the particular psalm before us be any reason to doubt that it was put together subsequently to the Babylonish captivity. Hengstenberg, even while maintaining it to have proceeded from David, does not abstain from remarking how well adapted it must have been to console and elevate the Church during the period after the return. Among the ancients Theodoret treats the psalm as having reference to the return from Babylon, and illustrates v. 8 by the assumed supremacy of Zerubbabel over all the Israelitish tribes.

The late date of the psalm receives confirmation moreover from the circumstance that it proves on examination to be compounded, with a few comparatively unimportant variations, of portions of two psalms of the original David; viz. Psalm lvii. 7—11, and Psalm lx. 5—12; the former portion being apparently introduced as a preface to the other. With regard to the contents of the latter of the two portions, they must be taken as a general expression of confidence in the ultimate triumph of the Church through the favour of God. To some of the particulars of the language which he borrowed Zerubbabel would find it scarcely less difficult

---

[1] Haggai i. 1, &c.; Ezra vi. 7.   [2] Haggai ii. 20—23; Zech. iv.

to attach a distinct meaning than we when we employ it in our own worship. The words of the psalm (especially vv. 7—9) had in David's time been little more than an enumeration of actual facts; nor did the enemies of the Jews much belie them to the Persian court when they declared that there had been mighty kings over Jerusalem, who had ruled over all countries beyond the river, and to whom toll, tribute, and custom had been paid[1]. Of the return of any such extent of dominion to the Israelitish nation there could in the days of Zerubbabel have been no visible prospect. The future conquests of Israel, by which the anticipations of the psalm were to be verified, were in truth to be triumphs of a different kind to those which David had won: the glory of Israel's future king was to shine forth not in temporal but in spiritual sway. Nor is it unreasonable to suppose that the expectations of Zerubbabel and of the more right-minded among his contemporaries respecting the mode in which God's promises would be ultimately made good had already been in some measure spiritualized, and that they did not simply look for a literal return of the olden times. However this may be, they piously held fast, in spite of all present appearances, to the assurance of the immutable truth of the divine word. God had "spoken in his holiness;" and therefore the language that had once been used by David, with all its prospective bearing, they would not abandon; a model of faith herein to the universal Church of all time, whose privilege it is to draw the substance of her devotional hopes not from the worldly circumstances of the periods in which her lot is successively cast, but from the unfailing and cheering promises, once made, of her divine Founder and Head[2].

---

[1] Ezra iv. 20.

[2] One modification of David's language, suggested to Zerubbabel by the altered circumstances of the times,

PSALM CIX.

If the superscription of this psalm, combined with the place which it occupies in the Psalter, would lead us to expect to be able to recognize Zerubbabel as its author, our anticipations will not be disappointed by an examination of the psalm itself. The words of v. 2, when correctly rendered, 'They have opened against me the mouth of the wicked and the mouth of the deceitful,' readily carry our thoughts to that passage in the book of Ezra where it is related that the people of the land "weakened the hands of the people of Judah, and troubled them in building, and *hired counsellers against them*, to frustrate their purpose, all the days of Cyrus king of Persia, even until the reign of Darius king of Persia[1]." In brief, the psalm belongs to that period of the return from the captivity during which the Samaritans were putting forth their efforts to hinder the rebuilding of the Jewish temple. There runs throughout the psalm the conception of a judicial trial, in which the psalmist's opponents are proceeding against him; a conception nowhere carried to the same extent in psalms of an earlier date, but which might yet well be suggested by the circumstances of the period following the return from the captivity, when the prosperity of the Jewish nation depended no longer, as during the period of the monarchy, on the victories they could gain in the field, but rather on the success of

should not be passed by without notice. In v. 9 the expressions respecting Moab and Edom remain the same as in Psalm lx.; for in one way or another the Moabites were still seducing God's people from their allegiance to him (cf. Neh. xiii.), and the Edomites still shewing themselves proud and malicious (cf. Ezek. xxxv.; Psalm cxxxvii. 7; and Josephus). But the warlike spirit of the Philistines had decayed, and as open foes they were no longer dangerous: the ironical challenge, "Philistia, triumph thou 'over' me," is therefore softened down into the simple declaration, "over Philistia will I triumph."

[1] Ezra iv. 4, 5.

their representations at **the** court of their suzerain the king of Persia. Those against whom the psalmist (apparently in the person of the whole Church) prays are no longer the "enemies," but the "adversaries;" for in that light the circumstances of the time obliged him to contemplate them. The Lord himself no longer appears as his people's "shield" or "fortress," but stands at the right hand of the poor as his advocate and judicial deliverer (v. 31); and correspondingly Satan stands at the right hand of the adversary as his accuser (v. 6)[1]. The aspect in which the evil spirit is here (and in Zech. iii. 1) regarded, and the name Satan (accuser) by which he is here and elsewhere designated both deserve attention. In the Mosaic writings he had appeared only **as the** serpent, the tempter; in the subsequent Old Testament scriptures he had for a time altogether disappeared from view except so far as they made mention of a spirit of madness, or of deceit, sent forth **by** God[2]. But **now** Chaldean influences had made themselves felt, and **the** belief in a spirit of evil had been revived among the Jews through their acquaintance with the Chaldean philosophy. The sacred Old Testament authors, writing by divine inspiration, **admitted** with the Chaldees the existence of an evil spirit, but gave no countenance to any views which implied for him a co-eternity, or perhaps co-equality, with the Spirit of good. They ascribed **to his** evil machinations what preceding writers had **referred** simply to God's anger, as appears from a comparison **of** the later 1 Chron. xxi. 1 with the earlier 2 Sam. xxiv. 1; but yet they represented him as acting only by the permission or sufferance of God (Job i, ii). And they gave

---

[1] Many translators here render, "and let an accuser stand, &c.," urging that Satan **cannot** here be a proper name, as it **lacks** the definite article. But the name has not the article in 1 Chron. xxi. 1.

[2] 1 Sam. xvi. 14; 1 Kings xxii. 22.

to him the name Satan or Accuser, thus sufficiently evidencing the light in which they viewed him. The adversarial character thus ascribed to the spirit of evil is in substantial accordance with the enmity which it was prophesied should exist between the tempter and the woman; and the identity of the Accuser of the later Jewish scriptures with the Tempter of the Book of Genesis is in the New Testament expressly asserted[1]. Yet the two forms under which his opposition to man is represented are sufficiently distinct to forbid us to suppose that the one portraiture of him could have been directly derived from the other; nor must we confound the two aspects of his character, both equally true and important, which the two different periods of the Old Testament dispensation thus served to bring out. We here assume the comparatively recent date of the composition of the Book of Job. The late date of the Books of Chronicles and of the prophecy of Zechariah, in which alone, except in the present psalm, the name Satan elsewhere occurs, admits of no dispute; and the very mention of Satan in the Book of Job thus furnishes strong evidence that the early date often assigned to it cannot be correct.

The psalm divides itself into two portions of unequal length. In the former (vv. 1—20) the psalmist, after setting forth the wickedness which is being practised against him, imprecates the divine judgments upon his adversaries. In the latter (vv. 21—31) he supplicates for mercy for himself. The imprecations of the former portion are well known as the most terrible in the whole of the Psalter. Yet they do not in spirit essentially differ from those of Psalm lxix, which have been already considered. The Jews might, during the period that their efforts to rebuild the temple at Jerusalem

[1] Rev. xx. 2.

were being wilfully hindered or frustrated, reasonably regard the Samaritans as types of the deliberate enemies of the Church of God. Certain modern commentators, more remarkable for their anxiety to remove from the Psalter what they deemed offensive than for the soundness of their judgment, have endeavoured to shew that the imprecations in vv. 6 seqq. are not those of the suppliant upon his adversaries, but of his adversaries upon him. It does not appear however that the mistaken ingenuity of these critics would even thus reconcile the spirit of the psalm with their own preconceived views; for in v. 17 the curses of the adversaries, whatever they may have been, are explicitly returned upon their own heads. The more obvious interpretation of the psalm is therefore undoubtedly correct; **nor** is there aught in it which may not be piously uttered by every worshipper, whether under the Old or under the New Covenant, who is filled with a holy jealousy **for** God's honour.

A deeper insight into the spirit of the imprecations which under divine inspiration the psalmist poured forth may be gathered from the reference which our Lord apparently made to this psalm in the words of his last prayer for his apostles: "While **I** was with them in the world, I kept them **in** thy name: those that thou gavest me I have kept, and none of them is lost, but **the son of** perdition; **that** the scripture might be fulfilled[1]." He foreknew **from the** first that Judas was a **devil**, an adversary; and it was probably not without reference to the language **of** the psalm before **us that** as such he in due **time** denounced him[2]; the verb which in this psalm **we** somewhat weakly render *to be an adversary* (vv. **4,** 20, "For my love they are mine adversaries," "Let this be the reward of mine

[1] John xvii. 12.   [2] John vi. 70.

adversaries") being both in Hebrew **and Greek the** correlative of the word *Satan, devil,* and the imprecation "Let Satan stand at his right hand" being only the imprecation of retribution on the sinner's own head for his adversarial, **devilish**, or Satanic conduct. The eventual overt treachery of Judas was therefore but the development **of that** wickedness of disposition which our Lord had forediscerned; the son of perdition was going forward in his perdition-course, **and** thereby bringing on his inevitable doom; and so the scripture was being fulfilled. We, who cannot, like our Lord, penetrate all the secrets of the hearts of men, have **no** right definitely to pronounce who are the sons of **per**dition, who not; but that there are many such in the **world** it would be idle to attempt to conceal; and in praying (as we are bound to pray) that God's will be done, **we** necessarily acquiesce in the judgments which **the guilty are** drawing down upon themselves. **If, not**withstanding the command to **judge not** before the time, we cannot **altogether dissociate our anticipations** of divine vengeance on the guilty from individual **per**sons who present themselves in one or another respect as types of wickedness to our eyes, still imprecations of judgment on the wicked *on the hypothesis of their continued impenitence* are not inconsistent with simultaneous efforts to bring them to repentance; and Christian charity itself can do no more than labour for the **sinner's conversion.** The law of holiness requires us **to pray for the fires of divine** retribution: the law of love **to seek meanwhile to rescue the brand** from the burning. The last **prayer of** the martyr Stephen was answered not **by** any general averting of doom from a guilty nation, **but** by the conversion of an individual persecutor to the service of God.

The apostle Peter seems to have recognized in v. 8

of this psalm a special prophetical reference to the fate of Judas[1]. Other verses (vv. 11 seqq.), which receive no literal illustration from the history of Judas, seem strikingly to set forth the judgments which should befall the Jewish nation. Of the subsequent guilt of the Jewish rulers the malice of the Samaritans in the days of Zerubbabel may indeed be regarded as a type: like the Samaritans, they let loose false witness against Him who had come to build the temple of the Lord[2], and without cause put themselves forward as his accusers in the presence of their Gentile ruler. In its substance, however, the psalm is of general, not of particular, reference; and the history both of the traitor-apostle and of the rejected covenant-people did at most but supply the imagery in which the terrors of the divine retribution on all wickedness might be expressed.

PSALM CX.

THE glories of the Messiah, enthroned on high after deliverance from his mortal strife, are now once more brought definitely before our gaze. He, and he alone, is the Lord of whom in this important prophetical ode the psalmist speaks. No portion of it is put into his mouth; we cannot therefore join with him in using it: he is here throughout, as in Psalms ii, xlv, either celebrated in the third person or addressed in the second; and we, in giving utterance to the words of the psalm, tell forth his sovereign praises. That therefore none but he can be the subject of the psalm is mainly evident from this, that if interpreted of any merely earthly ruler, it would necessarily lose its religious character. The victories and triumphs of a purely human sovereign

---

[1] Acts i. 20.   [2] Zech. vi. 12.

contain nothing permanently sacred; nor is it to worship a dead king, after the example of the heathen Romans, but to pay adoration to one who liveth for ever and ever, that in Christian solemnity we meet together. The language of the psalm is, moreover, inapplicable to any but the Messiah. None but he could be said to sit at God's right hand, implying as that phrase does, a participation in the divine government, according to the analogy of the Eastern usage with respect to the right hand of earthly sovereigns[1]. None but he could require that his people should follow him in the beauties of holiness, i. e. in holy attire. No king but he ever claimed to be a priest after the order of Melchizedek: none but he could be a priest for ever. From the question which our Saviour put to the Jews of his own day, and to which they made no objection, it is evident that they acknowledged the psalmist's Lord to be none other than the Messiah; and our Saviour himself, by his question, confirmed the correctness of their belief.

The correct determination of the subject of this psalm will help us to the solution of a less important but more intricate question—that of its authorship. Was it composed, as is generally assumed, by the original David? Or may we rather ascribe it, like the two preceding, to one of David's descendants? From the invectives of Chrysostom against the Jews of his day for asserting Zerubbabel to be the subject of the psalm, it may perhaps be not illegitimately surmised that some of them maintained Zerubbabel to be the author. If so, the place occupied by the psalm in the Psalter affords presumptive proof that they were right. But we need not here rest on mere presumption. Sufficient internal evidence is contained in the psalm to shew that

[1] Cf. Gen. xli. 40—44; 1 Kings ii. 19; Matth. xx. 21.

we must seek the author in Zerubbabel rather than in David.

In **the first place,** the text of the psalm in its original language **affords** grammatical indications of a comparatively late date. These are given in the note below[1].

Passing to **the contents,** we observe that the psalm foretells the union of the royal and priestly offices in the same person: "Thou art a priest for ever after the order of Melchizedek." It is extremely improbable that these words should have been uttered by David. There was nothing in the historical events of his life or reign to lead men's thoughts to the priestly office of the future Messiah. Notwithstanding David's pious attention to the ordering of the tabernacle-service, the dignity of the priesthood was in his time rather thrown into the background by the interest which centred in the person of the king. The comparatively recent institution of the **kingdom,** and David's own threefold royal anointing enabled him to discern how God should one day "set his king upon his holy hill of Zion;" but of the priestly office of that king no hint appears. **Nor,** it is almost needless to say, had there been any trace of the future union of the royal and priestly offices in the previous Israelitish history; neither had prophets in David's time given forth any utterance on the subject. The complete isolation, therefore, from both contemporary history and prophecy in which this important announcement of the psalm would stand, sup-

---

[1] The paragogic ' in דברתי (v. 4), by whatever name it may be called, is paralleled in Psalm ci. 5 (the work of Josiah), and in the later psalms, but nowhere in the psalms of the original David. The word דברה itself is only found elsewhere in the books of Job and Ecclesiastes, both, probably, later by centuries than the age of David and Solomon. One critic has also noticed the use of עַל with יָמִי in v. 5, cf. Psalm cix. 6: but the argument drawn from this is more questionable.

posing it to have been uttered by David, militates strongly against the theory of his authorship. The divine plan of teaching by means of type prevailed so universally in ancient times that any assumed violent departure from it strikes us as strange and unnatural; and though the psalm, it is true, finds a type of Christ in Melchizedek, it still remains to be explained for what reason the figure of that patriarchal sovereign-priest should be brought prominently forward in the days of David. Not less strange is it, if David be the author of the psalm, that no recognition of the important announcement and doctrine which it contains should occur in the writings of any subsequent prophet for a space of five hundred years.

If on the other hand we assign the authorship of the psalm to Zerubbabel, all becomes plain and simple. The union of the royal and priestly offices in the future Messiah was in his day distinctly prophesied by Zechariah, and was set forth in type by the placing of crowns upon the head of the high-priest Joshua[1]. At such a time the thoughts of holy men would naturally recur to the former recorded joint-representative of royalty and priesthood. And indeed when once the priestly office of the Messiah had been declared, (and there is another passage in the prophecy of Zechariah in which he makes reference to it[2],) the combination of priesthood and royalty necessarily followed, as the Messiah's royal character had been repeatedly announced by David, Solomon, and other psalmists, as well as by the earlier prophets.

We may remark moreover, in illustration of the exalted dignity ascribed to the Messiah in this psalm, that it is in the contemporary prophecies of Zechariah that we find some of the most remarkable Old Testa-

---

[1] Zech. vi. 11—13.   [2] Zech. iii. 8.

ment intimations that the Messiah should be a partaker of **the divine nature.** "According to Zech. xii. 10," observes Hengstenberg, **in** his *Christology,* "Jehovah himself **is pierced in the** Messiah. **In** Zech. xi. 13 Jehovah **calls the** miserable wages paid **to** the good shepherd **or Messiah** the "goodly price at which he, the LORD, was prised at of them." In Zech. xiii. 7 Jehovah calls the **good** shepherd "the man that is my fellow," **and thus points to the** fact that he is connected **with him by a secret unity of** nature." To these passages may be added **those in the same prophetical book in which** the divine character of **the** Son of God is **virtually asserted when he is spoken** of as "**the** angel of **the LORD:**" **such for example** is the account, in Zech. i., **of** that vision **in which he** appears riding upon a red horse, the symbol **of** fury against the hostile nations.

One striking parallelism between the psalm before **us** and **the** writings of Zechariah can hardly fail to arrest attention. The sins of the people are represented by Zechariah under the image of filthy garments worn by the high-priest[1]. These filthy garments are removed, and clean garments put upon him; and thus it is that the people (who share as **a** body in the benefit thus obtained) are **represented in** the psalm as accompanying their leader **in holy attire, or** as our English Version has it, "in the beauties of holiness."

Again **the** writings of **the** prophet Haggai, the contemporary of Zechariah, seem to have partly sup**plied the** basis of that portion **of the** psalm which delineates the overthrow **of** the heathen[2]. And it is worthy of notice that **the** particular prophecy of Haggai from which the psalmist must have drawn **was** specially directed to Zerubbabel, by whom, if

[1] Zech. iii. 3, 4.   [2] Hagg. ii. 20—23.

by any other than David, the psalm must have been written: "Speak to Zerubbabel, governor of Judah, saying, I will shake the heavens and the earth; and I will overthrow the throne of kingdoms, and I will destroy the strength of the kingdoms of the heathen; and I will overthrow the chariots, and those that ride in them; and the horses and their riders shall come down, every one by the sword of his brother."

In opposition to this mass of evidence for attributing the psalm to Zerubbabel the descendant of David rather than to David himself, there is probably but one argument which will generally carry any considerable degree of weight, or on which the upholders of the more commonly received view will care to rely. The argument is this: that our Blessed Saviour has, by his question "How then doth David in spirit call him Lord," himself recognized David as the author of the psalm. A full examination therefore of the justice and cogency of this argument, even at the risk of some degree of repetition of what has been already advanced in reference to other psalms, will here be not out of place. If indeed it can be shewn that in quoting the psalm our Saviour determinately acknowledged it to have proceeded from David the son of Jesse, all controversy respecting the authorship must forthwith cease: the truth of what he has uttered cannot be called in question. But on the other hand it can never be the part of true reverence to draw from his words an inference which they will not legitimately bear; still less to invest that inference with the sacred authority which really belongs to our Lord's own words alone. And therefore when reasons of considerable force lead us to the conclusion that the psalm is of far later date, we are bound to inquire whether the hypothesis that the psalm was written by a subsequent representative of David's house be not thoroughly consistent with the truth of all that our Lord uttered. It may perhaps be fairly allowed that the name David could in our Lord's question be hardly construed so widely as in Heb. iv. 7, so as to embrace the whole of the Psalter; but is there any sufficient reason why it should not be taken as including all those descendants of the original David who figure in the gospel genealogy as the heirs of David's line?

The admissibility of the view already maintained in this work respecting the authorship of this and other psalms which bear the name of David in their superscriptions will be best tested by examining whether it lead to any improbable result. Let the case then be fairly stated, the correctness of the view being for the moment assumed. David the son of Jesse, the psalmist-king of Israel, bequeaths to the Israelitish church more than sixty psalms, two-thirds of which are expressly arranged by himself for public holy use. They bear his name in their superscriptions; and, taken as a whole, they are largely pervaded by the hope which he entertained, that, according to the promise made him by God, the future Messiah, the everlasting king of Israel, should spring out of his loins. After the original psalms of David had been to some extent complemented by the productions of the Levites who ministered in the temple, the strain is at different times taken up by some of the more eminent of David's own descendants; by Hezekiah, by Josiah, by Zerubbabel; who, cherishing their ancestor's hopes and breathing their ancestor's spirit, and viewing themselves as the heirs of the promise made to him and as intermediate links in the genealogical chain between him and the Great Descendant in whom the promise was to be fulfilled, treat their own productions as substantially his, and entitle them like his, "Psalms of David." As such they are collected into the **Psalter** and go down to posterity: the traditional knowledge respecting their actual authors is gradually lost, and so the "Psalms of David," whether composed by David himself or by one of his descendants, stand, as indeed was intended, on the same footing. It is not unlikely that in popular belief they all passed for David's own compositions: whether it were so or not we have no means of ascertaining, nor is our ignorance on this point a matter of moment. Now in one of the later of these "Psalms of David" the psalmist speaks of the future Messiah as his Lord. That psalm our Saviour, in conversing with the learned Jews who had sought to entangle him in his talk, selects as his theme. He asks how Christ can stand to the same person in the double relation of Lord and Son. It is necessary to his argument that he should assume that psalm to have been written by his own ancestor; but it is not necessary that he should define whether that ancestor were David or some later descendant. He therefore speaks of the author of the psalm, broadly, as David: the Jews would have spoken of him in like manner: to have spoken of him otherwise would have been to open a question which was not to the point. Human intercourse in language could not be carried on if precision were always needed in every particular. We may fairly speak of the sun's rising and setting even to an auditor less informed than ourselves respecting the true motions of the solar system. The validity of our Saviour's argument was not affected by the circumstance that the psalm to which he referred was probably composed by Zerubbabel; and this being the case, he styled the author of the psalm David as legitimately as the psalm itself bore the name of David in the superscription. He argued in short from the superscription, and so, it may be, acknowledged and confirmed its authority; but he did not criticize or interpret it.

The subject and authorship of the psalm being thus sufficiently determined, we proceed to a few critical remarks on its plan and contents.

The analogy of other psalms would lead us *a priori* to expect that in the central verse we should find the marrow of the whole. And accordingly on examining the Hebrew text as arranged by the modern critical editors[1], we find that while all the other verses consist of two lines, v. 4 is distinguished by a threefold division; while in respect of the subject-matter, the central character of that verse is perhaps even yet more strongly marked by the circumstance that it records the oath which God has sworn:

> The LORD hath sworn, and will not repent,
> Thou art a priest for ever
> After the order of Melchizedek.

Thus is Melchizedek, the king of Salem, and priest of the most high God, made a type of Him in whom the kingly and priestly offices were to be united for evermore. In the primitive simplicity of patriarchal times the two offices had been frequently combined in the same person. It is probable that at the first the same natural law which had, before the name king

---

[1] Kennicott, Jahn, Rogers; whose authority I follow in making v. 3 consist of but two lines, in opposition to the arrangement given by the Jewish accentuators. I would not indeed to the judgment of the former attach too much weight; yet it will be remembered that *they*, in adopting their own arrangement, were not influenced by any ulterior views of the general structure of the psalm. Render v. 3 thus:

> Thy people shall be as free-will gifts in the day of thy power, in the beauties of holiness:
> Beyond that of the womb of the morning shall be to thee the dew of thy youth.

was heard, designated the head of the family as the one to whom the rest were to pay obedience, had also, before the institution of a special order of priesthood, marked out the head of the family as the fitting person to present the devotions of the rest before the throne of God; and even after kings and priests had appeared whose rule or ministration extended beyond the limits of a single family, the identity of the ruler in things civil and the minister in things sacred was in some degree perpetuated. In the history and institutions of the Israelites the distinction between the two offices had been clearly and purposely brought out; but the very object of this was that when in Jesus Christ all contradictions were once more reconciled, the new unity might be recognized not as the unity of confusion, not yet as the unconscious unity proceeding from non-development of difference, but as the higher divine unity presupposing a manifoldness of relations and yet harmoniously embracing them all. The Messiah, while he appeared as the representative of men before the throne of God, was also, as the representative of God, to assert universal dominion over men; being thus the mediator between God and men in their mutual relation to each other.

This union of royalty and priesthood in the Messiah, distinctly announced in v. 4, lies at the root of all the doctrine contained in the other verses; the general theme of the psalm being not the triumphs of Christ in his own person, but rather those which God should grant to him in the person of his Church. The lot of Christ and his Church being the same, the ransomed people, sharing in the royalty divinely conferred upon their representative priest, will rule and triumph even in the very midst of their enemies. Vv. 1—3 announce the source of the prospects that await them: **vv.** 5—7 delineate their career of victory.

That this is the correct interpretation of the psalm may be **proved from our** Lord's answer to the high-priest, **when bidden** declare whether he were the Christ, the **Son of God.** His words were these: "Thou hast said: nevertheless I say unto you, Hereafter shall ye see the Son of man sitting on **the** right hand of power, and coming in the clouds of heaven[1]." The **reference** in these words to **v.** 1 of the psalm before us is sufficiently obvious; **and** although the "coming in the clouds of heaven" may denote the final coming at the day of judgment, it can hardly be doubted that the "sitting on the right hand of power" **sets** forth the glorification of **Christ** during the entire period commencing with his death, resurrection, and ascension into heaven. This is indeed distinctly expressed **in** the Greek phrase improperly rendered in our English Version *hereafter*, but more strictly signifying *from this time forward*. How then, we may ask, during **the** period of his heavenly reign, was the Jewish high-priest, an unbelieving man, **to see** him sitting on the **right** hand of power? The **answer is clear.** He was to see him not in his own personal glory above, but as represented in his Church below; and the marvellous **successes** of the Christian Church from the great day of Pentecost onward might well furnish proof to all of the majesty of Him who had been crucified.

The **words of** the psalm itself are, however, almost equally **decisive.** For after the exaltation of Christ to God's right hand has been announced in **v. 1,** there follows in v. 2, "The LORD shall send the **rod** of thy strength *out of Zion.*" The Hebrew term here rendered

---

[1] Matth. xxvi. 64.

rod denotes the rod not of government but of victory over resistance[1]; and it is represented as sent forth out of Zion, not as though either the local Jerusalem or the Christian Church on earth were the source of strength to One who was himself seated at God's right hand above, but because it was in the Zion of the New Covenant, the Christian Church, that the victorious might of Christ was to be manifested abroad. Thence it would issue forth to the eyes of the world, though the secret fountain might exist above; and even the sceptic, whatever might be his views respecting the personal exaltation of the risen Saviour to the right hand of God, would be compelled to own that the Christian faith had obtained a remarkable victory over the established religions of the earth. It is accordingly in the history of the Christian Church that we trace the fulfilment of that divine charter of conquest, "Rule thou (or rather, 'Subdue thou') in the midst of thine enemies." Whether in countries where Christianity is professed as the religion of the people, or in lands avowedly heathen, it has been in the very heart of her enemies that the Church has in all ages gained her most remarkable triumphs; boldly pushing forward her work of evangelization abroad even when most furiously assailed at home, and everywhere finding in the hearts of men a new base of operations from which by the grace of God her influence may extend itself, with the invariable result that her efforts, so far from impairing, serve rather to draw forth and nurture her strength.

As it is thus the Church that will prove the instrument whereby Christ will subdue the world, we have in v. 3 the prophetical representation of his people, in the day of his power,—the whole period from the Ascen-

---

[1] Cf. Isai. x. 5; Ezek. vii. 11; Micah vi. 9.

sion to the **Day** of Judgment,—offering themselves **as** freewill gifts to be employed in his service, as numerous and as fair (after that by grace their filthy rags have been **exchanged for the** beauties **of** holiness) **as** the dewdrops **on the morning** grass. They have run unto him, their appointed leader and commander, because of the glory which the Holy One of Israel hath laid upon him; and he their king and priest has made them kings and priests, like himself, unto God and his Father[1].

The cause of Christ and his people having been **thus** identified, we **pass to** the description in vv. 5—7 of the career of victory that shall ensue. The **imagery,** in which Christ appears as a warrior pressing on **with** resistless prowess to the work of conquest, and crushing all **that** oppose his path, **is** probably **drawn** from the history of **Samson,** to whom indeed **much** of the description **would be** literally applicable. How entirely figurative is the language of the entire psalm in respect **of** the subject of which it treats, is evident from the **circumstance** that while **v.** 1, which **speaks of** Christ's exaltation, represents him as raised to **the right hand** of God, v. 4, which delineates his career of conquest, reverses the position: "The Lord at thy right hand." The last verse, "He **shall** drink, &c." (which can not **with any** propriety **be** explained of Christ's passion) only becomes intelligible when **it is** understood that the career **of victory** here described **is really** that of the Church, and when a tacit reference to the events in the history **of** Samson is assumed. **As** Samson, after **slaying** a thousand Philistines with the jawbone of an **ass,** found himself ready to perish for thirst, and thus, notwithstanding his victory, to fall into the hands of the uncircumcised, **so** must Christ's people expect that even in the very midst of the greatest successes that

[1] Isai. lv. **4, 5**; Rev. i. **5, 6.**

shall be granted to them they will yet frequently be faint for weariness of spirit, and will be tempted even in the hour of victory to yield themselves up to despair. And then they will remember how God at Samson's cry brought forth water for him on the spot, and how his spirit came again and he revived; and they will learn that even "in the way," in the road along which it has been their task vigorously to press, God will provide for them a "brook," supplies of his grace whereof they may drink, that so refreshed they may lift up their heads to further exertions in their pursuit; the same God, who at their right hand smites down their foes before them, knowing also their inward weakness, and delivering them from the temptations of their own hearts within as well as from the fury of the world without.

When we compare the boundless magnificence of the prospects which this psalm opens out with the depressed condition of the Jewish nation at the time at which it was written, and take also into account the remarkable concentration of the psalmist's thoughts on the future Messiah as the Great Priest-King through whom God's people were to subdue the opposing world, we may question whether even the sacred writings themselves exhibit any more striking instances of earnestness of faith. It is also worthy of note that more frequent reference is made in the New Testament to this psalm than to any other passage of the older Scriptures. It is directly quoted no fewer than eight times[1]; but the number of these quotations will of itself convey but a very inadequate impression of the extent to which its language is more or less directly there embodied[2].

---

[1] Matt. xxii. 44; Mark xii. 36; Luke xx. 42, 43; Acts ii. 34; Heb. i. 13; v. 6; vii. 17, 21.

[2] Reference has been already made to Matth. xxvi. 64. Among other passages may be mentioned Mark xvi. 19; Rom.

PSALMS CXI, CXII.

The formal arrangement of these two psalms is the same. Each contains ten verses, of which the first eight consist of two, the last two of three lines each; and the twenty-two lines of which each psalm is thus made up commence with the twenty-two successive letters of the Hebrew alphabet. But the resemblance between the psalms does not end here. In several instances the language of particular verses in the one is made to harmonize with that of the corresponding verses in the other. Thus the expression "his righteousness endureth for ever," used in Psalm cxi. 3 of God, is applied in Psalm cxii. 3 to the God-fearing man; the meaning here being, not that the man described shall necessarily *continue righteous* for ever, but that the righteous man, because of his righteousness, shall himself continue for ever, and that so righteousness shall obtain an enduring reward[1]. In v. 4 the words which are in the one psalm applied to God are in like manner again transferred in the other to the godly. In v. 7 of both psalms the leading idea is that of *sureness;* in v. 8, that of *stedfastness;* and thus the correspondence between the details of the psalms is sufficiently sustained.

The general contents of this pair of psalms are easily stated. The faithfulness and mercy displayed by God in rescuing the Jews from captivity and restoring them to their own land induced them to take, in Psalm cxi, a retrospect of that faithfulness and mercy which he had displayed towards them from the earliest period

---

viii. 34; 1 Cor. xv. 24 seqq.; Eph. i. 20—22; Heb. i. 3; viii. 1; x. 12, 13; and also Rev. xix. 11—16, which is however principally drawn from Psalm xlv.

[1] The phrase *his righteousness*, which is thus a circumlocution for "the righteous man," might perhaps be compared with the modern titles of honour, *his majesty, his grace,* &c.

of their history. They praised him for that his covenant, his precepts, and his purposes were alike unchanging. As Psalm cxi. thus set forth the praise of God, so Psalm cxii, which sprang from it, was made to set forth the blessedness of the God-fearing man; the two psalms together thus inculcating the lesson "Be ye merciful, as your Father also is merciful[1]." It may be useful to compare Psalm cxii. 4, "Unto the upright there ariseth light, &c." with Psalm xcvii. 11, and with Isaiah lviii. 7, 8.

PSALM CXIII.

A LIVELY psalm of praise to the Lord, who though high and lifted up, condescends to favour the lowly, regarding it as his peculiar employment to advocate their cause, and to conduct them from the dust to glory. Its contents may be compared with those of the songs of Hannah and of Mary[2]; from the former of which indeed the three concluding verses are partly borrowed. We may also compare Isaiah lvii. 15, "Thus saith the high and lofty One that inhabiteth eternity, whose name is Holy; I dwell in the high and holy place, with him also that is of a contrite and humble spirit, to revive the spirit of the humble, and to revive the heart of the contrite ones;" although in the language of the psalm before us explicit regard is had only to the outward poverty, not to the inward penitence of the person visited with divine favour.

An analysis of the psalm will establish more fully which sentiment in it should be regarded as the leading theme. In the general structure the relation of the

---

[1] Luke vi. 36. Cf. also the quotation of Psalm cxii. 9, at 2 Cor. ix. 9; especially in connexion with the context, 2 Cor. ix. 8.

[2] 1 Sam. ii. 1—10; Luke i. 46—55.

verses to each other is the same as in Psalm xx. The first part is formed of vv. 1—4, the after-part of vv. 7, 8, crowned by v. 9 as the conclusion of the whole. The emphatic verses are thus vv. 5, 6, which should be rendered as follows:

> Who is like the LORD our God
> (SO EXALTED IN DWELLING!
> SO CONDESCENDING IN SURVEY!)
> Whether in heaven or in earth?

And of these four introverted lines the main force is evidently concentrated in the second and third[1]; the purport of the two verses being that as none can be compared unto God in respect of the heavenly majesty wherein he dwells, so also has he no equal in respect of that watchful mercy wherewith he cares for even the meanest of his earthly creatures.

There can be little doubt that the psalm was composed in immediate reference to the gradual restoration of the prosperity of the Jewish people after the return from the Babylonish captivity; and in the barren woman, made to dwell in a house and to be a joyful mother of children, the Targumist rightly recognized the Church of Israel. But lately she had sat solitary, spreading forth her hands and finding none to comfort her: she was now once more established in her appointed dwelling-place, and made a name and a praise among the nations of the earth. We may of course understand the psalm to be substantially put into the mouth of the Church of every age, comparing the prophecy of Isaiah, liv. 1 seqq. That we cannot however in vv. 7, 8, particularize the poor and needy man as Israel, but must understand those verses to give utterance to a more general truth, seems to follow from the

---

[1] Cf., for the introversion, the central verse of Psalm lxviii.

words "that he may set him...*with the princes of his people,*" which as applied to Israel would be destitute of any precise meaning. The words "that he may set him with princes" are taken from Hannah's hymn: the following words "with the princes of his people" are apparently (so to speak) an after-thought of the psalmist, introduced to add force to the previous image.

PSALMS CXIV—CXVII.

That a close connexion subsists in this part of the Psalter between several consecutive psalms terminating with Psalm cxviii, may be fairly inferred from the circumstance that of them was composed that *Hallel* or Hymn of Praise which was regularly sung by the Jews of later times at their principal feasts, and which is therefore usually supposed to be the hymn recorded in the Gospels to have been sung by our Lord and his disciples after the eating of the Last Supper.

The traditions respecting the number of psalms constituting the Hallel differ, like all Rabbinic traditions, considerably from each other. According to the best account, it comprised Psalms cxiii—cxviii; and was sung at the beginning of the month, at the feast of the dedication, and at the feasts of the passover, of weeks, and of tabernacles. It was divided into two portions; the one consisting of Psalms cxiii, cxiv, the other of the four remaining psalms; and at the passover the former portion was sung before commencing the meal, the latter after drinking the last cup. And here it becomes us to remark that if these psalms had originally not only a mutual connexion, but also a festal character, it is easily conceivable that the employment of them might be subsequently deemed appropriate at all the more solemn feasts; while yet we should still have to gather from internal evidence alone **the** knowledge of the occasion at which they were in the first instance produced.

We turn therefore from the traditions of the Jews to an **examination** of the psalms themselves. And here the first noticeable circumstance respecting them is that each of the three psalms cxv, cxvi, cxvii. terminates with the word Hallelujah, "Praise ye the LORD;" while the same word **is prefixed to each of** the three psalms cxi, cxii, cxiii. This shews sufficiently the appropriateness of the name Hallel, "Praise," **as** a designation for the whole series; while it also suggests that it may be with Psalm cxi. that the series may be most properly reckoned to begin. Each of the eight psalms **beginning with** Psalm cxi. **and** ending with Psalm cxviii. would indeed be well fitted to form a portion of a composite hymn of praise.

When however we pass the several subjects of these psalms under review, it is not so far back as Psalm cxi, or even as Psalm cxiii, that it becomes easy to discover any determinate traces of connexion. The claims therefore of Psalms cxi, cxii, cxiii. to be reckoned as belonging to the series we cannot definitely either deny or allow. But, on the other hand, that from Psalm cxiv. onward a connexion **exists seems** to admit of sufficient proof. It is to the long concluding psalm, Psalm cxviii, that our attention must here be primarily and mainly directed. Of the importance of **this** psalm there can be little doubt. It stands out with the same prominence from those by which it is preceded as the great personal epinikion of David, Psalm xviii, and the grand festival anthem, Psalm lxviii, in the earlier portions of the Psalter. Moreover, as regards its position, it is separated from the one of these by exactly one hundred, from the other by exactly fifty places; and that **this is chiefly** due to a designed contrivance on the part of the final editor of the Psalter we can scarcely doubt when we remember the importance attached by the Jews to combinations of numbers. There are other indications of a spirit of numerical contrivance on the part of the collectors of the Fourth and Fifth Books; viz. the provision that the series of Advent-psalms in Book IV. should terminate with Psalm c; the separation of Psalm cxix. from Psalm xix. by exactly one hundred places, these being the two psalms which set forth the excellence of the divine law; and again, the provision that the whole number of psalms should amount to exactly one hundred and fifty. We may assume then that it was intended that the importance of Psalm cxviii. should be marked by the place which it occupies. We shall, on arriving at it, find that it was composed for the occasion of the laying of the foundation of the second temple. It thus stands in appropriate correspondence with Psalm lxviii, which was composed for the occasion of the festival at which the materials for the first temple were collected and the temple-site inaugurated. Now it will be remembered that Psalm lxviii. was preceded by three introductory psalms, Psalms lxv—lxvii, in which were respectively celebrated the sovereignty of God over the material universe, the divine work of redemption, and the divine spread of the knowledge of God's truth through enlightening and sanctifying grace. To those three psalms the psalms by which Psalm cxviii. is·preceded are strictly analogous; although the insertion of a supplementary psalm has increased the number from three to four. Psalm cxiv, to which Psalm cxv. must be regarded as appended, answers to Psalm lxv; Psalm cxvi. to Psalm lxvi; Psalm cxvii. to Psalm lxvii. Thus much will suffice for a brief indication of the reason of the positions which they occupy: we must now proceed to speak of them singly and in order.

First then, Psalm cxiv. sets forth the sovereignty of the God of Jacob over all the works of creation. The history selected as a vehicle for the conveyance of this truth—the history of the liberation of Israel from Egypt—was probably chosen with reference to the more recent deliverance of the Jews from their long captivity in the land of Babylon; yet it forms little more than the mere outward drapery in which the real substance of the psalm is clothed. Mention is indeed expressly made in v. 2 both of the tribe of Judah in particular and of Israel in general; and that designedly, for the purpose of declaring more distinctly that it was the God of Judah and of Israel, and none other, whom the elements of nature obeyed. The royal tribe and the chosen nation have each their distinctive glory: Judah being here styled God's sanctuary, or 'holiness,' as being the embryo Shiloh, to whom, in due time, the gathering of the people was to be, and whose claim to that honour was to be anticipatorily indicated by the eventual establishment of God's visible dwelling-place at Jerusalem; while Israel is in like manner designated God's dominion, as being the people by his visible protection and deliverance of whom God was anticipating the assertion of his own dominion over the nations of the earth. But it is in the following verses that the more proper subject of the psalm breaks forth. And here we should remark the elegance and force of the poetical arrangement by which the name of God is purposely withheld till the last verse but one. Through all the earlier portion of his song the psalmist playfully refrains from giving utterance to the truth which yet his tale sufficiently proclaims. The waves of the Red Sea retire to make way for the Israelites on their march: what can be the cause of their retirement? The rushing waters of the Jordan stand on an heap for the people of Israel to pass over: who arrested their course? Sinai is in a smoke while the people congregate round its base, and quakes with unusual agitation: who commanded its quaking? At length the answer comes. The cause, the sufficient cause of all those convulsions is God's all-holy presence; for He who has vouchsafed his presence in the midst of his chosen people is lord also of the entire universe; mountains and seas, rocks and streams, all are subject to him; he created them, and he can change them, nor is there aught amongst them that must not acknowledge the absolute sovereignty of his power.

The historical reminiscences introduced into this psalm would obviously render it an appropriate hymn for the passover-season. Yet it by no means necessarily follows that it was for the feast of the passover that it was originally written.

Psalm cxv. may be not inaptly described as a controversial supplement to Psalm cxiv; appended to it as a protest against the idolatry into which the Israelites had fallen before the Babylonish captivity. Its purport is that the LORD alone is the true sovereign of the universe; and that in that dignity none of the false objects of heathen adoration must be imagined to share with him. It may thus be said to embody the substance of Isaiah xl. 12 seqq. The connexion of the two psalms is outwardly testified by the circumstance that, unlike any other two consecutive psalms from Psalm cxi. to Psalm cxviii. inclusive, they are not parted from each other by a Hallelujah (Praise ye the LORD). Indeed in seventy-one Hebrew manuscripts, and in the Septuagint and all the versions derived from it, including the Syriac, they are joined together as one psalm. And although this affords no sufficient ground for disregarding the more ordinary Hebrew division and numbering, it nevertheless furnishes abundant illustration of the extent to which the two psalms have been practically associated, notwithstanding their *apparent* diversity of subjects.

The psalm is symmetrical, or nearly so, in its structure. It may be divided into five parts, ranged backwards and forwards from the centre; viz. vv. 1—3, the opening; vv. 4—7, terminating with the three-line verse, v. 7; vv. 8—11, the central portion; vv. 12—15, commencing with the three-line verse, v. 12; and vv. 16—18, the conclusion. Of these, vv. 8—11 set forth the Lord as the true object of trust: vv. 4—7 are taken up with exposing the utter vanity of idols, vv. 12—15 with repeating, again and again, the assurance of the blessings which the Lord will bestow on those that are content to trust him, and with proclaiming the privilege of being the blessed of Him who is the only true Maker of heaven and of earth. This mention of heaven and earth suggests the further sentiment of v. 16; in which there is an evident allusion to the restoration of the land of God's promise to the Israelites after the captivity; the very possession of that land by Israel being a witness to the glory of Him to whom alone the heavens on high and indeed the whole universe pertain. The two subsequent verses may be viewed as naturally springing out of the Hallelujah with which the psalm finally closes; and here again there is a manifest reference to the political revival of the Israelites as a nation, their resuscitation from their seventy years' sleep and consequent redemption from the death by which they had been well-nigh overtaken. These verses form the natural transition to Psalm cxvi; and the sentiments in them may be also compared with those in Psalms vi, xxx, lxxxviii, and in Psalm cxviii. 17, 18.

Psalm cxvi. is emphatically a psalm of redemption. Reading it in the English translation, one might not unreasonably conjecture it to have been written by King Hezekiah after his recovery from sickness; not only on account of its general subject, but also on account of the easy relation in which v. 9 would then stand to Isaiah xxxviii. 18—20, vv. 10, 11 to ibid. 10, 11, vv. 18, 19 to ibid. 20—22, and also the expressions in v. 16, "thy servant, and the son of thine handmaid," to those in v. 16 of Psalm lxxxvi, of which last we have already recognized Hezekiah as the author. But to all such conjectures respecting the authorship of the psalm a single perusal of it in the original Hebrew is absolutely fatal. The Chaldaisms of the language lie beyond the reach of dispute, and are more numerous than in almost any other piece of similar length throughout the Psalter; and to the Chaldean age therefore the psalm must manifestly be assigned. The speaker in it is the Church of the Redeemed, as typically represented in the first instance by the Jewish nation restored from its Babylonish captivity. The immediate "land of the living" was to them the restored land of their inheritance, the "rest" unto which their soul had returned after that God had "loosed" their "bonds;" and they were now about to pay their vows in the presence of all God's people, or rather to prepare the way for the payment of them, by rearing again the sacred house of the presence of God and of their national worship. The use of the first person singular throughout the psalm may be compared with the similar use of it in the corresponding hymn of redemption, Psalm lxvi; many of the sentiments of which are indeed here virtually repeated: cf. v. 3 with lxvi. 11; vv. 4—7 with ibid. 17—20; v. 8 with ibid. 9; v. 10 with ibid. 16; vv. 14, 17 with ibid. 13, 15. It may, however, at the same time be allowable to suppose that the writer, designing to represent the restoration of the Jewish people under the figure of the recovery of a single person from sickness, bethought him of the historical deliverance from death which had been vouchsafed to Hezekiah, and on this account purposely imitated the language of the records of that date. The resemblances of the present psalm to Psalm lxxxvi. and Isaiah xxxviii. would thus be sufficiently explained. Without, however, confining himself to these, the psalmist laid also the older psalms of David under contribution: cf. vv. 3, 4 with xviii. 4—6; v. 7 with xiii. 6; v. 8 with lvi. 13; v. 11 with xxxi. 22. The large extent to which the tenses of the verbs in the earlier portion of the psalm have been unwarrantably altered in all the ordinary translations may render the following version acceptable: it will also shew clearly the general structure of the whole. The usual Hebrew parallelisms are here few in number; and the psalm is mainly composed of long lines which the Jewish editors have improperly divided.

1 I am well pleased that the LORD should hear the voice of my supplications;
2 For he hath inclined his ear to me; and as long as I live will I call.
3 The cords of death compassed me round, and the straits of hell reached to me:
I shall reach to trouble and heaviness, and on the name of the LORD will I call:
Ah prithee, LORD! deliver thou my soul!
5 Gracious is the LORD and righteous: yea, our God is merciful:
6 The Lord preserveth the simple: I was brought low; yet will he help me.
7 Return, O my soul, unto thy rest, for the LORD hath dealt bounteously with thee;
8 For thou hast delivered my soul from death, mine eyes from tears, my feet from falling.

9 I shall walk before the LORD in the lands of the living.
10 I have believed, to the end that I might speak:
Though indeed I was afflicted very sorely;
11 Indeed I said in my haste, "All mankind¹ is a delusion."

¹ Or, *All manhood*: not as E. V. *All men*; in which case the Hebrew article would not be required.

12 What shall I render to the LORD for all his bounteous dealings with me?
13 The cup of salvation will I take, and on the name of the LORD will I call.
14 My vows will I pay to the LORD, yea in the presence now of all his people:
15 Precious in the sight of the LORD is the death of his saints.
   Ah see thou¹, LORD! for I am thy servant!
   I am thy servant, the son of thine handmaid, thou hast loosed my bonds:
17 To thee will I offer the sacrifice of thanksgiving, and on the name of the LORD will I call.
18 My vows will I pay to the LORD, yea in the presence now of all his people,
19 In the courts of the **LORD's house**, in the midst of thee, O Jerusalem.
   Praise ye the LORD.

The **psalm** evidently consists of a **strophe and** antistrophe, separated by a central piece **or mesode**. The **theme of** the strophe is God's bounteous dealings with **the worshipper**: that of the antistrophe the worshipper's thankful return to God. In the mesode the worshipper contrasts the impatience with which in **the** midst of his affliction he **had** given vent to an exclamation of despair with the faith which now prompted him to pour forth this **hymn** as **a tribute** of praise to God's loving-kindness. In his fear and forgetfulness he had suffered himself to murmur (with David in Psalm xxxix. 4, 5) that all mankind was a thing of nought, that human life was a vanity; but he had now been taught to believe that there were truly lands of the living, in which God's faithful servants might joyfully walk before him; and in this conviction he could not but utter a song, **and** proclaim aloud **the** lessons of his own experience. And these **lessons would in the** psalmist's day be more striking if drawn from the national, or rather, **churchly life of** Israel than from **the private** earthly life of any individual suppliant; **for the prophets had already given** assurance that the former should never end; whereas the latter, even though by God's **mercy it** might be occasionally somewhat prolonged, **was yet** to all appearance ultimately bounded **by the darkness** of the tomb: the gospel had

---

¹ The Hebrew word is **the same** as in v. 4; **but** bears apparently a slightly different meaning.

not yet brought life and immortality to light. We may here seize the opportunity of remarking that the Greek rendering of the former half of v. 10, as quoted by St Paul[1], and as adopted by our English Translators, ἐπίστευσα διὸ ἐλάλησα—"I believed, therefore have I spoken,"—cannot be regarded as grammatically correct: the sentiment conveyed, however, in the Hebrew and in the Greek is substantially the same, viz. that utterance is the result of faith; and the apostle might therefore have made the same use of a correct rendering of the psalmist's words that he has actually made of the version of the LXX.

With regard to the "cup of salvation" of v. 13, there can be little doubt that the original allusion was strictly to the drink-offering of wine, which, according to the Jewish law was combined with the daily meat-offering[2]. In favour of this is the obvious correspondence of the cup in v. 13 to the sacrifice in v. 17; which correspondence is also decisive against the notion that the *cup* of salvation here denotes simply the salvation which the worshipper receives as his *lot*. When the psalm came to be regularly used at the passover, as part of the Hallel, the Jews would naturally and not improperly connect the cup of salvation with that customary festal cup, of which, as he drank, the master of the house blessed God, the Lord of the world, for creating the fruit of the vine. To which cup itself also accrued a new and more sacred significance when our Lord Jesus Christ after his last supper re-imparted it to his disciples with the words, "This cup is the new testament in my blood, which is shed for you."

Psalm cxvii, the shortest, but not on that account the least noticeable composition in the Psalter, is the post-exilic counterpart of Psalm lxvii. It is a hymn

---

[1] 2 Cor. iv. 13.   [2] Numb. xxviii. 7, 8.

of praise to God the Sanctifier. In it the **ultimate gathering of the Gentiles into the Church is seen by the Christian expositor to be** virtually implied; though it is by no means distinctly foretold, and though even the psalmist himself **would** perhaps scarcely have admitted it as a legitimate consequence of his own doctrine. His **was still** the old, exclusive, Israelitish point of **view: thus much** only he knew, **that** the salvation of the world was somehow to be accomplished through the medium of God's dealings with Israel, and that therefore God's mercy to Israel, and the faithfulness with which he would in due time make good his promises to Abraham and David, were blessings for which all **nations** might well be invited to give thanks. The **wondrous restoration of the Jews** from **their** seventy years' captivity was a sufficient **token, to give** it no higher name, that the **promises** had not been forgotten. Nor is **it indeed for** the Christian, even while glorifying God **for his** own admission into the **Church**, or while contemplating the Catholic Church **as** the great present instrument of divine blessing **to the world,** to forget the manner in which the literal Israel of the old covenant was made subservient to God's grand purpose of the universal spread of the knowledge **of** his truth. He will recollect that **it** was of the stock of the literal Israel that his own **Redeemer came, the son of David,** the son of Abraham; born under the law; "a minister *of the circumcision* for the truth of God, to confirm the promises made *unto the fathers*" *of the Jews,* that *so* "the Gentiles might glorify God for his mercy[1]." It is to illustrate this **that St Paul** quotes the present psalm[2]; thus shewing that the "mercy" and "truth" exhibited in the divine dealings under the older covenant were the channels through which God's blessing had streamed

---

[1] Rom. xv. 8, 9.   [2] ibid. 11.

forth upon the Gentile world, and were therefore to be remembered and celebrated with gratitude by all his Christian people.

Nor should **we part** from this psalm without further remarking **that** even in the Old Testament we have more than one instance of a recognition on the part of those who were without the pale of the Church that God's favour to Israel was a source of blessing to themselves. Such were probably to some extent the sentiments of Hiram and the Queen of Sheba, the contemporaries of Solomon; such the experience of Naaman; such the virtual acknowledgments of Nebuchadnezzar and Darius the Mede. They beheld "his merciful kindness" toward his servants of the house of Israel, **and** they praised him accordingly.

PSALM CXVIII.

Four strophes, each of seven verses, together with one additional verse at the end, complete the psalm. I. "I was in distress, and God was my helper" (vv. 1—7)[1]. II. "Enemies compassed me, and God was my deliverer" (vv. 8—14). III. "I was near to death, and God was my saviour" (vv. 15—21). IV. "**His** mercy has now displayed itself, and God is my God" **(vv.** 22—28). In the concluding verse (v. 29) the opening words of the psalm are repeated by way of refrain.

If there **be** cases in which any symbolical importance is to be attached to the number of verses of which psalms consist, it may be worth remarking that the number of verses in David's personal epinikion, Psalm xviii, **was** seven times seven, completed by one in ad-

---

[1] Cf. the quotation **of v.** 6 in Heb. xiii. 6.

dition; that in Israel's epinikion at the close of **David's** reign, Psalm lxviii, five times seven, with no **extra** verse; that in the present psalm four times seven, and again with one verse in addition. The seven-fold seven of Psalm xviii, together with its completing verse, indicated the fullest **degree of** completeness: David had been delivered from the hand of **all** his enemies and **from the hand of Saul,** and the sovereignty of Israel had been **made** hereditary in his house. **On** the other **hand** in Psalm lxviii. the five-fold seven, **with** no extra verse, indicated a degree of incompleteness, five being the half of ten, the unfinished decade; and in fact that psalm belonged to the time when only the materials **for** the temple had been collected, and when the temple itself **was yet uncommenced:** the rearing of the permanent sanctuary, to which **for some time past all** Israelitish national life had been tending, was still only **planned, not in** process of actual accomplishment. The four-fold **seven** of Psalm cxviii, **with** the extra verse, **again** betokens **a** work already effected: **the** captive Israel have been **gathered from the four** quarters of the lands of their dispersion[1]; and, **as we** shall see, the new sanctuary is already in progress which is to mark the fresh dedication of the nation to the service of the Lord their God.

Yet a large number of critics, including even some of the most recent, have not hesitated to treat this **psalm** as the composition of **David**; and they have the **authority of the** Targumist **to** plead in their favour. **They** have however seldom offered much in the way of argument in support of their view, **nor do** they at all agree as to the period of the royal psalmist's life at which they suppose it to have been written. It would in general be a **needless as** well as a wearisome and

---

[1] Cf. Psalm cvii. 3.

profitless task to enter on a formal refutation of untenable views in favour of which so little that is positive has been advanced; but in this instance the prominence of the psalm, the importance which has always for various reasons been justly attached to it, and the extent to which the true interpretation of it, whether historically or prophetically regarded, would be compromised by the admission of the Davidic authorship, will justify a few controversial observations which had otherwise been with advantage omitted.

It is almost fatal to the theory of the psalm having proceeded from David that no superscription is prefixed to it naming David as the **author.** Nowhere, on examining the Davidic psalms, have we found such superscriptions lacking, except only in the case of those few that were manifestly connected with others to which such superscriptions were prefixed. Again, the late place of the psalm in the Psalter indicates a corresponding lateness of date, and naturally leads to the conclusion that it belongs to the period of the return from the captivity. On this it will not be necessary to enlarge: it will be sufficient to observe, that to those who have thus far traced, steadily and uninterruptedly, the arrangement of the different portions of the Psalter, the argument derived from the place occupied by the psalm will carry almost irresistible weight. Again, if the original connexion between Psalm cxviii. and the psalms immediately preceding can be clearly established, the Chaldaisms in the language of Psalm cxvi. will necessarily bring down the date of the rest to the Chaldean age. But it has been already shewn that Psalms cxiv.—cxvii. form the prelude to Psalm cxviii, as Psalms lxv.—lxvii. to Psalm lxviii. In further proof of the connexion we have only to note the parallelism between Psalm cxv. 9, 10, 11 and Psalm cxviii.

2, 3, 4, and the embodiment of the whole substance of Psalm cxvi. in Psalm cxviii. 17. Nay, the recurrence of the same unusual Hebrew words[1] in Psalms cxvi. and cxviii. indicates, not obscurely, an identity of authorship.

When we pass to the internal evidence which Psalm cxviii. itself furnishes, all still tends to negative the hypothesis of a Davidic authorship. Thus the special invitation to the house of Aaron to give thanks (v. 3), although not inappropriate after the return from the captivity when the position of the priesthood became one of greater prominence, is unparalleled in the psalms of David; and if introduced at all, could hardly but have been accompanied by a similar special invitation to the king himself, who does not refrain from referring to himself plainly in other psalms[2]. Again, that the speaker in the psalm is not any single individual, but the entire Israel, is evident from the use of the first person plural in vv. 23—27; but then, on reading v. 9, we naturally inquire, What temptation had Israel in David's time to put any confidence in princes? So also with reference to vv. 10—13: is it historically true that in David's time all nations had compassed Israel about? Lastly, v. 22, "The stone which the builders rejected, &c." seems almost necessarily to imply that the building of the temple had been at least commenced; but this was certainly not the case during any part of David's reign.

What then is the true account of the historical origin of this psalm? The answer is that given by Hengstenberg; and the main arguments by which it is supported may be best presented in his own words. There can be no reasonable doubt that the deliverance for which the psalm gives thanks—"The LORD hath

---

[1] אנה, דחה, מצר

[2] Cf. Psalms xx, xxi, lxi, lxiii.

chastened me sore: but he hath not given me over unto death"—was the deliverance from the Babylonish captivity. That the psalm was composed *immediately after this* deliverance is evident from the fervour of the thanks. That moreover it was destined for use at some important national undertaking appears from the words of v. 25, "Save now, I beseech thee, O Lord: O Lord, I beseech thee, send now prosperity," the coincidence of which with the words of Nehemiah i. 11 (more especially when compared in the Hebrew) shews that they embody the formula ordinarily employed in imploring the divine blessing on such occasions. And v. 22 sufficiently indicates that this undertaking was the laying of the foundation-stone of the temple in the second year of the return. So far we are conducted by the psalm itself. To a yet more definite result we are guided by the passage Ezra iii. 10, 11: "And when the builders laid the foundation of the temple of the Lord, they set the priests in their apparel with trumpets, and the Levites the sons of Asaph with cymbals, to praise the Lord, after the ordinance of David king of Israel. And they sang together by course in praising and *giving thanks unto the* Lord; *because he is good, for his mercy endureth for ever* toward Israel. And all the people shouted with a great shout, when they praised the Lord, because the foundation of the house of the Lord was laid." It is here implied that at the laying of the foundation-stone of the temple a song was sung, the kernel of which consisted of those very words which begin and end the psalm before us. So fresh indeed was the recollection of this that even the author of the Books of Chronicles describes with similar words the contents of the songs sung at the dedication of the first temple[1]. And although the words

---

[1] 2 Chron. v. 13, vii. 3.

in question are found also in Psalms cvi, cvii, cxxxvi, yet the contents of those psalms forbid us to suppose that it is to them that reference can be made; so that we necessarily infer that the words in the Book of Ezra were taken from Psalm cxviii.

To the foregoing observations (which Hengstenberg himself has supplemented by others of more questionable value) we may add that the words of v. 15, "The voice of rejoicing and salvation is in the tabernacles of the righteous," seem to point to a time when the people, but recently returned from captivity, were still for the most part dwelling themselves in tents. V. 9, "It is better to trust in the LORD than to put confidence in princes," is a virtual acknowledgment that Cyrus had been but an instrument in God's hands for the deliverance of Israel, and that it was to God, not to any Chaldean, Median, or Persian sovereign courted apart from him, that they would have to look for a revival of their former national prosperity. The historical occasion of the psalm is further illustrated by the dependence of vv. 14, 28 on Exod. xv. 2: the song of deliverance from Babylonish captivity would naturally borrow some of its strains from Moses' song of deliverance after that the passage of the Red Sea had freed the forefathers of the Israelites from Egyptian bondage. It is at periods of solemn national thanksgiving that men's thoughts especially recur to the records of their early national history: it was thus that the former great festival-psalm, Psalm lxviii, was made in its opening sentence to recall the words used by Moses at the outset of each march through the wilderness.

From these general remarks on the historical origin and purport of the psalm we naturally proceed to more minute inquiries in respect of certain particulars. That verse (v. 22) to which such interest attaches on account of its wondrously prophetical import, "The stone which the builders refused is become the head stone of the corner[1],"—what were the circumstances, if any, to which literal reference is made? The reply, though of necessity more or less conjectural, would be somewhat as follows. The first care of the restored exiles, on the occasion of their primary assemblage at Jerusalem after their return, had been to rebuild the altar. There are good grounds for believing that they had the means of identifying the exact spot on which it had previously stood; and that the new altar occupied the site of the old[2]. When in the next year they proceeded to commence the erection of the temple, we may easily suppose that their limited resources would induce them to plan a building of smaller dimensions than that which Solomon had raised with the wealth of an empire at his command. But in clearing away the ruins and débris of the former edifice (in itself no trifling task), and in excavating for the new foundations, we may suppose that the large foundation-stone on which the corner of Solomon's walls had rested, the chief cornerstone of that magnificent and venerated pile, came unexpectedly to light. To the workmen this was a circumstance of no moment: they would have covered it up again and buried it in oblivion. The priests, however, and the seniors of the people, who remembered Zion in her former glory, regarded it with different eyes. Here was that which they might well designate a rock of ages, undestroyed, uninjured, unremoved, a clear witness to the extent of the site which the holy house of the original temple had actually covered. Here was the very stone which had been

---

[1] Cf. Matth. xxi. 42; Mark xii. 10, 11; Luke xx. 17; Acts iv. 11; 1 Pet. ii. 7.
[2] Cf. my *Ancient Jerusalem*, p. 349.

already immortalized by the greatest of the Hebrew prophets, who in one of his evangelical predictions had treated it as a type of the future Messiah: "Thus saith the Lord God, Behold, I lay in Zion for a foundation a stone, a tried stone, a precious corner stone, a sure foundation[1]." Nay, what a beautiful image did this corner-stone, so unexpectedly rescued from the darkness of the earth, present of the Israelitish nation, so suddenly and marvellously delivered from their captivity in a foreign land! It was no matter for surprise that under such circumstances the priests should have given their voice for enlarging their previous designs, in spite of the smallness of their present resources, and for raising the walls of their new sanctuary on the foundation-stone of the old. The people sided with them; and, in spite of the opposition of the builders, the former dimensions of the temple of Solomon were respected. The building was commenced in the full assurance of faith: by faith the priests and people viewed it as already complete, and proclaimed, in anticipation of the fulfilment of their prayers, that the stone which the builders had refused was become the head-stone of the corner. We may well believe that they consciously attached a figurative import to their words. In that material temple which they had just commenced they beheld the type of a future edifice of universal blessing to the world. This edifice was not to be reared by the worldly ambition, the grasping dominion, and the destructive selfishness of Chaldean monarchs, who, animated by the same spirit in which their forefathers had vainly laboured at the olden tower of Babel, madly imagined that they might render Babylon the corner-stone of universal empire. The Lord's word against Babylon, as uttered by the

---

[1] Isaiah xxviii. 16.

prophet Jeremiah, had spoken explicitly with respect to this: "They shall **not take** of thee a stone for a corner, **nor a stone** for foundations; but thou shalt be desolate **for ever,** saith the LORD[1]." An older divine announcement, which still awaited its fulfilment, had indicated Israel as the chosen channel of blessing. In Jacob, and in Jacob's seed, were all the families of the earth to be blessed[2], **and on** Israel as the corner-stone of blessing **must** the edifice of blessing be divinely reared. Already had the rescue of Israel from national death and oblivion betokened that God's promise had not been **forgotten;** and as the corner-stone of Solomon's temple was a type of Israel, so was Israel in turn a type of Christ, in whom in due time all the promises were **to** culminate; who, in spite of his rejection by **the** unbelieving builders of **his** own nation, was yet, to the astonishment of all, **to** issue forth triumphant from the sepulchre of death wherein he had been laid, the chief corner-stone of the **new** universal household and temple of God. Hence the propriety of the Christian use of this psalm as **an Easter** festival-hymn: the Christian believer, contemplating the resurrection of Christ **as** the already accomplished pledge of his own future deliverance from death, may well acknowledge this to be "the LORD's doing," "marvellous in our eyes."

It may be proper here to observe that to a people rescued like Israel from national perdition, every succeeding **festival** would, in common with **the** day on which the rebuilding of their temple was commenced, **be** in some sort **a** fresh celebration of their marvellous deliverance. On every such day they might not unreasonably exclaim, 'This **day** hath the LORD made:' "It is the Lord's doing that **we, so** long the children **of** captivity, should be **spending this** present day in

[1] Jer. li. 26. [2] Gen. xxviii. 14.

renewing to him our homage on the holy mountain of our former solemnities." Hence this psalm was adopted for use on all the principal Jewish festivals; and it is only on insufficient grounds that some critics have endeavoured to connect it exclusively with one or other of the three great yearly feasts. For the same reason the psalm may be legitimately sung at every Christian season of worship whatsoever; inasmuch as the whole life-time of the Christian Church on earth may be regarded as one great festival wherein Christ's people unite to give thanks that they have, "as lively stones," been "built up a spiritual house, an holy priesthood, to offer up spiritual sacrifices, acceptable to God by Jesus Christ."

As we pass on to the succeeding verses of the psalm, vv. 25, 26, the question arises whether in the familiar words, "Blessed be he that cometh in the name of the LORD," there be any special reference to the Messiah. The manner in which these words are recorded in the New Testament to have been employed, not only by the Jews, but also by our Saviour himself, might at first sight seem to render such a reference probable; and many critics moreover have sought in them the explanation of the title "He that should come"—ὁ ἐρχόμενος—by which the Jews designated the Redeemer whose advent they awaited. But the origin of this phrase, thus applied, can equally well be traced to the prophecy of Malachi[1]. And it must be owned that the more natural interpretation of the above words, when taken in connexion with the rest of the psalm, would be simply this: Blessed in the name of the LORD be *every one* that cometh to worship in this temple. Indeed the plural *you*—"We have blessed *you* out of the house of the LORD"—in the succeeding part of the

[1] Malachi iii. 1.

verse, shews that no single person can be exclusively or specially intended; though the same form of salutation would admit of being individually applied, and even, as was in fact done by the Jewish multitude, to the Messiah himself[1]. The true view of the matter is this: the community had already in vv. 19, 20 viewed themselves as entering the temple-gates: once within those gates, they bid in v. 26 a welcome to all who shall enter after them to join them. The zeal with which any seek to draw others into the household of God is an obvious testimony that they have already themselves gained a standing therein. And in fact this interpretation will be found perfectly to accord with the use made of the words by our Saviour, when having finally declared to the Jews that their house was left unto them desolate, he added, "For I say unto you, Ye shall not see me henceforth, till ye shall say, Blessed is he that cometh in the name of the Lord[2]." From that time forward the Jewish nation were no more to be reckoned God's peculiar people. That gracious longsuffering which had hitherto, in spite of their sins, continued them the exclusive Church of God was now finally withdrawn; and *their* house—for *God's* house it must no longer be called—was left *unto them* desolate. God was now at last building up (upon the True Israel as the corner-stone) the foundation of a new and more extended spiritual fabric. Into this admission must henceforth be sought by all, whether Jew or Gentile, who desired to be everlastingly saved: here were henceforth the true gates of righteousness, the gate of the LORD, into which the righteous should enter; it was on those who came in hither, and on them alone, that God's ministers were henceforth authorized to pro-

---

[1] Matth. xxi. 9; Mark xi. 9; Luke xix. 38; Joh. xii. 13.
[2] Matth. xxiii. 39; Luke xiii. 35.

nounce blessing in his name. Not till the Jews **individually** entered the precincts of that catholic temple, **on an** equality with the redeemed of every other race, not therefore till standing themselves within **those** precincts they were **in a position** to greet **with** blessings all who might **enter after them,** must they henceforth expect **to realize in their** own **experience** those divine promises **of salvation,** which, as an entire **house,** and in their national capacity, they had unhappily **rejected.**

The last verse calling for special remark is **v. 27**; which should be thus rendered[1]:

> The LORD is God; and he **hath** kindled for us the flame
> (Bind the festal sacrifice **with** cords)
> Even unto the **horns of the altar,**

i. e. **even unto the corners of the altar, so** as to consume **the** whole **of the victims that** had been placed upon it. For the illustration of this it should be observed, **that on** several historical occasions God is recorded to have testified **his acceptance of** his people's offerings by himself **sending forth the fire to** consume **them.** It was so at the consecration of Aaron to the priesthood[2]; it **was so on** the occasion of David's sacrifice on the threshing-floor of Ornan[3]; it was so at

---

[1] All the attempts to make the preposition עַד depend on the verb אִסְרוּ have proved unsuccessful. Our E. V. evidently gives no sense. The Targum thus interprets: "Bind the sacrifice with cords, *till it be slain and the blood sprinkled* on the horns of the altar." But how can עַד imply all this? Ewald explains: "**so as to lift** it up to the horns of the altar." But was the sacrifice ever so lifted? According to another explanation חַג is to be taken for a number of victims, collectively viewed: these are to be fastened one to another in so long a row that they shall reach to the altar. But then why should the *horns* of the altar be mentioned? All translators have unfortunately omitted to note that הָאִיר מִזְבֵּחַ is the proper phrase (at any **rate the** post-exilic phrase) for *to kindle fire on an altar;* cf. Mal. i. 10. As regards the interruption of the syntax by the middle line **of the verse,** the student may compare Psalm lxviii. 8, 18, &c.; or in English, Gray's *Bard*, III. 1, the first three lines, "Edward, lo!" &c.

[2] Lev. ix. 24.

[3] 1 Chron. xxi. 26.

the dedication of Solomon's **temple**[1]. Hence the mode by which, through faith, Elijah on Mount Carmel put publicly to the proof the rival claims of the LORD and Baal. It is indeed from the record of the exclamations of the people on that occasion on beholding the fire descend that the opening words of the verse before us are borrowed[2]; for the slight variation between "The LORD, he is the God (Elohim)" as the words stand in the history, and "The LORD is God (El)" as they occur in the psalm, is too unimportant to cause any serious difficulty. It is not indeed recorded that God answered his people's sacrifice by fire at either the foundation or dedication of the second temple; nor in any case could such a fresh fiery answer be well referred to in the present psalm, which must necessarily have been prepared beforehand. But yet the psalmist may have intended to declare by anticipation the certainty that the present devotions of the Israelites would be accepted; and if so, he did this in a phraseology suggested by the fiery answers that God had actually vouchsafed on former occasions. Nor should the symbolical and typical meaning of those fiery answers be overlooked. The fire that went forth from the Lord to consume the proffered sacrifice had been in each case a testimony that the worshipping people were accepted, and that no fire should go forth upon them in vengeance for their sins. And, in like manner, in the manifestations of the divine wrath poured forth upon the Crucified Redeemer of mankind, those that believe are permitted to behold the pledge of their own deliverance from wrath to come. The sacrifice on which the Lord's fire descended was therefore, equally with the corner-stone which the builders rejected, a type of the atoning Saviour. It is a curious circumstance, not perhaps

---

[1] 2 Chron. vii. 1.   [2] 1 Kings xviii. 39.

altogether accidental, that to the victim for sacrifice of v. 27 the Targumist applies the same word by which he designated the boy among the sons of Jesse whom he conceived to be represented by the stone of v. 22; and the deep truth of the identity of Him in whom all the types were fulfilled we need not hesitate to accept, even while rejecting the more fanciful features of the interpretation in which it lies shrouded.

PSALM CXIX.

THE suggestion that the long and unique meditation to which we now proceed should be regarded as the composition of Daniel has been but recently put forward[1]. Yet if internal evidence (and we have here little else on which to depend) is in this instance to be allowed that due weight which in proportion to its copiousness and distinctness we generally feel no scruple in according to it, there seems to remain but little ground for hesitation in recognizing Daniel as the author. He, above all men whose lives are in the Old Testament recorded to us, had in his youth cleansed his way by guarding it according to God's word (cf. v. 9). Cast as a stranger and a pilgrim in a foreign land (vv. 19, 54), yet still assured that God's mercies would be vouchsafed to his servants wheresoever in the wide earth they might dwell (v. 64), he had found God's testimonies far dearer to him than all manner of worldly wealth (vv. 14, 36, 37, 72, 127). Reproached (vv. 22, 23), derided (v. 51), slandered (v. 69), and plotted against (vv. 78, 85, 86, 95, 110, 161) by the proud princes whom he had never wronged, (how vividly does the acknowledgment of the Median presidents and princes rise up before us, that they should find

[1] By Jebb, II. p. 274.

no occasion against Daniel except concerning the law **of** his God!) he **yet** had spoken **of** God's testimonies even **before** kings, **and** had not been ashamed (**v.** 46). He had seen an **end** of all perfection (v. 96); guilty Jerusalem **and** haughty Babylon had during Daniel's life-time, each **in** her turn, yielded up their spoils to their conquerors; but his trust was reposed in God's word, which abideth for ever. To this he remained stedfast; and day by day and night by night **he** unintermittingly persevered in his practice of pious devotion, meditating in God's word, crying for God's help, and praising God's name (vv. **147**, 148, 164). The whole psalm bespeaks **the character of** one who, **like Daniel,** lived in close and habitual communion with **God; one** habitually trained from his youth upwards in secret self-discipline, the peaceful flow of whose saintly career was not marked by the ruggedness which would generally follow, as in the case of St Paul, from sudden conversion, or by the fitfulness attaching to lives that, like David's, have been once disordered by acts of heinous transgression; **one** indeed who was not without spot, who confessed his sin[1], who relied only on God's grace to reclaim him from the many strayings of which he was conscious (v. 176); but yet "a man greatly beloved[2]," one of the pure in heart who might see God, and whom therefore God **numbered,** along with the patriarch Joseph and the evangelist St John, among the special few to whom he partially unlocked the secrets of the times and seasons of the future.

The prophetical office of Daniel would furnish sufficient authority for the reception into the Psalter of any psalm composed by him. In this respect the psalm before us will fall under the same category with Psalm cii, **if** that be assumed to be the composition of the prophet

---

[1] Dan. ix. 20.   [2] Dan. x. 11.

Jeremiah. Both of these psalms moreover were undoubtedly consigned to public use as giving utterance to the devotions of the entire Church of God. Both Jeremiah and Daniel were, in their afflictions, types and representatives of the whole nation of Israel, and thus, indeed, of the Church of God through every age.

The alphabetical arrangement in this psalm is carried out in the same manner as in the Book of Lamentations, only to a yet greater degree. The whole is divided into twenty-two portions of eight verses each; and the several verses of the respective portions all commence with the same Hebrew letter. This artifice of arrangement was doubtless partly designed as an aid to the learner who, exercising himself daily in God's statutes, should wish to commit the whole to memory. The same sententious character which pervades the other alphabetical psalms forces itself here also at once upon us. Each separate verse possesses a certain completeness in itself. But to the proposition frequently put forth, and lately iterated by Hengstenberg, that the psalm consists of a collection of individual sayings, and that there is no room for attempting to discover any connexion, or to trace any consecutive train of thought, we must demur. It is even in itself not easily conceivable that a piece requiring so much care in the elaboration should prove a mere compendium of unconnected sayings, a mere aggregation of units. Without necessarily conforming to the law of a strictly logical consecutiveness, the different parts of a meditation may yet be moderately connected; and it seems reasonable to suppose that in the working out of each separate strophe a train of thought would generally suggest itself to the psalmist's mind. In some indeed of the strophes (as for example the 12th, Lamed, and 13th, Mem) such a connexion of the several verses is plainly discernible, and **stands** out beyond the reach **of** dispute.

Nor is this **all.** The very structure of each strophe, when fairly examined, will generally shew that its eight several **verses** cannot be regarded as independent of each other. For in this psalm the more ordinary law of Hebrew parallelism does not generally obtain. **The** two clauses of the same verse do not, as a rule, mutually correspond. Instances may indeed be found; thus in verse 105,

> Thy word is a lamp unto my feet,
> And a light unto my path;

but they are nevertheless here comparatively rare. **Instead** therefore of **this,** we have **an** arrangement by which the pair of parallel clauses **(for** within certain bounds **the** principle of parallelism is still carried out) must **be** respectively searched for in the same strophe, **but in** different **verses.** Sometimes **two** entire verses will be found to correspond to each other: sometimes the order of correspondence is more complicated. The fourth strophe **will furnish** a favourable example of the **kind of** arrangement which will be found to prevail **more** or less **in each** separate strophe of the psalm. We **therefore** here exhibit it, with the corresponding clauses **marked by** the initial word of the **one** being ranged exactly **even with** that **of the other.**

> My **soul** cleaveth unto the dust:
>   Quicken thou me according to thy word.
>   I have declared my ways, and thou heardest me:
>   Teach me thy statutes.
>   Make me to understand the way of thy precepts:
>   So shall I talk of thy wondrous works.
> My soul melteth for heaviness:
>   Strengthen thou me according unto thy **word.**

> Remove from me the way of lying:
>   And grant me thy law graciously.
> I have chosen the way of truth:
>   Thy judgments have I laid before me.
>   I have stuck unto thy testimonies:
>   O Lord, put me not to shame.
>   I will run the way of thy commandments,
>   When thou shalt enlarge my heart.

It is evident that this principle of arrangement, even though but partially carried out, precludes the theory of an original want of connexion between the verses.

Neither again is it true that the several strophes of the psalm have no mutual bond of union. The order of the themes respectively treated in them is undoubtedly not apparent at first sight; but this is no more than might be fairly anticipated in a psalm of an almost purely meditative character; the more especially as the logical connexion of the strophes is to some extent overshadowed and so obscured by the artifice of the alphabetical arrangement. It will be therefore expedient to give here an outline of the contents of the psalm. The first strophe (Aleph) is the exordium. Like Psalm i. at the commencement of the Psalter, it pronounces blessedness on those who walk in God's law. In the succeeding strophes we have the successive stages in the pilgrimage of such towards perfection. The second strophe (Beth) furnishes the starting-point: "Wherewithal shall a young man cleanse his way?" By guarding it according to God's word. So the pilgrim begins his career; but at the very outset he throws himself in prayer upon God's mercy; for he is a stranger (str. 3, Gimel), and in much affliction (str. 4, Daleth), and needs a strength beyond his own in which to journey forward. And now follows the direct prayer for divine instruction (str. 5, He); in the receipt of which the pilgrim will be able, in singleness of heart, to stand, unabashed, in the presence either of his reproachers or of his earthly superiors (str. 6, Vau). His course must indeed be one of perseverance; he must continually himself remember God, he must continually pray **that God will** remember him (str. 7, Zain); and it is thus that he will learn more and more to recognize the Lord as his portion (str. 8, Cheth). And now godly experience begins to yield her lessons; and the pilgrim looks back upon his past career, and acknowledges the goodness of God's dealings with him, **and the** spiritual blessedness of his temporal affliction (str. 9, Teth). Yet he must continue to prove himself, and to pray that his heart be sound in God's statutes (str. 10, Jod); for after all, how far is he still from the **goal!** When will the full fruition of the Lord's salvation visit him? When will he be rescued from the dangers in which he is hourly environed? His present condition is to all outward appearance one of extreme peril: viewed from without, he is well-nigh exhausted **by** what he has had to endure; and the efforts of his enemies to destroy him have already only just failed of success (str. 11, Caph).

Here the climax of the delineation of the suppliant's pilgrimage is reached. We have arrived at the centre of the psalm, and the thread of the connexion is purposely broken off. The substance of the first eleven strophes has evidently been, "Hitherto hath the Lord brought me: shall it be that I now perish?" To this the eleven succeeding strophes make answer, "The Lord's word changeth not; and in spite of all evil forebodings, the Lord will perfect concerning me the work that he hath already begun."

Here then is the pilgrim's comfort, the comfort of sure hope. The Lord's word changeth not. It is settled in heaven: its unfailing truth is attested even by the abiding of the earth according to his ordinance (str. 12, **Lamed**). God's law has not deceived the affections which the pilgrim fastened upon it (str. 13, **Mem**): God's word has not failed to guide aright his feet (str. 14, **Nun**): **on God** therefore he will still lean for support (str. 15, **Samech**). "**I am thy servant**," he will continue **to say**, "leave me **not to** mine oppressors (str. 16, **Ain**), nor suffer me to fall **into** the iniquity into which they fain would allure me (str. 17, **Pe**): thou, O God, art righteous; and to thy everlasting righteousness I cleave (str. 18, **Tzaddi**). Hear thou therefore my cry (str. 19, **Koph**); consider mine affliction (str. 20, **Resh**): the **joy** which I feel at thy word, even as one that findeth great spoil, proclaims how I **have** hoped **for thy** salvation (str. 21, **Schin**); deliver thou me therefore; seek **me** out in whatsoever I have **gone astray**; let my soul live, and my lips shall utter forth thy praise (str. 22, **Tau**)."

That there is thus a train of consecutive thought running through the whole sufficiently appears from **the** above analysis. **In** tracing it out we need not attach to it an undue degree of importance. We have no right to expect to find it very strongly marked; nor is it necessary to suppose that the place of each strophe in the psalm was determined solely with reference to its logical connexion with that which preceded. In the latter half of the psalm the order of many of the **strophes** might perhaps be changed without any violent injury **to the** connexion **of the** whole. In some instances, as in that of the eighteenth strophe, where the Tzaddi **is** the initial of the Hebrew words for *righteous* and *righteousness*, the theme has been undeniably in part dictated by the alphabetical arrangement. Moreover in the structure of the psalm the psalmist seems **to** have desired **to** conform to a second artificial rule, viz. that the themes of the several strophes reckoned backwards and forwards from the centre shall in some measure respectively correspond; in accordance with that principle of inversion which is in other psalms illustrated by the arrangement of the lines or of the verses. If in the psalm before us we begin by examining the two strophes Caph and Lamed which mark the termination of the first and the commencement of the second half, we find in the latter an obvious reference, in the end which the psalmist had witnessed of all earthly perfection (v. 96), to the end which, as the former related, his enemies had almost made of him (v. 87). In the Jod strophe we have the pilgrim's prayer that his heart may be sound in God's statutes (v. 80): in the corresponding Mem strophe we have the confession that God's law has not deceived the love of his heart. The Teth and Nun strophes both speak of the snares of the wicked against him; while the two pairs of strophes Zain-Cheth and Samech-Ain both describe his horror at the wickedness of the ungodly and his anticipation of the judgments that must overtake them. Then again as the theme of the Vau strophe is the singleheartedness "which maketh not ashamed," this is also introduced into the corresponding strophe Pe (v. 130); while the strophes He, Tzaddi both bear witness to the perfect righteousness of God's law and the pilgrim's desire to have understanding therein. The strophe of crying, Koph, and that of affliction, Resh, may be joined together as a pair, and will then correspond to the strophe of crying, Gimel, and that of affliction, Daleth, which may be similarly joined. The Beth and Schin strophes both imply a truthfulness in the testimony of the lips (vv. 13, 163). Lastly the Aleph and Tau strophes are both characterized at the conclusion by the pilgrim's prayer that God would not forsake him; the which indeed it would scarcely be wrong to regard as the fundamental prayer of the entire psalm. These marks of design in the arrangement it was worth while to exhibit at some length that they might not be lightly passed over; and in the face of them it is difficult to conceive that the theory of the psalm being a mere collection of unconnected sayings will for the future be seriously maintained.

The psalm bears strong witness throughout to man's need of divine help to preserve him from transgression. Testimony to the same effect had been previously borne in that Davidic psalm which treated of God's law, Psalm xix. The doctrine is however unfolded in a somewhat different form in the one psalm from that in which it appears in the other. Psalm xix. sets forth the need of divine grace to effect that which the law could not effect: in Psalm cxix. the prayer is rather for grace to discern the wonders of the law itself. Insofar as they differ, the doctrine of each psalm is supplementary to that of the other.

There are in this psalm eight several names by which, according to the different aspects in which it is regarded, the law of God is designated; nor are there more than four verses, vv. 3, 37, 90, 122, in which one or other of these names will not be found. They are the following; and for convenience' sake we annex a tabular statement of the original terms, and of the renderings *generally* given to them in our English translation, and in the ancient versions. As the renderings of each term in the several versions, however, are not *uniformly* the same, the critical student must turn to the Hebrew in order to compute accurately the number of times that each term occurs.

	Hebrew	E. V.	LXX.	Aquila.	Symmachus.	Vulgate.	Jerome.
1	תורה	Law	νόμος	νόμος	νόμος	lex	lex
2	עדות	Testimonies	μαρτύρια	μαρτύρια	μαρτύρια	testimonia	testimonia
3	מצות	Commandments	ἐντολαί	ἐντολαί	ἐντολαί	mandata	mandata
4	חקים	Statutes	δικαιώματα	—	—	justificationes	praecepta / justitiae
5	פקודים	Precepts	ἐντολαί / δικαιώματα	προστάγματα / ἐντολαί	παραινέσεις	mandata / justificationes	praecepta
6	משפטים	Judgments	κρίματα	κρίσεις	κρίματα	judicia (justificationes)	judicia (justitiae)
7	דבר	Word	λόγος	—	—	verbum / sermo	irregular
8	אמרה	Word	λόγιον	ῥῆμα	λόγος	eloquium	irregular

Among other terms to **be met** with in this psalm may be noted the **two** following, the former of which is by some critics, on account of its occurrence in vv. 3, **37,** set on a par with **the** eight preceding.

9	דרך	Way	ὁδός	ὁδός	ὁδός	via	via
10	ארח	Way	ὁδός	—	ὁδός	via	semita

There are, moreover, yet others to which special attention might be directed, such **as** Faithfulness, Truth (אמת, אמונה), the one of which has been sometimes treated **as the** characteristic word of v. 90. But in frequency of occurrence none of these can be compared with the eight first mentioned. Five of these terms had already occurred in consecutive verses in Psalm xix. They might there have been treated as synonymous: it would here be impossible so to regard them; and the question therefore arises, what are the **several** shades of meaning which we must attach to **them?**

Of all these terms *Law* seems to be the most general, and to include all the rest. It denotes the law of God in all its parts; and is frequently applied to the **law** delivered to the Israelites by God through Moses, as also to the books in which that law is contained, or even to the preparatory dispensation under which the Israelites lived from the days of Moses until the com**ing of** Christ. By the *Testimony,* or *Testimonies,* we must understand the **Law, or** the several injunctions of the Law, viewed in their prohibitory aspect, as testifying against sin[1]. As such Moses himself regarded them when he delivered the final injunction, "Take this book of the law, and put it in the side of the ark of the covenant of the LORD your God, that it may be there for a witness against thee. For I know thy rebellion, &c.[2]" But when contemplated in their contrary aspects, the injunctions of the Law are either *Commandments*, in respect of their moral obligation; *Statutes*, in respect of their positive obligation; or *Precepts*, in respect of their religious expediency, as aids and means to the attainment of holiness. The same injunction might in many cases bear any one of these three names according as its moral, positive, or expediential obligation came more prominently into notice; but in general the term *Commandments* would be more properly applied to the several parts of the decalogue; *Statutes* to all ordained observances of a public, churchly, or national character, and more particularly to those which formed the divine code of the Israelitish people; *Precepts* to all rules for the individual believer's private guidance. The term *Judgments*, when applied to injunctions, differs from all the preceding terms in that it designates them with reference not to the persons obliged nor to the quality of the obligation, but to the source whence they proceed: it marks them as the manifestations of the will of an All-wise, All-holy, and All-loving Being. Having reference thus only to the author, and being wholly independent of the object, it may be equally applied to those rules which God lays down for his own observance in his dealings with men. It is so employed in v. 132,

---

[1] Theodoret: μαρτύρια δέ, ὡς διαμαρτυρόμενον, καὶ δεικνύντα, οἴαις ὑποβληθήσονται τιμωρίαις οἱ παραβαίνοντες. See this fully vindicated by Hengstenberg, *Genuineness of Pentateuch*, II. pp. 524 seqq. (Eng. Tr.)

[2] Deut. xxxi. 26, 27.

where, in order to express the force in English, we are constrained to resort to a paraphrase: "Look thou upon me, and be merciful unto me, **as** *thou usest to do* unto those **that love thy** name." Or again it may be applied (as in **v.** 91, **where our** English Version renders *ordinances*) to the natural laws to which by divine appointment the several creatures of the material universe conform: "They continue this day according to thine ordinances." The most nearly related to it among the preceding terms is *Statutes*, which has reference to the positive obligation of the injunctions so designated. Hence in the **Book** of Deuteronomy Statutes and Judgments are more than once joined together[1]; **and** the former name is itself also sometimes applied **to** the **natural laws** which **God** has ordained[2]. Of the **two** Hebrew words rendered Word, the first *(dabar)* is the more general, and denotes every kind of revelation of God's will whether **by** way of commandment or promise. **The** other *(imrah),* which for the sake of distinction might be translated *saying,* and which etymologically denotes the actual articulation, implies in its present **usage a more** personal and immediate address; whether **that** be **"a** special revelation, **a** peculiar promise, over and above the ordinary revelation of God's law[3]," or whether it **be** a special and personal bringing home to the believer's heart **of** that revelation which God has generally promulgated. The latter seems to be the meaning here intended. And thus that which when contemplated in respect **of its** divine utterer is a Word becomes **a** Saying when contemplated in respect **of the** person addressed: **the** one term has reference to the general promulgation, the other to the individual application; **a** distinction which may be to some extent

---

[1] Deut. **iv.** 1 ; **v.** 1.   Psalm cxlviii. 6 (id.).
[2] Job **xxviii.** 26 (E. V. *decree*);   [3] Cf. Jebb, II. p. 292.

illustrated by the frequently recurring scriptural passage, "The *word* of the LORD came unto him, *saying*."

Between the two Hebrew words rendered *Way* in our English Version it is scarcely possible to trace any real difference of import. And with respect to the remaining terms which recur in the psalm, their use is not sufficiently systematic to permit us to define with precision any exact shade of meaning that shall be found invariably to attach to them. Being less frequently employed by themselves, they are often used, as in the phrase "the word of thy truth," to qualify the principal terms; and in each separate passage in which they are found their sense will in general be easily ascertained.

PSALMS CXX—CXXXIV.

WE now arrive at the series of psalms which have been variously designated, according to the theory that different translators have formed of the meaning of the Hebrew title, Songs of Degrees, of Steps, of Ascents, of Goings up, or of Pilgrimages. They are fifteen in number. Four of them bear in their superscriptions the name of David; one that of Solomon. This last (Psalm cxxvii.) forms the central ode round which the rest are grouped; in proof of which it is urged by those who attach importance to the symbolical arithmetic in connexion with the use of the divine names, that both the sequence of seven psalms by which it is preceded and that by which it is followed contain the sacred name Jehovah exactly twenty-four times. It has been also remarked that although the length of the individual psalms of the series considerably varies, the aggregate length of those which precede the central ode is nearly the same with the aggregate length of those which come after it.

Common to all these psalms is the minuteness of artifice and symmetry displayed in their structure. But this is not the only bond of connexion between them. They are all more or less similar in tone; they exhibit, as a whole, a patient and hopeful endurance of present scorn and affliction, unmarked by any violent or momentary outburst of entreaty or exclamation; and short as many of them are, their subdued character contrasts with the exuberant sprightliness of the shorter odes in the previous parts of the Psalter. It will be at once evident that we must take this similarity of subject and of internal character into account in examining the different explanations that have been offered of the meaning of their common title; and we may therefore fairly assume that those are in error, who deem it to relate merely to some peculiarity either in the rhythmical structure of these psalms, or in the music to which they were sung.

This being premised, we have the following accounts of these psalms from which to choose. 1. Either that they were intended to be sung on the steps of the temple: so apparently most of the older authorities; the Targum, and the Talmud; the translation of the LXX, and the Vulgate; Hilary; and Jerome. 2. Or that they were designed for the use of the Israelitish people when travelling up to the feasts at Jerusalem: such was perhaps the view of Aquila, Symmachus, and Theodotion[1] among the older translators, while it has been also adopted by some of the most distinguished among modern critics. 3. Or that they were songs of the "going up" or return from Babylon: so the Syriac

---

[1] Aq. Symm. ᾠδὴ εἰς τὰς ἀναβάσεις. Theod. ᾆσμα τῶν ἀναβάσεων.

translator, and perhaps one of the Hellenists[1]; so also Chrysostom, Theodoret, and others. 4. A more definite view of the origin of this collection of psalms has been recently put forward by a writer in the *Journal of Sacred Literature*[2]. Retaining as the translation of the title "Songs of the Steps," and conceiving the steps intended to be not only the temple-steps but also those in other parts of the city of Jerusalem[3], he argues that the psalms were those in constant use by the builders of the walls of Jerusalem in the days of Nehemiah, and were collected together as a memorial of that part of the Jewish national history.

Those who adopt the second of the foregoing views defend their translation "Pilgrimage-songs," by observing that though step is the usual meaning of the word which they here render pilgrimage, yet the corresponding verb "to go up" is continually used in Scripture in reference to the Jewish festival-journeys. But even granting the admissibility of this translation, it does not appear that the psalms of the collection contain in general any distinctive features or allusions to mark them as pilgrimage-psalms. Not more than six out of the fifteen, viz. Psalms cxxi, cxxii, cxxv, cxxxii, cxxxiii, cxxxiv. could be fairly referred to as suggestive of any such theory; and even these, though they may in some degree fix our thoughts on the sanctuary at Jerusalem, make scarcely any reference to a *journey* thitherward. In Psalm cxxii. 2, not "Our feet *shall* stand," but "Our feet stand," is the more natural rendering of the Hebrew text. On the other hand there are evidently in Psalms cxx, cxxiv, cxxvi, and even in others, definite allusions to historical circumstances of which the pilgrimage-theory gives no account.

---

[1] ᾠδὴ τῆς ἀναβάσεως. [2] October, 1854, and April, 1855.
[3] Neh. iii. 19; xii. 27.

Unless supplemented therefore by an auxiliary hypothesis—as that these psalms belong to the period of the return from Babylon—the theory is manifestly untenable; and on the other hand should such auxiliary hypothesis be adopted, the pilgrimage-theory itself is then unneeded. For the title may in that case be translated "Psalms of the goings up from captivity, i. e. of the Returns;" and the advocates of this rendering have the advantage of being able to point to one passage of Scripture, Ezra vii. 9, in which the Hebrew word, although it never for certain denote a pilgrimage, is clearly used of the return from Babylon.

But can this—the third of the explanations enumerated above—be itself accepted? The language of one of the fifteen psalms, Psalm cxxvi, undoubtedly favours it: that of others is almost fatal to it. For taken as a whole, the psalms of this series bespeak a settled constitution of affairs: if of post-exilic date, they require that the re-establishment at Jerusalem (Psalm cxxii. 3) and the rebuilding of the sanctuary (Psalm cxxxiv. 2) should be viewed as already accomplished; what joyousness they possess is everywhere chequered with mournfulness, unlike the joyousness of captives on their first liberation; sometimes (as in Psalms cxx, cxxiii, cxxx) it deepens into positive gloom; while again the deliverance recorded in Psalms cxx, cxxiv, cxxix, is evidently deliverance from temporary distress, or from some recent display of hostile malice, not from a captivity of seventy years' duration.

With regard to the first explanation given above, the translation "Songs of the Steps" is philologically unexceptionable; but that the psalms thus designated were sung on the steps of the temple is in itself a mere conjecture, owing its importance rather to the number of authorities by whom it was traditionally received than to any intrinsic probability. It throws no light whatever on the origin, character, or import of these psalms; and when further unfolded becomes a germ of mere profitless speculation; as when the Jewish authors assign one psalm to each of the several fifteen steps mentioned—seven as belonging to the outer gates and eight to the inner gates—in the description of the vision-temple of Ezekiel; or as when the Christian Fathers view these fifteen steps as emblematical of the spiritual ascent to Christian perfection. The writer in the *Journal of Sacred Literature*, whose account of the origin of these psalms will presently come before us, has not been more successful than others in extracting any real information out of their title. In vain he attempts to trace a special connexion between these psalms and the steps of the temple and city of Jerusalem. His arguments, elsewhere just and convincing, are here farfetched and weak: his conclusions, elsewhere clear and definite, are here confused and vague. His explanation of the title is in short a mere encumbrance to an otherwise valuable investigation.

Of the title then of these psalms it can only be said that all endeavours to illustrate it have hitherto ended in failure; and that its very meaning is, at best, uncertain. Under these circumstances it seems the better course to ascertain in the first instance, if possible, the origin of this series of psalms from internal evidence alone. We shall then have the opportunity of further examining whether the view we take of the psalms themselves can suggest any explanation of the title which shall be at the same time philologically tenable.

Our attention must first be directed to the central psalm, Psalm cxxvii:

If the Lord build not the house,
In vain have its builders laboured thereon

If the LORD guard not **the city**,
In vain hath the watchman **waked.**

Here **at least the** historical indications, which meet us with such obvious significance in the very forefront of the psalm, cannot well be gainsaid. There was a period in **the** Jewish history when in building and in watching the greater part of the people were employed; the period of the restoration of the walls under Nehemiah. That work was accomplished in the very face of the enemy; the workmen were all armed; those who were not themselves labouring in the building were holding the spears by their side, "from the rising of the morning till the stars appeared;" and the inhabitants of the country round, along with their servants, were gathered for the time into Jerusalem, that they might help **to** guard by night and to labour by day. What more fitting words could at such a time be put into the people's lips than those which admonished them to trust in God by reminding them that he was the true Builder, he the real Watchman of their city? Nor is the rest of the psalm less illustrated by the circumstances of that period. At a time when the Jews were in need not only of walls but of men, and were feeble from the smallness of their numbers[1], and when they were daily liable to encounters with Sanballat, Tobiah, and their other foes, not at a distance, but beneath the very stones of the fortifications they were erecting, a psalm which spoke of the blessings of children, which compared them to arrows in the hand of a warrior, and which declared that their presence should make their parents bold to "speak with the enemies in the gate," contained lessons of encouragement the force of which could not well be missed.

Nor is it the central ode alone that thus abounds in

[1] Neh. iv. 2; vii. 4.

allusions to the period of the restoration of the walls. Let it be but once assumed that to this period the whole series of psalms belong, and the historical references immediately display themselves throughout to a striking and convincing extent. We may without much difficulty picture to ourselves the Jewish people all lodging together within the precincts (cxxxiii. 1) and labouring together upon the fortifications of their once glorious city (cxxii. 7); going out and coming in to take their turns at their tasks (cxxi. 8); toiling in the heat of the sun (cxxi. 5, 6) or keeping guard through the night (cxxi. 3, 4; cxxx. 6), some along the circuit of the city, some within the courts of the temple (cxxxiv. 1); gazing from the walls on which they stood towards the familiar hills by which Jerusalem was surrounded (cxxi. 1; cxxv. 2), or up towards the clear blue sky against which the outline of the hills was marked (cxxiii. 1), or down towards the rock of Zion on the edge of which the fortifications of the temple were being raised (cxxv. 1), or looking inward upon the courts of the sanctuary which rendered Jerusalem itself so dear to them (cxxii. 1, 9; cxxviii. 5; cxxxii; cxxxiv. 3), or on the hill of the City of David, hallowed by all its associations with the life of the great psalmist-king (cxxii. 5), or on the more extended range of the inhabited city (cxxii. 2, 3, 6; cxxviii. 5), on the palaces which had already begun to rise from its ruins (cxxii. 7), or on the grass-grown housetops of its more desolate parts (cxxix. 6). It was still indeed to them a season of mournfulness; but they were carrying on their present work in the hope of being ultimately rewarded: they were sowing in tears: they trusted to reap in joy (cxxvi. 4—6). Dangers still surrounded them: enemies of lying lips (cxx. 2, 3) and uncompromising hostility (cxx. 7) were close upon them (cxx. 5, 6), threatening even Jerusalem itself, which as the capital of the Jewish nation excited their bitterest hatred (cxxix. 5); enemies whose pride had not yet been quenched by the ill success that had lighted on their endeavours (cxxiv), and **who** still scorned and despised the little people of God (cxxiii); but even under these trials the Jews were reassured by their past experience of God's mercies (cxxix. 1, 2); their restoration from captivity, already accomplished (cxxvi. 1—3), was a pledge of further blessings, yet to come; and even the narrow escapes which they had had from their present enemies (cxx. 1; cxxiv) testified that God's hand still rested over them to defend them.

But while the numerous historical allusions in these psalms thus furnish the key to their date, it is almost equally clear from their general shortness that they were not the mere incidental effusions of the psalmists of that age, but were composed in pursuance of some special design, and with some special object in view. That they were not intended in the first instance for liturgical use, or for any solemn occasion of national thanksgiving, is shewn both by their brevity and by the didactic character which pervades them. We may therefore well suppose that they were designed for the use of the people while actually engaged in repairing or defending the walls; devotional accompaniments to the people's necessary labours, **which** could easily be committed to memory and repeated while the work of fortification proceeded. How fitting that that which was emphatically styled the Lord's work[1] should be sanctified **in** its progress by the sacred prayers and meditations of the labourers! And here a suitable explanation of the much controverted title suggests itself. The literal rendering of it is "Songs of the

[1] Neh. iii. 5.

goings up." Why then should it not denote those psalms which were intended to be sung by the workmen and guards of Nehemiah's days, when they "went up" (as the Hebrew phrase is) upon the city-walls? Such a meaning has the advantage of being not only appropriate, but also determinate: it indicates at once the historical circumstances under which the psalms were probably composed, and at the same time signally marks one of the most exciting scenes in the post-exilic Jewish history.

The investigations which we have conducted thus far into the authorship of the different portions of the Psalter will have already prepared us to conclude that neither David nor Solomon can be deemed the actual authors of any of the psalms in the series before us. Internal evidence sufficiently decides that Psalm cxxii. (see v. 5) cannot have flowed from David's pen. This psalm and also the other three which bear the name of David in their superscriptions exhibit perhaps somewhat more of personal feeling than most of the rest, but do not otherwise essentially differ from them in character. That ascribed to Solomon is somewhat more akin in its sententiousness to the Book of Proverbs. We may reasonably assume that all these were composed by a member of David's family; most likely by Nehemiah himself, if, as seems probable, he belonged to that royal house[1]. Although not, perhaps, the senior

---

[1] The office of cupbearer which he filled at the Persian court, and the commission which he subsequently received as governor of the Jews, seem to indicate that he was of royal lineage; and the way in which he speaks of Jerusalem as the city of his fathers' sepulchres (Neh. ii. 3, 5) points to the same conclusion. Eusebius (*Can. Chron. an.* 1584) asserts him to have been ἐκ φυλῆς Ἰούδα; and a later chronologer, quoted by Georg. Cedrenus, calls him Νεεμίας Ἰουδαῖος, ἐκ τοῦ σπέρματος Δαβίδ. Scaliger and Carpzov observe that the Princes of the Captivity were always taken from the tribe of Judah; and that Nehemiah may not improbably have been set over the Jews in Judea as having already exercised the like dignity among his countrymen at Babylon. Carpzov, *Introd. V. T. I.* p. 339.

representative of David's line, he would yet as governor of Judea take precedence for the time being of the other members of the family; and while exhibiting on the one hand in his piety the feelings of a genuine son of David, he might not inappropriately, as the restorer of Jerusalem, deem himself a sort of second Solomon, and thus entitle that psalm which alluded more distinctly to the "building" of "the house" a psalm "of Solomon." Without discussing at any length whether the designation of "the second Solomon" might be more justly claimed by Nehemiah or by Zerubbabel, we may easily apply to the former the remarks which Theodoret, in discoursing on the superscription of Psalm cxxvii, makes upon the latter: "The temple of God was indeed in the first instance built by Solomon, but it was by Zerubbabel that it was restored after it had been destroyed by the Babylonians. And it is to him, I think, that the name Solomon is here given, both as deriving his descent from Solomon, and as renewing Solomon's work. For the inspired utterance now before us does not suit the building of the original Solomon, although it agrees with that which was carried on after the return."

After this general introduction to the "Songs of Goings up," we shall need to say but little respecting the individual psalms of the series. The historical references, accompanied by a few occasional remarks, will be all that is required.

Psalm cxx. The difficulty which some interpreters of this psalm have experienced in taking Mesech as a proper name, on account of the distance by which the Caucasian tribe of that name were removed from the Israelites, is obviated by the consideration that both Kedar and Mesech are here used, not literally, but figuratively, to denote the nearer enemies of the Jews;

who by reproaches (Neh. ii. 19; iv. 1—5), by open warfare (Neh. iv. 7 seqq.) and by craft (Neh. vi.) were variously endeavouring to hinder the restoration of Jerusalem. And in this sense Israel might all the more truly be said to be dwelling among Mesech and Kedar, inasmuch as even among the Jews themselves there was a considerable party in league with the enemy (Neh. vi. 17—19; xiii. 28).

Psalm cxxi. See the previous general Introduction; and cf. Neh. iv. 9—23. In v. 6 the moon stands as the emblem of the night: those stationed on the walls were exposed to the effects of the cold of night as well as of the heat of day.

Psalm cxxii. describes the joy of the psalmist at being permitted to dwell or lodge within the precincts of that city which had long been the seat of God's sanctuary; the city whither, by divine ordinance, all the tribes of Israel had of old been wont to come up to worship. The sentiments of v. 6, and the prayer "Peace be *within* thy walls" in v. 7, "may be considered doubly significant, in the view of the internal disturbances mentioned in Nehemiah, chapter v, and of the troublesome enemies *without*[1]." The psalmist's mind would probably also lay a special emphasis on the phrase "the tribes *of the* LORD[2]" in v. 5; the bitter hostility of the Samaritans arising from the circumstance that their claim to be reckoned as belonging to the community of Israel, and therefore to have part in the sanctuary at Jerusalem, was denied by the Jews. The psalmist looked forward to the time when all Israel should again resort, as in the olden days of David, to Jerusalem to worship; but he would not defile the sanctity of Israel by admitting into its pale those who

---

[1] *J. S. L.* Oct. 1854. [2] Heb. "the tribes of JAH."

had no just **title to be included** among the chosen people of God.

Psalm cxxiii. **Cf.** Neh. ii. 19; iv. 1—6.

Psalm cxxiv. Cf. Neh. iv. 15: "And it came to pass, when our enemies heard that it was known unto us, and God had brought their counsel to nought, that we returned all of **us to the** wall, every one unto his work." In every age of **the** Church this psalm has come forth with fresh force on the occasion of any striking deliverance. With respect to the superscription, the peculiar grammatical forms, which are unparalleled in the psalms of the original David, shew that it cannot be ascribed **to him.**

Psalm cxxv. The historical allusions in this psalm are matters of no recent discovery. **The** language of the last verse long ago prompted the inference that the psalm was composed **at** a time when secret attempts were being made to draw away the people of Israel from their allegiance; and it was also seen that these attempts could **not** well be any other than those of Sanballat and Tobiah, whose private communications with the nobles of Judah Nehemiah has recorded (Neh. vi. 17—19). The psalm is remarkable for the distinctness with which it openly narrows the applica**tion of** the name Israel to those who were Israelites in **heart as** well as by race, who persevered in their uprightness instead of turning aside to the crooked ways of the workers of iniquity.

Psalm cxxvi. The restoration from captivity could not fail to be a most encouraging earnest to the Jews of the blessings which they might expect from God's hand. It stood in the same relation to their later history as the deliverance from Egypt to their earlier; **or as** our redemption in Christ to our whole Christian **life.** It must have been peculiarly inspiring to the

Jews, when toiling on the walls of Jerusalem in the face of the enemy, to call to mind the acknowledgments of divine favour towards them which even from the heathen their restoration had called forth. That these acknowledgments were repeated when the walls of the city were finished we know from Neh. vi. 16. Of the simile in v. 4, "as the streams in the south," various explanations, probably more erudite than correct, have been given by those conversant with the peculiarities of the Euphrates and the Nile. The real allusion is, without much doubt, to the torrent-beds in the parched regions of the southern territory of Judah; to the replenishing of which by the winter rains the return of prosperity to the Jewish nation is here compared.

Psalm cxxvii. has already been sufficiently illustrated.

Psalm cxxviii. has many points of contact with Psalm cxxvii: the references to the house, the children, the enjoyment of the results of labour. It is a pleasing delineation of the blessings which God's people, under the protection of their Almighty Sovereign, would desire to behold. The psalmist speaks first of the blessing of an abundant produce, so often promised in the law. From this he passes to the more domestic blessings of family life, which however he associates with the former, by comparing the wife in the recesses of the house to the fruitful vine that grew without it, and the children round about the table to the numerous olives on which the husbandman looked forth. The blessings of the household were obviously higher in degree than those of the mere domain; and the celebration of them would be peculiarly appropriate when the Jews, who for the first ninety years after their return from captivity had been little more than mere settlers in the land, were now at length rebuilding the walls of Jerusalem, and looking forward to the re-establishment of citizen-life. From these the psalmist again ascends to the yet higher blessings of national and churchly prosperity. Each family was in itself a type of the entire nation; and the true Israelite would desire happiness and peace not only for the inmates of his own dwelling but also for the whole house of Israel. It may be interesting, in connexion with this psalm, to observe that the family and the house were in the imagination of the Jew very strongly associated; the Hebrew words for *build* and *son* being etymologically connected, and the children being viewed as the building which the father of a family was by God's favour permitted to rear.

Psalm cxxix. fitly follows after Psalm cxxviii. The fundamental image in both psalms is that of the house; but in the one we have the prosperity of its occupants described, in the other the discomfiture of its assailants. Israel's foes have been long drawing their furrows across his back; but it is all as though they had been ploughing on the roof of his house. The Lord has put a sudden end to their ploughing by cutting the cord of the oxen in twain; and all the fruit of their labours has come to nought. While the righteous resemble the fruitful vine and the numerous olives, the enemies,—or rather the result of their endeavours, for that is the thing really intended,—are merely like the rootless grass which sprang upon those ruined housetops that formed the memorial of the Chaldean desolation of Jerusalem. While the occupants of the renovated house within were eating the labour of their hands, this wretched herbage with its few intermingled corn-blades was all that the desolators could claim as the produce of their ploughing; herbage not worth the gathering, inasmuch as all that so grew withered before it put forth the ear, and thus never, like the rich produce of the cornfield, afforded the opportunity to the mowers or reapers of collecting it in their hands or their bosoms amid the welcome salutations of those that passed by.

There was probably never a nation in the world that could say with so much truth as Israel after the return from the captivity, Many a time have they afflicted me from my youth, yet they have not prevailed against me. That so small a nation should have been successively humbled and oppressed by almost every one of the neighbouring tribes, should have been finally transplanted from its land into captivity, and should yet survive and rejoice in the hope of a prosperous future is, it may be not too much to assert, unparalleled in history. There is but one body that inherits the same vitality; the antitype of the ancient Israel, the universal Church of Christ.

Psalm cxxx. As in the preceding psalm Israel had taken a retrospect of their many afflictions, so in this they look back upon the long catalogue of their past iniquities. Hence this psalm is the most mournful in the whole series. It is in the contemplation of their own transgressions that men may truly feel themselves to be crying to God "*out of the depths.*" Correspondent to the different points of view from which this and the preceding psalm are uttered are the aspects in which the attributes of God are in them respectively presented to us. In Psalm cxxix, which speaks but of the nation's outward sorrows, we have his *righteousness* declared: "The LORD is righteous: he hath cut asunder the cords of the wicked." In Psalm cxxx, which opens up the nation's more inward griefs, his mercy is brought into prominence: "With the LORD there is mercy, and with him is plenteous redemption; and he shall redeem Israel from all his iniquities." It is his mercy which obtains for him the worship and reverence of his guilt-stricken people: "There is forgiveness with thee, that thou mayest be feared." That the psalm is uttered in the name of the whole people is evident both from vv. 7, 8, and also from the general character of the cycle of psalms of which this forms one. The language of the earlier portion of it is however equally suited to express the penitential supplications of every individual believer.

We have not hitherto paused to dwell upon the remarkable minuteness of artifice displayed in the structure of the psalms of this cycle. There was the less occasion to do so, inasmuch as the subject has been treated in one of the articles in the *Journal of Sacred Literature* already referred to. We may however notice some of the peculiarities of arrangement in Psalm cxxx. as a specimen of the rest. The psalm readily divides itself into four portions of two verses each. Verses 5, 6 answer to vv. 1, 2: vv. 7, 8 correspond to vv. 3, 4. Verses 5, 6, when distributed into clauses, shew an inverted arrangement which may be thus symbolized, *a, a, b; c, d, d;* the repeating clause coming at the beginning of v. 5 and at the end of v. 6:

5 I wait for the LORD,
My soul doth wait,
And in his word do I hope.

6 My soul waiteth for the LORD,
More than they that watch for the morning,
They that watch for the morning.

A comparison of vv. 7, 8 with vv. 3, 4 shews a similar inversion. The word *iniquities* (an important word in the psalm) comes (in the Hebrew) at the *beginning* of v. 3, and therefore at the *close* of v. 8. In vv. 3, 4 we have the mention first of sins, then of forgiveness, then of the feelings with which God will be regarded by his people: in vv. 7, 8 we have the mention first of the feelings with which God should be regarded by his people, then of forgiveness, then of sins. Care has also been taken that the length and structure of the lines shall (in the Hebrew) correspond in vv. 4, 8, inasmuch as they respectively close the two halves of the psalm.

Inversions and similar artifices mark the whole of the fifteen psalms now before us. Although it would be an error to assume that attention to this symmetry of structure originated at a late date, it is yet possible that in regard of the mere position of words more attention was paid to it in the later than in the earlier age of Hebrew psalmody. The minute details of this symmetry would also naturally be more brought out in the shorter than in the longer psalms.

Psalm cxxxi. may possibly have been written by Nehemiah after the accusation had been preferred against him by his enemies that he had sought to render himself a king[1]. Still, by whatsoever occasion suggested, it was certainly intended for the direct use of Israel at large; as is shewn by the last verse. The perfect realization in the person of our Blessed Saviour of the spirit here portrayed has been often noted: cf. among many other passages, Matth. xi. 29; Joh. vi. 15.

Psalm cxxxiii. The symmetrical arrangement of this psalm (as exhibited in the work to which reference has already been made[2]) helps to throw light upon its contents. After dividing vv. 11, 12 into four lines each (in accordance with the Jewish accentuation), and all the other verses into two lines, and separating the first

---

[1] Neh. vi. 5 seqq.   [2] *Journal of Sac. Lit.* April, 1855.

and last verses off from the rest, as forming the prelude and conclusion to the whole, we find the ode to consist of two portions of equal length (vv. 2—10, 11—17) marked as correspondent to each other by their respective openings, by the resemblance of v. 16 to v. 9, by the mention of David in the first clause of both v. 10 and v. 17, and by the termination of both with the word "anointed." The theme of the one portion is David's vow to the Lord: that of the other, the Lord's promise to David. And as God is evidently introduced as speaking even to the very end of the latter portion, so we may also assume, unless there be any strong reason (which there is not) for insisting on the contrary, that vv. 3—10 are all intended to be assigned to David. The language in which the sentiments are clothed is of course not taken directly from the history, but is due to the invention of the psalmist; and even the few verses 8—10 which are extracted from the Second Book of Chronicles consist strictly of the words of Solomon, which are here, by a necessary inaccuracy, put into the mouth of David, in order that the unity of the former half of the psalm might be preserved.

If we cast aside the poetical form into which the psalm is thrown, we find that its main contents may be reduced to these: the zeal of David in establishing the ark of the covenant on Mount Zion, and the divine assurance, which could not fail, that David's race should reign and that God would dwell in Zion for evermore. How full of the liveliest interest these themes to those who were rebuilding the walls of Jerusalem after the captivity, it needs no great stretch of discernment to perceive. To us, who recognize in the present earthly reign of our exalted Saviour, and in his continued presence with his universal Church, the long-expected fulfilment of the promises made to David of old, they should be not less deeply interesting. A second and more awful overthrow of the literal Jerusalem, from which we have no reason to suppose that she will ever in her ancient splendour arise, has taught us that it was not she to whom the divine promises in all their fulness belonged. "It is not," says Hilary, "that deserted and useless mount, not that overthrown and demolished city, that God hath chosen. God is not confined by any local bounds; nor does the Omnipotent and Eternal Substance make his rest either in the desert solitudes of hills, or in mere names such as constitute the only remains of cities now long since defaced. But he has chosen for a rest those of whom the Lord says in the gospel, 'No man can come to me, except the Father which hath sent me draw him.' He has chosen that holy Zion, that heavenly Jerusalem, to wit the harmonious company of the faithful, and the souls hallowed by the sacraments of the Church; to the end that in them, as in a reasonable and intelligent habitation, thoroughly cleansed, and eternal through the glory of resurrection, the reasonable and intelligent and undefiled and eternal nature of his ineffable divinity may rest. Not that he should abandon aught of that vastness in which his own infinity consists, so as to be straitened within the confined limits of human minds; but to the end that by means of the settlement of a habitation worthy of himself, who is everywhere and the same and everything and always, he should rest in his saints in whom he taketh delight; where offences may cause no further change, but where, world without end, that is, for periods of eternity, a worthy and acceptable abode may display itself as his choice."

The divine promises expanded in the latter half of

this psalm are not the only portions of it that have a prospective reference. The history of the ark is essentially typical. Lying in obscurity at the commencement of David's reign in the suburbs of an Ephrathite village, it was removed by him with solemn pomp to its resting-place on the holy hill of Zion: an image of Him who, born King of the Jews in another Ephrathite village, by name Bethlehem, and there laid in the manger because there was no room for him in the inn, was exalted thirty years later, after his resurrection from the dead, with great triumph unto his kingdom and royal resting-place in heaven. It is to preserve this typical allusion that the psalmist (who had the prophecy of Micah respecting Bethlehem Ephratah before him) speaks, somewhat unusually, of the ark resting in *Ephratah;* thus naming the district in which its temporary abode was situate, rather than the exact spot; which however he otherwise indicates, the expression "the fields of the wood" having a manifest reference to Kirjath-jearim, "the city of woods[1]."

Psalm cxxxiii. The difficulties, not to say the whole contents, of this little psalm have by commentators been rather glozed over than explained. On this account the following version may be acceptable, both as shewing the structure of the psalm, and also as assisting in its interpretation:

---

[1] The limits of the district of Ephratah are unknown. In the Book of Genesis the name is used, less accurately, as synonymous with that of Bethlehem. It must, however, have properly belonged to the district: cf. Ruth iv. 11, and the use of the word Ephrathite in Ruth i. 2; 1 Sam. i. 1. Hengstenberg explains v. 6 of the psalm thus: that when David was living as a young man in Ephratah, people knew of the ark only by hearsay, no one visiting it. But such a reference to that part of David's personal history which was not really connected with the ark would be out of place. More probable is the same author's next remark, that the expression "the *fields* of the wood" indicates that the ark stood not in the city but in the suburbs of Kirjath-jearim.

Lo! how goodly
    And how pleasant
      To **dwell as** brethren
  In very unity!
Like the goodly oil upon the head
  Which floweth down upon the beard,
    The beard of Aaron,
Flowing down upon the border of his garments;
  Like the dew of Hermon
Coming down upon the mountains of Zion;
For there the Lord commanded the blessing,
  Life for evermore.

The two similes here employed correspond respectively to the two epithets in the first verse. The oil illustrates the goodliness, the preciousness, the richness, the intrinsic value of brotherly unity: the dew its pleasantness and continual freshness. With respect to these similes it should also be observed that certainly the one, most probably both, are drawn, in part at least, from the imagination. The dew of Hermon could never have actually descended upon the hills of Zion; and it is very doubtful whether Aaron or any other person were ever anointed in such a manner that the oil ran down upon him to the border of his garment. Nor does the psalmist assert this. The renderings of our E. V. "that went down" (in the last part of v. 2), "that descended" (v. 3), are incorrect[1]: the true force of the Hebrew is represented by our English participle, which expresses what occurs in the imagination equally with what occurs in fact. We read indeed of the anointing oil being *sprinkled* along with blood upon Aaron's garments; and it is possible that this sprinkling may have been deemed to represent the less convenient ceremony of perfusion, just as with us at the

---

[1] For these we should have had in Hebrew not שירד, but הירד. The relation implied by the שׁ is quite indeterminate.

administration of the sacrament of baptism the sprinkling of water is ordinarily substituted for complete immersion; but in the account of the earlier part of the ceremony it is merely recorded that Moses having decked Aaron in his high-priestly attire poured of the anointing oil upon his head, and anointed him to sanctify him[1]. By heightening therefore the natural picture the psalmist draws our attention the more forcibly, as in Psalm xl. 6[2], to its symbolical significance.

For when we come to examine more minutely into the similes, it seems impossible to avoid recognizing in this psalm a prophecy of that brotherly unity which should be the distinguishing feature of the Christian Church. . The points of resemblance between the brotherly unity described and the precious ointment to which it is compared, are these: the flowing of unity from Christ, as the oil runs down from the head; the general diffusion of it over the whole mystical body of Christ, like the imaginary diffusion of the ointment over the whole person of Aaron; the spiritual and heavenly character of that unity, inasmuch as it is the direct work of the Holy Spirit of God, of whom oil is throughout the Scriptures the constant emblem; and lastly its holiness, signified by the sacred preciousness of the oil with which Aaron was anointed, an oil compounded of the most costly ingredients, according to a divine prescription, which none were permitted, under penalty of death, to imitate for any other purpose[3]. The border of the high-priestly garments may be taken to represent the humbler members of the Christian Church, whom Christ, the great high-priest, hath graciously folded round himself; while to complete the interpretation, the beard of the high-priest may, as by

---

[1] Lev. viii. 12, 30. [2] See above, Vol. I. p. 222, note 2.
[3] Exod. xxx. 22 seqq.

Augustine, be deemed symbolical of the apostles, on whom the Great Head of the Church first poured forth his gifts, and who were the instruments in perpetuating to others that divine unity which they had themselves received from their Master Christ. This interpretation, viewed as a whole, is no mere Christian application or pious adaptation of the psalmist's language: on the contrary it is the only interpretation which fully brings out its legitimate meaning. If it be asked, by way of objection, whether this meaning was fully present to the mind of the psalmist himself, and of the first Israelite worshippers who made use of his words, we answer that it was present to their minds to the same extent to which they recognized the real import of the ceremonies of the law which they observed. The oil of anointing with which first Aaron and afterwards the kings and prophets were inaugurated to their offices was essentially and intentionally typical of that Holy Spirit who was eventually to be poured out upon all flesh. It had no virtue in itself. Its diffusion from the head downwards (so far as it was practically diffused) could hardly fail to indicate the diffusion of God's grace from the Chief who first received to those who were associated with him; and in the case of the unction of Aaron there can be the less cause for hesitation in recognizing a type of the communication of grace from Christ the Head to the members of the Church his seamless garment, inasmuch as the high-priest wore in his dress, both on his breast and on his shoulders, the names of the twelve tribes of Israel in whose behalf he appeared before God.

The image in the other simile is the fresh and plenteous dew of Mount Hermon, which the psalmist represents to himself as coming down upon the mountains of Zion. A natural impossibility may yet be emblematical of a great spiritual truth; and the thing here intended is, without much doubt, **the** freshness of divine **fellowship as resting** upon the Christian Church. **It is** *there,* **in Zion, the** Church Catholic of Christ, **that** the **Lord has commanded** the blessing; **it is** there that he has vouchsafed **to pour** out his most blessed spiritual gift, **even life for evermore.** There is in the original of the **psalm a** designed paronomasia between the Hebrew word for *commanded* and the name Zion; and attention is thus drawn to the etymological meaning of the latter name, *sunny, arid;* the moral being that the Church is not to be judged by her natural or external appearance; that parched as **she** may appear in the fire of toil and persecution, she is yet **in** receipt of the spiritual richness of the fertilizing **dew** from above; and **that** of whatever blessings men may have heard as descending upon the most favoured regions of the earth, these and greater than these are hers, her members forming in the unity of the Spirit that one sacred body which is the fulness of him that filleth all in all.

Psalm cxxxiv. appropriately concludes this series. Amid the watchings of the Jews on their newly-rising city-walls against the attacks of the enemy it was well that the watchings **of** the Levites in the temple to their Almighty Sovereign should **not** be forgotten. Employed as the sacred singers **were** day and night in the task assigned them[1], it belonged to them especially to lift up by night, in the name of **the** whole people, their hands in the sanctuary, and bless the Lord. Hengstenberg argues from the call to praise and to supplicate the Lord, and from the phrase "The LORD that made heaven and earth" at the conclusion, which directs the Church, conscious of her own impotence, to her Lord's almightiness, that the psalm was composed at a season

[1] 1 Chron. ix. 33.

of depression. We arrive at the same result from the special mention of the night, in which one cannot well avoid acknowledging, along with Augustine, a typical allusion to the night-season of either personal or national life. Even in the Gospel of St John the mention of the night has a similar import; where it is related that Judas "having received the sop went immediately out: *and it was night*[1]." And assuredly it was a season of great national gloom at which the Jews at the bidding of Nehemiah rebuilt the walls of Jerusalem. Important as was the work in which they were engaged, they executed it in the midst of tribulation and danger; which was however so far of service to them, that it taught them to bend their eyes more directly and earnestly upward to God, and to rely less upon themselves. They felt that they needed God's blessing; and thus minded, they would be comforted by the doctrine of even this little psalm, which teaches "that in the depressing and difficult circumstances of the Church of God, the sure way to obtain the Lord's blessing is to bless him[2]."

PSALMS CXXXV, CXXXVI.

THE late date of these two psalms may be inferred from the manner in which they are compacted of passages from the earlier portions of the Psalter. In respect of the formal arrangement, the first consists of three strophes of seven verses each, of which the historical strophe, vv. 8—14, stands out by its central position as the most important. The other psalm, although not divided into strophes, is marked by the occurrence in every verse of the well-known refrain "for his mercy endureth for ever," itself borrowed, either immediately

[1] Joh. xiii. 30.   [2] Hengstenberg.

or mediately, from Psalm cvi. 1. The contents of the two psalms are however to a great extent the same; and they may therefore be conveniently treated of together. Both set forth the almighty power of God: both contain strong protests against idolatry: both recount the deliverance of Israel from Egypt: both make special mention of the divine overthrow of Sihon and Og, and of the assignment of their land as an heritage to Israel. A further comparison of both psalms with the solemn confession of sins contained in the ninth chapter of Nehemiah will leave little doubt that it was in connexion with the national fast therein recorded to have been observed that these psalms were composed. For convenience' sake it may be well to annex a table of the principal parallel passages.

Psalm cxxxv.	Psalm cxxxvi.	Neh. ix.
1—3, 19—21	1, 26	5.
5—7		6.
4		7, 8
8, 9	10—12	9, 10.
	13—15	11.
	16	12—21.
10—12	17—22	22—24.
	23, 24	27—31.

As the preceding fifteen psalms are historically connected with the rebuilding of the walls of *Jerusalem*, so do the two psalms now before us carry our thoughts back to the re-occupation of the Israelitish *territory*. Their historical starting-point is not indeed the first return from captivity; but rather Nehemiah's assemblage of the whole people that they might be reckoned by genealogy[1]; that genealogy undoubtedly furnishing in many instances the key to the territorial inheritance to which each family was entitled. At the end of the chapter of Nehemiah which contains the genealogies

[1] Neh. vii. 5.

we have this notice: "So the priests, and the Levites, and the porters, and the singers, and some of the people, and the Nethinims, and all Israel, dwelt in their cities; and when the seventh month came, the children of Israel were in their cities[1]." This apparently implies that Nehemiah had to some extent redistributed the people throughout the land, placing the several families in possession of the estates which had formerly belonged to their forefathers. Thus this occasion might be regarded as the great allotment of the land of Israel after the captivity; corresponding to the original allotment in the days of Joshua after the conquest. And it appears that the opportunity was seized to renew, for the first time, the primitive observance of the feast of tabernacles: "All the congregation of them that were come again out of the captivity made booths, and sat under the booths: for since the days of Jeshua the son of Nun unto that day had not the children of Israel done so[2]." It was a token that the people felt that they had once more been gathering in the fruits of their own land.

Their joy was not however unmingled with regret. They were indeed themselves settled again, according to the former allotment, in the land of their inheritance; but how contracted the limits of the district over which they were spread, when compared with those of the territory originally assigned to them! Samaria was occupied by a hostile race; Galilee too, for the present, was no longer theirs; and the fertile regions to the east of the Jordan, which had been so triumphantly won from Sihon the Amorite conqueror of Moab, and from Og the last of the old giant-race, chieftains whose renown had made the story of their defeat one of the most attractive of the tales of olden Israelitish history,

[1] Neh. vii. 73.   [2] Neh. viii. 17.

were now, according to all human appearance, almost irretrievably **lost**[1].

Under these circumstances the celebration **of** the ancient conquest of Canaan, while it furnished an appropriate theme of praise to those who were resettled in the land, contained also a stirring appeal to the people's faith. Knowing as they did that the whole land **had** been promised to Abraham and his seed after him, they must still believe in the perpetuity of the promise; they must look forward to the time when the blessing should be renewed in no measure of diminution; they must believe that God would yet plead the cause of his people, and repent him concerning his **servants**. Samaria and Galilee, Bashan and Gilead, must not be given up for lost; the day **should** yet come when they that sat in darkness should see a great light. Even in former days God, although he had given *all* Canaan, with Bashan, for his people's inheritance, had yet at various times suffered the Israelites to fall into the hands of their enemies for their sins; and so at the present season he was permitting the land of their inheritance to yield increase to the kings whom because of their sins he had set over them. Yet he had, in the days of the **judges,** been merciful to them on their repentance; and so even now, if they would return to him, and keep his law, he would doubtless again make good to them his promise in **all its fulness.**

---

[1] The suggestion has been recently thrown out that Psalm cxxxvi. is peculiarly adapted **to** the trans-jordanic tribes it being "difficult else **to account** for the stress laid on the conquest of Sihon and Og, to the entire exclusion of the conquest of Canaan." This **hypothesis is sufficiently negatived by the** obvious similarity of Psalm cxxxvi. to Psalm cxxxv, in which mention is made **not only of** Sihon and Og **but also of** "*all* **the kingdoms** of Canaan," and which **was evidently** designed, as the opening verses shew, to be sung in Jerusalem. If the language of Psalm cxxxvi. be deemed less exact **or complete** than that of Psalm cxxxv, it may perhaps be explained by assuming that Psalm cxxxvi. was designed to present the chief contents of Psalm cxxxv. in a somewhat more popular form.

We shall not need to dwell on the spiritual manner in which God is now at last vindicating his faithfulness. To the Church Catholic, the true antitype of the ancient Israel, he has assigned for an inheritance every heathen realm throughout the world; nor ought she to rest content till every one be subjugated to her sway. We celebrate with joy the first triumphs of the gospel through the different quarters of the globe; we may exult in the career of success which in far off lands is still being granted to it; but meanwhile, along with the Jews in Nehemiah's day, we have to bewail the provinces that we have lost; and those the very provinces, alas! over which the dominion of Christ was earliest asserted. Must the scenes of the first apostolic conquests be for ever abandoned to the darkness of superstition and the bane of misbelief? Must the regions of the east which Greece and Rome once subdued to civilize, and which Christianity in her turn subdued to enlighten, relapse into the semi-barbarism from which we hoped they had been rescued? Will God not yet repent himself concerning his servants and remember us in our low estate?

PSALM CXXXVII.

The two preceding psalms were an expression of confidence that God would ultimately make good in their fullest extent his promises of blessing and dominion to the Church. In the strain before us is announced the no less confident expectation that he will award the promised recompense of destruction to those by whom the Church has been hated and oppressed. The one expectation is the necessary complement of the other; and in the prophetical scriptures of both the Old and New Testaments they are always intimately associated.

The kernel of the psalm is thus contained (as Hengstenberg has justly remarked) in the last three verses. The first six (the more familiar portion of the psalm) form but the preface. They depict the constancy of the Church in the days of her sorest trials; her preference of the joys which she remembered as her own to all that the world could offer her; her refusal to dishonour the name of the Lord or to desecrate her own sacred songs by ministering with them to either the malice or the frivolity of those who held her in subjection. It was this patient endurance of the furnace of affliction by which she had been so purified as to be able to pray, alike with sincerity and earnestness, for the outpouring of God's judgment upon the foe: it was this by which she had been trained to purge the fire of godly indignation from that of private vindictiveness, and to demand vengeance upon Edom and upon Babylon from a holy jealousy for the honour of God.

This righteous cry for the accomplishment of divine vengeance is strong and undisguised. In one particular however our English Version imparts—perhaps unavoidably—to the language an aspect which it hardly seems legitimately to bear. The sentences "Happy shall he be that rewardeth thee, &c.," "Happy shall he be that taketh and dasheth, &c.," read to us as though a *general* blessing were pronounced on those whom God should select as the instruments of his wrath. It is probable that they imply no more than a desire for a full success of the avengers *in the work of vengeance:* "God speed the avenger, whosoever he may be, in rewarding thee as thou hast served us: God speed him in taking and dashing thy little ones against the stones[1]." Vengeance is prayed for upon Edom for her malignant

---

[1] שישלם, שיאחז. The שׁ implies relation of any kind, and should here be viewed less as a relative pronoun than as a conjunction: "*in that*."

joy in the ruin of her kindred-nation of Israel: vengeance is welcomed against Babylon for that ruin of Israel which she herself accomplished. In both cases the Church already knew, from the previous predictions of her own prophets, the nature of the avenging judgments that she was to expect[1].

An endeavour has been made by Hengstenberg to arrive from internal evidence at the precise date at which the psalm was written. It manifestly belongs to the period after the return from captivity; not to the period of the captivity itself. On the other hand it would seem to have been uttered in the early years of the return. "We have still before us the generation that had been in exile. The expressions *we sat, we wept*, are not, it is true, of themselves decisive for that; but yet the whole tone of the psalm shews that the speakers are not such as knew of the exile merely by hearsay. The state of exile still appears vividly before the eyes of the people, and in the foreground of their contemplations. Still fresh, and not obliterated by any later sufferings, is the thought of what had been endured at the hands of Edom and Babylon; and these two, Edom and Babylon, have not yet come to the lowest depth of misery: the divine justice has still farther to manifest its retributive dealings towards them." We must therefore conclude that in date of composition this psalm is much prior to those by which in the Psalter it is immediately preceded.

The more exact determination of the date is connected with the story of Babylon's fall. The decay of Babylon was gradual. It was first taken by Cyrus. From that time it never recovered its previous splendour, though it continued a place of considerable importance, and formed the winter residence of its con-

---

[1] See for Edom, Obadiah; for Babylon, Isaiah xiii.

queror Cyrus during seven months of each year. Berosus and Eusebius relate that Cyrus destroyed the outer walls. In the reign of Darius Hystaspis the Babylonians broke out into a revolt for which they had made previous preparations; and, once embarked in their rebellion, they put to death the greater part of their women in order to guard against a scarcity of provisions. The result was a siege of eighteen months, at the end of which time the city was taken through the stratagem of Zopyrus, and the walls which Cyrus had spared were overthrown. Another revolt, if we may credit the authority of Ctesias, occurred in the reign of Xerxes, and was followed by a third capture. It was by Xerxes also that the golden statue was removed from the temple of Belus, and the temple itself afterwards pulled down. Babylon however was still a flourishing city in the days of Alexander the Great: and it was not till the foundation of Seleucia by the first Syrian king of the Macedonian dynasty, that the period of its decay set finally in. The contiguity of a rival metropolis gradually effected what successive overthrows had left unaccomplished; and that which earlier princes had conquered in order to possess was neglected by those who had removed to a new capital. Indeed Seleucia itself was built with materials derived from the edifices of Babylon; and after the precedent of plunder had been once established, the ruins of the residence of the destroyer of Jerusalem became the quarry from which all the neighbouring cities successively arose. At the date of the Christian era Strabo wrote of Babylon, "The vast city is a vast desert;" and what in his days was still the language of metaphor became three centuries afterward the literal truth.

The calamities denounced against Babylon in the last verse of the psalm before us are spoken of as though they were yet future; and we may therefore best assume that the psalm was written before the capture of the city by Darius; which probably occurred eighteen years after its first capture by Cyrus. The date would thus fall before the eighteenth year of the return from the captivity. Hengstenberg indeed argues that the expression in v. 8, 'O daughter of Babylon, thou wasted (or, destroyed) one' (English Version, wrongly, *who art to be destroyed*) implies that the overthrow of the city by Darius had been already effected. But we may fairly construe that expression as the prophetic past. The wasting of Babylon had been long predicted, and was therefore to the eye of faith already certain. The capture of the city by Cyrus had moreover already been an earnest of the divine fulfilment of the judgments denounced; while on the other hand even in the reign of Darius the wasting was far from finally or literally accomplished.

PSALM CXXXVIII.

To this and the succeeding seven psalms the name of David is prefixed. They were therefore undoubtedly composed by a member of the Davidic house; but here our knowledge respecting them ends. There is no sufficient evidence to establish their more determinate authorship, or even to convince us that they all proceeded from the same hand. And moreover, inasmuch as the descendants of David after the return from captivity had but little personal history of their own distinct from that of their fellow-countrymen at large, the sentiments to which in these psalms they give utterance were virtually those of the entire Jewish nation. They only contemplated their own position in so far as it represented the position of the entire community. The tone and language of the psalm now before us would well agree with the supposition that it proceeded from Nehemiah; and on the hypothesis of his **belonging to the** family of David it may be not unreasonably ascribed to him.

That it was composed after the return from the captivity may be fairly inferred from the expression in v. 1: "Before the gods (powers, *elohim*) will I sing praise unto thee." The *elohim* denote here in the first instance the earthly powers, the princes and nobles of the surrounding heathen nations; but along with these they include also the false gods whom the heathen worshipped[1]; whose very names were frequently compounded into the names or titles which the earthly princes bore, and whose adoration, with all its heathenish ceremonies, was necessarily much introduced into the details of the government which they exercised. And it is plain that the force of the expression "before the elohim" **lies in this;** that Israel was now in a position of political inferiority to the powers of heathendom, and existed, for the present, only as the dependency of a great heathen empire; and one of the hardest problems in Israel's present career, as also in the private lives of courtiers such **as** Daniel and Nehemiah, was **how to** combine an uncompromising service and faithfulness to the Lord God and a dutiful abhorrence of all idolatry with a loyal subjection **to the** heathen princes who bare rule over them and a patient endurance of the idolatrous forms in which their acts of administration were clothed. This was indeed only **one** branch of the more extensive problem how to live to God while

---

[1] Stier takes the same view. "Ferner lässt sich neben den menschlichen Vicegöttern der Völker, was daran geknüpft ist, sehr wohl an die sogenannten eigentlichen **Götter** oder Götzen der Heiden denken." He illustrates the former part of the meaning by comparing Psalm cxix. 46, the latter by referring to Psalm cxxxv. 5.

moving in the midst of a sinful world; and in the general Christian usage of the psalm the expression "before the gods" might be thus paraphrased: "in the presence of the world, its worldly society, worldly principles, and worldly fashions."

A similar indication of the late date of the psalm may be traced in v. 4: "All the kings of the earth shall praise thee, O LORD, when they hear the words of thy mouth." So long as the chiefs of the Israelitish nation were the superiors or equals of the kings with whom they had to deal this sentiment would hardly have been uttered. But little importance would then perhaps have been attached to the influence of God's word on the hearts of those whom the Israelites were continually subduing, not indeed without God's help, yet still in an earthly manner, by feats of warlike prowess. It would not be till the splendours of Israel's political history had passed away, and till the chosen people of God were only existing by sufferance, and were living as dependents under the sovereignty of a heathen sovereign, that the eye of faith would take pleasure in discerning how the fiercest conqueror should bend before the feet of the God of the lowly and the captive, and should learn from a vassal nation the revealed word of divine truth.

The main points of the psalm are contained in the three long verses, vv. 2, 7, 8. V. 2 sets forth how God has already in his dealings with his people surpassed even the former wonders of his acts in their behalf: vv. 7, 8 express the confident hope that he will still carry on the work of grace that he has begun, and will by the final deliverance of his people bring it to completion. Nowhere, it is clear, could the Christian Church find language better adapted for her own worship. The words "Thou hast magnified thy word above all thy name," i.e. "Thou hast vindicated the faithfulness of thy promises to us by means unequalled in all the stories of thy olden achievements," seem to have been originally suggested by the contemplation of the marvellous return of the Jewish nation to the land from which they had been transplanted: they bear a new meaning to us, who have beheld our redemption accomplished by the death of the Son of God upon the cross, and have been sealed with the Holy Spirit of promise, the earnest of our inheritance. And it is because God has exalted himself above his name Jehovah, in revealing himself to us no longer merely as Jehovah, but as Father, Son, and Holy Ghost, that the Church has added to the end of the psalms of Israel her own Christian doxology; thus implying that she accepts them as expressing her own gratitude for those richer mercies poured forth from above since the time that they were written.

PSALM CXXXIX.

WE now arrive at the most familiar, yet withal the most marvellous, the most beautiful, yet withal the most difficult, of all the hymns by which the latter portion of the Psalter is adorned. Standing where it does, Psalm cxxxix. seems to show that though that golden age of Israelitish history on which we dwell with such spontaneous delight had long since passed away, a destiny as mysterious as ever still hung around the chosen nation: God's dealings with Israel, if less outwardly miraculous, were not less deeply wondrous; and events in Israel's career which might wear a commonplace aspect to the ordinary observers of the world were still adding to that accumulated mass of types which, slowly though surely, were awaiting in the Incarnation of the Son of God their perfect and simultaneous fulfilment.

The authorship of the psalm has indeed been frequently assigned to David, partly on the strength of the superscription, partly from internal evidence; but as respects the latter, apparently on no other ground than that of its extreme beauty. That it cannot be David's is shewn by the numerous Chaldaisms of the language, with which, beyond any other in the Psalter, this psalm is replete. Moreover its philosophical tone of thought is alien to the psalms of David; and its parallelism with and dependence upon the Book of Daniel sufficiently bespeak its late date.

The following is a revised, and it is hoped, a more accurate rendering:

1 O Lord, thou hast searched me and known me.
2 Thou knowest my downsitting and mine uprising:
   Thou discernest my thoughts from afar.
3 Thou hast sifted my path and my bed,
   And art familiar with all my ways;
4 For without a word on my tongue,
   Lo, O Lord! thou knowest every thing.
5 Thou hast beset me behind and before,
   And laid thine hand upon me:
6 Such knowledge is too wonderful for me,
   It is exalted beyond my reach.

7 Whither shall I go from thy spirit,
   And whither shall I flee from thy presence?
8 If I mount the heavens,—thou art there;
   Or make hell my couch,—still behold thee!
9 Should I rise on dawnward wings,—
   Should I lay me down in the farthest waves of the west[1],—

---

[1] The two clauses of v. 9 stand in contrast to each other: so Theodoret, and Lowth. It is impossible to convey in English the exact force of the language here employed, on account of the double meanings attaching to several of the Hebrew words. We speak of *expanding* our wings for flight: the psalmist speaks of *lifting up* his wings; thus indicating by a single word both the raising of his wings so as to prepare himself for flight, and the soaring aloft

10 Even there shall thy hand lead me,
    And thy right hand shall hold me.
11 Again I said, Yet shall the darkness **loom around me**[1];
    And even **the** night is light about me!
12 Yea the darkness darkeneth not from thee,
    But the night is light as the day:
    Alike the darkness and the light.

13 For thou didst possess my reins
    Ere thou coveredst me in my mother's womb[2].
14 I will praise thee, for that I am fearfully and wonderfully made:
    Marvellous are thy works; and **my** soul well knoweth it.
15 Not hidden from thee was my substance, whereof I was secretly made
    And fitly joined together in the lower parts of the earth.
16 Thine eyes beheld my embryo substance,
    And the days were predetermined
    When in thy book all my members should be written[3],
    Though as yet not one of them existed.
17 So to me how precious are thy friends[4], O God!
    How many are they in number![5]
18 If I should count them, they are more numerous than the sand:
    I have awaked, and **am** again with thee.

---

by means of those wings. The word יָם denotes both the *sea* (in contrast to the *sky*) and the *west* (in opposition to the *dawn*). Again אַחֲרִית combines the meanings of *distance* and *behindness*. The psalmist sets his face toward the dawn, consequently the west is behind him: indeed the normal position of a Hebrew was towards the east, the same Hebrew word קֶדֶם signifying both *before* and *eastward*.

[1] The root שׁוּף is well connected by Rosenmüller and others with נֶשֶׁף the *twilight* or *dusk*. The particle אַךְ =*yet at least*.

[2] The future tense of the verb תְּסֻכֵּנִי has been reprehensibly neglected by most translators: it plainly depends on the previous verb, טֶרֶם or בְּטֶרֶם being understood.

[3] Here again the future יִכָּתֵבוּ has been usually treated as a past, to the great injury of the sense.

[4] So all the ancient versions: viz. the Targum (which also so translated רֵעַ in v. 2), the LXX, Vulgate, Syriac, two anonymous Hellenists, and Jerome: also Jarchi; and in modern times, Schultens. The sense is here confirmed 1° by the word רָאשֵׁיהֶם in the next clause; and 2° by the reference to God's enemies in v. 20.

[5] Literally, "How numerous are their heads," or "polls," *i. e.* "persons": cf. Judg. v. 30; 1 Chron. xii. 13.

19 O that thou, O God, **wouldest** slay the wicked[1],—
　 Yea, ye men of blood, depart from me!
20 The men who speak of thee for purposes of malice,—
　 Thy enemies, who have taken thy name in vain.
21 Shall not I hate them, O LORD, that hate thee,
　 And shall not I abhor them that rise up against thee?
22 I hate them with perfect hatred:
　 They are enemies to me.
23 Search me, O God, and know my heart;
　 Try me, and know my thoughts:
24 Behold that there is no idol-way in me,
　 And lead me in the way eternal.

The Lord Jesus Christ, the true Israel, is the speaker in this psalm; and with him the new Israel that has sprung forth from him, his mystical body the Church, consisting of those who have been baptized into his death, have been "renewed in the spirit of their minds," and have "put on the new man which after God is created in righteousness and true holiness." Both are typified by the historical Israel, brought forth from the darkness of the Babylonish captivity, and re-endowed by divine grace with national life. "My mother's womb," says Augustine, in discoursing on v. 13, "was the custom of my former city. What city? She who first bare us in captivity. We know that Babylonish city of which in our sermon on the last psalm but one we spoke, the city whence all depart who believe and who sigh for that light, the heavenly Jerusalem.......Hie thee out from the womb of the Babylonish state, commence thou a hymn of praise to the Lord: come thou forth, and be born: so will the Lord take thee up even from thy mother's womb."

The scheme of the contents of the psalm is shortly this: God's all-seeing Providence (vv. 1—12), exemplified in bringing forth his people from the darkness

---

[1] אִם cannot mean *surely:* though it may by usage mean *surely not.*

of the **womb** (vv. 13—16) to a new life of righteousness (vv. 17, 18), the holiness of which involves a **perfect** hatred and casting out of all sin (vv. 19—24). The chief point of the whole is contained in v. 16, distinguished from the rest by its length. It will **be seen** that the translation adopted above gives to that verse **a** sense very different **from that** which it is usually, at the expense of grammatical consistency, made to bear. **In** the **historical type** the days which God had prede**termined were the** seventy **years** which were to elapse from the date of **the** captivity **to** the time of Israel's restoration. These days God **had** not only predetermined, but had revealed beforehand **to** the prophets: Jer. xxv. 11, 12; xxix. 10: cf. Daniel ix. 2. In like manner, at the date **of the** composition **of** the psalm, God had not only predetermined, but also revealed by his prophet Daniel (see Daniel ix. seqq.) the number of days that should elapse before everlasting righteousness should be brought in, and they that slept in the dust of the earth should awake to everlasting life.

The leading theme of the psalm, whether historically or prophetically viewed, being thus indicated, the reader will find the less difficulty in following out the details. The mother's womb of the restored Israel was historically, **as** has just **been** explained, the Babylonish captivity. Fearfully and wonderfully **had** God brought Israel forth from that land of gloom, **in** which, as in the lower parts of the earth, the nation **had** been buried. He had predetermined the time when the Jewish state should be re-established, and when every order of men, rulers, priests, prophets, should be registered afresh in the divine covenant-book; though previously to the occurrence none would, humanly speaking, have believed it. And as he had predetermined, even so had all come **to** pass: Israel had awaked from his national death-sleep, and was again with God; and in the persons of his noblest members was exulting in beholding the number of those who were proving themselves in their lives the true friends of God. The best historical illustration of vv. 17 seqq. will be found in Malachi iii. 16—iv. 1: "Then they that feared the LORD spake often one to another: and the LORD hearkened, and heard it, and a book of remembrance was written before him for them that feared the LORD, and that thought upon his name. And they shall be mine, saith the LORD of hosts, in that day when I make up my jewels; and I will spare them, as a man spareth his own son that serveth him. Then shall ye return, and discern between the righteous and the wicked, between him that serveth God and him that serveth him not. For behold, the day cometh that shall burn as an oven; and all the proud, yea and all that do wickedly, shall be stubble: and the day that cometh shall burn them up, saith the LORD of hosts, that it shall leave them neither root nor branch."

But while recognizing in the restoration of the nation of Israel after the Babylonish captivity the immediate occasion of the psalm, we ought not to overlook the individual character in which Israel is here represented, as a *man*, endowed with a human body, the handywork of God, planned beforehand by him in all its several parts, compacted together, and brought forth by him at a predetermined time from the maternal womb. So thoroughly and consistently indeed is this imagery carried out, that the principal aim of the psalm has been often erroneously understood to be the delineation of the wondrousness of God's dealings in the formation of the human body. The real aim of the psalmist seems to be rather to shew that the individual man and the entire nation virtually participate in the same lot: both have their state of deadness; both have their divine awakening. Each is a type of the other; they are united together by subjection to a common law; and their union is an emblem of the union of Christ the ideal man, and of the ideal society, Christ's mystical body, the Church.

This brings us to view the psalm in its prophetical aspect; wherein first of all it forms a remarkable prelude to the Incarnation of the Son of God. We need not go so far as to say that it can be called an express prophecy of that great central fact in the dealings of God with men; but certainly the stress which the language of this psalm (a psalm, be it remembered, "of David," and therefore fully realized in the person of Christ) lays, in its most literal acceptation, on the divine formation of the human body is at once sufficiently explained by the circumstance that it was with a human body that Christ himself was to be clothed. He was in due time to assert the true dignity of human flesh by himself assuming it; and was thereby to bear witness against all those ultra-spiritualists who imagine that by disparaging or neglecting the body and its functions they are pressing onward to perfection. We have already observed that it may have been the teaching of this psalm that suggested the prophecy of the Incarnation inserted in the Greek version of Psalm xl: "A body hast thou prepared me."

But the actual fleshly body of Christ was itself the type of his mystical body the Church, and is as such continually represented in Scripture. His bodily agonies on the cross were a warning of the afflictions to which the Church should be continually exposed, alway delivered unto death for Jesus' sake; his unbroken bones betokened the undiminished strength which throughout her afflictions the Church should retain; the blood and water which flowed from his pierced side exhibited to view what subsequent generations cherished in the two Christian sacraments. It would be impossible therefore, with due regard to the analogy of other Scripture-teaching, to read in the psalm before us a prophecy of the incarnation of Christ, and yet not to behold in it also a picture of that more spiritual body of his, in which, and in the different members of which, his glory was to be displayed forth to the world from the period of his first to that of his second coming.

And it is when we view Christ as speaking in the person of his mystical body the Church, that the prophetical character of the psalm shines out most clearly. In secret, in the darkness of his own grave, that Church was fearfully and wonderfully made: the corn had to fall into the ground and die ere its much fruit could be brought forth. Then, after his resurrection from the dead and his ascension to his Father in heaven,—"I have awaked, and am again with thee,"—did his new life on earth in the person of the company of his redeemed people begin. It was then, when in his own person he had left the world and gone to the Father, that he openly contemplated both the preciousness and the number of the friends of God, the members of his body. Their preciousness was shewn by the fulness of measure in which he poured forth his gifts upon them: their number was the divine fulfilment of the promise originally made to Abraham, "I will make thy seed as the dust of the earth: so that if a man can number the dust of the earth, then shall thy seed also be numbered."

This was undoubtedly the view taken of this psalm by the apostle St Paul, as shewn by the commentary which he has supplied on it in his Epistle to the Ephesians, Chap. iv. Having had occasion to speak in that chapter of the one Christian body (v. 4), and having illustrated from Psalm lxviii. the ascension of Christ (v. 8), he thus proceeds, with continual allusion to the psalm now before us: "Now that he ascended, what is it but that he also descended first into the lower parts of the earth"—those lower parts of the earth in which, as the psalm testifies, his mystical body was to be wrought or compacted together—? "He that descended is the same also that ascended,"—not merely mounted the heavens, as the psalm says, "If I mount the heavens, thou art there"; but ascended—"up far above all heavens, that he might fill all things. And he gave some, apostles; and some, prophets; and some, evangelists; and some, pastors and teachers; for the perfecting of the saints, for the work of the ministry, for the edifying of the body of Christ: till we all come in the unity of the faith, and of the knowledge of the Son of God, unto a perfect man," (here the psalmist's metaphor of the human body is evidently introduced,) "unto the measure of the stature of the fulness of Christ: that we henceforth be no more children, ... but .... may grow up into him in all things, which is the head, even Christ: from whom **the** whole body fitly joined together"—the word here used is probably intended by St Paul for a translation of that employed in v. 15 of the psalm—"and compacted by that which every joint supplieth, according to the effectual working in the measure of every part, maketh increase of the body unto the edifying of itself in love." There follows a strong protest against every kind of sin, in which the influence **of vv.** 19—24 of the psalm may on close examination be detected.

In reference to this latter portion of the psalm a writer who has not otherwise taken an altogether correct view of the imprecations in the psalms observes:

"The psalmist pauses, and completely overwhelmed with feelings of adoration towards so marvellous a God, indignantly separates himself *from the fellowship of those* who sin against him. He is conscious that love to God is sincere in proportion to our hating those who have fallen to so low a state that they are actually capable of hating God. This passage explains the hatred of the psalmists towards their enemies: they are *their* enemies because they are *the enemies of God.*" To this we may add that the spirit which pervades this psalm throughout is the same with that which pervades the first Epistle of St John. The closing verses of the one accord almost exactly with the closing verses of the other. And in this circumstance alone we find a sufficient confutation of the arguments of those who attack the spirit of the psalms as contrary to the spirit of the gospel. Under the new covenant equally as under the old we cannot but hate for God's sake those that sin against him. We hate them however only insofar as they sin, and on the hypothesis of their impenitence; and our hatred is not inconsistent with the most loving and earnest efforts to bring them to repentance.

PSALM CXL.

That this and the three following psalms proceeded from the same author will be almost universally allowed. In many respects they are not unlike the original psalms of David; although their place in the Psalter and the number of borrowed passages in Psalm cxliii.[1] shew that they cannot well be ascribed to him. The use in

---

[1] With v. 2 cf. Job xiv. 3; with v. 4 Psalm lxxvii. 3; with v. 5 Psalm lxxvii. 5; with v. 6 Psalm lxiii. 1; with v. 7 Psalm xxviii. 1. Psalms cxlii. and cxliii. present many points of mutual resemblance, which testify to the connexion between them.

Psalm cxl. 3 is one of the passages referred to by St Paul, Rom. iii. 13.

Psalms cxl, cxliii. of the Selah, which occurs nowhere else throughout the last two Books of the Psalter, is probably due to a designed imitation of the arrangement of the older hymns. And it is to the closeness with which the later psalmist has here adhered to the Davidic model that we also owe the superscription of Psalm cxlii, "Maschil of David, when he was in the cave, a prayer;" the import of which is that the situation and feelings of the psalmist, and of all in whose name he speaks, are the same with those of David when blockaded by Saul in the cave of Engedi.

The interpretation of particular passages in these psalms is attended with much difficulty, which does not however affect their general purport. They form in regard of their subjects a connected series. In Psalm cxl. the suppliant prays to be delivered from the machinations of his enemies, in Psalm cxli. from their assaults on his life: in Psalm cxlii. (the psalm of the cave) his soul is in prison; from the darkness of which he asks in Psalm cxliii. to be led forth into the land of uprightness. It is not to be denied that this sequence of subjects would well accord with the successive phases of David's early life, Psalm cxl. representing the period of his attendance at Saul's court, Psalm cxli. the period of his flight from that court, and of the slaughter of the priests at Nob (cf. v. 7), Psalms cxlii, cxliii. the period of his outlawry and exile among the mountains. But they may with equal propriety be viewed as a general embodiment of the trials of the true-hearted of the nation of Israel during the period of the captivity; the two earlier psalms exhibiting the more personal tribulations to which such men as Daniel were exposed, while they carefully eschewed the "wicked works" and even the tempting "dainties" of the workers of iniquity; the two latter setting forth the general desire of the chosen people to return from the prison-land of Babylon to that "land of uprightness" which had been given them for an inheritance. We must bear in mind that for wellnigh a century after the return of the first caravan of restored exiles by the permission of Cyrus, there were Jews still detained by various hindrances in the lands of the Gentiles, and still cherishing the same desires which had animated the whole Israelitish people during the earlier and more general portion of the captivity. The reception of the Book of Esther into the canon of Old Testament Scripture, and the later observance by the whole nation of the Feast of Purim in memory of the great deliverance therein recorded, sufficiently indicate that the history of the chosen people during the Persian period must include the account of the fortunes of those dwelling without as well as of those dwelling within the limits of Judea. Nor can it be reasonably doubted that the position of Mordecai and Nehemiah at the court of the Persian monarchs was still virtually the same as that of Daniel or the three holy children at the court of the rulers of Babylon. It may be—the view appears at least probable, although it be out of our power to substantiate it—it may be that the psalms before us, so far as they are drawn from personal experience, reflect the trials of Nehemiah during the earlier period of his life. But however this may be, there are none in the Psalter of which the language so easily adapts itself to the trials of every Christian man during his earthly pilgrimage; none in which the believer may so obviously read the alternate persecutions and seductions of the world, or in which he may so readily express his longing to be led from his present state, in which when he would soar aloft he finds himself fettered down by the bond-chains of worldliness, forth into that land of perfect uprightness where God's will shall meet with no resistance, and where they that **afflict the** souls of the righteous shall no more appear.

We proceed to speak more particularly of the first **psalm in the series,** Psalm cxl; of which the following version **will be useful,** as exhibiting its poetical structure. The outline of the arrangement is similar to that of Psalm v; the psalm consisting of a comparatively short strophe and antistrophe, and of a longer epode, the central verses of which stand out with marked prominence. The Selahs mark the respective ends of the strophe, the antistrophe, and the first division of the epode.

1 Deliver me, O LORD, from the evil **man,**
 From the violent man preserve me,
 Who have meditated mischiefs in their **heart!**
 Continually are they gathered together for wars;
 They **have** sharpened their tongue like a serpent;
 Adder's poison is **under** their lips. Selah.

4 Keep me, O LORD, from the hands of the wicked,
 From the violent **man** preserve me,
 Who **have** meditated to overthrow my steps!
 In their pride they have hid for me a snare and cords;
 They **have spread a** net by the wayside;
 They **have set traps** for me. Selah.

6 I have said to the LORD, Thou art my God!
 Give ear, O LORD, to the voice of my supplications!
7 O GOD the Lord, the strength **of my** salvation,
 Thou hast covered my head **in the day of** arms.
8 Grant not, O LORD, the **desires of the** wicked;
 Further not his wicked device. **Selah.**
9 Men shall shoot at them the poison of their own table;
 They shall clothe them with the mischief of their own lips;
10 They shall cause live coals to fall upon them;
 Into the fire shall one hurl them, into torrents that they rise not again[1].

[1] See on the Hebrew text of vv. 8, 9, 10 the article by me in the *Journal* *of Class. and Sacr. Philology,* Vol. IV. pp. 260—261. I had not, when I

11 Let not an evil speaker be established in the earth;
  The violent man, let evil hunt him to overthrow him:
12 Sure I am that the LORD will maintain
  The cause of the afflicted, the right of the poor:
13 For yet shall the righteous give thanks unto thy name,
  And the upright dwell before thee.

We have here only to ask whence the images of vengeance in v. 10 were drawn. The live coals and the fire bring up to our remembrance the furnace into which the three holy children were cast; and it may be that to that event a special allusion was intended; the authors of the malicious plots against the persons of the righteous reaping in all their fulness and effectiveness the terrible punishments to which they had fruitlessly consigned their own victims. The Persian monarchs, however, together with their subordinate officers, were unquestionably guilty of terrible atrocities in the various forms of torture and death to which they subjected offenders; and it may be that persecutions of the Jews scattered throughout the Persian realm, of the particulars of which we are not informed, had furnished occasion for the details of the psalmist's language more exactly than any of the historical events with which we are acquainted. All however tends to shew that it was in connexion with what passed in other lands than that of Judea that this and the following psalms were written.

PSALM CXLI.

OF this psalm vv. 1, 2 form the opening, vv. 7—10 the concluding strophe: the central and emphatic portion is vv. 3—6, consisting of two long verses, similar

wrote it, discovered how important in respect of the formal arrangement of the psalm were the emendations which I advocated.

to each other in structure, enclosed **by two** of ordinary length. Vv. 3, 4 contain the believer's prayer to be kept from carelessly or waywardly falling into imitation of the workers of evil: vv. 5, 6 set forth his delight in the **company of** the godly[1], even though at the cost of being exposed to rebuke and correction. It will be noticed moreover that as v. 5 contrasts with v. **4**, the oil of hospitable welcome in the one keeping up the image of the feast suggested by the dainties of the other, **so also v.** 6 specially contrasts with v. 3, both **these** latter having reference **to the** propriety of what is uttered with the lips:

3 Set a **watch, O Lord, to** my mouth,
   A guard **upon the door** of my lips:
4 Incline not my **heart to** any evil thing,
To practise wicked works with men that **work** iniquity;
   And let me not eat of their dainties!
5 Let the righteous smite me,—'t shall be kindness;
And let him reprove me,—oil for the head which my head shall
   not refuse;
       For **still** even in their calamities shall be my
       prayer!
6 Their judges were thrown by the sides of the cliff,
   And they heard my words, that they were sweet.

The **reference in** the first line of this last verse is to **the** barbarous punishment, prevalent among Eastern nations, of hurling **men or children down** from the top of an **elevated rock, and so dashing them to** pieces. It is perhaps **out** of our power to determine whether the psalmist **had** actually beheld this punishment inflicted on the leaders of his former persecutors, **or** whether it **be** an imaginary picture that is here drawn, for the **purpose of** setting forth the pious constancy of the

---

[1] It **is** to be noted that many, by the "righteous" of v. 5, understand God himself; comparing an alleged similar use of the word in Isaiah xxiv. 16, where, however, it has the article.

Church of God, even when in the extreme calamities of others she beholds evidence of the perils to which she is herself exposed. The lesson however inculcated is that under no circumstances should the holy prayers of God's people cease: stedfast in their allegiance to God, yet withal affectionate in their sympathy towards men, they should constrain the worldly in the midst of whom they dwell, whether in the hour of their pride or of their fall, to recognize the fragrance of the incense of supplication which is continually ascending from their hearts to the throne of grace above. They should make the world feel that there is a heaven-taught harmony which no earthly violence can effectually mar; the harmony of perpetual communion with Him who is the Lord of the spirits of men.

PSALM CXLII.

If by the superscription prefixed to this hymn the psalmist designed to shew how deeply his soul was penetrated by the spirit of the older supplications of David, the attention which he bestowed upon the formal structure of this as well as of the last two psalms shews how he also endeavoured to conform to those rules of poetical composition which David had observed. We have here, first, a prelude, vv. 1, 2; of which two verses the former is imitated from the opening verse of the Asaphic Psalm lxxvii. The prelude being once separated off, the remainder of the psalm is easily seen to consist of a verse of three tritonic lines (v. 5), enclosed by two pairs of verses of two long lines each (vv. 3, 4; 6, 7), the whole of these long lines being marked by distinct breaks in the syntax in the middle. The longer verses describe the sense of loneliness which weighs upon the suppliant's soul: the central verse, as also the prelude, expresses his resort to God for comfort in this hour of trouble.

And it is for support in his present distress rather than for actual deliverance from it that in this psalm the suppliant more especially prays. In the last verse indeed, which forms the natural transition to the ensuing psalm, he ventures to look forward to a time when his soul shall be brought out of prison, and the righteous shall compass him about; but otherwise his solicitude is rather how he may hide himself in God, and may be upheld by his almighty love, while the desolate gloom of his prison makes his heart sad, and the powers of darkness are yet upon him. The public devotions of the Church in her captivity here reflect the inward struggles of many an individual believer. The sense of present abandonment is oftentimes too intense to admit of being relieved by the mere prospect of future blessings: expectation of the day-break can not of itself dispel the blackness or avert the perils of the night. But God is still there, a very refuge and strength, even though his presence be outwardly unattested; and under the shadow of his wings, though he discern not any gleams of deliverance, the pilgrim may yet find his shelter till the tyranny be overpast.

PSALM CXLIII.

This psalm, the last of the series to which it belongs, is divided into two halves by the Selah, but is otherwise, apparently, not regular in its structure. In respect of its contents it contrasts strongly with Psalm cxlii, to which it forms the natural complement. It is a picture of godly hope, gazing from a state of great distress forward to a blessed future: it is a supplication for such deliverance as shall enable the worshipper to enter on a new life of uprightness. On the prosecution of this new career of godly activity his thoughts are concentrated: hence the petition (v. 2) not to be condemned for the past; hence also the petition (vv. 10, 11) for enlightening, sanctifying, and quickening grace. This new life, moreover, must be a life in God: to God the worshipper stretches forth his hands, for God his soul thirsts (v. 6); and thus it is that meditation on all God's past works quickens the fervour of his present devotions (v. 5).

And of this new life,—the new life of every individual believer in Christ,—the restoration of each successive company of Israelites to the land of their forefathers was the legitimate type. The inheritance of the chosen nation was, as has been already remarked, the visible pledge of the covenant which God had made with them; and for each several captive, exile, and wanderer, return to that inheritance was the outward expression of return to a life in covenant with God. The ratification, through the blood of Christ, of the covenant between God and man, having brought out more determinately its spiritual character, has rendered the former temporary symbol of it obsolete; yet history, however limited the theatre on which its events were transacted, can never lose its value; God's dealings are in every age essentially the same; and even to the Christian it must ever remain a task full of profit, with the volume of the Old Testament records before him, to "remember the days of old" and to muse on the former work of God's hands.

PSALM CXLIV.

The earlier portion of this psalm, so different in its tone to those immediately preceding, is almost entirely compacted of passages borrowed from previous parts of the Psalter: **chiefly from** the great epinikion of David, Psalm **xviii**; **also from** other psalms of David, Psalms viii, xxxiii, lxix; and in one instance from a **piece of** much later date, Psalm civ[1]. This last circumstance, **together with a** grammatical peculiarity unknown **to** the earlier psalms[2], points directly to a late date; which is also indirectly evidenced **by** the composite character of the psalm. As regards vv. 12—14, **the** transition **to** them **is** remarkably abrupt; and it has been fairly argued **by** Ewald, (who is by no means alone in **his** opinion,) that "the description in them is so singular, so genuinely and boldly poetical, so thoroughly indicatory of an earlier and more outwardly prosperous period, that we may unhesitatingly assume that **the** poet has borrowed it (like most of the other verses of the psalm) from some older poem, now lost, connecting **it** by one single word with what precedes." **This** word, the first word of v. **12**, may, instead of being rendered **as** in **our** English **Version** *that*, i.e. *in order that*, **be treated** as a relative **pronoun**, referring to the speakers understood; and then, **if we** supply throughout vv. 12—14 verbs in the indicative, not the optative, **mood**, the psalmist's meaning will be, "***We***, that people of whose happiness **an** older poet paints so noble a picture, *we* need not give way to doubts!"

---

[1] Compare vv. 1, 2 with Psalm xviii. 2, 34, 47; v. 3 with viii. 4; v. 5 with xviii. 9, civ. 32; v. 6 with xviii. 14; v. 7 with xviii. 16, lxix. 14; v. 9 with xxxiii. 2, 3; v. 10 with xviii. 50.

[2] The use of שֶׁ for אֲשֶׁר.

We, "**whose sons** are like plants well-grown in their youth,
Whose daughters like corner-pillars sculptured after the fashion of a palace;
Whose garners are full, supplying all manner of **store**,
Whose sheep bring forth thousands and ten-thousands in our fields,
Whose oxen are equal to their burdens, with **no** hostile irruption,
No going forth into captivity, no wail through **our streets**!"

The **view that these lines** form a quotation from an older poem is strongly confirmed by the **language of v. 15**, where the "**in such a case**" would **refer** more naturally to a description which the psalmist had **found** ready to his hand than **to** one which he had himself produced. An unfortunate mistake was committed **by the LXX.** and **the patristic interpreters when they** supposed the "**strange children**" to be **the subjects of this** description, and thus **imagined a contrast to be intended** between the material **blessings** of the enemies and **the** spiritual blessings of the people of **God**. It is **a** sufficient refutation of this **to** observe **that** the blessings promised by the Old Testament prophets to God's people almost uniformly include—as **far** as words go —those of material prosperity; blessings of the **lower** kind being in fact images or shadows of those of the higher.

The character **of the strange children** as drawn in this psalm exactly accords with that **of the neighbour**ing enemies of the **Jewish** people after their return from **the** captivity. There **can** thus be little doubt that it belongs to that period, to which indeed it is deemed by **Theodoret to refer;** but the question of its authorship is one of somewhat greater difficulty. If we assign it, as indeed we necessarily must, to **one of the repre**sentatives of **David's** house,—as for instance to Nehemiah on the **hypothesis** that he **was** descended from that family,—what **are we to** make of the words of v. 2, "who subdueth my people under me[1]," implying, as they apparently do, a royal authority on the part of the utterer? Theodoret quietly remarks that these words apply to Zerubbabel, and to Joshua the high-priest, who ruled the people immediately after the captivity: we might of course with equal propriety put them into the mouth of Nehemiah; but the question is, would any mere governor **or** viceroy, not being himself a king, venture to **speak** of the people of Israel, or of any **people** whatever, as *his* people?

Our answer to this question, **may** serve, if its correctness be admitted, to throw light upon the spirit in which the later psalms of the Psalter **were** penned. Their authors well knew that the promised kingdom of Israel had never yet been realized. The true king of Israel had yet to come. He was to spring, according to the divine announcement, of the house of David; but David's house had not yet produced any one comparable, in combined power and piety, to David himself. It had gradually, with some alternations **of** fortune, declined till the period of the captivity; nor had it **since** wielded the sceptre of royalty, though the nation had been in some degree restored. Yet even in this its period of depression (and before the coming of Christ **it** was destined to sink into **yet** greater obscurity) its

---

[1] We have here moreover a question of textual criticism to deal with. **Certain** MSS., fewer altogether than one-quarter, and, if fairly reckoned, fewer than one-sixth of the whole number, read for עַמִּי *my people*, עַמִּים *peoples;* which latter agrees with the rendering of the Targum, Syriac, Roman Psalter, and Jerome. These however can hardly justify us in rejecting the more difficult reading when supported by the large majority of MSS. and by the LXX, as well as by the Gallican Psalter. Nor indeed can we be certain that they did not really read עַמִּי, regarding it (although wrongly) as an apocopated plural. Indeed from a Masoretic note and from the marginal avowal of some of the MSS. it would appear that the reading עַמִּים originated in the desire to interpret by the regular plural form that which was erroneously believed to be also a plural form of rarer occurrence. There would also be a desire to assimilate the text to that of Psalm xviii. 47.

members, and especially those who took a leading part in the administration of the affairs of the nation, could not but view themselves as links in the chain of continuity from David to the future Messiah. Their royalty might be in abeyance, but royalty yet remained divinely stamped upon their house. In theory therefore, and in faith of the ultimate fulfilment of God's promises, they deemed themselves still **kings; and even** the various degrees of authority which under **various** titles they exercised, from whatsoever source proximately derived, seemed to them the natural fruits of the dignity of their lineage, the witness that to their family had been irrevocably assigned the office of ruling God's people Israel. And accordingly, without limiting **their** language to the measure of the authority which they actually possessed, they **continued, as** heirs of David and as ancestors of the Messiah, to speak **in** the same terms as those in which David would have spoken. Modern Europe furnishes abundant illustration of the reluctance of the illustrious by descent or by station to recede from the dignity that once pertained to those whom they followed or replaced. But from any merely frivolous or mendacious claims which hereditary pride or personal vanity might suggest, the royal language of the psalm **before us** is distinguished by the belief **of** its author that every claim that he made **in it** would **in** due time be to **the very** fullest extent realized—realized with a **grandeur** and a completeness of which he could form but a **very** faint conception. It was no mere reminiscence of the past: it was an anticipation by faith **of** the glories in store. The psalmist identified himself in spirit not merely **with** the departed David, but with **the** future Christ. Even David's own words were not all **true of** himself: it was in the person of **his** Great Descendant that he spoke. And in the same person, by virtue of the same faith, spoke the author of the psalm before us; not abating, even under the present depression, one jot or one tittle of the magnificence of the language that David's more prosperous circumstances had suggested; nay, rather increasing it; so that where David wrote "it is God that subdueth *the nations (peoples)* under' me[1]," the later psalmist substitutes "who subdueth *my people* under me;" thus viewing all the Gentile nations as collected in some sort into one great people for obedience to that Son of man of whom a prophet had already written, "There was given him dominion, and glory, and a kingdom, that all people, nations, and languages, should serve him: his dominion is an everlasting dominion, which shall not pass away, **and** his kingdom **that** which shall not **be** destroyed[2]."

As regards the use of this psalm by the Christian Church, we have no need to repeat the remarks already made upon the analogous Psalm xviii.

PSALM CXLV.

WE have already noticed the indications of such a designed arrangement of the later psalms as that their several subjects should, where it were possible, correspond to those **of** the earlier **psalms from** which they were removed by exactly **one hundred** places[3]. Traces, however faint, **of such a design here** again meet us. Psalms xliv. and cxliv, strongly **as** their tones contrasted with **each other,** agreed in this, that a leading theme of both was God's going forth with his people's armies; while Psalm cxlv. so far recalls Psalm xlv, that it shines conspicuously forth **in** its place in the Psalter

---

[1] Psalm xviii. 47.   [2] Dan. vii. 14.
[3] See above, pp. 221, 222.

as a grand hymn of praise, and that it even borrows from it particular words or collocations of words[1]; the subject of both being the glory of the divine kingdom, although in the one it is contemplated as the kingdom of the divinely exalted Messiah, in the other as the kingdom of the Almighty Creator.

The psalm before us is appropriately styled in the superscription, "A hymn-of-praise of David:" the word in the Hebrew being that which was afterwards adopted as the generic name for a *psalm*, although this is the only superscription in which it is actually found. It is "a song of thanksgiving and praise on the part of the house of David and the Church after all their tribulations have come to a close[2];" doubtless written at a season when through the mercy of God tribulation had temporarily given way to general joy, and when men could therefore the more easily anticipate the advent of the promised blessings of the latter days. Theodoret, relying on the expressions in vv. 9, 12, 21, urges that it contains a prophecy of the calling of the Gentiles; nor is the remark altogether unjust; though we should be straining the force of those expressions were we to press a more definite meaning on them than on many others in the Psalter which we have passed unnoticed. In its structure the psalm is alphabetical; but by the absence of any verse commencing with the letter Nun the number of verses is restricted to twenty-one. It thus divides into three equal portions or strophes, of which the first celebrates God's greatness, the second his goodness, the third his righteousness. The first strophe is obviously in a measure introductory to the other two; and in its concluding verse, v. 7, expressly announces their respective subjects: "They shall publish forth a memorial of thy great *goodness*, and shall

---

[1] Cf. vv. 5, 6 with xlv. 3, 4.   [2] Hengstenberg.

celebrate aloud thy *righteousness*." This verse is not however on that account to be detached from the first strophe: it is God's *great* goodness that is insisted on, it being in the display of the other attributes that his **greatness unfolds** itself; and it is in fact only by circumlocution or paraphrase that we can in English convey the exact force of the original text of the verse, in which a special emphasis is thrown on the adjective *great* by placing **it before** the substantive: "They shall **celebrate** the memorials of thy goodness and of thy **righteousness with** utmost powers of voice and liveliest transports **of joy; and** then in **the** inadequacy **of** the highest human strains to express how tenderly and how justly thou hast dealt with **us**, shall the excellence **of thy** incomparable greatness most fully **appear."**

It **was** not to **be** expected that tamperers with the Biblical text would in **any** age suffer the imperfection of the alphabetical arrangement in this psalm to remain; and accordingly **in** the translation of the LXX. **and** in its derived versions, including the Syriac, **we** find inserted after v. 13 a verse which if rendered in Hebrew would begin with the omitted letter: "The LORD **is faithful in** his words, and holy in all his works." **Of** the spuriousness of this there can be no reasonable doubt. How can **we, even** making the most undue allowance for the supposed **carelessness of** transcribers, believe **in the** loss of one **entire** verse from a psalm, the alphabetical arrangement **of** which afforded the strongest guarantee of the preservation of its integrity? The inserted verse is implicitly condemned by the authority of the Targum and of Jerome, of every Hebrew manuscript[1] and of every Jewish commentator; it bears evident traces of having been manufactured, with a

---

[1] **Its** appearance on the *margin* **of a** single MS. **furnishes, of course, no occa**sion for modifying this statement.

slight alteration, from v. 17; and lastly it is not in place in the second strophe of the psalm, of which not God's righteousness, but his goodness, is the subject.

PSALM CXLVI.

THE five concluding psalms of the Psalter all begin and end with the Hallelujah; thus solemnly marking the book of which they form the close as one great offering of praise to Him that dwelleth in Zion. They are themselves essentially psalms of praise: the last four exuberant and unchequered in their joyfulness; the first—that with which we are now concerned—tinged with a gleam of melancholy from the remembrance of previous sufferings, yet still a psalm of praise, sure in its hope, and devout in its thankfulness. We can but guess at the exact occasion on which it was written. There is none with which its language would better agree than that of the return to Judea, by permission of king Artaxerxes, of the second caravan under Ezra: compare more especially the sentiments of vv. 3—5 with Ezra's acknowledgments of the divine mercy on the issue of the royal decree: "Blessed be the LORD God of our fathers, which hath put such a thing as this in the king's heart, ... and hath extended mercy unto me before the king, and his counsellers, and before all the king's mighty princes. And I was strengthened as the hand of the LORD my God was upon me, etc.[1]" The words of v. 5 of the psalm, "Happy is he that hath the God of Jacob for his help," —not "helper," the more usual expression,—would form a natural confession for one who himself bore the significant name Ezra, *Help*.

[1] Ezra vii. 27, 28.

We have no distinct warrant for supposing the present psalm to have proceeded from any but the Sons of Asaph. Should any suggest that Ezra himself were the author, our first observation in reply must be that Ezra was not a temple-singer but a priest. Still it is not to be denied that his high office may have marked him out as the legitimate leader and director of the public devotions of Israel[1]; and if it were by him that this and the following four psalms were produced,—though those four were certainly not written till the period of the governorship of Nehemiah,—he would not unnaturally for this reason, if for no other, as the final editor of the Psalter and indeed of the whole canon of Old Testament Scripture, take care to assign to them the concluding place. Our present copies of the LXX. ascribe this psalm, together with those immediately succeeding, to the prophets Haggai and Zechariah. The same superscription appears also in the Syriac translation: it is however of no authority, and in the case of Psalms cxlvii, cxlviii. undoubtedly incorrect.

Not undeserving of notice are the coincidences of language or sentiment between the psalm now before us and that which we last examined. Verse 2 may be compared with cxlv. 2; v. 5 (in the Hebrew) with cxlv. 15; vv. 7, 8 with cxlv. 14—16; v. 10 with cxlv. 13. There are also several resemblances in it to passages of Isaiah: cf. vv. 3, 4 with Isaiah ii. 22, v. 5 with xxvi. 4, vv. 7, 8 with lxi. 1.

---

[1] It may also be noted that in Neh. xii. 27—43 the priests as well as the Levite singers come before us as assisting in the sacred musical service.

PSALM CXLVII.

The Old Testament history closes, in point of time, with the administration of Nehemiah. The great work accomplished by Nehemiah was the restoration of the walls of Jerusalem. It was by this that he was afterwards remembered: "among the elect," says the son of Sirach, "was Neemias, whose renown is great, who raised up for us the walls that were fallen, and set up the gates and the bars, and raised up our ruins again[1]." That a memorial of that work would be preserved in the closing strains of the Psalter is no more than we might expect to find; and we may reasonably conclude both from their language and place that it was for the occasion of the thanksgiving procession after the completion of the walls that Psalms cxlvii—cl. were written. It was evidently no ordinary assemblage. "At the dedication of the wall of Jerusalem," we read[2], "they sought the Levites out of all their places to bring them to Jerusalem, to keep the dedication with gladness, both with thanksgivings, and with singing, with cymbals, psalteries, and with harps. And the sons of the singers gathered themselves together, both out of the plain country round about Jerusalem, and from the villages......; for the singers had builded them villages round about Jerusalem." The names of the priests' sons who blew the trumpets are carefully recorded, as also those of the other Levite musicians who marched "with the musical instruments of David the man of God, and Ezra the scribe before them;" while lastly a sort of epilogue at the end of the chapter in which this account is contained seems to imply that

---

[1] Ecclus. xlix. 13.   [2] Neh. xii. 27 seqq.

every effort was on this occasion made to re-establish the sacred musical service on the basis of the rules of the original foundation of David as nearly as the circumstances of the time would permit. And in this there was an obvious fitness. The rebuilding of the walls of Jerusalem was looked upon as the return to the days of David, by whom that city had been first erected into the Israelitish capital. The trials and humiliations of the captivity seemed at length to have passed away. All was once more new; and the Israel of the restored Jerusalem was the type of the Church triumphant of the last days, the glorious company of victorious saints, ransomed from the captivity of an imperious world, into whose lips this very psalm is virtually put, and whose praises a yet struggling Christendom anticipates, looking forward with the certainty of divine assurance to the season of the final exaltation of the meek and of the final casting of the wicked down to the ground.

The psalm has its points of resemblance to Psalms xxxiii, civ; but almost every verse in it is marked by the restoration-character which belongs to the whole. Jerusalem built up after her desolation, the bars of her gates made fast; the children of God that were scattered abroad gathered together in one, and the denizens of Zion filled with the richest of blessings within her; the wounded bound up, the heart-broken healed; these are all images the relation of which to the general theme of the psalm can hardly be mistaken. But when we further read of God telling the number of the stars, these words are equally intended to convey the consoling lesson that He who according to his promise to Abraham made his people as the stars of heaven for multitude, will not overlook the needs of even the least amongst them. When we read of the clouds and the rain, and of the grass which by their means is made to grow on the mountains as pasture for the cattle[1], and of God's consequent supply of food to the beasts, yea and even to the young ravens that call upon him, all this is intended to signify that he who thus provideth for the brute creation cannot forget the wants of his nobler subjects, much less of his own chosen and redeemed people who invoke him. When lastly we read of the melting of the snow and ice by his word and his breath, this also was no unfit emblem of the dissolution of the Jewish captivity; while to the Christian Church it speaks in yet more emphatic language; for (to use the beautiful words of a recent commentator) "when the creatures God has made become cold and hardened for lack of his love within their hearts, and when their affections are colder than the snow, and their consciences harder than the morsels of ice, and their souls are dying like living things in a piercing frost which they cannot bear,—then he sendeth forth his all-loving Son, crucified for their salvation, and loving them unto the end; and he bloweth upon them with his wind, the soft breathings of his Holy Spirit; and their frozen heart, hardened like ice in the long cold night of this cheerless world, is melted through the shining of the Sun of Righteousness, and their softened soul dissolves into repenting and longing tears with the warmth of the Saviour's love, and under the gentle influence of that Spirit of grace, which bloweth where he listeth."

Thus are all God's wondrous operations in the material world viewed as emblems and pledges of his acts of love to the members of his Church.

---

[1] The addition of the LXX. to v. 8, preserved in our Prayer-book version, "and herb for the use of men," destroys the whole force of the passage. It was easily borrowed from Psalm civ. 14, where it is in place.

PSALM CXLVIII.

The former psalm rehearsed the grounds of praise: the present psalm is the conveyance of it. And as it is God's Church alone by whom this reasonable sacrifice of praise can on earth with understanding be offered, the real purport of the psalm is comprised in the last verse. In this respect the calls for praise upon the inanimate creation, and even upon the angels, who are here introduced for the sake of completeness, are but introductory to the final call upon Israel, the "all people" of every rank and condition of vv. 11, 12 forming the intermediate link; so that the psalmist ascends from the inanimate to the animate, from the animate to the redeemed: man is the priest of nature, Israel the priest among men. If the preceding psalm had shown that God's works in nature were emblems of his acts of grace to his Church, so now the emblemed Church must remember not to yield to the material emblems in the depth of her praises; and the homage which to the imagination of faith all nature unceasingly renders must stimulate the faithful themselves to purer and more fervent devotion. There is however another leading idea running through the psalm which requires to be unfolded. It is this; that as the sun, moon, and stars, and the firmament of clouds are to the eye of men the great witnesses of God's glory above, so is the exaltation of the horn of his people, or in other words, the triumph accorded to the Church, the great revelation of his glory on earth. Hence the division of the psalm into two parts· "Praise ye the Lord from the heavens," vv. 1—6: "Praise the Lord from the earth," vv. 7—14. The one is of course introductory to the other; and v. 13 supplies the reason why God should be praised from the earth; viz. because his splendour *rests upon*[1] the earth as it does upon the heavens; and this, in that (v. 14) he hath manifested forth his glory in his chosen people Israel. And therefore once more, as the Church is to be the great choir of the universe for the celebration of God's praises, so is the glory bestowed upon the Church, which is the great earthly testimony to the glory of God, to be the universal theme of praise; and as all nations of the earth, and even earth herself, join with untrained voices in the strains which chorister-saints have been specially instructed to lead, and the nave and aisles of the great universal temple re-echo the chants which the white-robed denizens of the chancel put forth with heaven-inspired skill, so are all to give thanks that God should thus have "a people near to him," to be his witnesses in the world, and to awaken spiritual harmonies in souls wearied with the baser turmoil of earthly life in which they have long been grovelling. Kings of the earth such as Nebuchadnezzar and Cyrus felt long ago the beauty of a service in which, as non-Israelites, they could take no direct part; and even in the season of the present catholicity of the Church, when all are freely received into the company of the highest Christian worshippers, perhaps among those who still linger without, with vacillating purpose or divided heart, there are yet many who feel it a blessing even to listen to Christian strains, and who can honestly praise God that there are others nearer to him than they have yet approached themselves.

---

[1] E. V. wrongly, *is above*.

PSALM CXLIX.

WE have here a fuller development of the last verse of the preceding psalm. A designed verbal coincidence links the two together: the "praise of all his saints" of Psalm cxlviii. 14 becomes in Psalm cxlix. 1 "his praise in the congregation of saints." Both passages are somewhat ambiguous; but with regard to the latter, as all the older translators concur in the rendering "His praise *is* in the congregation of saints," we may conclude the meaning to be that it is in the glory which he hath bestowed on the congregation of his saints that God's praise chiefly displays itself: well therefore may those saints themselves employ their skill in praising him. It is God by whom Israel hath been made an Israel, a chosen and glorified people: well may the Church rejoice in Him from whom her churchly character proceeds.

The analogy of all sacred history would sufficiently warrant us in expecting that the praises vented on such an occasion as the thanksgiving for the rebuilding of the walls of Jerusalem would be deeply and markedly prophetical. The psalm before us is essentially prophetical. From the very first its whole substance rested upon prophecy. The Jews of the days of Nehemiah were never engaged in executing judgment upon the heathen. They never handled the sword but for purposes of defence. *For defence* indeed, history records how, while labouring at the fortifications of their city, they with the one hand wrought in the work, and with the other hand held a weapon[1], but the time yet lay hidden in the womb of the future when with

---

[1] Neh. iv. 17.

the high praises of God in their mouth, and a two-edged sword in their hand, they should go forth "to execute vengeance upon the heathen, and punishments upon the people, to bind their kings with chains, and their nobles with fetters of iron." Three centuries onward brought to the Jews a certain outward and typical fulfilment of this language in the victories of the Maccabees; of which the psalm is accordingly treated by Theodoret as a prophecy. For the real fulfilment we must, it is almost needless to say, look to the spiritual victories of the Christian Church. It is these through which, by the strength of Christ, the judgment of this world is effected, and the prince of this world cast out[1]: these, through which the strong man is bound and spoiled by the might of the stronger than he. When the apostle Paul spoke to his Christian converts of the judgment which was being accomplished by them, "Do ye not know that the saints shall judge the world? and if the world shall be judged (rather, 'is judged') by you, &c."[2] he doubtless implicitly referred either to the psalm now before us, or to the other scriptures on which that psalm is based.

What then are those other scriptures? Evidently the writings of the prophet Daniel; in which, unfolding the mysteries of the vision of the four beasts, he had declared that the saints of the Most High should take the kingdom, and should possess the kingdom for ever, even for ever and ever; that for a time indeed the horn of blasphemy should make war with the saints and prevail against them, until the Ancient of days should come, when the judgment should sit, and they should take away the blasphemer's dominion to consume and to destroy it unto the end[3]. The expression employed in the last verse of the preceding psalm, "He exalteth

---

[1] Joh. xii. 31. [2] 1 Cor. vi. 2. [3] Dan. vii. 18 seqq.

the horn of his people," was probably chosen with reference to this **vision** of Daniel respecting the horn of blasphemy. Nor when the psalmist speaks of executing **upon the** heathen **the** judgment *written*, **does** there seem to be any good ground for assuming the special reference to be to the commands issued or the strains uttered by Moses in the Pentateuch. There is no special resemblance between the language of this psalm and that of either the seventh or thirty-second chapters of Deuteronomy, with which it **has** been sometimes compared. **The** writings of Daniel must in the days of Nehemiah have already taken their place amid the recognized sacred prophetical **Jewish** literature. Even **were** they only first received into the sacred **canon by** Ezra at the date of the composition of this psalm, there would still be no inconsistency in at once referring to them as a revelation from God. The admission of any prophetical writing into the canon was not, so to speak, **the** first consecration of it, but only the formal acknowledgment of that divine sacredness which it had from the first **possessed.**

And with regard to the description, both in Daniel and in the psalm before us, of the saints executing judgment **upon the worldly power,** we may remark that it could hardly have been written **in** earlier days, such as those of **David.** Israel **did not then** come into conflict with **the** principal representatives of the power of the world. **It** was not till Israel **had been** confronted with Assyria and with Babylon that the future triumphs of God's Church could be fully depicted. The struggles with those mighty empires, and more especially the Babylonish captivity and the return from it, were thus in God's good providence made the occasion for those promises of the victory of the saints over the worldly power by which they were oppressed, for which in earlier times (except only in the deliverance from Egypt) a historical basis would have been wanting.

One further remark by way of caution. These anticipations of saintly triumphs, although connected with the historical crises through which Israel was passing, were no mere enthusiastic visions kindled by the all-engrossing excitement of present conflict. Far from it: they were revelations made to men of chastened lives, singing aloud "upon their beds," the scenes of quiet meditation and undisturbed divine communing. No earthly alloy mingled with the divine announcement of the judgment which the saints should in due time execute upon the enemies of God. Not to a Joshua or a Judas Maccabeus, not even to a Nehemiah, the zealous reformer of internal corruption, the privileged repairer of the walls of Jerusalem, was the first utterance of it confided; but to a captive ascetic, who passed all his days far away from the land of his fathers, and who there in his exile "had a dream and visions of his head upon his bed," and "wrote the dream, and told the sum of the matters[1]."

PSALM CL.

Quicquid sonat, Deum sonet. Such is Bossuet's account of this psalm. A call to praise God, with each several instrument of music which the Levites employed in the temple-worship forms a most appropriate conclusion to the hymn-book which comprised the burdens of their strains. With instruments of every variety of timbre, from the deafening trumpet to the fascinating harp; with instruments adapted to every purpose, whether used to accompany the dance or the song; with instruments of every gradation of tone,

[1] Dan. vii. 1.

with cymbals of a piercing and with cymbals of a clanging sound; let God be praised. So far Bossuet's argument **is correct.** Yet as the concluding verse invites **not** all that **hath** sound, but **all** that hath breath, to join in the praise; and as we can hardly suppose that man would be intentionally introduced as **a** mere appendage to the lifeless instruments which **he** himself hath fashioned; it would seem that that which is capable of sound is here to be viewed as the type of that which is filled with the breath of life; **a** fact the less to be questioned, since even in the New Testament St Paul draws from the lifeless instruments **a** parable respecting the utterances of men[1]. And **thus** the moral **of** the psalm will be that all mankind, whatever be their natural varieties of mind **or of** temper, whatever the pursuits in life in **which they** severally best may glorify God, whatever the character **of** their powers and faculties are summoned to unite **in** that great swell of praise which shall then ascend **to** Almighty God from the universal earthly company of his redeemed Church. And thus will God be praised by men in the sanctuary of his Church **below as** by angels in his mighty firmament above. **It is** his will to be praised: be his will done **in** earth **as it is in** heaven. Amen.

[1] 1 Cor. xiv. 7 seqq.

APPENDIX I.

ON THE NAMES OF GOD IN THE PSALMS.

THE two names by which both in the Psalms and in the rest of the Old Testament the Almighty Being is most frequently designated are: 1. *Elohim*, in English *God*; 2. *Jehovah*, the sacred name which the later Jews refused to pronounce, which the Greek translators accordingly replaced by Κύριος, and which in consequence still generally appears in our English Bibles as LORD, distinguished by capital letters. It is well known that these two names are not found promiscuously; but that in some parts of the Old Testament the use of the one, in others the use of the other, is preferred; those parts consisting in some cases of entire books, in others of smaller sections of the same book. Thus the student will search in vain through the book of Ecclesiastes for the name Jehovah, or through that of Obadiah for the name Elohim. In the Pentateuch the passages in which the one name or the other is employed generally alternate. Thus in the passage Gen. i. 1.—ii. 3 we have everywhere Elohim; in Gen. ii. 4 —iii. 24 we have generally the composite name Jehovah Elohim; in Gen. iv. Jehovah. And here where an exceptional Elohim occurs in the midst of a passage exhibiting the habitual use of the Jehovah, or *vice versâ*, the reason is frequently obvious; as for example in Gen iii. 1—5, where we have the simple Elohim instead of Jehovah Elohim, because the tempter is speaking.

Now in the different parts of the Psalter we find, with some limitations, this same preference for the use of the one or of the other name. The following table, extracted from the *Symbolæ ad Psalmos Illustrandos Isagogicæ* of Delitzsch will shew the number of times that either name occurs in each psalm. It does not extend to the superscriptions of the psalms, nor to the doxologies at the ends of the several Books; nor yet to those passages in which the name Elohim is combined with a possessive suffix (*my God, our God*, &c.), or is applied to any but the true God. It will be proper also to observe that the

APPENDIX I.

accuracy of the table cannot be conveniently tested in an English Bible, as the word *God* there represents the Hebrew term *El* as well as the more frequent *Elohim*.

BOOK I.			BOOK II.			BOOK III.			BOOK V.		
	No. of occurrences of the name			No. of occurrences of the name			No. of occurrences of the name			No. of occurrences of the name	
PSALM	Jehovah.	Elohim.	PSALM	Jehovah.	Elohim.	PSALM	Jehovah.	Elohim.	PSALM	Jehovah.	Elohim.
i.	2	0	xlii.	1	6	lxxiii.	1	3	cvii.	12	0
ii.	3	0	xliii.	0	4	lxxiv.	1	4	cviii.	1	6
iii.	6	1	xliv.	0	4	lxxv.	1	2	cix.	7	0
iv.	5	0	xlv.	0	3	lxxvi.	1	2	cx.	3	0
v.	5	1	xlvi.	3	5	lxxvii.	0	6	cxi.	4	0
vi.	8	0	xlvii.	2	7	lxxviii.	2	8	cxii.	2	0
vii.	7	3	xlviii.	2	5	lxxix.	1	1	cxiii.	6	0
viii.	2	1	xlix.	0	2	lxxx.	2	5	cxiv.	0	0
ix.	9	1	l.	1	7	lxxxi.	2	1	cxv.	10	0
x.	5	2	li.	0	5	lxxxii.	0	2	cxvi.	15	0
xi.	5	0	lii.	0	3	lxxxiii.	2	2	cxvii.	2	0
xii.	5	0	liii.	0	7	lxxxiv.	7	4	cxviii.	22	0
xiii.	3	0	liv.	1	4	lxxxv.	4	0	cxix.	24	0
xiv.	4	3	lv.	2	5	lxxxvi.	4	2	cxx.	2	0
xv.	2	0	lvi.	1	9	lxxxvii.	2	1	cxxi.	5	0
xvi.	4	0	lvii.	0	6	lxxxviii.	4	0	cxxii.	3	0
xvii.	3	0	lviii.	1	2	lxxxix.	10	0	cxxiii.	2	0
xviii.	16	0	lix.	3	5				cxxiv.	4	0
xix.	7	0	lx.	0	5	BOOK IV.			cxxv.	4	0
xx.	5	0	lxi.	0	3				cxxvi.	4	0
xxi.	4	0	lxii.	0	7	xc.	2	0	cxxvii.	3	0
xxii.	6	0	lxiii.	0	2	xci.	2	0	cxxviii.	3	0
xxiii.	2	0	lxiv.	1	3	xcii.	7	0	cxxix.	3	0
xxiv.	6	0	lxv.	0	2	xciii.	5	0	cxxx.	4	0
xxv.	10	1	lxvi.	0	7	xciv.	9	0	cxxxi.	2	0
xxvi.	6	0	lxvii.	0	5	xcv.	3	0	cxxxii.	6	0
xxvii.	13	0	lxviii.	2	24	xcvi.	11	0	cxxxiii.	1	0
xxviii.	5	0	lxix.	5	7	xcvii.	6	0	cxxxiv.	5	0
xxix.	18	0	lxx.	2	3	xcviii.	6	0	cxxxv.	15	0
xxx.	10	0	lxxi.	3	6	xcix.	7	0	cxxxvi.	1	0
xxxi.	10	0	lxxii.	0	1	c.	4	0	cxxxvii.	2	0
xxxii.	4	0				ci.	2	0	cxxxviii.	6	0
xxxiii.	12	0				cii.	7	0	cxxxix.	3	0
xxxiv.	16	0				ciii.	11	0	cxl.	7	0
xxxv.	8	0				civ.	8	0	cxli.	3	0
xxxvi.	2	2				cv.	5	0	cxlii.	3	0
xxxvii.	15	0				cvi.	8	0	cxliii.	4	0
xxxviii.	3	0							cxliv.	4	1
xxxix.	2	0							cxlv.	9	0
xl.	9	0							cxlvi.	9	0
xli.	5	0							cxlvii.	5	0
									cxlviii.	4	0
									cxlix.	2	0
									cl.	0	0

If we reckon up the total number of times that the two names occur in each of the five Books into which the Psalter is divided, the result will be

	Book I.	Book II.	Book III.	Book IV.	Book V.
Jehovah.........	272	30	44	103	236
Elohim	15	164	43	0	7

APPENDIX I.

From this it appears that in Book IV. the name Jehovah is used to the entire exclusion of Elohim; that, save in two psalms out of forty-four, the same is also the case in Book V; and that in Book I. also the use of the same name vastly preponderates. On the other hand in Book II. the Elohim occurs more than five times as often as the Jehovah; while in Book III. the preponderance of the Elohim in the earlier psalms of that Book is balanced by the preponderance of the Jehovah in its later psalms.

Now these cannot be the results of mere chance. They may point to a predilection for one or other of the divine names at different periods of history, or in different styles of composition. They may point to some hidden device by which the psalms were ranged in their present order. They may point to systematic alterations made in the texts of different portions of the Psalter. But whatever be the true explanation of them, one thing is certain, that by any one who would pursue the right path in a critical examination of the Psalter, they cannot be lightly passed over or neglected. They may not have attracted the notice of those who merely read the psalms devotionally, nor even of a great majority of those who have investigated their several characters, their order, and arrangement: still, once discovered, they are palpable to our gaze, and display themselves as sacred facts, the reverent study of which can hardly fail to prove both interesting and instructive.

In examining the conclusions which have been drawn from these facts by others, it would be a profitless and wearisome task to enter minutely into all the complicated theories respecting the history of the Psalter to which they have given rise. It will be sufficient for our immediate purpose to notice the explanations that have been given of them by two orthodox Christian expositors, Delitzsch and Hengstenberg; which, though not themselves altogether admissible, will yet prepare us to render a more correct account respecting the facts before us. In criticizing the views of these two scholars it must be premised that they both, in common indeed with all hitherto who have maintained the genuineness of the superscriptions of the psalms, assume David to be the author of all those psalms which are marked with his name.

The theory then of Delitzsch is briefly this; that the oldest collection of psalms comprised the present Books I. and II, and that in it the forty-one which exhibited the divine name Jehovah were designedly placed first, the other thirty-one made to follow; that the first permanent appendix to this collection consisted of the present Book

III, and that here the Elohim-psalms were placed first in order that they might follow immediately on the Elohim-psalms of the original collection; and that, thirdly, at a still later period all the remaining psalms, comprising those which had been preserved either by memory or else in appendices similar to Book III, were rearranged and constituted into Books IV. and V. As regards the distinction of psalms some exhibiting the one divine name, some the other, he argues that this did not arise from their being composed at different periods or by different authors, nor yet from any grammatical or logical necessity of using the one name rather than the other, since the two might be frequently interchanged without injury to the sense. He conceives therefore that just as we recognize different metrical, rhythmical, poetical, and musical styles, so also we must simply admit the existence of two kinds of Hebrew psalmody differing from each other in the divine name employed; the distinction between them being perhaps based on the distinction between the passages in the Pentateuch which differ in the same manner. He allows however that the Elohim-psalms belong chiefly to the age of David; and that in consequence of the subsequent idolatrous use of the term *elohim*, the later psalmists, following the example of the prophets, preferred the employment of the name Jehovah.

Had Delitzsch pursued this last observation to its legitimate consequences, he might have been led still nearer to the truth. As his theory stands, it is beset by one insurmountable difficulty. How came it to pass that amid the remains of the Davidic period which were not included in Books I, II, III, and which it was consequently left for the collector of Books IV, V. to arrange, there should be found but one Elohim-psalm (Psalm cviii)? Had Delitzsch been but able to perceive that no such remains existed, and that the simple reason for the non-appearance of the name Elohim in the last two Books of the Psalter is that those Books consist entirely, or almost entirely, of the psalms of the later periods, in which, for certain reasons, the divine name Jehovah was almost universally employed in preference to Elohim, his general explanation would then be not very far removed from the truth. But he was fettered by the assumption that all psalms marked with David's name must be ascribed to David's pen; an assumption hitherto unquestioned by those who believe in the genuineness of the superscriptions, and which has proved the chief source of perplexity and cause of failure in the attempts that have been hitherto made to analyse the arrangement of the Psalter. For this reason the attempt of Delitzsch fails as a whole in common with the rest; though in some respects it is destitute neither of merit nor of partial success. His account however of the origin of the two classes of psalms is shallow and unsatisfactory.

Hengstenberg, more profound, but less cautious, has framed an altogether different theory. He unreservedly rejects the view that the present Books of the Psalter represent collections of psalms formed at different periods: it is according to him "certain that our present collection presents no traces of being formed out of such early collections: it has in no respect the character of a work done piecemeal, but **is** arranged from points of view that embrace the whole field: its author, living at a time when psalmodic poetry had already ceased, had the entire body of existing psalms before him, **and formed** the collection after those points of view." In forming it, he made Book I. to consist of the Jehovah-psalms of David; in Book II. he gave to the Elohim-psalms **of the** Levite singers the first place, to the Elohim-psalms of David the second; in Book III. **he** comprised the Jehovah-psalms of the Levite singers; and **in Books** IV. and V. he put, in exact chronological order, all that remained from Moses to the captivity and from the captivity to Nehemiah, including in each case those Davidic psalms which had been interwoven into the cycles of psalms composed in those periods.

We need not discuss the reasons which Hengstenberg assigns for the proceedings of his assumed collector. Even could the proceedings themselves be proved, the reasons would necessarily remain conjectural. Let us simply test the theory by examining how far it accords with the known facts which it purports to explain.

It will be observed that according to this theory the arrangement of the first three Books was mainly influenced by the distinctions existing among the psalms in regard of their respective use of the divine names; that of the last two Books by considerations of chronology. We should therefore naturally expect to find the phenomena respecting the use of the divine names more marked in the first three Books than in the other two. But what are the facts of the case? In Book IV. the exclusive use of the name Jehovah is absolute and universal, in Book V. all but universal: respecting Books I, II. assertions quite so strong could certainly not be made, while in Book III, *viewed as a whole*, the phenomenon altogether disappears. Our incredulity is at once excited.

Proceed we more particularly to the psalms of Book III. To the maintenance of Hengstenberg's theory it is indispensable that these should all be reckoned as Jehovah-psalms, in contrast to the Elohim-psalms of Book II. **That** the first ten (Psalms lxxiii—

lxxxii.) would hardly so be reckoned by an unprejudiced inquirer is, at a glance, sufficiently evident. Most undauntedly does Hengstenberg argue that "their Elohistic character rests merely upon appearance." But is not the whole distinction between the two classes of psalms very much a distinction of appearance? For surely in its deepest essence every Elohim-psalm is a Jehovah-psalm, every Jehovah-psalm an Elohim-psalm: this could scarcely be denied even by Hengstenberg himself. The LORD, he is God: there is but One Almighty and All-loving Being, whether he be contemplated as the God of the universe or as the God of his people Israel. The remarks made by Hengstenberg on the psalms of which we are speaking are not without their value, but those who have entered into them will find no difficulty in equally applying them to Psalms xlvi—xlviii. In the case of Psalm lxxvii. he not unjustly argues that "the precious name is found exactly in the words which form the beating heart of the psalm, 'I will remember the works of Jah,' in v. 11; and that the one Jah in this passage, more emphatic than Jehovah, weighs more than the six Elohims which serve only to make it shine forth more brightly." But how came he to overlook the similar phenomenon of Psalm lxviii. (in which we must include also its introductory trilogy Psalms lxv.—lxvii.), where the repeated Elohims bring out with greater force the emphatic Jah—the concentrated Jehovah—of vv. 4, 18?

Such, as regards the arguments drawn from the use of the divine names, are the objections to Hengstenberg's theory of the arrangement of the Psalter. To speak more particularly of the psalms of the Levite singers, there are really no grounds for denying that those of Book II. stand on precisely the same footing with the earlier ones of Book III. in respect of their preference for the name Elohim. It is far more natural to suppose that that preference is connected with the circumstances of the times within the limits of which all those psalms were written. Hengstenberg is in fact in error when he assigns any of the psalms of the Levite singers to the age of David. Even when they are severally examined, the evidence is in every single instance in favour of a later date. Nor again, if only the more obvious difficulties can be otherwise explained, is there any substantial ground for Hengstenberg's assumption that the several Books of the Psalter were simultaneously arranged: it was doubtless far otherwise. In his view of the chronological principles upon which the last two Books were collected it is satisfactory to be able more nearly to concur; though it is here a rash assertion of his that the psalms in those Books are arranged in *exact* chronological order.

A simpler account has in the body of this work been given than that to which he was compelled to resort of the appearance of psalms "of David" in those Books; and it may, without breach of modesty, be hoped that the discovery of the true meaning of the superscriptions of those psalms may prove of considerable importance to future students of the Psalter. In thorough and striking agreement with the view of their authorship there propounded is the account which Hengstenberg has in his commentary generally given of the spirit and significance of those later Davidic psalms; and such an agreement of two independent lines of reasoning lends to both no slight degree of confirmation.

In endeavouring to unfold the true causes of the phenomena respecting the use of the divine names in the Psalter, we must first gain a clear view of the general relation of those names to each other. The basis of the distinction between them is that while Elohim is not necessarily more than man's name for the object of his worship, known or unknown, Jehovah represents a revelation made by God of himself to men.

In the great process of divine revelation which the Bible sets before us we may discriminate three principal stages or periods[1]; those of the Promise, the Law, and the Gospel. At each successive period it pleased God to make a revelation of himself in the form of a Revelation or Declaration of his Name. To Abraham he revealed himself as El Shaddai, The Almighty God, or Almighty Power[2]; to the Israelites as Jehovah, or more fully as I AM THAT I AM[3]; to the Christian Church as the Father, the Son, and the Holy Ghost[4]. The revealed name of the Promise bore witness of God's power to fulfil his promises; that of the Law, of his Eternal Being, the fountain-head whence all law proceeds; that of the Gospel, of his Perfect Fulness, manifested forth upon earth to give life to the world.

The first of these revelations was comparatively simple in its character: the second, with which we are now more immediately concerned, presents more points of difficulty. It is in the first place to be remarked that the revealed name, Jehovah, was not entirely new, for it had been employed by the patriarchal recipients of the former revelation. But its full significance was now for the first time brought out; and it is with reference to this that we are to understand God's declaration that he had not been known to Abra-

---

[1] Cf. Moberly's *Law of the Love of God*, pp. 100 seqq.
[2] Gen. xvii. 1, cf. Exod. vi. 3.   [3] Exod. iii. 14; vi. 3.
[4] Matth. xxviii. 19.

ham, Isaac, and Jacob by that name. In the next place we observe that the name was not intended to denote the Eternal Being of God as wrapped up in itself, but as exhibited forth in its all-effective energy; God's revelation of the name being expressly connected with the announcement of **what he** would accomplish, Exod. vi. 6. And moreover **as** the name **evidently** implied that God changeth not, but is everywhere and **at all** times the same, it followed that every manifestation upon earth of this divine energy must be in itself a true declaration of the character of God, being not merely an exhibition of what he is at a particular time or place, but rather a projection on the mundane theatre of events of what he is eternally. Hence the connexion of the name Jehovah with the **moral** attributes of God, Exod. xxxiv. 6, 7. Then again we must specially notice that God's formal revelation of himself by the name Jehovah was accompanied by **the** first formal announcement of his taking the Israelites to be his people, Exod. vi. 7, "And I will take you to me **for a** people, and **I** will be to you a God;" it being in the special guardianship and sovereignty **of his people** Israel that he was about to display himself both to them and to the **surrounding heathen as** the One Only True and *Living* God.

In consequence of the connexion between God's revelation **of himself** by the name Jehovah, and his assumption of the Israelites **to** be his peculiar people, the name Jehovah became the name **by which** the Israelites regularly spoke of God. It was their privilege to use the name: it was his memorial among them unto all generations. The habitual employment of it was one of the outward means whereby they realized their position as his covenant-nation, as the people who were called by his Name. There was no intrinsic reason of convenience why they should disuse it; and it is in point of fact by far the more frequent appellation of God both in the historical books, and in the **Prophets,** and in the Psalms of the Old Testament. Our problem therefore is not to explain in the Psalter **the use of the** name **Jehovah,** but to assign the reasons of the more **exceptional use of the** name Elohim.

Elohim is in itself, as **has been** already stated, no more than man's name for the object of his worship. But as such it will bear any latitude of meaning. The idea conveyed by it is entirely dependent on the degree of religious education of the man using it. With the untutored savage it may denote no more than the spirit of his departed ancestor, on whose grave he lays his offerings. **With** the Israelite worshipper it denoted the One Almighty and **Eternal** Being who had revealed himself to Israel by his name

APPENDIX I.

Jehovah: it therefore conveyed to him no lower idea than was conveyed by the sacred name Jehovah itself.

Such being the case, when through any cause the significance of the name Jehovah was obscured, the sacred writers recurred to the name Elohim, in order to convey by it the full idea which the name Jehovah failed to **convey**.

1. Thus, first, **as** regards the moral attributes of God. We have traced the connexion between these and the name Jehovah. The acts of Jehovah were so many declarations of his moral character, they brought his moral attributes to light; and the righteousness and lovingkindness which were inherent in the idea of Elohim present **to** the mind **of** an Israelitish worshipper were practically derived from the divine education which **at** the hands of Jehovah he had received, and from the contemplation of the righteous and loving dealings of Jehovah with those **whom he** had taken to be his people. It may sound to us an axiom **to** say that God is perfect holiness, perfect love; but this is in real truth the **result of our** Christian training. Natural religion has never shone very brightly except where she has been enabled to borrow, however indirectly, the doctrines that revealed religion had previously taught. But on the other hand it is undoubtedly the fact that to a religiously educated mind much of what has been practically derived from revela**tion wears,** when once apprehended, the appearance of necessary and axiomatic truth. And this is especially the case with regard to the conceptions formed respecting the character and attributes of God; which, once formed, become thenceforward independent of the peculiarities of the source from which they were derived. So that though the moral attributes of Elohim were, in the main, only known from the manifestation of those attributes in Jehovah, yet the name Elohim thenceforward implied the instinctive recognition of them as eternal and immutable, while the name Jehovah directly involved only the cognition of them as limited **by** the conditions of the mode in which they had been manifested.

But such a limitation, or even the appearance of it, would have been in practice insupportable. The lovingkindness of Jehovah had been manifested in deeds as a lovingkindness towards his chosen people *as a people;* but the individual offender who had justly forfeited his title to be reckoned any longer among Jehovah's people felt constrained to appeal expressly to that deeper and more radical divine lovingkindness which was the same under all circumstances, and of which the lovingkindness of Jehovah to his people as a people was only one form or manifestation. And if the name

Jehovah were liable to suggest this one conditioned and restricted form of lovingkindness, there would be an obvious reason why the penitent should address his prayer to God by the more general name Elohim. This is precisely the case which meets us in Psalm li. Again, the righteousness of Jehovah had been specially manifested as a righteousness delivering the Israelites from the persecutions of their heathen enemies. No doubt such manifestations would prepare them to recognize that eternal righteousness of God which must equally judge between the persecutors and the persecuted within the commonwealth of Israel; but the use of the name Elohim indicates more directly than that of Jehovah that it is to this essential, fundamental righteousness that the appeal is made. Hence in Psalm lviii. the name Elohim occurs twice, the name Jehovah but once. The Elohim has the more force, though the Jehovah through which the knowledge of the righteousness of Elohim had been developed is not inadmissible. When however the relations of Israel to the heathen are distinctly contemplated as typical of the relations of the godly to the wicked, as in Psalm lix. 5, (where the heathen must, even historically, be sought *within* the commonwealth of Israel,) there the manifestation of the righteousness of Jehovah towards his people rises *ipso facto* into a type of his essential righteousness, and the name Jehovah is in its proper place.

We need not pursue these remarks. Little difficulty will be found in explaining on the foregoing principles David's repeated use of the name Elohim in each of the psalms li—lxiv; except, perhaps, in the case of Psalm lx, where the reason for the preference of the Elohim to the Jehovah is less obvious. But when such psalms as these were adapted by David himself to the sanctuary service, the name Elohim was generally replaced by the name Jehovah; and hence the prevalence of the name Jehovah in Book I. of the Psalter, which forms David's sanctuary-hymnal. The reasons for this substitution may have been, first that the Jehovah, being the name by which the Israelites usually addressed God, could not well be refused its place in a hymnal expressly intended for the temple use; secondly, that though to a soul of strong passions the Elohim might more directly suggest the eternity of God's moral attributes, yet to the great body of the people it was needful that the memorial of the manifestations of his attributes should be continually brought home by the repetition of the Jehovah; and thirdly, that as the consignment of the psalms to the use of the Church was closely connected with their prospective reference, it was desirable to mark that the fuller manifestation of God's attributes which men were to expect

APPENDIX I.

would be the continuation and completion of those more limited manifestations which as Jehovah he had already made in the midst of his people Israel.

2. But we proceed to point out a second cause which introduced into many of the psalms the name Elohim rather than Jehovah. The name Jehovah was in itself the very strongest protest against all worship of strange gods. It proclaimed the absolute being of the One True God, and therefore, by implication, the absolute nothingness and vanity of all deities beside. But when, the meaning of the name being forgotten, Jehovah came to be in any wise treated only as the national God of the Israelites, and as such to be set on a par with the objects of adoration of the surrounding nations, it then became necessary to enter a fresh protest against all such profanation of his majesty by a resort to the employment of the name Elohim. Now this was precisely what came to pass during the greater part of the period of the schism; the schism itself contributing in no slight measure to that result. The existence of the two rival kingdoms side by side throw the theocracy into the shade; and as the kingdom of the ten tribes put itself gradually, through the apostasy of its princes, on a level with the kingdoms of Tyre and of Syria, while the mistaken compromises of such rulers as Jehoshaphat helped to sink the kingdom of Judah to the level of the kingdom of the ten tribes, the Israelites lost sight, more or less, of their character as a chosen and peculiar people, a people "dwelling alone" and "not reckoned among the nations," as well as of the dignity of their calling as witnesses to the world for the truth of God. Men in Israel halted between two opinions, hesitating whether they should follow Jehovah or Baal, or perhaps in many cases endeavouring to reconcile the worship of the one with the worship of the other; and even the pious Jehoshaphat, when asking at the court of Ahab for a prophet of Jehovah, enquired in words which implied such a condescending recognition of the status of those prophets who were not prophets of Jehovah as an adequate zeal for God's honour could never have tolerated. Elijah and Elisha testified loudly against this compromise with evil: nevertheless it continued. To the day of their captivity the ten tribes of Israel "followed vanity, and became vain, and went after the heathen that were round about them;" and so long as the kingdom of the ten tribes was permitted to exist, Judah also "walked in the statutes of Israel" (2 Kings xvii. 15, 19). Then at last a change was brought about; partly through the removal of the contagious example of the ten tribes, and the warning afforded by their punishment; partly through the personal influence of the

zealous Hezekiah; partly through the altered political relations of the Jews to the surrounding heathen; the manifest worldly inability of Judah to struggle against the might of Assyria bringing out into full relief that churchly character of the chosen people which had been thrown into the shade so long as they had been equally matched in point of worldly strength against their former Syrian enemies. And this change was, on the whole, permanent; at least so far permanent, that in spite of the multiplied transgressions which followed, and which drew down from God the judgment of the Babylonish captivity, the better part of the nation never lost sight to the same extent as before of their essentially churchly character. The period then when we should *a priori* expect that there would be most occasion for guarding against the debased popular view of Jehovah, as a mere national God of the Hebrews, by a recurrence to the use of the name Elohim, is the period from the separation of the kingdoms up to the middle of the reign of Hezekiah. And it is precisely to this period that the Elohim-psalms of the Levite singers, viz. Psalms xlii—l, lxxiii—lxxxiii. have been shewn to belong. From the middle of the reign of Hezekiah the predominant use of the name Jehovah becomes re-established,—cf. Psalms lxxxiv—lxxxvii; while in the psalms of later date, from Psalm lxxxviii. onwards, the Jehovah not merely predominates, but entirely excludes the Elohim. Psalm cviii. is obviously not to be accounted as of really later date, being compacted of portions of two older hymns, nor does the single occurrence of the Elohim in Psalm cxliv. need to be reckoned, as that psalm also consists chiefly of passages strung together from previous strains.

Stress has been laid by both Delitzsch and Hengstenberg on the variations in the doxologies of the several Books of the Psalter, as though the divine names employed in those doxologies were designedly intended to mark the characters of the Books to which they were attached. But it is more simple to assume that the doxologies, equally with the psalms themselves, depended for their form on the age which gave birth to them. In the Davidic doxology of Book I, and in the post-Hezekianic doxologies of Books III, IV, we have the name Jehovah alone: in the doxology of Book II. the sacred collector, living in the *early* part of the reign of Hezekiah, abstained from using the name of Jehovah unaccompanied by Elohim.

3. A third reason for the occasional use of the name Elohim was to render the recurrence of the Jehovah less frequent, and so to bring out that sacred name with greater emphasis and solemnity. To this, and to the chief exemplification of it, in the connected

psalms lxv—lxviii, we have already adverted. But the Elohim might obviously be used with this effect in psalms where it was partly introduced on **other** grounds.

On one or other of the above principles may thus **be** sufficiently explained the use of **the** Elohim in almost all the psalms in which that **use** predominates. As to Psalms lxix—lxxi, it **is** perhaps enough to say that they exhibit that mixed use of both the divine names which was probably habitual to the royal psalmist, and which would have been exhibited to us in many of the psalms of Book I. to a greater **extent than** at present had they been consigned by David to **the use** of the Church in the **exact** form in which they **were** originally **composed by** him. Lyrical poetry from its very nature demands variety; nor can we see why such variety may not reverently extend even to the different appellations by which God **is** designated; and we may reasonably conceive that the poetry **of** David would be no less full of native variety in this than in other respects. It is less easy to discern the reason for **the exclusive use** of the name Elohim in Psalm lx. Yet may it not have **been to** remind Israel, who looked back with humiliation and shame on their past season of depression, that they were after all, in very truth, God's people? There remains the psalm of Solomon, Psalm lxxii, in which the Elohim occurs once, the Jehovah not at all. Now this psalm seems to contemplate the reign of the Messiah as a revelation *to all nations* of the righteousness and lovingkindness of that God whom they had hitherto hardly known. If this be so, the name Elohim is more appropriate than Jehovah; and it is accordingly the name employed.

APPENDIX II.

ON THE MUSICAL INSTRUMENTS OF THE JEWISH PSALMODY.

MUSICAL Instruments may be generally divided into String-instruments, Wind-instruments, and Instruments of Percussion. These last are in most cases not capable of being easily made to produce more than one note each, and are therefore principally employed in company with other instruments, to enhance the general effect of the performance. For melody we depend on instruments of the former two kinds; and here there are three different methods by which a variety of notes may be obtained:

1. By a modification of action upon the instrument, by means of which, of the different harmonic notes which it is capable of simultaneously producing, one is elicited in preference to the rest; as in the simple unkeyed trumpet.

2. By a modification of the instrument itself, consisting for the most part in such an artificial increase or diminution of its length as can, owing to the peculiarity of its construction, be rapidly made with the fingers; as in the flute, or the single-stringed violin.

3. By the juxtaposition of a number of simple instruments, involving a partial combination of them into a single whole; as in the organ, pianoforte, or harp.

Of these three expedients the last was the most obvious, and therefore probably the first adopted. It was this, perhaps, which was devised by Jubal, "the father of all such as handle the harp (*kinnor*) and organ (*ugab*);" the former instrument standing as the type of all those formed by a combination of strings, the latter, in its simplest form, the Pandean pipes or syrinx, as the type of all formed by a combination of wind-tubes. It can hardly be doubted, however, that when music was cultivated, the second method of producing a variety of notes would be also brought into play; while, furthermore, the first method would be also introduced wherever trumpets were extensively employed.

This being so, we proceed to the enumeration of the different instruments mentioned in the texts or superscriptions of the psalms, or of which it is otherwise probable that **they were used** in the temple-service.

I. STRING-INSTRUMENTS. Of these there were among the Jews two main kinds: the *kinnor*, E. V. *harp*, in the LXX. generally κιθάρα or κινύρα, occasionally ψαλτήριον, once ὄργανον; and the *nebel*, E. V. *psaltery*, or in the prophets *viol*, in the Prayer-book *lute*, in the LXX. generally νάβλη or ψαλτήριον, once κιθάρα, in Amos ὄργανον. **The accounts** that have in modern times been given of these two **instruments, and** of the difference between them, are, as might be supposed, very various; and the only evidence on which we can thoroughly rely as to their respective characters is the scanty evidence indirectly supplied **by** the Hebrew scriptures **themselves**.

It seems in the first place almost certain that both instruments were portable, and capable of being played while they were carried along; a circumstance which forbids us to suppose that either could have been so ponderous as a modern harp. Thus we read of Samuel warning Saul that he should "meet a company of prophets coming down from the high place with a *nebel*, and a tabret, and a pipe, and a *kinnor*, before them" (1 Sam. x. 5). Again, when the procession was formed to bring up the ark from Kirjath-jearim, "they carried the ark of God," we read, "in a new cart out of the house of Abinadab: and Uzza and Ahio drave the cart. And David and all Israel played before God with all their might, and with singing, and with *kinnoroth*, and with *nebalim*, and with timbrels, and with cymbals, and with trumpets" (1 Chron. xiii. 8; 2 Sam. vi. 5). Similar is the account of the renewed procession from the house of Obed-edom: "All Israel brought up the ark......making a noise with *nebalim* and *kinnoroth*" (1 Chron. xv. 28). Again, when Judah marched out under Jehoshaphat to the wilderness of Tekoa to encounter the Moabites and Ammonites, the singers went out before the army; and on their return "they came to Jerusalem with *nebalim* and *kinnoroth* and trumpets unto the house of the LORD" (2 Chron. xx. 28). As regards the *kinnor* in particular, it was not too heavy to be carried by a singing-woman about a city (Isaiah xxiii. 16), nor yet to be hung upon the willow-trees by those that desired not to use it (Psalm cxxxvii. 2).

Furthermore both the *kinnor* and the *nebel* were made, in whole or in part, **of wood**. Whether or no 2 Sam. vi. 5 be so construed as to imply that **both were, in David's** earlier days, formed of fir (or rather 'cypress'), it is **at least clear**, from 1 Kings x. 12, 2 Chron. ix. 11, that Solomon made both of the more precious wood of the almug-tree.

The **difference between the two instruments** may be partly gathered from the words used in connexion with them. We read in 1 Chron. **xv. 20, 21,** in the account of the temple-orchestra, of "*kinnoroth* on the Sheminith," and of "*nebalim* on Alamoth." **The word** *sheminith*, or "eighth," answers probably to our **"octave"; and as** Psalms vi, xii, both of a very lugubrious character, are appointed in the superscriptions to be sung upon the sheminith, there seems good reason to concur with Gesenius in supposing the octave intended to be the *lower* octave, in other words, the notes of graver tone, the solemn effect of which would be in keeping with the mournfulness of **the** theme. "On Alamoth," i. e. "after the manner of virgins," **would then** express the higher **or soprano notes, such as are** within the compass of women's **voices: Psalm xlvi. is superscribed "upon** Alamoth," and is of a joyful, inspiriting character. The natural sound of the *kinnor* was thus in all probability deeper than that of the *nebel*.

Of the number of strings of the *kinnor* the Bible supplies no hint; but we learn from it that the *nebel*, either universally, or in one of its kinds, had ten strings; the instrument which is in Psalm xcii. 3 called simply the *asor*, *i. e.* the ten, or decachord, being designated more fully in Psalm xxxiii. 2, cxliv. 9, as the *nebel asor*, *i. e.* the ten-stringed *nebel*. (The *and* supplied in the English Version of these latter two passages has no existence in the Hebrew, and should be omitted). Josephus indeed speaks of the *kinnor* as having ten strings, the *nebel* twelve[1]; but this is at variance with the evidence supplied by the psalms themselves; and the assertion therefore, if it be not due to ignorance or carelessness, must be explained by Josephus' habitual desire **to** magnify in the eyes of the Gentiles everything connected **with his own** country; which possibly he might in this case be able **to do without wholly** contravening the **truth, by** describing the largest known forms **of the** two instruments instead of those generally employed.

As regards the manner in which these instruments were played,

---

[1] Jos. *Ant.* VII. 12. 3 : ἡ μὲν κινύρα, δέκα χορδαῖς ἐξημμένη, τύπτεται πλήκτρῳ· ἡ δὲ νάβλα, δώδεκα φθόγγους ἔχουσα, τοῖς δακτύλοις κρούεται.

it is observed by Jebb (II. pp. 145, 146) that the Hebrew verb *nagan* to play (whence the words *neginath*, *neginoth*) is the technical word used in 1 Sam. xvi. 16, 23, Isaiah xxiii. 16, in connexion with the *kinnor*, but that it is never employed in reference to the *nebel*. He might have added that the word *neginoth*, which occurs in the superscriptions of Psalms iv, vi, liv, lv, lxvii, lxxvi, is found **once** in connexion with the "upon Sheminith," Psalm vi, but never with the "upon Alamoth". His inference, legitimate so far as an inference may be drawn from such scanty evidence, is that the above technical term was applied to the more artificial method of playing on an instrument with a plectrum; an inference supported by the assertion of Josephus that the *kinnor* was struck with the plectrum, the *nebel* with the fingers[1]. I have taken the liberty of substituting "with a plectrum" for Jebb's "with a bow, or plectrum"; for while we have abundant evidence of the use of the plectrum both in Egypt and in Greece, the bow, for friction instead of percussion, seems **to** be entirely a discovery of modern times.

For an account of the difference in form **between** the *kinnor* and the *nebel* we must have recourse to later testimony; which indeed, if the knowledge of the difference were preserved to Christian times, and if we may depend on the authority of St. Augustine, is not wanting **to us.** That father repeatedly asserts, in his discourses on the psalms, that the hollow part of the instrument over which the strings were stretched in order to impart to them the greater resonance was, in the *kinnor*, below; in the *nebel*, above. In connexion with this we must attend to the testimony of Jerome, repeated by Isidorus and Cassiodorus, that the shape of the *nebel* was that of the Greek letter Δ inverted. Both these descriptions probably refer rather to that which would appear the natural position of the instruments than to that in which they were actually played: an unprofessional person of the present day would, in speaking of the top and bottom of a violin, conceive it as placed in an upright position like a violoncello, a very different position, it need hardly be remarked, from that in which it is held by a performer. Now if the *nebel* were of the shape of the inverted Δ, the uppermost of the three sides forming the sounding-board,

---

[1] The word נגן is generally used in the Piel: it occurs however in the Kal in Psalm lxviii. 25. In this verse, Jebb, referring נֹגְנִים to the *kinnoroth*, ingeniously takes עֲלָמוֹת not of the damsels, but of the *nebalim*. But would it not somewhat mar the poetry of the passage to our ears to speak of the procession of the "trebles,"—this being the exact English equivalent of *alamoth* in its technical sense? **That women were** present, striking the timbrels, is clear from the gender of תוֹפֵפוֹת.

and the strings stretching from that board, either from its under-part, or else across it, from its summit, downwards, probably in an oblique direction, to one of the other sides, it seems to follow from the length of the sounding-board, which would otherwise have been useless, that the instrument had several strings, not fewer, for instance, than ten, or eight at the least. On the other hand it may well be that the *kinnor*, with its sounding-board below, was a kind of lyre; and the lyre, though it often had seven strings, had also, in other cases, but three or four. The figure of a lyre with three strings, possibly the Hebrew *kinnor*, is found on coins ascribed to **Simon Maccabeus** (Kitto's *Cyclopædia*, Art. Musical Instruments, where the representation is given).

And here another probable difference between the two instruments suggests itself. As the *nebel* had a comparatively large number of strings, and those of acute sound, none of its strings would be required to give forth more than one note: the instrument would have as many notes as strings, and no more. On the other hand if the *kinnor* had but few strings, and those of deep tone, we may reasonably surmise that it was so constructed as to allow of the strings being stopped, by which means a large variety of notes, of different degrees of acuteness, might be obtained, according to the skill of the player. For that this method of extending the compass of a string-instrument was adopted by the ancients can scarcely be doubted. The guitar-like instruments represented in the Egyptian hieroglyphics, some of them not adapted for more than two strings, must have been played in this manner. A relic of ancient sculpture mentioned by Hawkins in his *History of Music* (I. p. 246, note), exhibiting Apollo playing on the lyre, bears witness to the same practice of manipulation among the classical nations; to which also Plato probably refers when he speaks of the joint employment of both hands in performing upon the lyre, the left hand being occupied on the instrument itself, the right hand in managing the plectrum (*De Legg.* p. 794 E).

The conclusions then to which we are conducted, and which, if not demonstrably correct in every particular, are at least both reasonable in themselves, and in harmony with every testimony on the subject except the untrustworthy assertion of Josephus regarding the number of strings, are as follows. The *kinnor* was an instrument with the hollow part below, with but few strings, of naturally deep tone, which were capable of being variously stopped with the fingers of the left hand, and which were struck with a plectrum. The *nebel*, on the contrary, was a triangle, of which the hollow part formed the uppermost side, while its strings were, for a portable instrument, comparatively numerous: they were moreover of acute tone, were played with the fingers, and did not admit of being stopped. If they were always ten in number, the *nebel* and the decachord were identical: if their number was variable, then the decachord was one form of the *nebel*. Of English terms, *viol*, by which our English Version occasionally renders *nebel*, would suit well for the *kinnor;* while *harp*, by which it uniformly renders *kinnor*, would be more appropriate to the *nebel*.

"On the sheminith" will signify on the notes of the lower octave, such as the deepest notes of the *kinnor*. "On alamoth," on the treble notes. "On neginoth," or rather "'with' neginoth," with the playings, i. e. to the music of the *kinnor* played with the plectrum. In Psalm lxi. alone we have "upon 'neginath'": the word is probably the singular of *neginoth*, but it has a different preposition before it. This may well signify "after the manner of playing," i. e. with music in the *style* of that of the *kinnor* played with the plectrum. The word *neginath*, playing, will explain the passages Lam. v. 14, Isaiah xxxviii. 20, Hab. iii. 19, Psalm lxxvii. 6. In Job xxx. 9, Lam. iii. 14, either this, or a cognate word *neginah*, which however never occurs uninflected, denotes a *song of mockery*, or *satire*.

There remains for explanation, "on the gittith," found in the superscriptions of Psalms viii, lxxxi, lxxxiv. Some, as the Targumist, suppose *gittith* to be the name of an instrument brought either from the city of Gath in Philistia, or from the Levitical city of Gath-rimmon. Others connect it directly with *gath*, "a winepress," and suppose it to have been the instrument used by the vintage-gatherers in their rejoicings; and as Psalms viii, lxxxi, lxxxiv. are all of a joyful character, this seems on the whole the most probable view. The latest explanation, that of Redslob, subsequently approved by Gesenius, derives the word from an assumed contracted infinitive of the verb nagan, the root of *neginath;* but it is not easy, on this hypothesis, to assign a difference of meaning between "on the gittith" and one or other of the superscriptions last explained, while it is scarcely likely that it did but express the same thing as one of them.

II. WIND-INSTRUMENTS.

The more powerful instruments of this class were two in number, the *hazozerah*, English Version *trumpet*, LXX. σάλπιγξ; and the *shophar*, English Version generally *trumpet*, but where a distinction is necessary, *cornet*, LXX. σάλπιγξ or κερατίνη. The difference between these is sufficiently clear. The *shophar* was curved, being either made of the actual horn of an animal or else in imitation of it: hence the word *keren*, "horn," is once used as its equivalent, Jos. vi. 5. "Pastoralis est, et cornu recurvo efficitur," says Jerome on Hos. v. 8. The *hazozerah* on the contrary was straight, and was properly made of silver. Josephus thus describes it as "a little less than a cubit in length; the tube narrow, a little thicker than a flute, and just wide enough to the performer's mouth to permit him to blow it; while it terminated, like other trumpets, in the form of a bell" (*Ant.* III. 12. 6). It appears that instruments answering to this description are represented, among the other spoils of the Jewish temple, on the Arch of Titus, at Rome.

Both the *hazozerah* and the *shophar* were employed in the Jewish temple-service. They are mentioned simultaneously in Psalm xcviii. 6, 2 Chron. xv. 14; and if various accounts in the Books of Chronicles dwell on the use of the *hazozeroth*, there is also the further testimony of Psalm cl. 3 to the employment of the *shopharoth*. The sacred use of the former had its warrant, if such were needed, in the divine command in obedience to which they were first fashioned in the wilderness (Numb. x.): that of the latter in the prominent part which had been assigned to them when the priests marched with them in advance of the ark around the walls of Jericho (Jos. vi.)

Of softer wind-instruments there occasionally comes before us in the Bible the *halil*, English Version *pipe*, LXX. αὐλός, doubtless some kind of pipe or flute: the Hebrew name has an etymological reference to its being pierced with holes. That this instrument was used for sacred purposes may be gathered from the Talmud, so far as we can trust its authority.

The temple-orchestra included further, as we learn from Psalm cl. 4, the *ugab*, English Version *organ*, in the Prayer-book *pipe;* LXX, here, ὄργανον, but in Gen. iv. 21 κιθάρα. The instrument is mentioned also in Job xxi. 12, xxx. 31. The Targum renders it by אבובא, *pipe*. It has by recent writers been identified with the bagpipe, on the ground of its being used in the Hebrew translation of Daniel for the Chaldee סומפניה, which is described in the Hebrew treatise Shilte Haggibborim as of the bagpipe character, and which, it is alleged, is perpetuated in an instrument of similar name in Italy and Asia Minor. But the premises on which this conclusion is based are far from certain. The Modern Greek for bagpipe is τζαμπούρνα, spelt, if Lexicons may be trusted, with a ρ; and as regards the Italian *zampogna*, more properly *sampogna*, Menagio's etymology

from *sambucina*, dim. of *sambuca*, is to be preferred; nor in fact does
the word denote exclusively a bagpipe, the true Italian for which is
piva or *cornamusa*. We seem therefore to be at least as safe in
supposing that in the *ugab* the sounding tube was blown directly
from the mouth. And as it could not well have been the same with
the *halil*, which the Targum, in three passages, renders also by
אבובא, there is good reason for allowing it to have been a composite instrument, formed by a collocation of reeds or tubes of different tones; an improved and refined form of the Pandean pipes or
syrinx. The coupling of it with the *minnim* or strings in Psalm cl.
4 will thus be not altogether unnatural; the one term standing as
the generic name for all string-instruments, the other representing
the most complicated form of wind-instrument then in use.

III. INSTRUMENTS OF PERCUSSION.

First among these comes the *toph*, English Version *tabret*, *timbrel*,
LXX. τύμπανον, once ψαλτήριον. It was what would now be called
a tambourine, being played with the hand; and was specially used by
women. It is thrice mentioned in the Psalms: lxxxi. 2, cxlix. 3,
cl. 4.

The *shalishim* of 1 Sam. xviii. 6 evidently perplexed our translators; who accordingly styled them simply "instruments of musick."
The ancient versions (LXX. κύμβαλα, Targ. צלצלין) regarded them
as cymbals or castanets; but as the name has to do with *three*,
triangles, alleged by Athenæus to be a Syrian invention, seem the
simplest explanation. The sistrum, with three transverse moveable
bars, has been also suggested, in accordance with the rendering of
Jerome. Our English marginal rendering, "three-stringed instruments," is improbable. Along with these note may be taken of the
menaaneim (English Version, improperly, *cornets*) of 2 Sam. vi. 5,
rendered in the Greek and Latin by the same words as the *shalishim*.
The Targum translates them רבייעין, similarly the Syriac; which
term, having to do with *four*, suggests that they may have been
instruments of the same kind as triangles, but of a square shape. Representations of metal rods, both square and triangular, may be seen
in Kitto's *Cyclopædia*; being charged with rings, they would be
shaken as well as struck; hence the propriety of the name *menaaneim*,
from the root נוע *to move to and fro*. As the *menaaneim* were used
in the sacred procession of the ark, it is likely that both they and
the *shalishim* were not excluded from the temple.

We come lastly to the genuine cymbals; called in 2 Sam. vi. 5,
and in Psalm cl. 5, *zelzelim*; but more generally, *meziltaim*; the dual

form implying **that a pair were used together.** Of the cymbals **employed in the** temple Josephus tells us that "they were broad **and large,** and made of brass" (*Ant.* VII. 12. 3). An importance was attached to these instruments in **the** temple-service which it is difficult for us to understand. They were played by the principal musicians of the orchestra, by **Asaph,** Heman, and Ethan themselves (1 Chron. xv. 19; **xvi. 5, 42). In the accounts** of the temple-performances, where mention is made of other instruments, that of the cymbals is never omitted; and in general they take precedence of the string-instruments. **They had** probably **different varieties of tone, that of some being** of a more piercing, that of **others of a more** clanging pitch; or if Psalm cl. 5 do not imply this, it at least indicates the manifold relish which the Israelites felt for the cymbal's sound. The *shushan* or "lily" of the superscriptions of Psalms xlv, lx, lxix, lxxx, **has been** already identified with the cymbal: no other equally probable explanation has ever been given of it; and of this **again it is to** be remarked, that if **it indicate a** particular kind of cymbal, it shews the care which was bestowed on their various forms; while on the other hand if it be a general name for a cymbal, it shews **the** playful love with which they were regarded.

INDEX.

The Arabic numbers refer to the pages. The letter n signifies that the reference is to a Note.

ABIGAIL, I. **314**
Ablutions, typical, I. 158.
Absalom, psalms of the period of his rebellion, I. 47, 62, **66,** 69, 78, 317, 342, 343.
Accents, Jewish, I. 16.
Achish, David's resort to, I. 185 seq.
Adonijah, demonstration of, I. 374 seqq.
Advent-psalms, II. 126 seqq.
Æthiopic version of the Psalter, I. 21.
Ahaz, psalms of his reign, I. 249, 255; II. 8 seqq.
Ahithophel, I. **317 seqq.**
Alamoth, II. **344 seq., 347.**
Alford's Greek **Test., referred to, I. 73 n,** 380 n.
Alphabetical psalms, I. 14, **90, 153, 189,** 199; II. 217, 246, 314 seq.
Al-taschith, I. 324 seqq.
Amalekites and David, I. 205 seqq., 215 seqq.
Amaziah, II. 41 seq.
Ambrose on the Psalms, I. 22, 54, 220.
Amen, repeated by the people, II. 181.
——— use of, in New Testament, I. 9.
Ammonites, their war with David, I. 35, 124 seq., 127; with Jehoshaphat, I. 276 seqq; their typical character, II. 67.
Amos, prophecies of, II. 58, 61.
"Ancient Jerusalem," referred to, I. 177 n, 275 n, 285 n, 363 n; II. 28 n, 237 n.
Angel of the Lord, I. 194; II. 165 seqq.
Apostles, from which tribes sprung, I. 372 seq.
Aquila, account of his version, I. 20.
Arabic version of the Psalter, I. 21, 195.
Ark, its removal and establishment upon Mount Zion, I. 147 seqq., 160, 164, 168, 172 seqq., 373.
Arnobius, **his** reading of the Psalms, II. 140 n.

Asa, his religious assemblage, I. 236, 290 seq.
Asaph, account of, I. 240; **source** of his authority, II. 182 seq.
———, **Sons of,** I. 240 seqq.; **II. 8,** 113, 182 seq.
Assyria, of what a type, II. 63 seq.
Athenæus, II. 349.
Augustine, his testimony respecting **an**cient versions, I. 21 seq.; II. 140 n; **his** style of interpretation, I. 30, 57, 394; II. 63, 173 seq.; quoted, I. 124, 146, 154, 167 n, 183 n, 251, 268 n, 313 n, 345; II. 294; otherwise referred to, I. 54, 176 n, 204 n, 331; II. 79 n, 278, 280, 345.
Azariah, son of Oded, probably a psalmist, I. 235 seq., 290 seq.

Babylon, history **of,** II. 286 seqq.
Bahrdt, editor of the Hexapla, I. 20.
Barnabas, his testimony to a reading, II. 140 n.
Bathsheba, David's sin with, I. 127, 297, 306.
Benjamin, one of the ten tribes, II. 38 n.
Bonar, A. A., his work on the Psalms referred to, II. 17 n. 74 n, 162.
Boniface and the Gallican Psalter, I. 22.
Bonomi, his Nineveh and its Palaces, II. 5.
Books of Psalms, I. 6.
Bossuet on the Psalms, I. 195; II. 71, 74 n, 326.
Bruce, Robert, anecdote of, I. 327.

Calvin on the Psalms, referred to, I. 103 n, 212 n, 256, 332, 340; II. 145.
Captivity, first intimation of, I. 369; of Ten Tribes, II. 20; return from, II. 187, 294, 308.
Cassiodorus, I. 22; II. 140 n, 345.
Celsus, II. 140 n.

Central verses, I. 19; examples of, I. 66, 167, 189, 219, 304 seqq., 327, 337; II. 7, 16, 35, 105, 160 n, 211, 228, 303, 304, 306, &c.

Chaldaisms of language, II. 82, 171, 205 n, 226, 292.

Chaldean influences, II. 171, 199.

Chief Musician, I. 61.

Christians at Pella, I. 95 seq.

Chrysostom, quoted, I. 273 seq., 283 n, 295 n; referred to, I. 256; II. 204, 258.

Condemnation of our Lord, I. 191 seqq.

Cowper, his hymns, I. 45.

Daniel, probably the author of Psalm cxix., II. 244 seq.; his prophecies, II. 324 seqq.

David, his psalms, I. 27 seqq., 296 seqq.; his character, I. 124, 230, 382; II. 245, &c.; his degree of knowledge, I. 37, 112, 151, 357; his history, I. 48 seqq.

David, later psalms bearing his name, II. 80 seqq., 209 seqq., 264, 288, 301, 310 seq.

Delitzsch on the Psalms, quoted or referred to, I. 67 n, 82 n, 114 n, 210, 226 n, 241 n, 262 n, 327 n, 396 n; II. 23 n. 81 n, 99 n, 129 n; his Symbolæ, II. 329 seq., 331 seqq., 340.

Divisions of the Psalter, I. 4 seqq.

Doeg, I. 309 seqq.

Doxologies, I. 5, 229, 397; II. 110, 181.

Edomites, David's war against, I. 301 seq., 333 seq.; character of, I. 338; II. 65 seq.

Elohim, I. 85 n; II. 58, 289, 329 seqq.

Engedi, scene at, I. 190, 195 seq.

English versions of the Psalms, I. 23 seq.

Enigmatical superscriptions, I. 58, 78 seq., 186, 230, 302, 314.

Erroneous arrangement, I. 15.

Esther, Book of, I. 270; II. 302.

Ethan, I. 243; II. 96 seqq., 103.

Ewald on the Psalms, referred to, I. 13 n, 180 n, 212 n, 214 n, 314 n; II. 18 n, 242 n, 309.

Ezra, possibly a psalmist, II. 317.

Ezrahite, meaning of the term, II. 97 seqq.

Faber, his Psalterium Quincuplex, I. 15.

Fairbairn, his Typology, I. 68 n, 158 n, 268 n; II. 47 seqq.; on Prophecy, II. 193 n.

Famine for the Gibeonites, I. 181, 350.

Fenwick, on the superscriptions, I. 57.

Forbes, his Symmetrical Structure of Scripture, I. 156 seq. 189, 199 n, 307 n; II. 107 n.

Forster, his Geography of Arabia, I. 394 seq.

Francke, A. H., II. 162 n.

French and Skinner's Version of the Psalms, II. 179 n.

Fulfilment of prophecy, I. 52, 97 seq., 137, 191, 301, 378 seqq.

Future life unrevealed to the psalmists, I. 112, 200, 214, 287, 289; II. 119.

Germain, bishop of Paris, I. 22.

Gifts of the wise men, I. 269.

Gittith, II. 71, 347.

Gloria Patri, I. 299; II. 291.

Goliath, David's combat with, I. 84, 91.

Good, Dr Mason, on the Psalms, I. 103 n, 205 n; II. 97.

Good Friday, Collects for, I. 306.

Gray's Bard, II. 242 n.

Gregory of Tours, I. 22.

Habakkuk, his prophecies, II. 129 seqq.

Hallel, II. 220.

Hannah, hymn of, II. 14 seq., 218.

Hawkins' History of Music, II. 346.

Heathenism within the Church, I. 90 seqq; II. 338.

Hebrews, Epistle to the, I. 75 n, 222 seqq., 263; II. 134 seq., 142, 160 seqq., 179.

Heman, I. 242 seq.; II. 96 seqq.

Hengstenberg, on the Psalms, quoted, I. 131 n, 278; II. 176, 234 seqq., 286; controverted, I. 309 seq.; II. 83, 333 seqq.; referred to comparatively briefly, I. 82 n, 100, 103 n, 114 n, 150, 172 n, 194 n, 212 n, 226 n, 241 n, 252 n, 280, 337; II. 20, 35, 38 n, 81 n, 96, 98 n, 125, 127 n, 138, 170 seq., 246, 275 n, 279, 280, 285, 288, 314, 340; on the Pentateuch, II. 254 n; on the Revelation, I. 170 n; his Christology, I. 194 n; II. 166 seq., 207.

Herodotus, II. 17.

Hervey, Lord A, on the Genealogies, II. 104 n.

Hezekiah, author of Psalm lxxxvi, II. 85 seqq.; his ordering of the temple-psalmody, I. 233, 293; psalms of his reign, I. 274; II. 3, 4; his message to the ten tribes, II. 24 seq., 70; his intercession for them, II. 76.

INDEX. 353

Higgaion, I. 9.
Hilary on the Psalms, quoted, I. 29; II. 274; otherwise referred to, I. 8, 20, 22, **54**, 311, 312 n, 331; II. 120, 257.
Historical **sense** of the Psalms, I. 48 seqq.
Horne, Bishop, on the Psalms, **I.** 54, 56, 176 n, **278, 353.**
Horsley, Bp., on the Psalms, I. **54, 57,** 67 n, 109 n, **130,** 176 n, 193; **II. 127 n,** 145, 163.
Houbigant, on the Psalms, I. **193.**

Imprecations in the Psalms, I. **380 seqq.**; II. 200 seqq., 299 seq.
Inspiration **of the Psalms,** I. **1, 40, 53,** 175.
Inversion, I. **18** seq.; examples of, **I. 362**; II. 88, 106 seq., 219, 251, 271.
Isaacs' Dead Sea, I. 250 n.
Isaiah, his probable genealogy, II. **103**; perhaps the author of Psalm **lxxxix,** *ibid.*
Ishmaelites, of whom types, II. **66** seq.
Isidorus, II. 345.
Israel **(Ten Tribes),** Kingdom **of, II. 19** seqq.

Jacob, life of, I. 152 seqq.
Jah, emphatic for Jehovah, I. 358; **II. 334.**
Jahaziel, probably a psalmist, I. **235 seq.,** 281 seq.; his prophecy, I. 278 n.
Jebb on the Psalms, quoted or referred to, I. 11, 226 n, 241 n, 243 n, 293; **II.** 9 n, 78 n, 122 n, 124 n, 127 n, 255, 345.
Jeduthun, I. 211, 244, 341. **See also** Ethan.
Jehoshaphat, psalms of **his reign,** I. **236,** 261 seq., 276 seq., 280; his character, I. 266; II. 87.
Jehovah, use **and meaning of the name,** II. 329 seqq.
Jeremiah, probably the author of Psalm cii, II. 156 seq.
Jerome, his versions of the Psalter, I. 22 seq.; referred to, *passim*; his manner of writing the psalms, I. 18; his reference to a Rabbinic canon, II. 120; his account of the south of Palestine, **I.** 216 n; do. of certain musical instruments, II. 345, 348.
Jerome, Breviary ascribed to, I. 176 n.
Jerusalem, building of, I. 307; rebuilding of, II. 261 seqq., 318 **seqq.**

Joab, a **type of heathenism within the Church,** I. **92.**
Job, **Book of, I. 100,** 207 seq., 213; II. 83, 99 n, 200.
John, St, Gospel of, II. 109, &c.
—— First Epistle, I. 109; II. 300.
Jonah, Book of, II. 191.
Josephus, II. 344, 346, 348, 350.
Josiah, author of two psalms, II. 150 seqq., 170 seqq.; his labours, II. 3, 118.
Journal of Class. and Sac. Philology, **I.** 134 n; **II.** 18 n, 303 n.
Journal of Sac. Literature I. 228 n; II. **258,** 260, 266, 271, 272.
Justin Martyr, his charge respecting Psalm xcvi, II. 140 n.

Korah, ancestor of the Korhites, I. 242.
Korhites, **I. 242** seqq., 257, 282; II. 3, **74 n, 91.**
Köster on the Psalms, II. 99 n.

Lactantius, his testimony **to a reading,** II. 140 n.
Latin hymn Vexilla Regis, II. 140 n.
Latin versions of the Psalms, I. 21 seqq.
Lee on Inspiration of Scripture, II. 193 n.
Levites, see Temple-singers.
Levitical inheritance, I. 106.
Lines in the Psalms, I. 15 seqq.
Liturgical arrangement of the Psalms, Christian, I. **4 seq.**; Jewish, I. 7 seq.; II. 130.
Lowth, Bp., his Prælectiones referred to, I. 245, 287 n; II. 177 n, 292 n; on Parallelism, I. 18.
Luther, his translation of Cusb, I. 78; his **hymn** Ein feste Burg, I. 276.

Mabillon, I. 22.
Maccabees, psalms erroneously referred to their times, I. **250** seqq.; II. 8; their victories foretold, II. **194,** 324.
Makkeph, I. 17, 259 n.
Manasseh, psalms of his reign, II. 95 seq., 96, 104.
Maschil, I. 179, 246 seq., 279; II. 4, &c.
Massillon, I. 288 n.
Maurer, his commentary referred to, I. 13 n, 64 n, 178 n; II. 131 n.
Melchizedek, a type of Christ, II. 211.
Mephibosheth, I. 343.
Metre of Hebrew poetry, I. 17.
Michaelis, J. D., II. 121 n, 162 n.

Michtam, I. 105 n, 247, 334.
Mizar, I. 250 n.
Moabites, **character of,** I. 338; II. 67.
Moberly, on the Law of the Love of God, I. 85; II. 335 n.
Moral attributes of God, II. 336 seq
Moral sense of the Psalms, I. 30.
Montfaucon, I. 20.
Moses, psalm **of,** II. 114 seqq.
Muis, De, on the Psalms, I. 332.
Musical instruments, II. 342 seqq.

Nabal, I. 313.
Nehemiah, rebuilder of the walls of Jerusalem, II. 265, 318; **his** probable lineage, II. 264 n; perhaps the author of several psalms, II. 264, 272, 302, 310 seq.; psalms collected and arranged in his time, II. 113, 187.
New birth, doctrine of, II. 95.
Nob, slaughter **of priests of,** I. 114, 309 seqq.
Numbering of the Psalms, I. 6 seqq.; design in reference to, II. 221 seqq., 313 seq.

Origen, **his** Hexapla, I. 20.

Pairs of psalms, I. 7.
Parables, II. 32.
Parallelisms, I. 14, 18; II. 247.
Paul, St, great influence of the language of the psalms on his arguments, I. 223 seqq.; II. 298 seq.; his epistles otherwise referred to, I. 24, 63 n, 119, 122, 148, 151, 201, 222 n, 257 seq.; II. 92, 132, 169, 229, 300 n, **324,** 327; his speeches referred to, I. 7, 36, 83, 105; II. 106 n; his character, **II. 245.**
Paulinus of Nola, I. 327 n.
Penitential psalms, I. 76 seqq.
Peter, St, his epistles referred to, I. 188 n, 320; **his speeches referred to,** I. 105, 110, 119; II. 202 seq.
Philistines, **character of,** I. 338; II. 67 seq.
Philo Judæus, II. 168.
Pius V., pope, I. 22.
"Plain Commentary," quoted, II. 320 seq.; referred to, II. 9 n, 124 n.
Plato, II. 346.
Prayer-book Version of the Psalms, I. 23, 24; referred to with approval, I. 305 n; II. 127.

Prophetical **sense of the Psalms,** I. 42 seqq.
Prosper of Aquitaine, I. 22.
Psalm (mizmor), use of the word, I. 245; II. 143, 151 n.

Rahab (Egypt), II. 92, 105.
Redslob, on musical instruments, II. 347.
Restoration of the Jews to their former land, not to **be expected,** I. 164, 269; II. 146, 157 seqq., 192, 274, 308.
Revelation, Book **of,** I. 41 n, 169 seq., 264, 266, 272, 394; **II.** 110, 148, 193.
Revelations made by **God of himself,** II. 335.
Rhyme, I. 11; instances of, I. 84 n, 322 n; II. 88.
Ritter, his Erdkunde, I. 216 n.
Robinson, his Biblical Researches, I. 195 seq., 216 n, 249 n, 337 n.
Rosenmüller, his **Scholia,** I. 268 n; II. 293 n.
Rowlands, on the site of Ziklag, I. 216 n.

Saadia, II. 114.
Sabatier, I. 22.
Sabbath, design of, II. 125.
Sacrifice, meaning of, I. 68.
Samson, reference to his history, II. 215.
Satan, doctrine respecting, II. 199 seq.
Saul, his character not made **prominent** in the Psalms, I. 230, 310, **323.**
Selah, functions of, I. 8 seqq.; noteworthy instances of its use, I. 211, 316, 330, 342; II. 17, 22, 301, 303.
Septuagint version of the Psalms, account of, I. 19 seq.; instances of its errors, I. 23 seq.; remarkable readings or renderings of, I. 221 seqq.; II. 18, 163, 167 seq., 179, 229, 297, 315; account given by it of various psalms, I. 170, 210, 390; II. 16, 130, 136, 142 seq.; its numbering of the psalms, I. 6; II. 224; referred to, *passim.*
Sermon on the Mount, I. 203.
Sheminith, I. 96; II. 344 seq., 347.
Shiggaion, I. 78, 247.
Shimei, his slanders, I. 78 seqq.
Shushan, or lily, I. 258, 334; II. 350.
Solomon, author of Psalm lxxii., I. 234, 390; his name prefixed to Psalm cxxvii., II. 256, 264 seq.; birth of, I. 127.

Song (shir), **use of** the word, I. 173, 246; II. 4, 151 n.
Soph-pasuk, I. 15.
Stanley, his Sinai and **Palestine referred** to, I. 166 n, 196, 250 n, **308 n; II. 17,** 178 n, 283 n.
Stier, on the Psalms, quoted or referred to, I. **102** seq., 356; II. 124, 162 seq., 289 n; on the words of the Lord Jesus, I. 73 n.
Strophes in the Psalms, I. 10 seqq.
Supernumerary psalm, I. 7.
Superscriptions of the psalms, I. **6;** character of some of them, I. **301 seq.;** their genuineness, II. 84.
Symbolism, I. 394; of numbers, II. 231 seq.
Symmachus, account of his version, **I.** 20.
Syriac version, account of, I. 20; its numbering of the psalms, I. 6 seq.; II. 224; its account of Psalm xxxviii., I. 205 n; referred to, *passim*.

Talmud, referred to, II. 104, 257, **348.**
Targum, **account** of, I. 20; remarkable interpretations of, I. 327, 377; II. 120, 162, 244; referred to, *passim*.
Tarshish, I. 395.
Te Deum, I. 179.
Temple, preparations for, I. 349 **seqq.;** second, foundation of, II. 234 seqq.
Temple-singers, account of, I. 234 seqq.; their labours among the ten tribes, II. 37, **55.** See also Asaph, sons of, and Korhites.

Tertullian, his testimony to a reading, II. 140 n; his view of the Psalms, I. 53.
Theodoret, peculiarity in his Commentary, II. 171; quoted, I. 135 n, 167 n, 220 n, 221 n, 268 n, 331 seq., 333; II. 161 n, 254 n, 265; referred to, I. 99 n, 100, 123, 195, 256, 269, 372, 377; II. 4, 122 n, 130, 133, 143, 196, 258, 292 n, 310 seq., **314,** 324.
Theodotion, account of his version, I. 20.
Tholuck, on the Psalms, quoted or referred to, II. 51, 102, 299 seq.
Titus, Arch of, at Rome, II. 348.
Trans-jordanic tribes, I. 366 seqq.; II. 283 n.
Trumpets, feast of, II. 46 seqq.
Tyrians, character of, II. 67 seq.

Verses in the Psalms, I. 13 seqq.
Versions of the Psalms, account **of, I. 19** seqq.

Walafrid Strabo, I. 22.
Westcott on the Canon, **I. 21.**

Zerubbabel, author of Psalms cviii—cx., II. 195 seqq., 204 seqq.
Ziba, I. 318.
Ziklag, destruction of, I. 205 seqq.; recovery of, I. **215 seqq.**
Zion, meaning of **the** name, **I.** 283 n; II. 279.
—— the Church **of** Christ, I. 36; II. 146 seq., 158; so referred to, *passim*.
Ziphites, I. 314 seq.

CAMBRIDGE: PRINTED BY C. J. CLAY, M.A.
AT THE UNIVERSITY PRESS.

LIST OF BOOKS

PUBLISHED BY

MACMILLAN AND CO.

Cambridge,

AND 23, HENRIETTA STREET, COVENT GARDEN, LONDON.

ÆSCHYLI Eumenides.
The Greek Text with English Notes, and an Introduction, containing an Analysis of Müller's Dissertations. By BERNARD DRAKE, M.A., late Fellow of King's College, Cambridge. 8vo. cloth, 7s. 6d.

ADAMS.—The Twelve Foundations and other Poems.
By H. C. ADAMS, M.A., Author of "Sivan the Sleeper," &c. **Royal 16mo.** cloth, 5s.

AGNES HOPETOUN'S SCHOOLS AND HOLIDAYS.
The Experiences of a Little Girl. A Story for Girls. By Mrs. OLIPHANT, Author of "Margaret Maitland." Royal 16mo. 6s.

AIRY.—Mathematical Tracts on the Lunar and Planetary
Theories. The Figure of the Earth, Precession and Nutation, the Calculus of Variations, and the Undulatory Theory of Optics. By G. B. AIRY, M.A., Astronomer Royal. **Fourth Edition,** revised and improved. 8vo. cloth, 15s.

ARISTOTLE on the Vital Principle.
Translated, with Notes. By CHARLES COLLIER, M.D., F.R.S., Fellow of the Royal College of Physicians. Crown 8vo. cloth, 8s. 6d.

BAXTER.—The Volunteer Movement: its Progress and
Wants. With Tables of all the Volunteer Corps in Great Britain, and of their Expenses. By R. DUDLEY BAXTER. 8vo. 1s.

BEASLEY.—An Elementary Treatise on Plane Trigonometry:
with a numerous Collection of Examples. By R. D. BEASLEY, M.A., Fellow of St. John's College, Cambridge, Head-Master of Grantham Grammar School. Crown 8vo. **cloth, 3s. 6d.**

BIRKS.—The Difficulties of Belief in connexion with the
Creation and the Fall. By THOMAS RAWSON BIRKS, M.A., Rector of Kelshall, and EXAMINING CHAPLAIN TO THE LORD BISHOP OF CARLISLE, Author of "The Life of the Rev. E. Bickersteth." Crown 8vo. cloth, 4s. 6d.

BLANCHE LISLE, and Other Poems.
Fcap. 8vo. cloth, 4s. 6d.

BOOLE.—The Mathematical Analysis of Logic.
By GEORGE BOOLE, D.C.L. Professor of Mathematics in the Queen's University, Ireland. 8vo. sewed, 5s.

BOOLE.—**A Treatise** on Differential Equations.
Crown 8vo. cloth, 14s.

BRAVE WORDS for **BRAVE SOLDIERS** and **SAILORS**.
Tenth Thousand. 16mo. sewed, 2d.; or 10s. per 100.

BRETT.— Suggestions relative to **the** Restoration of Suffragan Bishops and Rural Deans. By THOMAS BRETT (A.D. 1711). Edited by JAMES PENDALL, M.A., Procter in Convocation for the Clergy of Ely. Crown 8vo. cloth, 2s. 6d.

BRIMLEY.—Essays, by the late GEORGE BRIMLEY, M.A. Edited by W. G. CLARK, M.A., Tutor of Trinity College, and Public Orator in the University of Cambridge. With Portrait. **Second Edition.** Fcap. 8vo. cloth, 5s.

BROOK SMITH.—Arithmetic in Theory and Practice.
For Advanced Pupils. Part First. By J. BROOK SMITH, M.A., of St. John's College, Cambridge. Crown 8vo. cloth, 3s. 6d.

BUTLER (Archer).—Sermons, Doctrinal and Practical.
By the Rev. WILLIAM ARCHER BUTLER, M.A. late Professor of Moral Philosophy in the University of Dublin. Edited, with a Memoir of the Author's Life, by the Very Rev. THOMAS WOODWARD, M.A. Dean of Down. With Portrait. **Fifth Edition.** 8vo. cloth, 12s.

BUTLER (Archer).—A Second Series of Sermons.
Edited by J. A. JEREMIE, D.D. Regius Professor of Divinity in the University of Cambridge. **Third Edition.** 8vo. cloth, 10s. 6d.

BUTLER (Archer).—History of Ancient Philosophy.
A Series of Lectures. Edited by WILLIAM HEPWORTH THOMPSON, M.A. Regius Professor of Greek in the University of Cambridge. 2 vols. 8vo. cloth, 1l. 5s.

BUTLER (Archer).—Letters on Romanism, in Reply to Mr. NEWMAN's Essay on Development. Edited by the Very Rev. T. WOODWARD, Dean of Down. **Second Edition,** revised by the Ven. Archdeacon HARDWICK. 8vo. cloth, 10s. 6d.

CAMBRIDGE.—A Cambridge Scrap Book: containing in a Pictorial Form a Report on the Manners, Customs, Humours, and Pastimes of **the** University of Cambridge. With nearly 300 Illustrations. Second Edition. Crown 4to. half-bound, 7s. 6d.

CAMBRIDGE.—Cambridge Theological Papers. Comprising those given at the Voluntary Theological and Crosse Scholarship Examinations. Edited, with References and Indices, by A. P. MOOR, M.A. of Trinity College, Cambridge, and Sub-warden of St. Augustine's College, Canterbury. 8vo. cloth, 7s. 6d.

MACMILLAN & CO.'S PUBLICATIONS.

CAMBRIDGE SENATE-HOUSE PROBLEMS and RIDERS, with SOLUTIONS:—

1848—1851.—Problems. By N. M. FERRERS, M.A. and J. S. JACKSON, M.A. of Caius College. 15s. 6d.

1848—1851.—Riders. By F. J. JAMIESON, M.A. of Caius College. 7s. 6d.

1854—Problems and Riders. By W. WALTON, M.A. of Trinity College, and C. F. MACKENZIE, M.A. of Caius College. 10s. 6d.

1857—Problems and Riders. By W. M. CAMPION, M.A. of Queen's College, and W. WALTON, M.A. of Trinity College. 8s. 6d.

1860—Problems and Riders. By H. W. WATSON, M.A. Trinity College, and E. T. ROUTH, M.A. St. Peter's College. 7s. 6d.

CAMBRIDGE ENGLISH PRIZE POEMS, which have obtained the Chancellor's Gold Medal from the Institution of the Prize to 1858. Crown 8vo. cloth, 7s. 6d.

CAMBRIDGE.—Cambridge and Dublin Mathematical Journal. *The Complete Work*, in Nine Vols. 8vo. cloth, 7l. 4s.
ONLY A FEW COPIES OF THE COMPLETE WORK REMAIN ON HAND.

CAMPBELL.—The Nature of the Atonement and its Relation to Remission of Sins and Eternal Life. By JOHN M°LEOD CAMPBELL, formerly Minister of Row. 8vo. cloth, 10s. 6d.

CICERO.—Old Age and Friendship.
Translated into English. Two Parts. 12mo. sewed, 2s. 6d. each.

COLENSO.—The Colony of Natal. A Journal of Ten Weeks' Tour of Visitation among the Colonists and Zulu Kaffirs of Natal. By the Right Rev. JOHN WILLIAM COLENSO, D.D. Lord Bishop of Natal. With a Map and Illustrations. Fcap. 8vo. cloth, 5s.

COLENSO.—Village Sermons.
Second Edition. Fcap. 8vo. cloth, 2s. 6d.

COLENSO.—Four Sermons on Ordination, and on Missions.
16mo. sewed, 1s.

COLENSO.—Companion to the Holy Communion, containing the Service, and Select Readings from the writings of Mr. MAURICE. Edited by the Lord Bishop of Natal. *Fine Edition*, rubricated and bound in morocco, antique style, 6s.; or in cloth, 2s. 6d. *Common Paper*, limp cloth, 1s.

COOPER.—The Nature of Reprobation, and the Preacher's Liability to it. A Sermon. By J. E. COOPER, M.A., Rector of Fornsett St. Mary, Norfolk, 8vo. 1s.

COTTON.—Sermons and Addresses delivered in Marlborough College during Six Years by GEORGE EDWARD LYNCH COTTON, D.D., Lord Bishop of Calcutta, and Metropolitan of India. Crown 8vo. cloth, 10s. 6d.

COTTON.—Sermons: chiefly connected with Public Events of 1854. Fcap. 8vo. cloth, 3s.

COTTON.—Charge delivered at his Primary Visitation, September, 1859. 8vo. 2s. 6d.

CROSSE.—An Analysis of Paley's Evidences.
By C. H. CROSSE, M.A. of Caius College, Cambridge. 12mo. boards, 3s. 6d.

DAVIES.—St. Paul and Modern Thought:
Remarks on some of the Views advanced in Professor Jowett's Commentary on St. Paul. By Rev. J. LL. DAVIES, M.A. Fellow of Trinity College, Cambridge, and Rector of Christ Church, Marylebone. 8vo. sewed, 2s. 6d.

DAYS OF OLD: Stories from Old English History of the
Druids, the Anglo-Saxons, and the Crusades. By the Author of "Ruth and her Friends." Imp. 16mo. cloth, 5s.

DEMOSTHENES DE CORONA.
The Greek Text with English Notes. By B. DRAKE, M.A. late Fellow of King's College, Cambridge. **Second Edition**, to which is prefixed AESCHINES AGAINST CTESIPHON, with English Notes. Fcap. 8vo. cloth, 5s.

DEMOSTHENES.—Demosthenes on the Crown.
Translated by J. P. NORRIS, M.A. Fellow of Trinity College, Cambridge, and one of Her Majesty's Inspectors of Schools. Crown 8vo. cloth, 3s.

DREW.—A Geometrical Treatise on **Conic** Sections, with
Copious Examples from the Cambridge Senate House Papers. By W. H. DREW, M.A. of St. John's College, Cambridge, Second Master of Blackheath Proprietary School. **Crown 8vo. cloth, 4s. 6d.**

FARRAR.—Lyrics of Life.
By FREDERIC W. FARRAR, Fellow of Trinity College, Cambridge. Author of "Eric," &c. Fcap. 8vo. cloth, 4s. 6d.

FISHER.—The Goth and the Saracen: a Comparison
between the Historical Effect produced upon the Condition of Mankind by the Mahometan Conquests and those of the Northern Barbarians. By E. H. FISHER, B.A. Scholar of Trinity College, Cambridge. Crown 8vo. 1s. 6d.

FORD.—Steps to the Sanctuary; or, the Order for Morning
Prayer, set forth and explained in Verse. By JAMES FORD, M.A., Prebendary of Exeter Cathedral. Crown 8vo. cloth, 2s. 6d.

FROST.—The First Three Sections of Newton's Principia.
With Notes and Problems in illustration of the subject. By PERCIVAL FROST, M.A. late Fellow of St. John's College, Cambridge, and Mathematical Lecturer of Jesus College. Crown 8vo. cloth, 10s. 6d.

GILL.—The Anniversaries. Poems in Commemoration of
Great Men and Great Events. By T. H. GILL. Fcap. 8vo. cloth, 5s.

GODFRAY.—An Elementary Treatise on the Lunar Theory.
With a brief Sketch of the History of the Problem up to the time of Newton. By HUGH GODFRAY, M.A. of St. John's College, Esquire Bedell in the University of Cambridge. 8vo. cloth, 5s. 6d.

GRANT.—Plane Astronomy.
Including Explanations of Celestial Phenomena, and Descriptions of Astronomical Instruments. By A. R. GRANT, M.A., one of Her Majesty's Inspectors of Schools, late Fellow of Trinity College, Cambridge. 8vo. boards, 6s.

MACMILLAN & CO.'S PUBLICATIONS.

HAMILTON.—On Truth and Error: Thoughts, in Prose and Verse, on the Principles of Truth, and the Causes and Effects of Error. By JOHN HAMILTON, Esq. (of St. Ernan's), M.A. St. John's College, Cambridge. Crown 8vo. cloth, 5s.

HARE.—Charges delivered during the Years 1840 to 1854. With Notes on the Principal Events affecting the Church during that period. By JULIUS CHARLES HARE, M.A. sometime Archdeacon of Lewes, and Chaplain in Ordinary to the Queen. With an Introduction, explanatory of his position in the Church with reference to the parties which divide it, 3 vols. 8vo. cloth, 1l. 11s. 6d.

HARE.—Miscellaneous Pamphlets on some of the Leading Questions agitated in the Church during the Years 1845—51. 8vo. cloth, 12s.

HARE.—The Victory of Faith.
Second Edition. 8vo. cloth, 5s.

HARE.—The Mission of the Comforter.
Second Edition. With Notes. 8vo. cloth, 12s.

HARE.—Vindication of Luther from his English Assailants.
Second Edition. 8vo. cloth, 7s.

HARE.—Parish Sermons.
Second Series. 8vo. cloth, 12s.

HARE.—Sermons Preacht on Particular Occasions.
8vo. cloth, 12s.

⁎ The two following Books are included in the Three Volumes of Charges, and may still be had separately.

HARE.—The Contest with Rome.
With Notes, especially in answer to Dr. Newman's Lectures on Present Position of Catholics. Second Edition. 8vo. cloth, 10s. 6d.

HARE.—Charges delivered in the Years 1843, 1845, 1846. Never before published. With an Introduction, explanatory of his position in the Church with reference to the parties which divide it. 6s. 6d.

HARE.—Portions of the Psalms in English Verse.
Selected for Public Worship. 18mo. cloth, 2s. 6d.

HARE.—Two Sermons preached **in** Herstmonceux Church, on Septuagesima Sunday, 1855, being the Sunday after the Funeral of the Venerable Archdeacon Hare. By the Rev. H. VENN ELLIOTT, Perpetual Curate of St. Mary's, Brighton, late Fellow of Trinity College, Cambridge, and the Rev. J. N. SIMPKINSON, Rector of Brington, Northampton, formerly Curate of Herstmonceux. 8vo. 1s. 6d.

HARDWICK.—Christ and other Masters.
A Historical Inquiry into some of the chief Parallelisms and Contrasts between Christianity and the Religious Systems of the Ancient World. With special reference to prevailing Difficulties and Objections. By the Ven. ARCHDEACON HARDWICK. Part I. INTRODUCTION. PART II. THE RELIGIONS OF INDIA. Part III. THE RELIGIONS OF CHINA, AMERICA, AND OCEANICA. Part IV. RELIGIONS OF EGYPT AND MEDO-PERSIA. 8vo. cloth, 7s. 6d. each part.

HARDWICK.—A History of the Christian Church, during the Middle Ages and the Reformation. (A.D. 590–1600.)
By Archdeacon Hardwick. Two vols. crown 8vo. cloth, 21s.

    Vol. I. **History from Gregory the** Great to the Excommunication of Luther. With **Maps.**

    Vol. II. History of the Reformation of the Church.

        Each volume may be had separately. Price 10s. 6d.

    . These Volumes form part of the Series of Theological Manuals.

HARDWICK.—Twenty Sermons for Town Congregations.
Crown 8vo. cloth, 6s. 6d.

HAYNES.—Outlines of Equity. By FREEMAN OLIVER HAYNES, Barrister-at-Law, late Fellow of Caius College, Cambridge. Crown 8vo. cloth, 10s.

HEDDERWICK.—Lays of Middle Age, and other Poems.
By JAMES HEDDERWICK. Fcp. 8vo. 5s.

HEMMING.—An Elementary Treatise on the Differential and Integral Calculus. **By G. W.** HEMMING, M.A. Fellow of St. John's College, Cambridge. **Second Edition.** 8vo. cloth, 9s.

HERVEY.—The Genealogies of our Lord and Saviour Jesus Christ, as contained in the Gospels of St. Matthew and St. Luke, reconciled **with each** other and with the Genealogy of the House of David, from Adam to **the close of the** Canon of the Old Testament, and shown **to** be in harmony with **the true** Chronology of the Times. By Lord ARTHUR HERVEY, M.A. **Rector** of Ickworth. 8vo. cloth, 10s. 6d.

HERVEY.—The Inspiration of Holy Scripture.
Five Sermons preached before the University of Cambridge. 8vo. cloth, 3s. 6d.

HOWARD.—The Pentateuch; or, the Five Books of Moses. Translated into English from the Version of the LXX. With Notes on its Omissions and Insertions, and also on the Passages in which it differs from the Authorised Version. By the Hon. HENRY HOWARD, D.D. Dean f Lichfield. Crown 8vo. cloth. GENESIS, 1 vol. 8s. 6d.; EXODUS AND LEVITICUS, 1 vol. 10s. 6d.; NUMBERS AND DEUTERONOMY, 1 vol. 10s. 6d.

HUMPHRY.—The Human Skeleton (including the Joints). By GEORGE MURRAY HUMPHRY, M.D. F.R.S., Surgeon to Addenbrooke's Hospital, Lecturer on Surgery and Anatomy in the Cambridge University Medical School. With Two Hundred and Sixty Illustrations **drawn** from **Nature.** Medium 8vo. cloth, 1l. 8s.

HUMPHRY.—On the Coagulation of the Blood in the Venous System during Life. 8vo. 2s. 6d.

INGLEBY.—Outlines of Theoretical Logic.
Founded on the New Analytic of SIR WILLIAM HAMILTON. Designed for Text-book in Schools and Colleges. By C. MANSFIELD INGLEBY, M.A., **of Trinity** College, **Cambridge. In** fcap. 8vo. cloth, 3s. 6d.

MACMILLAN & CO.'S PUBLICATIONS.

JAMESON.—Analogy between the Miracles and Doctrines of Scripture. By F. J. JAMESON, M.A., Fellow of St. Catharine's College, Cambridge. Fcap. 8vo. cloth, 2s.

JAMESON.—Brotherly Counsels to Students. Four Sermons preached in the Chapel of St. Catharine's College, Cambridge. By F. J. JAMESON, M.A. Fcap. 8vo. limp cloth, red edges, 1s. 6d.

JUVENAL.—Juvenal, for Schools. With English Notes. By J. E. B. MAYOR, M.A. Fellow and Assistant Tutor of St. John's College, Cambridge. Crown 8vo. cloth, 10s. 6d.

KINGSLEY.—Two Years Ago. By CHARLES KINGSLEY, F.S.A. Rector of Eversley, and Chaplain in Ordinary to the Queen. **Second Edition.** 3 vols. crown 8vo. cloth, 1l. 11s. 6d.

KINGSLEY.—"Westward **Ho**!" or, the Voyages and Adventures of Sir Amyas Leigh, Knight of Burrough, in the County of Devon, in **the** Reign of Her Most Glorious Majesty Queen Elizabeth. **New and Cheaper Edition.** Crown 8vo. cloth, 6s.

KINGSLEY.—Glaucus; or, the Wonders **of the** Shore. **New and Illustrated Edition,** corrected and enlarged. Containing beautifully Coloured Illustrations of the Objects mentioned in the Work. Elegantly bound in cloth, with gilt leaves. 7s. 6d.

KINGSLEY.—The Heroes: or, Greek Fairy Tales for my Children. With Eight Illustrations, Engraved by WHYMPER. **New Edition,** printed on toned paper, and elegantly bound in cloth, with gilt leaves, Imp. 16mo. 5s.

KINGSLEY.—Alexandria and Her Schools: being Four Lectures delivered at the Philosophical Institution, Edinburgh. With a Preface Crown 8vo. cloth, 5s.

KINGSLEY.—Phaethon; or Loose Thoughts for Loose Thinkers. **Third Edition.** Crown 8vo. boards, 2s.

KINGSLEY.—The Recollections of Geoffry Hamlyn. By HENRY KINGSLEY, Esq. 3 **Vols. 1l.** 11s. 6d.

LATHAM.—The Construction of Wrought-Iron Bridges, embracing the Practical Application of the Principles of Mechanics to Wrought-Iron Girder Work. By J H. **LATHAM, Esq.** Civil Engineer. **8vo.** cloth. With numerous detail Plates. 15s.

LECTURES TO LADIES ON PRACTICAL SUBJECTS. **Third Edition,** revised. Crown 8vo. cloth, 7s. 6d. By Reverends F. D. MAURICE, CHARLES KINGSLEY, J. LL. DAVIES, ARCHDEACON ALLEN, **DEAN** TRENCH, PROFESSOR BREWER, DR. GEORGE JOHNSON, DR. SIEVEKING, DR. CHAMBERS, F. J. STEPHEN, Esq., and TOM **TAY**LOR, Esq

MACMILLAN & CO.'S PUBLICATIONS.

LITTLE ESTELLA, and other **TALES FOR THE YOUNG.** With Frontispiece. Royal 16mo. extra cloth, gilt leaves, 5s.

LUDLOW.—British India; its Races, and its History, down to 1857. By JOHN MALCOLM LUDLOW, Barrister-at-Law. 2 vols. fcap. 8vo. cloth, 9s.

LUSHINGTON.—La Nation Boutiquière: and other Poems, chiefly Political. With a Preface. By the late HENRY LUSHINGTON, Chief Secretary to the Government of Malta. **Points of War.** By FRANKLIN LUSHINGTON, Judge in the Supreme Courts of the Ionian Isles. In 1 vol. fcap 8vo. cloth, 3s.

LUSHINGTON.—The Italian War 1848-9, and **the** Last Italian Poet. By the late HENRY LUSHINGTON, Chief Secretary to the Government of Malta. With a Biographical Preface by G. S. VENABLES. Crown 8vo. cloth, 6s. **6d.**

MACKENZIE.—The Christian Clergy of the first Ten Centuries, and their Influence on European Civilization. By HENRY MACKENZIE, B.A. Scholar of Trinity College, Cambridge. Crown 8vo. cloth, 6s. **6d.**

MANSFIELD.—Paraguay, Brazil, and **the Plate.** With a Map, and numerous Woodcuts. By CHARLES MANSFIELD, M.A. of Clare College, Cambridge. With a Sketch of his Life. By the Rev. CHARLES KINGSLEY. Crown 8vo. cloth, 12s. 6d.

M'COY.—Contributions to British Palæontology; or, First Descriptions of several hundred Fossil Radiata, Articulata, Mollusca, and Pisces, from the Tertiary, Cretaceous, **Oolitic, and Palæozoic** Strata of Great Britain. With numerous Woodcuts. By FREDERICK M'COY, F.G.S., **Professor of** Natural History in the University of Melbourne. 8vo. cloth, 9s.

MASSON.—Essays, Biographical **and Critical**; chiefly on the English Poets. By DAVID MASSON, M.A. Professor of English Literature in University College, London. 8vo. cloth, 12s. 6d.

MASSON.—British Novelists and their Styles; being a Critical Sketch of the History of British Prose Fiction. By DAVID MASSON, M.A. Crown 8vo. **cloth**, 7s. **6d.**

MASSON.—Life of John Milton, narrated in Connexion with the Political, Ecclesiastical, and Literary History of his Time. Vol. I. **with Portraits.** 18s.

MAURICE.—Expository Works on the Holy Scriptures. By FREDERICK DENISON MAURICE, M.A., Chaplain of Lincoln's Inn.

I.—The Patriarchs and Lawgivers of the Old Testament. **Second Edition.** Crown 8vo. cloth, 6s.

This volume contains Discourses on the Pentateuch, Joshua, Judges, and the beginning of the First Book of Samuel.

MAURICE.—Expository Works on the Holy Scriptures.
By FREDERICK DENISON MAURICE, M.A., Chaplain of Lincoln's Inn.

II.—The Prophets and Kings of the Old Testament.
Second Edition. Crown 8vo. cloth, 10s. 6d.
This volume contains Discourses on Samuel I. and II., Kings I. and II., Amos, Joel, Hosea, Isaiah, Micah, Nahum, Habakkuk, Jeremiah, and Ezekiel.

III.—The Gospel of St. John; a Series of Discourses.
Second Edition. Crown 8vo. cloth, 10s. 6d.

IV.—The Epistles of St. John; a Series of Lectures on Christian Ethics. Crown 8vo. cloth, 7s. 6d.

MAURICE.—Expository Works on the Prayer-Book.

I.—The **Ordinary** Services.
Second **Edition.** Fcap. 8vo. **cloth, 5s. 6d.**

II.—The Church a Family. Twelve Sermons **on the** Occasional Services. Fcap. 8vo. cloth, 4s. 6d.

MAURICE.—What is Revelation? A Series of Sermons on the Epiphany; to which are added Letters to a Theological Student on the Bampton Lectures of Mr. MANSEL. Crown 8vo. cloth, 10s. 6d.

MAURICE.—Sequel to the Inquiry, "What is Revelation?" Letters in Reply to Mr. Mansel's Examination of "Strictures on the Bampton Lectures." Crown 8vo. cloth, 6s.

MAURICE.—Lectures on Ecclesiastical History.
8vo. cloth, 10s. 6d.

MAURICE.—Theological Essays.
Second Edition, with a new Preface **and other** additions. Crown 8vo. cloth, 10s. 6d.

MAURICE.—The Doctrine of Sacrifice deduced from **the** Scriptures. With a Dedicatory Letter to the Young Men's Christian Association. Crown 8vo. cloth, 7s. 6d.

MAURICE.—The Religions of the World, and their Relations to Christianity. Third Edition. Fcap. 8vo. cloth, 5s.

MAURICE.—On the Lord's Prayer.
Third **Edition.** Fcap. 8vo. cloth, 2s. **6d.**

MAURICE.—On the Sabbath Day: the Character of the Warrior; and on the Interpretation of History. Fcap. 8vo. cloth, 2s. 6d.

MAURICE.—Learning and Working.—Six Lectures on the Foundation of Colleges for Working Men, delivered in Willis's Rooms, London, in June and July, 1854. Crown 8vo. cloth, 5s.

MAURICE.—The Indian Crisis. Five Sermons.
Crown 8vo. cloth, 2s. 6d.

MAURICE.—Law's Remarks on the Fable of the Bees.
Edited, with an **Introduction** of Eighty Pages, by FREDERICK DENISON MAURICE, M.A. **Chaplain** of Lincoln's Inn. Fcp. 8vo. cloth, 4s. 6d.

MAURICE.—Miscellaneous Pamphlets:—

I.—Eternal Life and Eternal Death.
Crown 8vo. sewed, 1s. 6d.

II.—Death and Life. A Sermon. In Memoriam C. B. M.
8vo. sewed, 1s.

III.—Plan of a Female College for the Help of the Rich and of the Poor. 8vo. 6d.

IV.—Administrative Reform.
Crown 8vo. 3d.

V.—The Word "Eternal," and the Punishment of the Wicked. **Fifth Thousand.** 8vo. 1s.

VI.—The Name "Protestant:" and the English Bishopric at Jerusalem. **Second Edition.** 8vo. 3s.

VII.—Thoughts on the Oxford Election of 1847.
8vo. 1s.

VIII.—The Case of Queen's College, London.
8vo. 1s. 6d.

IX.—The Worship of the Church a Witness for the Redemption of the World. 8vo. sewed, 1s.

MAYOR.—Cambridge in the Seventeenth Century.
2 vols. fcap. 8vo. cloth, 13s.
Vol. I. Lives of Nicholas Ferrar.
Vol. II. Autobiography of Matthew Robinson.
By JOHN E. B. MAYOR, M.A. Fellow and Assistant Tutor of St. John's College, Cambridge.
*** The Autobiography of Matthew Robinson may be had separately, price 5s. 6d.

MAYOR.—Early Statutes of St. John's College, Cambridge.
Now first edited with Notes. Royal 8vo. 18s.
*** The **First** Part is now ready for delivery.

MAXWELL.—The Stability of the Motion of Saturn's Rings.
By J. C. MAXWELL, M.A. Professor of Natural Philosophy in the University of Aberdeen. 4to. sewed, 6s.

MOORE.—A New Proof of the Method of Algebra commonly called "Greatest Common Measure." By B. T. MOORE, B.A., Fellow of Pembroke College, Cambridge. Crown 8vo. 6d.

MORGAN.—A Collection of Mathematical Problems and
Examples. Arranged in the Different Subjects progressively, with Answers
to all the Questions. By H. A. MORGAN, M.A., Fellow of Jesus College. Crown 8vo. cloth, 6s. 6d.

MORSE.—Working for God, and other Practical Sermons.
By FRANCIS MORSE, M.A. Incumbent of St. John's, Ladywood, Birmingham. **Second Edition.** Fcap. 8vo. cloth, 5s.

NAPIER.—Lord Bacon and Sir Walter Raleigh.
Critical and Biographical Essays. By MACVEY NAPIER, late Editor of the *Edinburgh Review* and of the *Encyclopædia Britannica*. Post 8vo. cloth, 7s. 6d.

NORWAY AND SWEDEN.—A Long Vacation Ramble in
1856. By X and Y. Crown 8vo. cloth, 6s. 6d.

OCCASIONAL PAPERS on UNIVERSITY and SCHOOL
MATTERS; containing an Account of all recent University Subjects and Changes. Three Parts are now ready, price 1s. each.

PARKINSON.—A Treatise on Elementary Mechanics.
For the Use of the Junior Classes at the University, and the Higher Classes in **Schools.** With a Collection of Examples. By S. PARKINSON, B.D. Fellow **and** Assistant Tutor of St. John's College, Cambridge. Crown 8vo. cloth, 9s. 6d.

PARKINSON.—A Treatise on Optics.
Crown 8vo. cloth, 10s. 6d.

PARMINTER.—Materials for a Grammar of the Modern
English Language. Designed as a Text-book of Classical Grammar for the use of Training Colleges, and the Higher Classes of English Schools. By GEORGE HENRY PARMINTER, of Trinity College, Cambridge; Rector of the United Parishes of SS. John and George, Exeter. Fcap. 8vo. cloth, 3s. 6d

PEROWNE.—"Al-Adjrumiieh."
An Elementary Arabic Grammar. By J. J. S. PEROWNE, B.D. Lecturer in Divinity in King's College, London, and Examining Chaplain to the Lord Bishop of Norwich. 8vo. cloth, 5s.

PHEAR.—Elementary Hydrostatics.
By J. B. Phear, M.A. Fellow of Clare College, Cambridge. **Second Edition.** Accompanied by numerous Examples, with the Solutions. Crown 8vo. cloth, 5s. 6d.

PHILOLOGY.—The Journal of Sacred and Classical Philology.
Vols. I to IV. 8vo. cloth, 12s. 6d. each.

PLAIN RULES ON REGISTRATION OF BIRTHS AND
DEATHS. Crown 8vo. **sewed,** 1d.; 9d. **per dozen**; 5s. **per 100.**

PLATO.—The Republic of Plato.
Translated into English, with Notes. By Two Fellows of Trinity College, Cambridge, (J. Ll. Davies M.A., and D. J. Vaughan, M.A.) **Second Edition.** 8vo. cloth, 10s. **6d.**

PRAYERS FOR WORKING MEN OF ALL RANKS;
Earnestly designed for **Family Devotion and Private Meditation and Prayer** Fcap. 8vo. cloth, red leaves, 2s. 6d. Common Edition, 1s. 9d.

PRINCIPLES of ETHICS according to the NEW TESTAMENT. Crown 8vo. sewed, 2s.

PROCTER.—A History of the Book of Common Prayer: with a Rationale of its Offices. By FRANCIS PROCTER, M.A., Vicar of Witton, Norfolk, and late Fellow of St. Catherine's College. **Fourth Edition,** revised and enlarged. Crown 8vo. cloth, 10s. 6d.
*** This forms part of the Series of Theological Manuals

PUCKLE.—An Elementary Treatise on Conic Sections and Algebraic Geometry. With a numerous collection of Easy Examples progressively arranged, especially designed for the use of Schools and Beginners. By G. HALE PUCKLE, M.A., Principal of Windermere College. **Second Edition,** enlarged and improved. Crown 8vo. cloth, 7s. 6d.

RAMSAY.—The Catechiser's Manual; or, the Church Cate-chism illustrated **and explained,** for the use of **Clergymen,** Schoolmasters, **and Teachers.** By **ARTHUR RAMSAY,** M.A. of Trinity College, Cambridge. 18mo. cloth, 3s. 6d.

REICHEL.—The Lord's Prayer and other Sermons.
By C. P. REICHEL, B.D., Professor of Latin in the Queen's University; Chaplain to his Excellency the Lord-Lieutenant of Ireland; and late **Don-nellan** Lecturer in the University of Dublin Crown 8vo. cloth, 7s. 6d.

ROBINSON.—Missions urged upon the State, on Grounds both of Duty and Policy. By C K. ROBINSON, M.A. Fellow and Assistant Tutor of St. Catherine's College. Fcap. 8vo. cloth, 3s.

ROWSELL.—THE ENGLISH UNIVERSITIES AND THE ENGLISH POOR. Sermons Preached before the University **of Cambridge.** By T. J. ROWSELL, M.A. Incumbent of St Peter's, Stepney. Fcap. 8vo. cloth limp, red leaves, 2s.

RUTH AND HER FRIENDS. A Story for Girls.
With a Frontispiece. **Third Edition.** Royal 16mo. extra cloth, gilt leaves, 5s.

SALLUST.—Sallust for Schools.
With English Notes. **Second Edition.** By CHARLES MERIVALE, B.D.; late Fellow and Tutor of St. John's College, Cambridge, &c., Author of the "History of Rome," &c. Fcap. 8vo. cloth, 4s. 6d.
"THE JUGURTHA" AND "THE CATILINA" MAY BE HAD SEPARATELY, price 2s. 6d. EACH IN CLOTH.

SANDARS.—BY THE SEA, AND OTHER POEMS.
By EDMUND SANDARS, of Trinity Hall, Cambridge. Fcap. 8vo. cloth, 4s. 6d.

SCOURING OF THE WHITE HORSE; or, The Long Vacation Ramble of a London Clerk. By the Author of "Tom Brown's School Days." Illustrated by DOYLE. **Eighth Thousand.** Imp. 16mo. cloth, elegant, 8s. 6d.

SELWYN.—The Work of Christ in the World.
Sermons preached before the University of Cambridge. By the Right **Rev.** GEORGE AUGUSTUS SELWYN, D.D. Bishop of New Zealand, formerly Fellow of St. John's College. **Third Edition.** Crown 8vo. 2s.

SELWYN.—A Verbal Analysis of the Holy Bible.
Intended to facilitate the translation of the Holy Scriptures into Foreign Languages. Compiled **for the use of the** Melanesian Mission. Small folio, cloth, 14s.

SIMPSON.—An Epitome of **the** History of **the** Christian Church during the first Three Centuries and during the Reformation. With Examination Papers. By WILLIAM SIMPSON, M.A. **Third Edition.** Fcp. 8vo. cloth, 5s.

SMITH.—City Poems.
By ALEXANDER SMITH, Author of "A Life Drama," and other Poems. Fcap. 8vo. cloth. 5s.

SMITH.—Arithmetic and Algebra, in their Principles and Application: with numerous systematically arranged Examples, taken from the Cambridge Examination Papers. By BARNARD SMITH, M.A., Fellow of St. Peter's College, Cambridge. **Seventh Edition.** Crown 8vo. **cloth,** 10s. 6d.

SMITH.—Arithmetic for the use of Schools.
New Edition. Crown 8vo. cloth, 4s. 6d.

SMITH.—A Key to the Arithmetic for Schools.
Crown 8vo. cloth, 8s. 6d.

SNOWBALL.—The Elements of Plane and Spherical Trigonometry. By J. C. SNOWBALL, M.A. Fellow of St. John's College, Cambridge. **Ninth Edition.** Crown 8vo. cloth, 7s. 6d.

SNOWBALL.—Introduction to the Elements of Plane Trigonometry for the use of Schools. **Second Edition.** 8vo. sewed, 5s.

SNOWBALL.—The Cambridge Course of Elementary Mechanics and Hydrostatics. Adapted for the use of Colleges and Schools. With numerous Examples and Problems. **Fourth Edition.** Crown 8vo. cloth, 5s.

SWAINSON.—A Handbook to Butler's Analogy.
By C. A. SWAINSON, M.A. Principal of the Theological **College, and** Prebendary of Chichester. Crown 8vo. sewed, 2s.

SWAINSON.—The Creeds of the Church in their Relations to Holy Scripture and the Conscience of the Christian. 8vo. cloth, 9s.

SWAINSON.—THE AUTHORITY OF THE NEW TESTAMENT; The Conviction of Righteousness, and other Lectures, delivered before the University of Cambridge. 8vo. cloth, 12s.

TAIT and STEELE.—A Treatise on Dynamics, with numerous Examples. By P. G. TAIT, Fellow of St. Peter's College, Cambridge, and Professor of Mathematics in Queen's College, Belfast, and W. J. STEELE, late Fellow of St. Peter's College. Crown 8vo. cloth, 10s. 6d.

TAYLOR.—The Restoration of Belief.
By ISAAC TAYLOR, Esq., Author of "The Natural History of Enthusiasm." Crown 8vo. cloth, 8s. 6d.

THEOLOGICAL Manuals.
    CHURCH HISTORY: DURING THE MIDDLE AGES AND THE REFORMATION (A.D. 590—1600). By ARCHDEACON HARDWICK. With Four Maps, 2 vols. Crown 8vo. cloth, price 10s. 6d. each.
    THE COMMON PRAYER: ITS HISTORY AND RATIONALE. By FRANCIS PROCTER. **Fourth Edition.** Crown 8vo. cloth, 10s. 6d.
    HISTORY OF THE CANON OF THE NEW TESTAMENT. By B. F. WESTCOTT. Crown 8vo. cloth, 12s. 6d.
    ** Others are in progress, and will be announced in due **time.**

THRING.—A Construing Book.
Compiled by the Rev. EDWARD THRING, M.A. Head Master of Uppingham Grammar School, late Fellow of King's College, Cambridge. Fcap. 8vo. cloth, 2s. 6d.

THRING.—The Elements of Grammar taught in English.
Third Edition. 18mo. bound in cloth, 2s.

THRING.—The Child's Grammar.
Being the substance of the above, with Examples for Practice. Adapted for Junior Classes. **A New Edition.** 18mo. limp cloth, 1s.

THRING.—Sermons delivered at Uppingham School.
Crown 8vo. cloth, 5s.

THRING.—School Songs.
A Collection of Songs for Schools. With the **Music arranged for** four Voices. Edited by EDWARD THRING, M.A., Head Master of Uppingham School, **and H.** RICCIUS. Small **folio,** 7s. 6d.

THRUPP.—Antient Jerusalem: a New Investigation into the
History, Topography, and Plan of the City, Environs, and Temple. Designed principally to illustrate the records and prophecies of Scripture. With Map and Plans. By JOSEPH FRANCIS THRUPP, M.A. Vicar of Barrington, Cambridge, late Fellow of Trinity College. 8vo. cloth, 15s.

THUCYDIDES, BOOK VI. With English Notes, and a Map.
By PERCIVAL FROST, Jun. M.A. late Fellow of St. John's College, Cambridge. 8vo. 7s. 6d.

TODHUNTER.—A Treatise on the Differential Calculus.
With numerous Examples. **By** I. TODHUNTER, M.A., Fellow and Assistant Tutor of St. John's College, Cambridge. **Third Edition.** Crown 8vo. cloth, 10s. 6d.

TODHUNTER.—A Treatise on the Integral Calculus.
With numerous Examples. Crown 8vo. cloth, 10s. 6d.

TODHUNTER.—A Treatise on Analytical Statics, with
numerous Examples. **Second Edition.** Crown 8vo. cloth, 10s. 6d.

TODHUNTER.—A Treatise on Conic Sections, with
numerous Examples. **Second Edition.** Crown 8vo. cloth, 10s. 6d.

TODHUNTER.—Algebra for the use of Colleges and Schools.
Crown 8vo. cloth, 7s. 6d. **Second Edition.**

TODHUNTER.—Plane Trigonometry for Colleges and
Schools. Crown 8vo. cloth, 5s.

TODHUNTER.—A Treatise on Spherical Trigonometry for
the Use of Colleges and Schools. Crown 8vo. cloth, 4s. 6d.

TODHUNTER.—Examples of Analytical Geometry of Three Dimensions. Crown 8vo. cloth, 4s.

TOM BROWN'S SCHOOL DAYS.
By AN OLD BOY. **Seventh Edition.** Fcap. 8vo. cloth, 5s.

TRENCH.—Synonyms of the New Testament.
By The Very Rev. RICHARD CHENEVIX TRENCH, D.D. Dean of Westminster. **Fourth Edition. Fcap.** 8vo. cloth, 5s.

TRENCH.—Hulsean **Lectures for 1845—46.**
CONTENTS. 1.—The Fitness of Holy Scripture for unfolding the Spiritual Life of Man. 2.—Christ the Desire of all Nations; or the Unconscious Prophecies of Heathendom. **Fourth Edition. Foolscap** 8vo. cloth, 5s.

TRENCH.—Sermons Preached before the University of Cambridge. Fcap. 8vo. cloth, 2s. 6d.

VAUGHAN.—Notes for Lectures on Confirmation. With suitable Prayers. By C. J. VAUGHAN, D.D., Head Master of Harrow School. **Third Edition.** Limp cloth, red edges, 1s. 6d.

VAUGHAN.—St. Paul's Epistle to the Romans.
The Greek Text, with English Notes. By C. J. VAUGHAN, **D.D. 8vo.** cloth, **7s. 6d.**

VAUGHAN.—MEMORIALS OF HARROW SUNDAYS.
A Selection of Sermons preached in Harrow School Chapel. By C. J. VAUGHAN, D.D. With a View of the Interior of the Chapel. Crown 8vo. cloth, red leaves, 10s. 6d.

VAUGHAN.—Sermons preached in St. John's Church, Leicester, during the years 1855 and 1856. By DAVID J. VAUGHAN, M.A. Fellow of Trinity College, Cambridge, and Incumbent of St. Mark's, Whitechapel. Crown 8vo. cloth, 5s. 6d.

VAUGHAN.—Three Sermons on The Atonement. With a Preface. By D. J. Vaughan, M.A. Limp cloth, red edges, 1s. 6d.

WAGNER.—Memoir of the Rev. George Wagner, late of St. Stephen's, Brighton. By J. N. SIMPKINSON, M.A. Rector of Brington, Northampton. **Second Edition.** Crown 8vo. cloth, 9s.

WATSON AND ROUTH.—CAMBRIDGE SENATE HOUSE PROBLEMS AND RIDERS. For the Year 1860. With Solutions by H. W. WATSON, M.A. and E. J. ROUTH, M.A. Crown 8vo. cloth, 7s. 6d.

WESTCOTT.—History of the Canon of the New Testament during the First Four Centuries. By BROOKE FOSS WESTCOTT, M.A., Assistant Master of Harrow School; late Fellow of Trinity College, Cambridge. Crown 8vo. cloth, 12s. 6d.
*** This forms part of the Series of Theological Manuals.

WESTCOTT. — Characteristics **of the** Gospel Miracles.
Sermons preached before the University **of Cambridge. With Notes.** By B. F. WESTCOTT, M.A., Author of "**History of the** New Testament Canon." Crown 8vo. cloth, 4s. 6d.

WHEWELL.—THE PLATONIC DIALOGUES FOR ENGLISH READERS. By W. WHEWELL, D.D. Vol. I. Fcap. 8vo. cloth, 7s. 6d.

WHITMORE.—Gilbert Marlowe and Other Poems.
With a Preface by the Author of "Tom Brown's Schooldays." Fcap. 8vo. cloth, 3s. 6d.

WILSON.—The Five Gateways of Knowledge.
By GEORGE WILSON, M.D., F.R.S.E., Regius Professor of Technology in the University of Edinburgh. Second Edition. Fcap. 8vo. cloth, 2s. 6d. or in Paper Covers, 1s.

WILSON.—The Progress of the Telegraph.
Fcap. 8vo. 1s.

WILSON.—A Treatise on Dynamics.
By W. P. WILSON, M.A., Fellow of St. John's, Cambridge, and Professor of Mathematics in the University of Melbourne. 8vo. bds. 9s. 6d.

WOLFE.—ONE HUNDRED AND FIFTY ORIGINAL PSALM AND HYMN TUNES. For Four Voices. By ARTHUR WOLFE, M.A., Fellow and Tutor of Clare College, Cambridge. Oblong royal 8vo. extra cloth, gilt leaves, 10s. 6d.

WORSHIP OF GOD AND FELLOWSHIP AMONG MEN.
A Series of Sermons on Public Worship. Fcap. 8vo. cloth, 3s. 6d.
By F. D. MAURICE, M.A. T. J. ROWSELL, M.A. J. LL. DAVIES, M.A. and D. J. VAUGHAN, M.A.

WRIGHT.—The Iliad of Homer.
Translated into English Verse by J. C. WRIGHT, M.A. Translator of Dante. Crown 8vo. Books I.—VI. 5s.

WRIGHT.—Hellenica; or, a History of Greece in Greek,
as related by Diodorus and Thucydides, being a First Greek Reading Book, with Explanatory Notes, Critical and Historical. By J. WRIGHT, M.A., of Trinity College, Cambridge, and Head-Master of Sutton Coldfield Grammar School. Second Edition, WITH A VOCABULARY. 12mo. cloth, 3s. 6d.

WRIGHT.—David, King of Israel.
Readings for the Young. With Six Illustrations after SCHNORR. Royal 16mo. extra cloth, gilt leaves, 5s.

WRIGHT.—A Help to Latin Grammar;
or, the Form and Use of Words in Latin. With Progressive Exercises. Crown 8vo. cloth, 4s. 6d.

WRIGHT.—The Seven Kings of Rome:
An easy Narrative, abridged from the First Book of Livy by the omission of difficult passages, being a First Latin Reading Book, with Grammatical Notes. Fcap. 8vo. cloth, 3s.

WRIGHT.—A Vocabulary and Exercises on the "Seven Kings of Rome." Fcap. 8vo. cloth, 2s. 6d.

*** The Vocabulary and Exercises may also be had bound up with "The Seven Kings of Rome." Price 5s. cloth.

ONE SHILLING, MONTHLY.

MACMILLAN'S MAGAZINE.
EDITED BY DAVID MASSON.
Volume I. is now ready, handsomely bound in cloth, price 7s. 6d.

R. CLAY, PRINTER, BREAD STREET HILL.

www.ingramcontent.com/pod-product-compliance
Lightning Source LLC
Chambersburg PA
CBHW030401230426
43664CB00007BB/692